CLARENDON LAW SERIES

Edited by

PETER BIRKS

CLARENDON LAW SERIES

Introduction to Roman Law
By BARRY NICHOLAS

Legal Reasoning and Legal Theory
By NEIL MCCORMICK

Natural Law and Natural Rights
By JOHN G. FINNIS

The Concept of Law (2nd edition)
By H. L. A. HART

An Introduction to the Law of Contract (5th edition)
By P. S. ATIYAH

Principles of Criminal Law
By ANDREW ASHWORTH

Playing by the Rules
By FREDERICK SCHAUER

Precedent in English Law (4th edition)
By SIR RUPERT CROSS AND JIM HARRIS

An Introduction to Administrative Law (3rd edition)
By PETER CANE

Policies and Perceptions of Insurance
By MALCOLM CLARKE

An Introduction to Family Law
By GILLIAN DOUGLAS

Discrimination Law
By SANDRA FREDMAN

The Conflict of Laws
By ADRIAN BRIGGS

The Law of Property (3rd edition)
By F. H. LAWSON AND BERNARD RUDDEN

INTRODUCTION TO COMPANY LAW

PAUL L. DAVIES

Cassel Professor of Commercial Law

London School of Economics

OXFORD

UNIVERSITY PRESS

OXFORD
UNIVERSITY PRESS

Great Clarendon Street, Oxford OX2 6DP

Oxford University Press is a department of the University of Oxford.
It furthers the University's objective of excellence in research,
scholarship, and education by publishing worldwide in

Oxford New York

Auckland Bangkok Buenos Aires Cape Town Chennai
Dar es Salaam Delhi Hong Kong Istanbul Karachi Kolkata
Kuala Lumpur Madrid Melbourne Mexico City Mumbai Nairobi
São Paulo Shanghai Taipei Tokyo Toronto

Oxford is a registered trade mark of Oxford University Press
in the UK and in certain other countries

Published in the United States
by Oxford University Press Inc., New York

© P. I. Davies 2002

The moral rights of the author have been asserted
Database right Oxford University Press (maker)

First published 2002

Crown copyright material is reproduced with the permission of the
Controller of Her Majesty's Stationery Office

British Library Cataloguing in Publication Data
Data available

Library of Congress Cataloging in Publication Data
Data available

ISBN 0–19–924940–7

5 7 9 10 8 6 4

Typeset in Ehrhartdt
by RefineCatch Limited, Bungay, Suffolk
Printed in Great Britain by
Biddles Ltd, King's Lynn, Norfolk

Preface

The aim of this book is set out in Chapter 1 and, accordingly, a preface might seem unnecessary. However, in a book of this type, which seeks to explain a subject in a relatively short compass and without full citation of references, it is inevitable that intellectual debts may appear inadequately acknowledged in the body of the text. Therefore, I should like to take the opportunity of a preface to mention a, now rather large, number of people from whose insights and understanding of company law I have learned much over the years—not necessarily in ways of which they would approve.

First, I was introduced to company law as a graduate student at the London School of Economics in 1967 by Bill (now Lord) Wedderburn, whose incisive Thursday evening lectures will long be remembered by generations of company lawyers. I am grateful, as well, to contemporaneous LLM students, among whom Tony (now Lord) Grabiner showed me how it was possible to read through all the material contained in the dense handouts attached to those Thursday evening lectures.

More recently, members of the Law Department of the LSE have provided a congenial context for serious work in the company law field, and I am particularly grateful to Sarah Worthington, who read and commented insightfully on the first half of the book.

Over the years I have benefited from membership of that shadowy and intermittent but highly rewarding (for its members) body, the International Faculty for Corporate and Capital Market Law and from interaction with its members, especially Bob (now Justice) Austin, Eddy Wymeersch, and the contributors to its comparative corporate law project: Henry Hansmann, Gérard Hertig, Klaus Hopt, Hideki Kanda, Reinier Kraakman, and Ed Rock. My intellectual debt to that project will be obvious in this book. Among others who have made major contributions to my education in comparative company law are Theo Baums, Guido Ferrarini, Marcus Lutter, and Rolf Skog.

My understanding of domestic company law was furthered enormously by membership of the Steering Group of the Company Law Review and of some of its Working Groups. I am grateful to fellow members of those Groups, to the DTI civil servants who supported the

Review, and, above all, to Jonathan Rickford, the Review's indefatigable Director.

Of course, books, as well as people, feed ideas into one's mind in ways that cannot always be reconstructed subsequently. I would like to acknowledge my debts in that regard to the various editions of Len Sealy's *Cases and Materials in Company Law*, to Brian Cheffins' *Company Law: Theory, Structure and Operation* (1997), and to the Second to Fifth Editions of Jim Gower's, *Principles of Modern Company Law*.

PLD   Dydd Dewi Sant, 2002

Contents

Preface   v
Table of Cases   x
Table of Statutes   xvi
Table of Conventions and Treaties   xxiv

1. **The Core Features of Company Law**   1
   The scope of company law   1
   Shareholders, directors and creditors   5
   The core characteristics of company law   9
   Separate legal personality   9
   Limited liability   10
   Centralized or specialized management   13
   Shareholder control   15
   Transferability of shares   21
   The core features and company size   24
   Companies as vehicles   30
   The structure of the book   33

2. **Corporate Personality**   36
   The exceptions to separate legal personality   37
   How does a company act and know?   38
   Conclusion   59

3. **Limited Liability: Rationale and Creditor Self-Help**   60
   Introduction   60
   The rationales for limited liability   63
   Creditor self-help   68
   Opportunistic behaviour on the part of secured creditors   76

4. **Limited Liability: The Limits of Creditor Self-Help**   78
   The case for mandatory rules   78
   General rules against debtor opportunism   80
   Creditor protection and company capital   83
   Opportunism and increases in the company's liabilities   93

Groups of companies   102
Conclusions   108

5. **Centralized Management I: Empowering
   Shareholders in Widely Held Companies**   111
   The legal basis of centralized management   111
   Centralized management and principal/agent problems   117
   A typology of legal strategies   118
   Shareholder involvement in decision-making   123
   Appointment rights   127
   Affiliation rights   144
   Conclusion   149

6. **Centralized Management II:
   Constraining the Board**   151
   The constraints strategy: introduction   151
   The duty of care   154
   The duty to act bona fide in the best interests of
      the company   159
   Obeying the constitution   160
   Delegation and fettering discretion   167
   Conflicts of interest: self-dealing transactions   170
   Part X of the Act   176
   Corporate opportunities and secret profits   183
   Forgiveness and enforcement   191
   Conclusion   196

7. **Centralized Management III: Setting the
   Board's Incentives**   198
   Trusteeship and non-executive directors   199
   The reward strategy   207
   Conclusions on board/shareholder strategies   209

8. **Majority and Minority Shareholders**   215
   Decision rights   217
   Appointment rights   226
   Affiliation rights   228
   Constraining majority decisions   231
   Setting incentives   245
   Conclusions   253

9. **Shareholder Control** 255
    The meaning of shareholder control and the need for its
        justification 255
    Does the law require control by the suppliers of risk capital? 258
    Why ordinary shareholders contract for votes 262
    The distribution of voting rights among shareholders and
        the loss of control 263
    Allocating governance rights to non-shareholder
        stakeholders 266
    Sharing control rights with stakeholders 267
    Sharing control rights with specific stakeholder groups 271
    Shareholder control and the interests of other stakeholders 276
    Conclusion 280

10. **Small Companies and Small Businesses** 282
    The nature of the small company issue 282
    The small business and the companies legislation 285
    Small businesses and alternative business vehicles 294
    Conclusion 297

    Index 298

Table of Cases

Australia

Daniels *v* Anderson (1995) 16 ACSR 607 157

Gambotto *v* WPC Ltd (1995) 127 ALR 417 236

Queensland Mines Ltd *v* Hudson (1978) 18 ALR 1 187

Canada

Canadian Aero Services *v* O'Malley (1973) 40 DLR (3d) 371 188

Edgeworth Construction Ltd *v* M D Lea & Associates Ltd [1993]
   3 SCR 206 53

Peso–Silver Mines Ltd *v* Cropper (1966) 58 DLR (2d) 1 187

European Commission and Court of Human Rights

Centros Ltd (Case C – 212/97) [2000] All ER (EC) 481 ....4, 201

New Zealand

Coleman *v* Myers [1977] 2 NZLR 225 232

New Zealand Netherlands Society 'Oranje' Inc *v* Kuys [1973]
   1 WLR 1126 187

UK

Adams v Cape Industries [1990] Ch 433 ....80, 105, 106

Allen *v* Gold Reefs of West Africa Ltd [1900] 1 Ch 656 ....234, 236,
   240–1, 294

Anglo-Continental Supply Co Ltd, Re [1922] 2 Ch 723 230

Armagas Ltd *v* Mundogas SA [1986] 1 AC 717 50

Attorney-General for Hong Kong *v* Reid [1994] 1 AC 324 191

Attorney-General's Reference (No 2 of 1999) [2000] QB 796 57

Automatic Self-Cleansing Filter Syndicate Co *v* Cuninghame
  [1906] 2 Ch 34 115

Bamford *v* Bamford [1970] Ch 212 30
Barings plc (No 5), Re [1999] 1 BCLC 433; [2000] 1 BCLC 523 158
Bishopsgate Investment Management Ltd *v* Maxwell (No 2) [1994]
  1 All ER 261 164
Blue Arrow plc, Re [1987] BCLC 585 240
Bratton Seymour Service Co Ltd *v* Oxborough [1992] BCLC 693 243
Brown *v* British Abrasive Wheel Co Ltd [1919] 1 Ch 290 235
Bushell *v* Faith [1970] AC 1099 132

Cade (J E) & Sons Ltd, Re [1992] BCLC 213 240
Caparo Industries plc *v* Dickman [1990] 2 AC 605 ....73, 122, 135
Cardiff Savings Bank, Re [1892] 2 Ch 100 155
Carlton Holdings Ltd, Re [1971] 1 WLR 918 248
Charnley Davies Ltd (No 2), Re [1990] BCLC 760 242
City Equitable Fire Insurance Co Ltd, Re [1925] Ch 407 154
Clemens *v* Clemens Bros Ltd [1976] 2 All ER 268 235
Cohen *v* Selby [2001] 1 BCLC 176 155
Company, Re A [1983] BCLC 126 294
Company, Re A [1986] BCLC 376 238
Company, Re A [1986] BCLC 382 233
Company, Re A [1987] BCLC 82 233
Connelly *v* RTZ Corporation plc [1998] AC 854 106
Cook *v* Deeks [1916] 1 AC 554 ....188, 190, 225
Crowther (John) Group plc *v* Carpets International plc [1990]
  BCLC 460 169
Cumbrian Newspaper Group Ltd *v* Cumberland and Westmorland
  Herald Newspaper and Printing Co Ltd [1987] Ch 1 222

Dafen Tinplate Co Ltd *v* Llanelly Steel Co Ltd [1920] 2 Ch 124 235
Daniels *v* Daniels [1978] Ch 406 250
Dawson International plc *v* Coats Patons plc [1990] BCLC 560 170
Dovey *v* Corey [1901] AC 477 157
Duckwari plc, Re [1999] Ch 253 181

Ebrahimi *v* Westbourne Galleries Ltd [1972] 2 All ER 492;
  [1973] AC 360 ....238, 239
Erlanger *v* New Sombrero Phosphate Co (1878) 3 App Cas 1218 182
Evans (C) & Sons Ltd *v* Spritebrand Ltd [1985] 1 WLR 317 54

First Energy (UK) Ltd v Hungarian International Bank [1993]
  BCLC 1409 45
Foss v Harbottle (1843) 2 Hare 461 ....194, 241
Framlington Group plc v Anderson [1995] 1 BCLC 475 188
Freeman & Lockyer v Buckhurst Park Properties (Mangal) Ltd
  [1964] 2 QB 480 ....44, 47
Fulham Football Club Ltd v Cabra Estates plc [1994] 1 BCLC 363 ..169

Gaiman v National Association for Mental Health [1971] Ch 317 164
Greenhalgh v Arderne Cinemas Ltd [1951] 1 Ch 286 235
Grierson, Oldham and Adams Ltd, Re [1968] Ch 17 248
Guinness v Saunders [1990] 2 AC 663 ....162, 163, 165, 167, 190

Halt Garage (1964) Ltd, Re [1982] 3 All ER 1016 171
Hampshire Land Company, Re [1896] 2 Ch 743 50
Harmer (H R), Re [1959] 1 WLR 62 238
Harrison (Saul D) & Sons plc, Re [1995] 1 BCLC 14 ....239, 241, 272¹
Heatons Transport (St Helens) Ltd v TGWU [1972] 3 All ER 101 49
Hellenic and General Trust, Re [1976] 1 WLR 123 ....218, 220
Heron International Ltd v Lord Grade [1983] BCLC 244 277
Hickman v Kent or Romney Marsh Sheep Breeders Association
  [1915] 1 Ch 881 244
Hogg v Cramphorn [1967] Ch 254 ....146, 162, 164, 166
Holders Investment Trust Ltd, Re [1971] 1 WLR 583 236
Houghton & Co v Nothard, Lowe & Wills [1927] 1 KB 246 45
Howard Smith Ltd v Ampol Petroleum Ltd [1974] 1 All ER 1126;
  [1974] AC 821 ....116, 164, 166
Hutton v West Cork Railway Co (1883) 23 Ch D 654 278
Hydrodam (Corby) Ltd, Re [1994] 2 BCLC 180 ....104, 153²

Imperial Mercantile Credit Association v Coleman (1871) LR 6
  Ch App 558 172
Industrial Development Consultants v Cooley [1972]
  1 WLR 443 ....187–8, 189, 190

Kleinwort Benson Ltd v Malaysia Mining Corp Bhd [1989] 1 All
  ER 785 103
Konamaneni v Rolls Royce Industrial Power (India) Ltd [2002]
  1 All ER 979 250

---

¹ Shown as . . . & Son **Ltd** . . . on p 272
² Shown as . . . BCLC 189 on p 153

Kuwait Asia Bank EC *v* National Mutual Life Nominees Ltd
  [1991] 1 AC 187..76, 168

Lee *v* Lee's Air Farming Ltd [1961] AC 12 38
Lennard's Carrying Co Ltd *v* Asiatic Petroleum Co Ltd [1915]
  AC 705 56
Lister *v* Hesley Hall Ltd [2001] 2 All ER 769 50
Lloyds *v* Grace, Smith & Co [1912] AC 716 50
Lubbe *v* Cape plc [2000] 1 WLR 1545 106

MacDougall *v* Gardiner (1875) 1 Ch D 13 245
Maclaine Watson & Co Ltd *v* Department of Trade and Industry
  [1988] BCLC 404 11
Macro (Ipswich) Ltd, Re [1994] 2 BCLC 354 241
Meridian Global Funds Management Asia Ltd *v* Securities
  Commission [1995] 3 All ER 918 ....41, 56
Merrett *v* Babb [2001] 3 WLR 1 53
Morris *v* Kanssen [1944] Ch 346; [1946] AC 459 41
Morris *v* Martin (C W) & Sons Ltd [1966] 1 QB 716 ....50, 52
Movitex *v* Bulfield [1988] BCLC 104 ....172, 185
Multinational Gas and Petroleum Co *v* Multinational Gas and
  Petroleum Services Ltd [1983] 1 Ch 258 112
Mutual Life Insurance *v* Rank Organisation Ltd [1985] BCLC 11 233

New Zealand Guardian Trust Co Ltd *v* Brooks [1995]
  1 WLR 96 ....49, 76
Noel *v* Poland [2001] 2 BCLC 645 53
North-West Transportation Co Ltd *v* Beatty (1887) 12 App
  Cas 589 ....220, 221

O'Neill *v* Phillips [1999] 1 WLR 351 ....239, 240, 242, 248

Panorama Developments Ltd *v* Fidelis Furnishing Fabrics Ltd
  [1971] 2 QB 711 45
Parke *v* Daily News [1962] Ch 927 ....20, 279
Pavlides *v* Jensen [1956] Ch 565 250
Pender *v* Lushington (1877) 6 Ch D 70 245
Percival *v* Wright [1902] Ch 421 ....231, 232
Permanent House (Holdings) Ltd, Re [1988] BCLC 563 74
Peskin *v* Anderson [2001] BCLC 372 ....153, 232
Phelps *v* Hillingdon BC [2000] 3 WLR 776 53
Phipps *v* Boardman [1967] 2 AC 46 190

Polly Peck International plc (in administration), Re [1996] 2 All
   ER 433 103
Posgate & Denby (Agencies) Ltd, Re [1987] BCLC 8 240
Produce Marketing (No 2), Re [1989] BCLC 520 96

R v British Steel Plc [1995] 1 WLR 1356 56
R v ICR Haulage Ltd [1944] KB 551 56
R v Panel on Take-overs and Mergers ex parte Datafin plc [1987]
   QB 815 ....3, 147
Rackham v Peek Food Ltd [1990] BCLC 895 169
Rayfield v Hands [1960] Ch 1 243
Regal (Hastings) Ltd v Gulliver [1942] 1 All ER 378 ....184, 185, 186,
                                                               187, 188, 189, 193
Regentcrest plc v Cohen [2001] 2 BCLC 80 159
Roith (W & M), Re [1967] 1 All ER 427 159
Rolled Steel Products (Holdings) v British Steel Corporation
   [1986] Ch 246 ....162, 164
Royal Bank of Scotland v Etridge (No 2) [2001] 4 All ER 449 70
Royal British Bank v Turquand (1856) 6 El & Bl 327 46
Russell v Northern Bank Development Corpn Ltd [1992] 1 WLR
   588 221

Said v Butt [1920] 3 KB 497 55
Salomon v Salomon [1897] AC 22 ....10, 28, 37, 69, 104, 108, 284
Scott v Frank F Scott (London) Ltd [1940] Ch 794 243
Scottish Insurance Corp v Wilsons & Clyde Coal Company 1948
   SC at 376 247
Secretary of State for Trade and Industry v Bottrill [2000] 1 All
   ER 915 38
Sevenoaks Stationers (Retail) Ltd, Re [1991] Ch 164 98
Shaw (John) & Son (Salford) Ltd v Shaw [1935] 2 KB 113 193
Shuttleworth v Cox Bros & Co (Maidenhead) Ltd [1927] 2
   KB 9 ....235, 244
Smith v Croft (No 2) [1988] Ch 114 ....219, 220, 226
Smith & Fawcett Ltd, Re [1942] Ch 304 ....24, 159, 294
Supply of Ready Mixed Concrete (No 2), Re [1995] 1 AC 456 56

Tesco Supermarkets Ltd v Nattrass [1972] AC 153 56
Tiessen v Henderson [1899] 1 Ch 861 ....133, 195
Toup Totara Timber v Rowe [1978] AC 537 178

Walker v Standard Chartered Bank plc [1992] BCLC 535 129

Wallersteiner *v* Moir (No 2) [1975] QB 373 219
Weller (Sam) & Sons Ltd, Re [1990] Ch 682 253
West Mercia Safety Wear Ltd *v* Dodds [1988] BCLC 250 265
Westmid Packing Services Ltd, Re [1998] 2 All ER 124 158
Williams *v* Natural Life Health Foods Ltd [1998] 1 WLR 830 51–4,
                                                                          55, 296
Wise *v* USDAW [1996] ICR 691 245

USA

Smith *v* Van Gorkam 488 A 2d 858 (1985) 158

Table of Statutes

Germany

Aktiengesetz 114, 115
    Art 23(5) 17
    Art 84 129

GmbH Gesetz 114

Konzernrecht 1965 107

WpÜG 149
    Art 33 149

New Zealand

Companies Act 1993
    ss 271–2 107

UK

Building Societies Acts 1986–1997 259

Civil Procedure Rules 250
    r 19.9(7) 219
Companies Act 1856 ....28, 68
    s 4 28
Companies Act 1948 73
    s 210 ....237, 238
    Sch 1 16
        Table A ....16 , 139
            Art 78 184
Companies Act 1967 284
Companies Act 1984
    s 346 177

Companies Act 1985 ....1, 2, 5, 9, 11, 12, 13, 31, 32,
87, 104, 108, 123, 128, 135, 174, 200, 211, 222,
223, 243, 246, 252, 258, 260, 282, 283, 285, 286
s 1(1) 7
(2)(b) 31
(c) 12, 69
s 2(5)(b) 7
s 3A 46, 165
s 4 ....124, 235
ss 5–6 235
s 8 ....16, 115
(3) 16
s 9 ....16, 116, 124, 243, 247
s 10(1) 16
s 13(1) 24
(3) 9
s 14 ....173, 243–4
s 22 7
(2) 293
s 24 ....66, 72
s 30 ....32, 72
s 34 72
s 35 ....163, 192
(1), (2), (3) 163
s 35A 41, 47, 48, 163
(2) 42
(3) 16
(4), (5) 163
s 35B 42, 47
s 36C 43
s 49(8) 224
s 54 247
s 80 ....125, 166
s 81 ....17, 125
ss 82–88 125
s 89 ....125, 166, 213, 253
ss 90–96 125
s 100 85
ss 102–111 85
s 117 85

s 125, (1), (2) 222
s 126 222
s 127 ....222, 247
ss 128–129 222
s 135 ....90, 247
(1) 90
ss 136–137 91
s 142 86
s 143 ....88, 93
s 151 93
s 159 88
s 160 ....88, 89
s 162 89
s 163(3) 88
s 164(2) 223
s 166 223
s 170 89
s 171 88
s 173 89
s 175 89
s 176 ....89, 247
s 177 89
s 183 ....7, 293
s 226 ....14, 134
s 233 134
s 235 134
s 238 ....134, 287
s 241 287
s 244 73
s 249A 290
s 252 287
s 253(2) 287
s 254 73
s 258 104
ss 263–264 87
s 282 ....13, 113
s 285 41
s 292 128
s 303 ....19, 23, 75, 116, 129, 130, 132, 133, 136, 137, 139, 146
(2) 137

(5) 129
s 309 ....271, 279
s 310 ....184–7, 196
s 311 161
ss 312–315 178
s 316, (3) 178
s 317 174–5
s 318 ....126, 130
s 319 130–1
ss 320–321 179
s 322 ....179, 182, 190
s 322A 41, 163
ss 330–340 171
s 341 ....171, 179
ss 342–344 171
s 346 179
(2)(c), (4) 180
s 348 72
s 349 72
(4) 72
s 351 72
s 352 293
s 366 136
s 366A, (3) 287
s 367 136
s 368 ....138, 146
s 369 137
ss 376–377 137
s 378 ....139, 222
s 379 ....137, 139
s 379A, (3) 287
s 381A 288
s 384 125
s 425 ....125, 247
s 429 248
s 430(4) 248
s 430C 247
s 458 95
s 459 ....158, 229, 237, 238, 239–42, 243, 245,
248, 253–4, 256, 289, 292–3, 294

(2) 293

s 460 237

s 461 237

(2)(c) 242

s 652 100

s 711A, (1), (2) 47

s 716 28

s 718 1

s 719 21

s 727 196

ss 736–736A 104

s 741 104

(1) 153

s 744 ....8, 154

Pt II 124

Pt V

Ch IV 125

Ch VI 125

Ch VII 21, 125

Pt VII 73

Pt VIII 21

Pt X 123, 125, 153, 176–83, 211, 236, 237

Pt XA 177, 219

Pt XII 110

Pt XVI 239

Pt XVII 237

Pt XXIII 4

Schs 4–4A 134

Sch 6 ....126, 177

Sch 8 291

Sch 8A 292

Sch 22 1

Companies Act 1989 ....1, 47

Company Directors Disqualification Act 1986 2

s 1 ....15, 98

s 2 98

s 6 ....15, 98, 157, 158

s 7(3), (4) 100

s 10 98

s 11 ....14, 98 s 15 98

Contracts (Rights of Third Parties) Act 1999
 s 6(2) 244

Employers' Liability (Compulsory Insurance) Act 1969 81
Employment Rights Act 1996
 Pt XII 81

Financial Services and Markets Act 2000 2
 s 143 147
Friendly Societies Act 1992 259

Health and Safety at Work etc Act 1974 ....55, 58

Industrial and Provident Societies Act 1965 ....258, 259
Insolvency Act 1986 ....2, 12, 60, 77, 81, 230, 238
 s 9 75
 s 29(2) 75
 s 40 76
 s 74 ....12, 95
 s 107 ....21, 84, 255
 ss 110–112 229
 s 122 11
   (1)(f) 102
     (g) 237
 s 123 11
   (1)(e) 102
 s 124 11
 s 143 84
 s 187 21
 s 212 193
 s 213 95
 s 214 ....95, 96–7, 104, 105, 106, 107, 155, 158, 265
   (4), (5) 155
 s 215 95
 ss 216–217 ....99, 100
 ss 238–241 81
 s 245 77
 ss 339–342 81
 s 386 76
 ss 423–424 81

Ch V 229
Pt III 68
Sch 6 76

Joint Stock Companies Act 1844 ....1, 63

Limited Liability Act 1855 ....28, 63, 68, 70, 86
s 1 68
s 13 86
s 142 86
Limited Liability Partnership Act 2000 ....29, 295
s 1(5) 295
Limited Liability Partnership Regulations, SI 2001 No 1090
Pt VI 295
Limited Liability Partnership Regulations, SI 2001 No 1091
reg 3 296
Sch 1 296

Partnership Act 1890
s 4(2) 11
Political Parties, Elections and Referendums Act 2000 ....177, 219

Road Traffic Act 1988 81

SI 1985 No 805 16
Table A 16, 21, 114, 115, 139, 167, 168, 185, 186
Arts 23–28 293
Arts 64–98 114
Art 70 ....45, 114, 115, 116, 139, 165
Art 71 43
Art 72 168
Art 84 173
Art 85 ....173, 184
(b), (c) 184
Arts 94–95 175
Art 109 133
Art 114 256

Traded Securities (Disclosure Regulations) 1994, SI 1994
No 188 136

USA

Delaware General Corporation Law
  § 351 ....13, 289

Model Business Corporation Act
  ss 8.05–8.08 129

New York Business Corporation Law
  s 717 270

Table of Conventions and Treaties

Council Directive 77/91/EEC Second Company Law Directive
    [1977] OJ L26/1 ....85, 92, 93, 166
    Art 25 166
    Art 29 166
Council Directive 79/279/EEC on the conditions for the admission of
    securities to official stock exchange listing
    Art 9 126
Council Directive 89/667/EEC Twelfth Company Law Directive on
    one-person Companies [1989] OJ L395/40 ....28, 69, 108, 285
Council Directive 2001/34/EC Combined Admissions and Reporting
    Directive
    Art 46 145
    Art 65(1) 252
Council Directive 2001/86/EC European Company Directive 276
    Annex, Pt 3 275
Council Directive on employee involvement 4
Council Regulation (EC) No 2157/2001 for the incorporation of a
    'European Company' [2001] OJ L294/1 ....4, 275

Directive 78/660/EEC Fourth Company Law Directive [1978]
    OJ L222/11 291
    Art 11 290
    Art 51 290

EC Treaty 3
    Art 44 3

I

The Core Features of Company Law

THE SCOPE OF COMPANY LAW

Those coming to the study of company law for the first time face a forbidding task. The difficulties are two-fold, and stem from the bulk and range of legal materials which have to be mastered and, for many people, from unfamiliarity with the activities which the law is trying to regulate.

As far as the legal materials are concerned, the new student quickly finds his or her way to the Companies Act 1985, a consolidating statute of some several hundred sections. This is the latest in a line of Acts which can be traced back to the emergence of modern company law in the middle of the nineteenth century. Modern company law dates from the Joint Stock Companies Act 1844, introduced by William Gladstone when he was President of the Board of Trade. That Act ushered in the crucial principle that citizens should be empowered to form companies by going through a relatively simple bureaucratic procedure, presided over by a state official, the Registrar of Companies. Previously, incorporation had been available securely only by following the cumbersome routes of obtaining a private Act of Parliament or a Royal Charter.[1]

Since 1844 statutory company law has been amended and then consolidated on a number of occasions.[2] However, consolidation is very

---

[1] These two routes to incorporation still exist but are rarely used, at least by trading companies. Yet examples of such companies can be found today and present, at least theoretically, an issue of competitive advantage. This arises because only parts of the Companies Act 1985 (notably the financial reporting provisions) apply to companies not registered under the 1985 Act (hereafter 'CA 1985') or any of its predecessors, and some 'unregistered' companies are exempt even from those limited parts of the Act (s 718 and Sch 22). Examples of totally or partly exempt companies are P&O and the Bank of Scotland, though they are kept in line, no doubt, by the knowledge that, if they abused their positions, the exchanges on which their shares are traded or the government would take action.

[2] Notably in 1855/6, 1862, 1908, 1929, 1948, 1967, and 1980/1. The 1985 Act itself has been the subject of further amendment, particularly by the Companies Act 1989. In 1998 the Secretary of State for Trade and Industry, the modern-day successor to the President of the Board of Trade, established an independent Company Law Review (hereafter 'CLR') whose reports may lead to a fundamental overhaul of the subject early in the twenty-first century. The publications flowing from that Review will be referred to at various points in this book.

different from codification, and it quickly becomes apparent that large parts of company law are not to be found in the 1985 Act but in the common law. Indeed, the common law at present provides the rules which govern some central parts of the subject, such as many of the legal duties of directors of companies and the rules about enforcement of those duties.

Even now, however, only part of the legal landscape has been identified. The law relating to the insolvency of companies, which used to be part of the companies legislation, was hived off in the 1980s and is now to be found mainly, though not entirely,[3] in the Insolvency Act 1986 (hereafter 'IA 1986'). This Act treats together the rules governing corporate and personal insolvency, which previously had been in separate legislation. Although handling corporate insolvency has become an immensely technical business, which most first courses in company law touch on only lightly, the insolvency legislation cannot be ignored entirely. Many problems, which lie undiscovered or can be ignored while the company is a going concern, become the focus of detailed analysis once the company is no longer able to pay its way and creditors and shareholders dispute with each other and among themselves for the maximum share of the company's inadequate assets. In consequence, some central issues of company law tend to be seen through the lens of insolvency law, as we shall see in subsequent chapters.[4]

A similar process of hiving off occurred in the 1980s in relation to public offerings of shares by companies. The relevant legislation is now the Financial Services and Markets Act 2000. In this case the government decided it was sensible to bring together under one Act and one regulator the oversight of all major financial markets. However, as with the insolvency legislation, while issuing and trading in the shares of companies constitute only a part of the operation of financial markets, company lawyers cannot ignore the rules regulating these markets. Company lawyers need to know some basic principles of securities law, because the decision to make a public offering of its shares and to trade them on a securities market (or to reverse those decisions at a later stage by 'going private') are major events in a company's life. Thus, companies whose shares are traded on the main market of the London Stock Exchange are subject to much greater public attention and to a much more demanding regulatory regime (via the 'Listing Rules') than companies which have

---

[3] Some important insolvency-related rules are in the Company Directors Disqualification Act 1986.

[4] For example, see the discussion of the standard of care required of directors, below at pp. 155 and 157.

not taken this step; but they also have available to them much more sophisticated mechanisms for raising capital than if they had never come to the Stock Exchange. The Listing Rules are now the responsibility of the Financial Services Authority (FSA) in its capacity as UK Listing Authority.

In addition, the rules of certain non-state bodies are part of the regulatory regime in which at least large companies have to operate. The most important of these rules are those of the City Panel on Take-overs and Mergers, which regulate the conduct of public offers to *acquire* the shares of large companies. Whether these rules may be termed accurately an example of 'self-regulation' is very much open to doubt, though that term is often used to characterize them.[5] What is clear is that these rules are not generated and administered in the same way as legislation, primary or subordinate, and so the company lawyer needs to acquire a further set of skills in order to grasp their significance.

Finally, company law is one of the areas of domestic law where European Community law has had a significant impact. The original drafters of the EC Treaty envisaged an ambitious programme of harmonization of the national company laws of the Member States under what is now Art 44 EC. Eleven harmonizing directives have been issued in the area of 'core' company law, and they have had a particular impact, in the UK, upon the rules relating to the protection of third parties dealing with the company, company accounts (for both individual companies and groups of companies), the auditing of accounts, and corporate capital. However, for more than a decade the harmonization process has made little progress, partly because of the difficulties of achieving agreement among the Member States on the harmonization of governance issues,[6] and partly because the intellectual argument that the achievement of the Community's goals required close harmonization of national company law systems lost conviction.[7] In recent years, Community harmonization efforts have turned in the more fruitful direction of capital markets law.

Along with closer harmonization of national laws, since the late 1960s the Commission also had a plan for a Community-level form of

---

[5] The Panel's decisions are certainly subject to (a light form of) judicial review on the grounds that the Panel performs a function which, if not discharged by that body, would be taken on by the state. See *R v Takeover Panel ex parte Datafin plc* [1987] QB 815, CA.

[6] See below in this chapter at p. 20, where the German board system is contrasted with that in the UK.

[7] For a discussion of the competing arguments in favour of harmonization of or, by contrast, competition among national company law systems, see B. Cheffins, *Company Law: Theory, Structure and Operation* (Oxford: Clarendon Press, 1997), ch. 9.

incorporation, so that large companies operating across borders could choose to incorporate under Community law rather than under the national laws of one or other of the Member States. Of course, incorporation under Community law is not necessary in order for a company to be recognized in a jurisdiction other than the one in which it is incorporated. All modern legal systems accept and provide for the operation within their jurisdiction of companies incorporated elsewhere, without requiring them to incorporate under domestic law.[8] However, incorporation at Community level was aimed to make it easier to overcome nationalistic opposition to cross-border tie-ups between companies, by removing the need for the resulting 'lead' company to identify itself with the law of one particular Member State. After many travails, in 2001 the Community adopted a Regulation for the incorporation of a 'European Company' (abbreviated to 'SE' after the Latin *Societas Europaea*), which will come into force in October 2004.[9] However, in the many years that have passed between proposal and adoption, the SE law has ceased to provide a near-complete code of company law for Community-level incorporated companies. Large parts of the applicable law for the SE have been delegated to the company law of the Member State in which the SE has its registered office. Consequently, the level of use of the SE is difficult to predict.

Although company law is not unique among legal subjects in the bulk and diversity of legal materials which it presents to those who will study it, there can be no doubt that a guide through the terrain is needed—and not only by the novice. It is the purpose of this short book to provide such a guide and to do so in a particular way. Company law in the UK benefits already from the existence of a number of full-scale textbooks, as well as from some well-established multi-volume practitioner works. One way of producing a short guide would be to follow the format and structure of these books, but to achieve brevity by leaving out much of the detail. The approach adopted in this book is somewhat more ambitious. The claim is that, despite the quantity and range of the legal materials, those materials are aimed at implementing, and addressing the problems generated by, a small number of core features of company law. The first task, therefore, is

[8] For the UK provisions, see CA 1985 Part XXIII, which deals with what are quaintly termed 'oversea' companies. However, some countries, unlike the UK, will not recognize a company merely because it is incorporated in another jurisdiction unless it has some significant 'real' connection with that jurisdiction. See Case C–212/97, *Centros Ltd* [2000] All ER (EC) 481 (ECJ).

[9] Council Regulation (EC) No 2157/2001, [2001] OJ L294/1, accompanied by a Directive on employee involvement. See Chapter 9, p. 275.

accurately to identify this small number of core features and their functional significance. That will be the primary task of this first chapter. Later chapters will analyse how the core features have been implemented in British[10] company law and how that law seeks to solve any consequential problems. The aim of the book as a whole is to equip the student with a set of intellectual tools which can be brought to bear on, and to analyse, any part of the subject, even though that part is not treated in detail in this book.

SHAREHOLDERS, DIRECTORS, AND CREDITORS

Before turning to the identification of the core features, however, it will be useful to say something about the second feature of company law which makes it initially a difficult subject, namely, possible lack of familiarity with and understanding of the roles performed by the people whose activities company law regulates. At least as far as British company law is concerned, it deals with the activities of three main groups of people: the shareholders (or 'Members') of the company; its directors and, to a lesser extent, its senior managers, whether they are directors or not; and its creditors, who may be secured or unsecured. The law seeks to regulate both the relations between these three groups (for example, shareholders as against directors or creditors as against shareholders) and within these groups (for example, majority as against minority shareholders or secured as against unsecured creditors). It also seeks to regulate the mechanisms by which people join, or leave, one of these groups as well as their rights and duties once they have joined a group. Thus, the law is interested in the processes by which investors come to be shareholders or creditors of a company as well as their legal status once they have acquired shares or lent money to the company.

Obviously, a company which runs a business will need to generate successful relationships with other groups of people as well, notably suppliers of various inputs (such as labour or components) and customers, not to mention government or the community in which the company operates. To look at customer and supplier relationships solely in terms of the protection of creditors is a very narrow viewpoint. The company laws of some countries do embrace a wider set of relationships, though, in

---

[10] The Companies Act applies throughout Great Britain and company law is not a devolved matter. There is separate, but similar, legislation in Northern Ireland. The common law of companies may vary as between England and Wales, on the one hand, and Scotland on the other, as may procedural matters.

terms of structures, few have gone beyond bringing some aspects of the relationship with employees within the fold of company law. We shall discuss in a later chapter the pros and cons of extending the reach of company law beyond shareholders, directors/senior managers, and creditors, as opposed to regulating these additional relationships through separate bodies of law. Let us stay for the time being with the traditional trinity.

It is not easy to put in one sentence the role of each of these groups, because, as we shall see, companies perform many different functions and the roles of shareholders, directors, and creditors vary accordingly. It is perhaps easiest to say something about the directors. Their legal function is to manage the company, though what that entails can vary, according to the size of company and the distribution of its shareholdings, from simply doing what a dominant shareholder tells them to do, to monitoring the execution of the management task by the senior employees of the company, via actually taking and implementing the strategic decisions themselves.

Shareholders, who may or may not be directors of the company as well, usually provide a particular type of finance to the company ('risk' capital) and, in return, their shares are usually thought of as giving their holders two types of right. One is to exercise ultimate control over the company, notably by selecting or removing the directors and setting the terms of the company's constitution; and the other is to receive a financial return on their investment in the shares, either in the form of a dividend when the company is a going concern or by way of a share in the assets of the company if it is wound up. In fact, the nature and extent of these entitlements can vary enormously from one company to another. The shareholders' rights are essentially a matter of contract with the company and so different companies may wish to issue shares on differing terms. Even within a single company, there may be more than one class of shareholder, with the different classes having different entitlements. Some shares carry voting rights at meetings of the shareholders, others not; some have an entitlement to a dividend, others do not have a claim to more than the directors choose to pay them; some shareholders may have priority over others in a winding-up, useful if there are not in fact enough assets to go around. In fact, the only substantial limit on the ingenuity of companies in formulating the rights of shareholders is the willingness or otherwise of investors to buy the shares at an acceptable price.

However, it is of the utmost importance to note that the law treats shareholders not just as a group of people with contractual rights of various sorts against the company but also as its 'members'. It is the initial shareholders of the company who bring it into existence by registering it with the Registrar of Companies and who become the first members of the organization thus created. Subsequent shareholders also become members of the company.[11] The point is of theoretical, even ideological, significance, because the train of thought which makes the shareholders the members of the company leads naturally to making the shareholders' interests predominant within company law. To the Victorian drafters of the companies legislation it was as natural to vest ultimate control of the company in the shareholders (members), at least as the default rule,[12] as it is still to us to think that the members of a cricket club or a students' union should be the ultimate repository of authority in those organizations.

However, this account does not explain why the law treated the shareholders as the members. Certainly, they provide an important input for the company's activities, namely a certain type of finance, but, as we have just noted, other groups of people provide arguably equally important inputs. Why not treat the directors as the members of the company or the employees or even its creditors? This is a crucial issue which we shall discuss in a later chapter. For the moment, all we need to see is that the shareholders' relation with the company is not simply a contract for the supply of finance to the company but also a contract of membership in the company.

Creditors, too, come in many varieties. The most obvious are those

---

[11] Technically, the company is formed by the subscribers to the company's memorandum of association (CA 1985, s 1(1)) but in the case of a company limited by shares each subscriber must take at least one share (s 2(5)(b)). Section 22 then defines the members of the company as the subscribers to the memorandum and those who subsequently agree to become members and whose names are entered in the company's register of its members. Finally, s 738 defines the allotment of new shares by a company as conferring upon the allottee an unconditional right to be included in the company's register of members; and the test for a successful transfer of a share from an existing shareholder to a new investor is the entry of the name of the new shareholder in the register of members (s 183). So, those shareholders who form the company or who subsequently buy shares from it or who buy shares from existing shareholders all become members of the company. The complexity of the statutory provisions is caused, at least in part, by the fact that a company may be formed with members who are not shareholders. See p. 31 below.

[12] A default rule is one which is applied by the law in a particular situation unless the parties involved agree upon a different rule. The law may make it easy or difficult for the parties to agree upon something different. Because of the dominance of ideas of freedom of contract in company law, default rules are a characteristic feature of our law. For further discussion of default rules see p. 68 below and Law Commission, *Company Directors: Regulating Conflicts of Interest and Formulating a Statement of Duties*, Law Commission Consultation Paper No 153 (London, 1998), pp. 36 and 41–4.

who have supplied goods or services to the company but have not been
paid for them; or who have suffered wrongs at the company's hands and
not yet been compensated. More significant for the financing of the company, however, are those creditors who have made medium- or long-term
loans to the company. The interests of all creditors feature among the
concerns of company law, but company law does not purport to provide a
complete code of rules for company/creditor relations. Much of this
regulatory task is left to commercial law, because the relevant rules do not
depend on whether the party to the transaction with the creditor is a
company or some other legal entity or an individual person. Company law
addresses only creditor issues which are unique to companies. In the
main, such issues arise out of the adoption by company law of the doctrine of 'limited liability'[13] or because the taking of security by creditors
gives them a potential role in the governance of companies. Thus, long-
term loans may be secured on the assets of the company, and certain types
of security[14] give the creditor the right to replace the directors with its
own nominee to run the company if the company defaults on the terms of
its agreement with the lender. In this way creditors become part of the
governance structure of the company and not just the holders of a
secured entitlement against the company.

The creditor may be a single person, for example a bank, but companies may offer their debt instruments to the public, as well as their
shares. In this case, there will be a class or classes of creditors of the
company, as well as of shareholders, and the debt instruments (often
called 'bonds') may be traded on the Exchange in the same way as shares.
If the loan is secured on the company's assets, then, whether the loan is
from a single or a class of lenders, it is common to refer to it as a 'debenture'.[15] In the case of secured loans raised from classes of creditor, especially where the debt instruments are traded on a public market, there
will normally be a trustee for the debenture-holders who can act swiftly
to protect their interests, if the need arises.

With this by way of preamble, let us turn to the task of identifying the
core characteristics of company law.

---

[13] See p. 10 below and Chapters 3 and 4.
[14] The 'floating charge', which is discussed in Chapter 3.
[15] In law the term 'debenture' embraces unsecured as well as secured loans (see CA 1985,
s 744) but commercial parlance differs: see *Gower's Principles of Modern Company Law*, 6th
edn (London: Sweet & Maxwell, 1997), pp. 322–4 (hereafter '*Gower*').

THE CORE CHARACTERISTICS OF COMPANY LAW

It is suggested that there are five core characteristics around which it is possible to organize an introductory analysis of company law. The New Zealand Law Commission has identified four of them in the following terms.[16]

- Recognition of the company as an entity distinct from all its shareholders.
- Limited liability for shareholders.
- Specialized management, separate from the shareholders.
- Ease of transfer of the shareholder interest.

In addition, it is suggested that there is a fifth characteristic, which the Commission perhaps omitted because it thought it too obvious, but which is in fact the most controversial feature of modern company law, at least in terms of the wider public debate. This is:

- Allocation of rights of control over the company and of rights to receive the profits, if any, of the company's operations to the members of the company.

Let us say a little about each of these now. They will be fully examined in the later chapters of this book.

SEPARATE LEGAL PERSONALITY

The notion that the company is a legal person separate from its shareholders, directors, creditors, employees, indeed from anyone else involved in it, is fundamental to the conceptual structure of company law. Functionally, it is also important because it facilitates, even if it does not require, the provision by company law of other core features such as limited liability and transferable shares. Nevertheless, it must be admitted that the legislative technique by which the Companies Act 1985 achieves this result is rather antiquated. Section 13(3), the wording of which dates back to the nineteenth century, provides as follows. Upon issuance of a certificate of registration by the Registrar of Companies, those who sign

---

[16] Law Commission, *Company Law Reform and Restatement*, Report No 9 (Wellington, New Zealand, 1989), para. 22.

the memorandum of association[17] 'shall be a body corporate by the name contained in the memorandum', together with any other persons who from time to time subsequently become members of the company. This rather suggests that the members are the company rather than that the process of registration creates a separate legal person of which those requesting its creation become the first members. Nevertheless, the latter is the sense in which the companies legislation has been understood to operate at least since the end of the nineteenth century,[18] and the Company Law Review has proposed that the statutory wording should be updated so as to reflect this fact.[19]

In the previous paragraph, we presented the function of the separate legal personality rule as being the performance of a rather subordinate role, that is, facilitating two other core features which we shall describe in a moment. However, the company's separate legal personality is a *general* feature of its legal status and is not confined to the areas of limited liability and transferable shares. The question then arises whether there are some circumstances in which the general rule should be ignored, that is, the separate legal personality of the company should be ignored.[20]

Further, the separate legal personality of the company enormously complicates some areas of legal reasoning, because an additional legal person has to be fitted into the analysis of legal relations between and among shareholders, directors, and creditors. In other words, company law may not establish legal relations directly between these groups, but instead may, and typically does, mediate them through another legal person, the company. Thus, directors will owe duties to the company rather than to the shareholders; shareholders may have rights against the company rather than against the directors. There are good functional reasons for proceeding in this way, but the interposition of the company person into the relationships between the groups of human beings involved in the company can generate as many analytical problems as it solves.[21]

LIMITED LIABILITY

Limited liability means that the rights of the company's creditors are confined to the assets of the company and cannot be asserted against the

[17] See above, n. 11.

[18] See *Salomon v Salomon* [1897] AC 22.

[19] CLR, *Company Formation and Capital Maintenance*, Consultation Document 3 (London, 1999), p. 81.

[20] See Chapter 2, p. 37.   [21] See Chapter 2, p. 38.

personal assets of the company's members (shareholders). Hence the common expression 'limited liability companies'. However, this is really a misnomer. The liability of the company is not limited at all. Creditors' rights can be asserted to the full against the company's assets. It is the liability of the members which is limited.

Separate legal personality facilitates limited liability in that it makes it easier to distinguish business assets (owned by the company) from personal assets (owned by the members), though it is not impossible to find effective ways of drawing this line in bodies which do not have separate legal personality. While the company is a going concern, separate legal personality can be said to guarantee limited liability. If a third party has a contract and the counter-party to the contract is a company as a separate legal person, English common law draws the consequence that liability on the contract is confined to the company and its assets and will not extend to the members of the company and their assets.[22] In English law, the real bite of the limited liability doctrine is revealed not in the context of a possible direct legal relationship between the creditor and the shareholders on the transaction giving rise to the debt or liability, because such a relationship is not recognized. Rather, the importance of limited liability shows itself in the legal relationship between the company and its members if the company becomes insolvent because it has insufficient assets to meet the overall claims of its creditors. In insolvent liquidation the question arises whether the liquidator, who now runs the company in place of the directors, can claim a contribution to the company's inadequate assets from its members. However, since an unpaid creditor has the power to put the company into compulsory liquidation[23] and since the liquidator owes his or her primary duties to the company's creditors, in fact the creditors will normally be the parties in interest if the liquidator is able to bring such contribution claims against the members.

Perhaps surprisingly, one cannot find the answer to the question of whether the members have limited liability in this further and crucial sense (i.e. as against the liquidator) in the Companies Act. It is necessary

---

[22] See *Maclaine Watson & Co Ltd v Department of Trade and Industry* [1988] BCLC 404, 456–7, CA. At common law there is thus a clear dichotomy: either a body is incorporated and it is liable to third parties and its members are not; or it is an unincorporated association with no legal personality and its members are liable. Some civil law systems, including in this context the Scottish law of partnership, recognize 'mixed' bodies, where the body is incorporated and liable but the members are nevertheless also (secondarily) liable (see Partnership Act 1890, s 4(2)). The CLR has recommended the inclusion in the Act of a statement of the English common law rule.

[23] IA 1986, ss 122–4.

instead to turn to the provisions of the Insolvency Act 1986. Section 74 begins with the proposition that in a winding-up the members are indeed liable to make such contributions as are needed to cover the company's debts and liabilities. Fortunately for the members, however, the section goes on to provide that, in the case of a company which has issued shares, no further contribution is required from the shareholders beyond the amount, if any, which is still owing to the company for the shares.

Thus, by a combination of separate legal personality (while the company is a going concern) and the provisions of the Insolvency Act (if it becomes insolvent), limited liability is effectively guaranteed to the members of companies. However, it is not obligatory to have limited liability. The Companies Act permits the incorporators to choose an 'unlimited company'.[24] In such a company the shareholders have the protection of the doctrine of separate legal personality, but the contribution principle of s 74 of the Insolvency Act applies to them in full force. Thus, so long as the company is solvent, the shareholders of an unlimited company need have no dealings with its creditors, but if the company goes into insolvent liquidation they should expect the liquidator soon to appear on the scene, seeking contributions to the company's assets. For this reason, perhaps, very few unlimited companies have been formed, even though unlimited companies are more lightly regulated than limited companies: of the over 1.2 million companies on the register in 1998 fewer than 4,000 were unlimited companies.[25]

In the previous paragraphs we have concentrated on the protection afforded to shareholders by the doctrine of limited liability. However, if the principle is that the creditors' claims are normally to be confined to the assets of the company, one might conclude that the assets of the directors (and indeed of employees and other groups) should be protected from the creditors' claims as well. As we shall see in Chapter 2,[26] the legal techniques by which the protection of limited liability is extended to directors are entirely different from those by which it is extended to shareholders, and the protection of directors is conceptually less securely based than it is in relation to shareholders.

---

[24] CA 1985, s 1(2)(c).

[25] In particular, unlimited companies do not have to file accounts and they are free to reduce their share capital without obtaining the authorization of the court. Within some corporate groups, where the parent company is happy to stand behind a subsidiary, the subsidiary may be formed as an unlimited company to take advantage of these relaxations.

[26] Below at p. 51.

CENTRALIZED OR SPECIALIZED MANAGEMENT

In companies of any size it is hardly surprising that the management of the company is not left with the shareholders but is entrusted to a small group of managers. Partly, this is a question of speed and cost. A large shareholding body can be convened fairly only after reasonable notice (say two weeks at a minimum) and at some expense. Partly, it is a question of expertise. Shareholders in large companies, even if they are professional fund managers, may be experts at taking investment decisions but are not necessarily skilled at managing companies. Individual investors may not be highly skilled at either, since their main occupation in life may be something entirely different. Partly, it is a question of motivation. A shareholder who knows he or she will be one of a body of, say, one thousand shareholders taking a particular decision may be tempted not to invest much time in working out the correct answer to the question, but rather to free-ride on the efforts of the others—but all the shareholders will be subject to the same incentive to shirk and so none may prepare properly. The dynamics of small group decision-making, which will govern decisions of the managers, are entirely different.

However, the arguments in the previous paragraph do not constitute a convincing case that company law should require a centralized management structure. One might say that, if these arguments are forceful, companies will develop their own structures, provided only they are given the legal freedom to do so. Such contractual structures could be customized to the needs of particular companies and, indeed, some companies, for example small ones, might decide that they did not need a centralized management structure at all: the shareholders might be a small enough group for them to constitute also the managers. In fact, however, British company law is prescriptive on this point. Section 282 of the Companies Act requires public companies to have at least two directors and private companies to have one,[27] and the Act is peppered with provisions which assume the existence of a board of directors. The Company Law Review floated the idea that British company law should follow the example of many US states and permit small companies to dispense with the separate board of directors,[28] but on consultation the idea did not prove attractive.

There is no doubt that the statutory requirement for a board of directors has some advantages. In particular, when it is desired to regulate the

---

[27] The distinction between public and private companies is explained below at p. 17.
[28] See, for example, Delaware General Corporation Law, §351.

top management of companies, whether by common law or statute, the board provides a focus for the attachment of the relevant rules. As we shall see, there is a very substantial corpus of statutory and common law rules applying to directors, the analysis of which traditionally constitutes a major part of company law courses. This explains why managers as such play a relatively small role in company law, no matter how large they may loom in the business schools. At centre stage, as far as the law is concerned, are the directors, either individually or collectively as a board of directors, though some of the directors will normally also be full-time managers of the company (usually termed 'executive' directors).

Nevertheless, the problem of inflexibility arising out of the law's requirement that companies have directors is still troublesome. The potential inflexibility relates not only to small companies, which may not want a board at all, but also to larger companies, which may have different views about the functions which their boards should fulfil. The traditional response of the law to this problem has been to stipulate very little about who the directors should be and what they should do. No qualifications are required for acting as the director of a company,[29] though directors can now subsequently be disqualified from so acting on various grounds.[30] Again, although the Act imposes many administrative duties upon the directors, of which the most important is probably the production of annual accounts,[31] it says very little about the management functions which the directors are to discharge.

In this way, the law seeks to accommodate the wide range of different business (and other) activities which are carried on through the company form. In some small companies there is no doubt that the board does indeed manage the company. In fact, the only managers in the company may be its directors. In large global businesses, on the other hand, the board can manage the company only in the rather broad sense of setting overall corporate strategy and monitoring the effectiveness of its execution by non-board management. In such a company only a few of the most senior managers will be on the board: the overwhelming majority of the army of full-time managers needed to run the company will never

---

[29] Except the negative one of not being an undischarged bankrupt: Company Directors Disqualification Act 1986, s 11.

[30] So everyone is entitled to at least one bite of the cherry of being a company director. See Chapter 4, p. 97.

[31] CA 1985, s 226. Contrary to popular belief it is the directors (rightly) upon whom the duty lies to produce the balance sheet and profit and loss account, not the company's auditors.

achieve board membership. In between these extremes many other divisions of function between the board and senior management can be found. The important point is that, in the absence of legal regulation, the functions of the board are determined by the company's constitution[32] or by resolution of the board itself, that is, by private rather than public ordering.

Nevertheless, the traditional abstention of the law from regulation of who directors are and what they do is coming under some strain, as we shall see later in the book. Among examples of this trend are the following. An increasing number of statutory and common law rules are applied to de facto or shadow directors,[33] which categories may embrace senior managers in certain situations. A court order disqualifying a person who has shown him- or herself to be unfit to act as a director will also prohibit that person from being involved in the management of the company, whether as a director or otherwise.[34] The common law and statutory rules relating to a director's duty of care are increasingly regulating not only how the director discharges the functions he or she chooses to undertake but also the choice of function, a tendency which has been taken further in the non-statutory corporate governance codes.[35] Finally, those corporate governance codes have also paid attention to one important issue relating to the composition of boards of listed companies, namely the split between executive and non-executive directors, that is, between those who are and those who are not also senior managers of the company.[36] The notion that, at least in listed companies, management is too important a matter to be left entirely to the directors and shareholders is beginning to gain ground.

SHAREHOLDER CONTROL

We have already noted that the Victorian draftsman regarded the shareholders, as members, as the ultimate repository of authority in the company. What concretely does this mean in terms of control rights for the shareholders? There are three principal areas of shareholder control: control over the company's constitution; control over the company's

---

[32] The meaning of this word is considered below at p. 16.

[33] These terms are discussed further below at p. 153.

[34] Company Directors Disqualification Act 1986, ss 1 and 6.

[35] See Institute of Chartered Accountants, *Internal Control* (London, 1999)—the 'Turnbull' Report.

[36] See Chapter 7, p. 200.

management; and control over the company's economic surplus. Let us say a little about each of these.

CONTROL OVER THE COMPANY'S CONSTITUTION

At present the company's constitution is contained in two principal documents: the memorandum of association and the articles of association, though the Company Law Review has proposed that they be replaced by a single document.[37] The memorandum is the shorter document, its content is largely specified by the Act, some parts of it cannot be changed after registration of the company,[38] and its original purpose was to provide information which it was thought the outside world needed to know. The articles, by contrast, deal with the internal arrangements of the company at some length and are very much under the control of the members, though they are also required to be sent to the Registrar on formation[39] and thus are publicly available. In particular, the articles allocate decision-making as between the shareholders' meeting and the board, except to the limited extent that the Act requires particular decisions to be taken by these bodies.[40]

Although the legislature has provided a model set of articles to help those wishing to form companies—the so-called Table A[41]—they constitute no more than a set of default rules.[42] The incorporators may choose to form the company with a set of articles completely different from the statutory model[43] and, whether they do or they do not, a three-quarters majority of the shareholders may subsequently alter the articles in any way they please.[44] A number of well-known commercial incorporation

---

[37] Above, n. 19, p. 9. CA 1985, s 35A(3) treats also shareholder resolutions and agreements as part of the company's constitution.

[38] In particular, the clause specifying jurisdiction of incorporation (England and Wales or Scotland) of the company falls into that category.

[39] Unless the company adopts Table A (see below) exclusively, in which case the company's articles do not have to be registered.

[40] See further, Chapter 5, p. 123.

[41] Currently contained in SI 1985 No 805. It contains some 118 regulations. There have been a number of earlier models, one of which may have influenced the articles actually adopted by companies which are still in existence. This is particularly true of the model which immediately preceded the current one, namely, that of 1948, and which was contained in Sch 1 to CA 1948. A change in the statutory model does not alter the articles of any existing company: CA 1985, s 8(3).

[42] See n. 12 above.

[43] CA 1985, s 8. Because the statutory model will apply in default of an alternative choice, the incorporators are not obliged to file articles with the Registrar, though they will need to file any departures they choose to make from the statutory model: CA 1985, s 10(1).

[44] CA 1985, s 9.

agents have founded now extensive businesses on the giving of advice to those who wish to form companies on how they should adapt the statutory model to meet their own particular needs.

The articles part of the constitution is thus highly flexible and its control by the shareholders correspondingly important. The flexibility of the constitution and its control by the shareholders are distinctive features of British company law. At least for large companies, both our continental European neighbours and some common law jurisdictions, such as the states of the USA, have been more prescriptive, at least historically. They have determined more things in the companies legislation and left fewer things for determination by the members in the company's constitution.[45] Probably, the flexibility of the articles in British law is the result of using a single Act to regulate all forms of company. In continental Europe it is common to have separate legislation for companies which offer their shares to the public and for those which do not;[46] whereas in the United States it is common to provide separate forms of incorporation or separate constitutional provisions for small companies. Either way, it is possible for the legislature in such systems to be prescriptive for the large companies, while conceding greater freedom of action to the smaller ones.

In Britain, by contrast, all sizes of company fall under a single statute. In such a system, it was probably necessary to grant freedom of action to the members, since no legislature could hope to lay down a single constitutional structure appropriate for all classes of company. At a deeper level, however, it may be that the 'single Act' approach represents a preference, historically, on the part of the British legislature for default rather than mandatory rules in the area of company constitutions, for freedom of contract over legislative prescription. After all, the *distinction* between companies which are permitted to offer their shares to the public and those which are not is to be found within our single Act. It is indeed the basis of the distinction made in the Act between a public company and a private company. A private company commits a criminal offence if it offers its shares to the public.[47] The public/private distinction is regarded as being so important that it is reflected in the suffix which most

---

[45] Thus art 23(5) of the German *Aktiengesetz* (see next note) provides: 'The articles may make a different provision from the provisions of this Act only if this Act explicitly permits.'

[46] In Germany the former type of company is called the *Aktiengesellschaft* (AG) and the latter the *Gesellschaft mit beschränkter Haftung* (GmbH); in France the equivalent division is between the *société anonyme* (SA) and the *société à responsabilité limitée* (Sarl).

[47] CA 1985, s 81.

companies are required to have as part of their name. A public company must carry the words 'public limited company' or 'plc' after its name (or their Welsh equivalents) and a private company the word 'limited' or 'ltd'.

Not only does the Act draw the distinction between public and private companies, it also regulates the former more closely. This is so, not just in the sense that some types of regulation are unnecessary for companies which do not offer their shares to the public, but also in the broader sense that the freedom to make public offerings is seen as an indicator of the public-interest significance of the company in a general way. Thus, public companies are more tightly regulated than private companies, even in matters which have no direct connection with the public offering of shares. Yet, the legislature never moved beyond drawing the public/private distinction within the single Act to developing separate constitutional frameworks for the two types of company (or, indeed, for other types of company).

CONTROL OVER MANAGEMENT

Control of the company's constitution and control of its management are separate but conceptually linked issues. Thus, the company law of a country might prescribe minutely the division of functions between shareholders and the board and the decision-making procedures within companies (so that the shareholders had no control over the constitution) but the prescribed constitution might nevertheless give the shareholders the power to appoint and dismiss the directors (so that it would be appropriate to say that they had control over the management).

It might be thought that the easiest way to give shareholders control over management would be to vest the management powers in them. Given the flexibility of British law in relation to the company's constitution, this is legally a feasible strategy and is followed in some small companies. In effect, the company is managed by its shareholders and the board, as such, plays only a minor role. The board does only the things which the Act requires to be done by the board; everything else is done by the shareholders. However, this strategy for giving shareholders control over management (by vesting it in them) at the same time deprives those shareholders of the advantages of centralized management, which we have already noted.[48] Moreover, vesting management in the shareholders solves one problem (the shareholder/directors problem) at the potential cost of creating another, namely, the risk of oppressive conduct on the

---

[48] Above, p. 13.

part of the majority of the shareholders as against the minority. It is perhaps not surprising that company law has developed rules against minority oppression most strongly in the small company context where control of the company is most likely to be in the hands of the majority shareholders, as we shall see in a later chapter.[49] As far as medium-sized and large companies are concerned, however, the question which company law has traditionally posed itself is how to maintain shareholder control in a context of centralized management.

Company lawyers have devoted considerable ingenuity over the years to developing techniques which enable shareholders to exercise some measure of control over centralized management, and we shall examine them, and their effectiveness, in Chapters 5 to 7 of this book. There are two basic approaches: enhancing the shareholders' control over the board and directly structuring the board's decision-making. As to the former, the Act gives an ordinary majority of the shareholders the right to remove all or any of the directors at any time and for any reason, irrespective of whether the shareholders have this right under the company's constitution.[50] The threat of a hostile take-over offer may also operate to keep the management up to the mark. In this case, protection of the existing shareholders is effected by the securities markets and the power of the shareholders to transfer their shares, and it is the bidder who will exercise the statutory power of removal, if the bid succeeds. As well as empowering the shareholders, the law may try to structure the decisions of the directors. Thus, the common law treats directors as fiduciaries and, in consequence, as bound to exercise their discretion in the interests of the shareholders, while various contractual mechanisms may be deployed (such as share option schemes) to align the directors' interests de facto with those of the shareholders.

When we come to examine these techniques later in the book, we shall see that it is debatable how effective some of them are. However, we should note here a further issue which will need to be examined, which is an almost contrary critique. This critique questions the value of making the lines of accountability of the management run to the shareholders or, at least, solely to the shareholders. All that we need to say at this point is that, as a matter of theoretical possibility, it is obvious that the lines of accountability could be different, and that other groups with a long-term commitment to the company could be brought within the control mechanisms of company law. There are examples of this near at hand. In

---

[49] Below, Chapter 8.   [50] CA 1985, s 303.

Germany the board of management of large companies (*Vorstand*) is accountable, at least in some degree,[51] to a supervisory board (*Aufsichtsrat*), one-third of whose members will be persons appointed by the employees of the company or the relevant trade union, where the company employs at least 500 workers. Where the company employs at least 2,000 workers, the employees appoint half the members of the supervisory board, though the chair has a casting vote and is always a shareholder representative. It is clear that, with this core feature, company law enters very firmly into the field of social and political values. We shall attempt to face head-on the questions raised by the clash of values in Chapter 9. It may be possible to identify rather better reasons for shareholder control than were ever articulated by the Victorians. On the other hand, modern theories of 'stakeholding' in companies pose a powerful challenge to the shareholder monopoly of managerial control.

ENTITLEMENT TO THE SURPLUS

The third element of control which we identified was control over the distribution of the surplus made by the company. The shareholders' entitlement to the surplus earned by the company results from the combined operation of two features of company law. The first is the principle that the directors have no authority—and possibly the company has no capacity—to distribute the company's assets to anyone other than the members of the company except in the discharge of a legal claim upon the company or in order to further the company's business.[52] This principle is strikingly displayed by the need to introduce a special statutory provision permitting a company which is ceasing to trade to pay voluntary severance payments to its employees. Since the payments were not in satisfaction of any legal claim on the company and a company which was ceasing to trade had no need to generate goodwill amongst its workforce, such payments were held to be unlawful at common law.[53] However, even

---

[51] Klaus Hopt suggests that the relative weakness of the supervision exercised by the *Aufsichtsrat* may be related to the presence of non-shareholder interests on it, i.e. shareholders would prefer a weak supervisory board to strong supervision by a body which includes 'outside' interests: 'Labor Representation on Corporate Boards' (1994) 14 *International Review of Law and Economics* 203. The text ignores the special regimes operative in the coal and steel industries.

[52] Of course, the company's business might consist in part of giving money away, for example in the case of a charitable company making grants to support certain activities. Here the problem dissolves, precisely because the company's authorized activities include giving money to non-members.

[53] *Parke v Daily News* [1962] Ch 927.

the modern statutory provisions permitting such payments require shareholder approval for them, thus underlining the point that any surplus is for the shareholders to dispose of.[54]

If payment of surplus to non-members is difficult, except with shareholder consent, the answer to the second question, of whether the members have an entitlement to the surplus when the company is a going concern, depends mainly upon the company's constitution and the terms upon which a particular class of shares was issued.[55] In fact, companies tend to be extremely cautious in granting legally enforceable entitlements to dividends to shareholders. Some classes of share, usually referred to as 'preference shares', may be given a contractual entitlement to a fixed and modest level of dividend, but ordinary shareholders are usually dependent upon the discretion of the board for any dividend they receive.[56] Thus, the board has a discretion whether it pays out a dividend or invests the surplus in new projects. As for the statutory provisions on the return of surplus to shareholders, whether by the obvious method of a dividend payment or in less obvious ways, such as a re-purchase of the members' shares, their aim is not to give shareholders entitlements but to ensure that, if the company chooses to take these steps, the interests of the creditors are not harmed and minority shareholders are not prejudiced.[57] Thus, it may be too strong a thing to say that the shareholders have a 'right' to the corporate surplus, but one can say that the law contains a structure which will encourage the surplus to flow in the shareholders' direction, unless the board is, unusually, dependent upon neither the shareholders' votes nor their willingness to subscribe for new share issues in the future.

TRANSFERABILITY OF SHARES

The principle of transferability of shares has two aspects. The first issue is whether the transfer by a shareholder of his interest in the company has an adverse impact upon the resources available to the company. This is ease of transfer from the company's point of view. The second issue is the

---

[54] CA 1985, s 719; IA 1986, s 187.

[55] The same principle applies on a winding-up. Any surplus available after the creditors have been paid is to be distributed among the members 'according to their rights and interests' which will be defined in the company's constitution or the terms of the share issue: IA 1986, s 107.

[56] Table A, art 102.   [57] CA 1985, Part V, Ch VII and Part VIII.

question of whether the shareholder is legally entitled or factually able to transfer his or her shares whenever it is wished to do so. This is ease of transfer from the shareholders' point of view.

FROM THE COMPANY'S POINT OF VIEW

The first aspect is perhaps most easily seen through an example. Suppose an investor buys shares from a company when that company makes a public offering of its shares. At that point money will move from the investor to the company and the investor will become a shareholder in the company. Later the shareholder may wish to sell his or her shares for personal reasons. It is vital to see that it is rare for such a sale to be effected by way of a re-purchase of the shares by the company. Indeed, until relatively recently the law prohibited a company from purchasing its own shares (in order, it was said, to protect creditors). Now, re-purchases are permitted, provided the company follows the prescribed procedure,[58] but, as we have just seen, it is not obligatory for the company to re-purchase a shareholder's shares when the latter requests it. Rather, the shareholder will normally seek out another investor to whom the shares may be sold and who will step into the seller's shoes as a shareholder in the company.

One can thus see why it is in the interests of a company which has made a public offering of its shares to secure that its shares are admitted to trading on a public market. This will enormously increase the efficiency of the process whereby shareholders in the company may dispose of their holdings if they wish to do so. Thus, the availability of a secondary market in the shares will also increase the willingness of investors to buy the company's shares in the primary offering. Just as important, the sale of the shares will take place without the company's assets being affected. On the sale, the shareholder converts the shares back into cash, but the cash comes from the purchasing investor and not from the company. Of course, the amount of cash received by the shareholder on the sale may be more or less than the amount initially paid for the shares to the company, depending on how the company has fared commercially in the interim, but that would be true even if the company bought back the shares.

As trading on the stock market continues, it may well be that the overwhelming majority of shareholders become people who have bought their shares from other investors, rather than from the company directly.

---

[58] See previous note and Chapter 4, p. 87, where 'redeemable' shares are also analysed.

All this trading can take place, however, without impugning the company's resources, even though many millions of shares change hands in the course of a single day. Thus, on 20 April 2000, admittedly during a take-over offer, over 280 million shares in the company, Blue Circle, changed hands, some of them obviously more than once. Although the management of Blue Circle may have been worried about who was buying the company's shares,[59] the integrity of the company as a business organization was not affected by the transfers. Building on the concept of separate legal personality, company law takes the view that the assets employed in the business are owned by the company and not by the shareholders, even collectively. In consequence, a disposal of the investor's interest in the company, measured by the share, does not involve any transfer of those underlying business assets. All this contrasts with the situation in relation to partnerships. Here, a partner who gives notice to withdraw from the partnership is normally entitled to have the capital invested in the partnership paid back, either immediately or within a relatively short time period, which may embarrass the other partners if they need the capital to support the partnership's existing level of business activity.

FROM THE SHAREHOLDERS' POINT OF VIEW

Company law does rather little to guarantee ease of transfer of the share from the shareholders' point of view. It could hardly give the shareholder a general right to transfer the shares, in the sense of imposing upon someone else the duty to buy them at a fair price, though shareholders who are in a particularly strong bargaining position may be able to secure such a provision in the company's constitution or in a separate contract with the company or the other shareholders.[60] Nor does the law guarantee to the shareholder the existence of a market upon which the shares can be traded, though, as we have just seen, it may be in the interest of companies which raise funds from the public to ensure that their shares are traded on a public market. In fact, for many private companies, there probably is no market, or no adequate market, for the company's shares. In such a case, the shareholder may find him- or herself in an unfortunate position, unable to exit the company or to do so only at an unrealistically low price.

---

[59] Because that person might subsequently use their s 303 power to remove the existing board. See above, p. 19.

[60] And the law does use compulsory purchase at a fair price as a remedy in some cases: see Chapter 8.

However, company law does not even guarantee that, if a buyer can be found, the shareholder may transfer the shares without the consent of others involved in the business. There is certainly a presumption at common law that shares are issued by a company on the basis that they are freely transferable, but that presumption may be rebutted by express provisions in the company's constitution or the terms of issue of the shares. In fact, in small companies, which are in effect incorporated partnerships, restrictions on the free transferability of shares are common, as the drafters of the company's constitution try to recreate in the company context the rule which normally obtains in a partnership, namely, that the admission of a new partner requires the consent of the existing partners.[61] In fact, until 1980, the Act required that, to qualify as a private company, the company had to place restrictions on the free transferability of its shares, though that is no longer the case.[62] Any guarantee of transferability without consent is to be found, not in company law but in the rules governing the operation of securities markets.[63]

THE CORE FEATURES AND COMPANY SIZE

We have now identified five core, structural features of company law. They are: separate corporate personality; limited liability; centralized management under a board structure; shareholder control; and free transferability of shares. The attentive reader will have noticed, however, a curious feature of these core features: it is possible to establish a company which fails to display all but one of the core features. That feature is separate corporate personality, which flows ineluctably from the fact that, upon registration, the statute incorporates the company,[64] and it is the feature which is, as we have seen, the least important in functional terms.

---

[61] *Re Smith & Fawcett Ltd* [1942] Ch 304 and see Chapter 10.

[62] The present test is whether the company is free to offer its shares to the public: see n. 47 above.

[63] Thus, the Listing Rules issued by the FSA state that: 'To be listed, securities must be freely transferable' (FSA, *The Listing Rules*, London, 2001, para. 3.15). Thus, listed companies cannot impose restrictions on the freedom of their shareholders to transfer their shares. Even here, exceptions have been made on privatization issues, where the government has retained a 'golden share', the rights attached to which in one way or another operate so as to restrict the freedom of the other shareholders to transfer their shares to someone the government thinks should not obtain control of the company. Such golden shares have normally had a finite and limited life so as to protect the company only in the immediate aftermath of the privatization.

[64] CA 1985, s 13(1).

The statute itself provides for unlimited liability companies[65] and in any event limited liability and the other three features can in fact be avoided by appropriate provisions in the company's constitution or contracts with the company or its shareholders.

The attentive reader will also have observed that the companies most likely not to display the four optional core features are the smallest ones. Take Smith & Jones (Decorators) Ltd, incorporated by Ms Smith and Mr Jones, who were and remain its only shareholders, to run a small decorating business. The money to fund the business they have probably borrowed from the local bank, which has required Smith and Jones to give personal guarantees of its repayment. So, at least in relation to this major liability, they do not have the benefit of limited liability. Smith and Jones, as the company's only shareholders, have appointed themselves its only directors and probably are not much aware, when they take decisions, whether they are doing so as shareholders or as directors. As shareholder/directors they do all the managing this small company requires, so that there are no senior managers who are not directors. In fact, there is unity of shareholding, board membership, and management in this company, rather than centralized management separate from the shareholders. The articles provide that the consent of all the existing shareholders is needed for the admission of a new member and that, if an existing shareholder wishes to sell his or her shares, they must first be offered to the other existing shareholders; and, of course, the shares in the company are not traded on a public market. So there is no free transferability of shares, at least from the shareholders' point of view.[66]

It might be thought, however, that this is clearly a company where shareholder control applies. Smith and Jones have all the shares, clearly control the board since they are the board, and no doubt take for themselves by way of dividend or directors' remuneration as much of the company's economic surplus as they think is prudent in the light of its needs for working capital or capital for expansion. At a deeper level, however, one may doubt that this is an example of *shareholder* control. Let us suppose, as would be common, that upon registration Smith and Jones agreed to subscribe each for one £1 share in the company, and they have not subsequently increased their holdings. So, Smith and Jones have acquired these control rights for the payment of a mere £2. Why should

---

[65] Above p. 12.

[66] If the articles contained a provision requiring the company to buy the shares of a shareholder who wished to leave the company, there would be no free transferability from the company's point of view either.

the bank be prepared to finance a company where the controllers have contributed apparently so little? The answer probably is because Smith & Jones' business plan reveals that they are going to be the people who get and do the work which the company is set up to carry on. In effect, they have been given control rights, not because they have made a major equity investment in the company (they clearly have not), but because they have promised to work for it. This small company displays a form of workers' control or, if you prefer, the shares have been allocated to them, not in exchange for capital contributions, but in exchange for an implicit promise to devote their full energies to developing the business. Smith and Jones are not shareholder-capitalists but shareholder-workers or shareholder-entrepreneurs.

Of course, it is equally easy to identify companies which display all five of the core features in a straightforward way. Such companies tend to be at the other end of the size spectrum from Smith & Jones (Decorators) Ltd. Companies, such as BP, whose shares are traded on public markets will fall within this category. They are likely to have hundreds, perhaps thousands or even tens of thousands, of shareholders, none of whom has given any personal guarantee of the company's debts or liabilities; the board is clearly distinct from both the shareholders and the senior management of the company; and the shares are freely transferable from both the shareholders' and the company's point of view. As far as the law is concerned, the shareholders also control the company in the ways defined above. However, by way of contrast with Smith & Jones Ltd, the sheer number of the shareholders raises a serious question whether the difficulties the shareholders will face in co-ordinating their actions mean that in fact they are incapable of exercising the control the law confers upon them. We shall examine this question in Chapter 5.

In addition to companies whose shares are traded on public markets, it is likely that nearly all public companies display the five core features, although the absence of a public market may make it more difficult for a shareholder to find a purchaser for his or her shares. Finally, a substantial number of private companies[67] will also display the five core features. A good example might be a company, originally built up by an entrepreneur, who has now died, where the shares are held by various members of the next generation of the founder's family. They may still have a keen financial and emotional interest in the fortunes of that company but may have decided not to run it themselves but rather to hire professional managers

---

[67] The distinction between public and private companies is given above at p. 17.

to do so, the senior of which managers they will have placed on the board. In such a case one can identify centralized management distinct from the shareholders but, in contrast to the publicly traded company, the problems of shareholder co-ordination are much easier to deal with and the accountability of the board to the shareholders will be real. Indeed, the shareholders may place one or more of the family members on the board in a non-executive capacity in order to improve the flow of information from the management to the shareholders. Where this has happened, the shareholders, directors, and managers will be distinct, but overlapping, groups. However, in the absence of a public market, free transfer of shares may again be a difficulty. Moreover, the family may be committed to keeping control of the company in their hands, even if some non-family members have been admitted as shareholders, and have included provisions in the company's constitution or have entered into a shareholders' agreement which formally restrict the transferability of the shares.

The above are only examples (or models) of types of company. In practice a bewildering variety of configurations can be found. However, both in this chapter and later in the book, it is worth keeping these simplified models in mind when testing the impact of particular legal rules. Proceeding up the size hierarchy, we have identified: the owner-managed company; the large private company; the public company whose shares, however, are not publicly traded; and the public company whose shares are traded on a public market and whose activities are thus regulated in addition by the rules of that market.

As far as the core features are concerned, there is a clear correlation between the size of the company and the likelihood of its displaying all five core features. It is suggested that this is not a random fact. As companies become larger, their needs for capital to carry on their business are likely also to increase, to the point where the public needs to be invited to provide risk capital to the company, either directly or via intermediaries such as pension funds or insurance companies. Public shareholders are unlikely to want or to be able to manage the company, so centralized management emerges, and they are likely to be significantly more willing to invest in the company if they can subsequently dispose of their shares on a market and if they benefit from limited liability. Finally, having provided investment with no legal guarantee of a return, they are likely to want the power to remove the management if it proves unsuccessful.

Reverting, however, to the owner-managed company, since the only core feature of the company form, of which Ms Smith and Mr Jones availed themselves when they established the company, was member

control, the obvious question which arises is whether small businesses
need, or should be granted, access to the corporate form at all. Should
they not be required to carry on business in the form of a partnership (or
some similar form) which does not benefit from limited liability but
does provide the one feature, member control, which Smith & Jones
(Decorators) Ltd clearly both need and want? The policy of the mid-
Victorian companies legislation was, indeed, that small businesses should
adopt the partnership form and only medium-sized and large businesses
the company form. Thus, an upper limit of 20 was placed on the
number of people who could form a partnership; beyond that they had
to form a company.[68] By contrast, incorporation with limited liability was
restricted to associations of at least 25 and later at least seven members.[69]

Thus, below seven members the partnership form was obligatory;
between seven and 20 either could be chosen; above 20 only the corporate
form was available. The story of the subversion of this legislative policy
of using the number of members as a proxy for the size of a business and
of excluding small businesses from the corporate form is one of the most
well known in the history of British company law. From the beginning
company practitioners set about undermining this policy, by the use of
nominee shareholders,[70] mainly in order to give small businesses the
advantages of limited liability. The House of Lords set its seal of approval
on this development in one of its most famous decisions in our field,
Salomon v Salomon,[71] and the legislature decided to accept the defeat
and did not seek to reverse *Salomon*. From that time onwards even the
smallest one-person business has had access to the corporate form.[72]

However, the issue of principle has not gone away. The smallest
businesses may now have access to the corporate form, but should the
legislature strive to make it positively attractive to small businesses to

[68] CA 1856, s 4. The rule is still stated in CA 1985, s 716, but is so riddled with exceptions
that the latter have swallowed up the former. In 2001 the government decided to do away
with the rule entirely.

[69] Seven was the number chosen in the 1856 Act, the Limited Liability Act 1855 having
originally stipulated the higher number.

[70] A nominee shareholder is one who holds the shares on behalf of another, often as a bare
trustee. So, the seven-member requirement could be subverted in practice by having one
beneficial holder and six other shareholders who held their shares, usually only one share
each, on behalf of the beneficial holder.

[71] [1897] AC 22.

[72] The minimum number of members had gradually been whittled away to two when
in 1989 Council Directive 89/667/EEC required the UK formally to introduce one-
member private companies. However, because of the previous possibility of using nominee
shareholders, this was a change of form, not substance.

incorporate as companies rather than operate as partnerships or, in the case of single entrepreneurs, as sole traders? Will small businesses in fact continue to use the company form now that Parliament has just created a form of the partnership which confers limited liability on all the partners and separate legal personality upon the partnership?[73] We shall discuss this issue further in Chapter 10.

It will be useful to conclude this section with some statistical evidence on the incidence of different types of company and business. In March 2001 there were some 1.4 million companies in Great Britain[74] which were registered under the Companies Acts, ignoring those which were in the course of liquidation or removal. Of these only some 13,000 (or less than 1 per cent) were public companies and the rest were private.[75] Of those public companies about 2,500 had their shares listed on the London Stock Exchange, though a further number had their shares traded on some other public market.[76] Thus, in numerical terms, though not in economic terms, private companies far outweigh the public ones, and this remains true even though, at any one time, about half the private companies on the register are not economically active. Looking at businesses as a whole, we see that 2000 statistics suggest that there were 3.7m. businesses in the UK, of which 825,000 were carried on through companies, 671,000 through partnerships, and 2.25m. as sole traders. Of course, one should not be mesmerized by the sheer number of businesses in each category because that may not be a true measure of their economic significance. Thus, companies constituted about 20 per cent of all businesses but provided two-thirds of the employment generated in the business sector; and over half the employment generated by companies was located in companies employing more than 500 workers (i.e. large companies), even though such companies constituted only 0.4 per cent of the corporate population.[77]

It is within the private category that the widest range of sizes can be

---

[73] Limited Liability Partnership Act 2000.

[74] The figures for Northern Ireland are kept separately because it has its own companies legislation, though it closely follows the Great Britain model.

[75] Department of Trade and Industry, *Companies in 2000–2001* (London, The Stationery Office, 2001), Tables A1 and A2.

[76] The best known of these other markets is the Alternative Investment Market (AIM), also run by the London Stock Exchange, upon which the shares of some 400 companies are traded. In this book 'listed' refers to companies complying with the Listing Rules issued by the FSA, whereas 'publicly traded' refers to a company whose shares are traded on any generally accessible market, whether in the UK or elsewhere.

[77] DTI, *Small and Medium Enterprise Statistics for the United Kingdom, 2000* (London, 2001), Table 6.

found. Some private companies are very big. Thus, JCB, a private manufacturing company, reported sales in the year to 31 December 1999 of £883 million.[78] However, the majority of private companies have turnovers which are but a tiny fraction of that figure. The CLR found that 65 per cent of companies which were actively carrying on business had an annual turnover of less than £250,000, which is a very small amount.[79] Most of these will have been owner-managed companies.[80] A pattern of a small number of large companies and a larger number of smaller companies is to be expected. If large companies are the result of the search for economies of scale or scope, then there are necessarily going to be rather few such companies in existence at any one time. On the other hand, if the entrepreneurial spirit is vigorous, one would expect a constant supply of new companies seeking to exploit fresh opportunities which the more leaden-footed large companies cannot quickly seize.

COMPANIES AS VEHICLES

It is implicit in the above account of the mid-Victorian legislation that policy-makers have always seen company law in rather instrumental terms. The company is one of a number of mechanisms made available by the state for carrying on business. In its various Consultation Documents the CLR captures this idea by referring to companies as 'vehicles'. We have argued that the company form is particularly well suited for carrying on medium or large-scale business where it is clearly the dominant form.[81] On the other hand, small businesses clearly have a real choice as to the vehicle through which the business is to be conducted: company,

---

[78] *Financial Times*, 23 March 2000, p. 36. This company was the subject of a famous piece of litigation in the late 1960s when another company run by other members of the family successfully repulsed a take-over bid from JCB: *Bamford v Bamford* [1970] Ch 212.

[79] CLR, *Developing the Framework*, Consultation Document 5 (London: Department of Trade and Industry, 2000), para. 6.8. Turnover is a measure of the value of the business done by a company during a period; it is not a measure of the company's profit which would have been much less, perhaps even non-existent.

[80] 70 per cent of companies have only one or two shareholders: ibid., para. 6.9.

[81] Thus, the Government's statistics reveal that at the beginning of 1997 only 145 sole traders employed more than 100 persons; 655 partnerships did so; but 15,365 companies achieved this level of employment. See DTI, *Small and Medium Enterprise Statistics for the United Kingdom, 2000*, Table 6. The partnership figure is inflated by the traditional self-regulatory requirement of some professions, notably lawyers and accountants, that their professional businesses be organized through partnerships (with unlimited liability for the partners). Although this requirement has now been repealed for most professions, its influence lives on in the dominance of the partnership vehicle in this area.

partnership, or sole trader. Of course, the choice of form in any particular case may be governed by many matters extraneous to the design of these vehicles, including notably tax considerations. Thus, at the bottom end of the market for business vehicles the company form faces competition from other vehicles, but that competition lessens as the size of the business increases.

However, the flexibility of the corporate vehicle in terms of the range of business sizes it is able to accommodate is not the only measure of its adaptability. In particular, it is not true to say that in Britain the company is available only for the purpose of carrying on business with a view to making a profit. On the contrary the 1985 Act provides a form of company which is particularly suitable for carrying on not-for-profit activities. This is the company 'limited by guarantee'.[82] Such a company has members but they are not shareholders, because such a company issues no shares. Instead, its members must agree to contribute a certain amount to its assets if the company is wound up as insolvent. The company limited by guarantee is, however, able to display the core features identified above, notably that of limited liability, except that there is less likely to be an economic surplus to distribute or, even if there is, its distribution to the members may be prohibited by the company's constitution.[83] Because of the existence of this form of the company (with members who are not shareholders) the generic term used in the Act to refer to those who are associated in the company is 'member', not 'shareholder', even though in most companies the members are shareholders.

It may be wondered why so many 'not-for-profit' companies choose to incorporate as companies limited by guarantee rather than as share companies. After all, shares can be issued with a nominal value as low as 1p, and it is difficult to think that the obligation to pay a few pence on joining (as opposed to undertaking the obligation to pay a few pence on winding-up if the company is insolvent) would alter many people's decision whether or not to join the company. In some cases, regulation is the answer. Thus, if a charity wishes to incorporate as a company, it must do so as a guarantee company. Even where there is no obligation to use the guarantee form, it seems that ceasing to be a member is a much easier process to handle in a guarantee company where there is no share to be

---

[82] CA 1985, s 1(2)(b).

[83] The phrase 'not for profit', which is not a term of art in British law, is used to refer both to the companies which do not aim to make a profit and to those which do so aim but which prohibit its distribution to the members.

dealt with, which must be either re-purchased by the company[84] or transferred to a new member, which is a cumbersome process in private companies.[85] Instead, the admission and departure of members can be governed solely by the company's own rules.

In addition, the Act permits companies limited by guarantee (but not companies limited by shares), which pursue certain defined public-interest objectives and whose constitutions prohibit the distribution of economic surplus to the members, to dispense with the obligation, which would otherwise apply to them, to include the word 'ltd' at the end of their name.[86] Thus, my employer describes itself thus on its notepaper: 'The London School of Economics is . . . a charity and is incorporated in England as a company limited by guarantee under the Companies Acts (Reg. No. 70527)'.[87] However, guarantee companies are not obliged to pursue not-for-profit objectives and, conversely, companies which have issued shares may also be used in the not-for-profit sector. Thus, the tenants of a block of flats may incorporate a company limited by shares in order to see to the upkeep of the common parts.[88] That is clearly not a charitable or even a public-interest objective. Equally, however, such a company may not be seeking to make a profit. Its aim may simply be to balance over time the receipts from the tenant-members by way of maintenance charges and expenditures on cleaning, decorating, and repairs.

The role of the company in the not-for-profit area is an increasingly important one. With the growing reliance by government on non-governmental organizations for the delivery of some kinds of social services previously provided directly by the state, charities and other bodies, such as housing associations, find themselves entering into contractual commitments of an increasing size. They thus have an incentive to incorporate in order to gain in particular the benefits of limited liability.

---

[84] On which the law has traditionally frowned: see Chapter 4, p. 87.

[85] Unlike in listed companies where the process is now largely computerized (through the London equity settlement agency CREST) and shares are often held in 'dematerialized' form (i.e. as computer entries).

[86] CA 1985, s 30.

[87] The CLR has proposed that charities which wish to incorporate should in future not be free to do so under the Companies Act, but should have their own form of incorporation, the Charitable Incorporated Institution. This represents an attempt to restrict the scope of Companies Act registration in favour of a more specialized vehicle for charitable companies. Even then, however, companies with public-interest but not charitable objectives could still use the form of the company limited by guarantee and, in appropriate cases, the s 30 exemption.

[88] Equally, they could use a company limited by guarantee for this purpose.

THE STRUCTURE OF THE BOOK

Now that the core features of company law have been identified, and also the range of uses to which the company vehicle can be put, it might be thought that the rest of this book should consist simply of analysing the way in which the core features are implemented in company law, noting as one goes along the types of company which do not make use of a particular core feature and seeking to explain why this should be. Indeed, discharging these tasks will constitute a substantial part of the rest of this book. However, the task is somewhat more complex than the above description might suggest, for the following two reasons.

First, the values which underlie the core features cannot be presented as overriding policy objectives which must defeat in all circumstances countervailing values. Take, for example, the doctrine of limited liability, that is, the rule that creditors' claims are limited to the company's assets. As we shall see in a later chapter, one powerful argument in favour of limited liability is that it encourages the purchase of shares by people who do not want to be involved in the management of the company. However, it is also a doctrine which may permit, or even encourage, opportunistic behaviour on the part of the controllers of the company as against its creditors, for example by spiriting out of the company assets which the company was represented as owning when the credit was advanced to the company. It is not in the interest of companies in general for limited liability to be used in this way, because such behaviour may make it more expensive for them to raise credit. For example, if abuse of the doctrine of limited liability were rife, banks lending to companies might be prepared to do so only at higher interest rates than would obtain if the shareholders' liability were not limited. So, the task for company law is not simply to implement limited liability. The task is not even necessarily to balance the interests of investors and creditors, though it may come to that if no better strategy can be identified. The most challenging task is to design a set of rules which achieves the desired benefits of limited liability (encouraging shareholder investment) while reducing or even eliminating the occasions for opportunistic behaviour as against creditors which those rules might otherwise generate. The task is a demanding one, in relation both to limited liability and to the equivalent issues arising under the other core features.

Second, the five core features do not inhabit separate universes. On the contrary, they interact with one another, so that the ideal solution for the implementation of one feature may score very poorly when considered from the standpoint of its promotion of another feature. We have already noted that shareholder control over management may be maximized by placing a wide range of decisions in the hands of the general meeting, but that such a rule would at the same time substantially deprive the company of the benefits of centralized management. For small companies, where centralized management is not a desideratum, this solution may be feasible. In large companies, on the other hand, general shareholder decision-making would be a disaster,[89] and in such companies the law must try to devise techniques which provide the benefits of shareholder control without at the same time imposing greater costs by way of loss of the benefits of centralized management.

As we apply the *five* core features (separate legal personality, limited liability, centralized management, shareholder control, and free transferability of shares) to the *four* model types of company which we identified (owner-managed, large private, public, and publicly traded) we will become aware that *three* relationships recur in our analyses. These three relationships are:

- The relationship between the shareholders as a whole and the board of directors.
- The relationship between majority and minority shareholders.
- The relationship between the controllers of the company (whether directors or shareholders) and those other groups whose contribution is potentially vital to the success of the company, such as investors, lenders, employees, suppliers, and customers.

The relationships which are the focus of attention vary according to the core feature and type of company we are concerned with. Thus, in a publicly traded company centralized management raises issues mainly concerned with the first relationship (how can the directors be made accountable to the shareholders?) but the solution to that problem may affect relationships in the third category (too close an accountability to the shareholders may discourage, for example, employees or suppliers from making appropriate investments in their relationship with the company). In a large private company accountability to the shareholders will be easier to provide because the shareholdings are likely to be more concentrated, but with concentrated shareholdings there is a greater risk that some of the shareholders will co-ordinate their activities so as to control the board and run the company without regard to the interests of the

---

[89] For the reasons given above at p. 13.

non-controlling shareholders, thus raising issues under the second relationship.

In short, the task of most of the remaining chapters is to analyse the way in which the law seeks to provide the benefits, and avoid the costs, of the core features of company law by focusing, across the range of companies, on the relationships among the corporate actors upon which the weight of the law's policy falls.

2

Corporate Personality

In the first chapter we saw that the idea of the company as a separate legal person facilitates two core features of company law.[1] These are the limited liability of the shareholders and the transferability of a shareholder's interest in the company to another person. Separate legal personality makes it easier to distinguish business assets from personal assets, a distinction upon which limited liability depends. It also permits shares, which belong to the members, to be transferred from one person to another, while the property and contractual rights and obligations of the company, that is, its business assets and liabilities, remain unaffected. With hard work and ingenuity, limited liability, and the transfer of interests can be (and have been)[2] achieved without separate legal personality, but only at a much higher cost of transacting, and so separate legal personality is the efficient rule. There is often debate within legal systems about the range of bodies which should be treated as having separate legal personality, and legal systems differ somewhat on this point among themselves,[3] but it is notable that no modern legal system fails to make readily available to businesses formed for commercial purposes a legal vehicle which has separate legal personality.

For this reason, contemporary debate in company law focuses on the problems generated by the acceptance of separate legal personality for the company, rather than upon the question of whether it should, in principle, be made available. In this chapter we shall examine two such issues. The first, which we shall analyse only briefly at this stage, is what

[1] See pp. 9 and 22.

[2] Thus, before the legislature created a simple form of incorporation by registration in the middle of the nineteenth century (see p. 1), business people aimed to achieve these features by means of the 'deed of settlement company', a form of partnership in which the assets of the business were held by trustees. See *Gower*, 6th edn, 1997, pp. 28–32.

[3] A matter on which different stances have been taken by legal systems is whether the partnership should have separate legal personality, an issue upon which, even within Great Britain, different views are taken in England and Wales (no separate legal personality) and Scotland (legal personality). See Law Commission and Scottish Law Commission, *Partnership Law: A Joint Consultation Paper*, 2000, pp. 6–9 and Part IV.

exceptions, if any, should be made to the rule of separate legal personality. The second, which will occupy the bulk of the chapter, is how a company, which is an artificial person, can be said to act or to know anything.

THE EXCEPTIONS TO SEPARATE LEGAL PERSONALITY

Two issues need to be distinguished here, the first arising within company law and the other more generally. Given the functions within company law of separate legal personality, it is obviously a matter of great interest to company lawyers if the legislature or the courts ignore the doctrine of separate legal personality, with the consequence that shareholders are made liable for the company's debts or the free transfer of shares is impeded. However, we intend to deal with this aspect of separate legal personality primarily in those chapters where we discuss limited liability and the transferability of shares. Especially in relation to limited liability,[4] we shall see that there is a narrow set of situations where, for good reason, the corporate veil is pierced (as the hackneyed phrase has it) and shareholders are held responsible for the company's debts or other liabilities. The reason for postponing discussion is that these examples of piercing the corporate veil can be analysed sensibly only within an overall understanding of the role of limited liability.

This leaves the general issue. When in *Salomon v Salomon*[5] the House of Lords emphasized the importance of the separate legal personality of companies, it did so, not only for the purposes of company law, but for all legal purposes. However, although this is the starting point for analysis, the courts have held that in some situations, outside company law, the separate legal personality of the company should be ignored. In fact, the list of such instances is now impressively long.[6] Much effort has been expended by company lawyers in trying to explain these instances. It is suggested that no single explanation for these cases will be found and that in any event company lawyers are not well equipped to provide the explanation or explanations.

I make this apparently radical suggestion on the basis that it is possible to decide whether to ignore the separate legal personality of the company

[4] See p. 105 below.
[5] [1897] AC 22. See above, p. 28.
[6] For a representative account see *Palmer's Company Law* (London: Sweet & Maxwell, looseleaf), vol. 1, para. 2.1519 ff.

in any particular case only on the basis of an understanding of the purpose of the rule which is alleged to require this step to be taken. This is true whether the rule in question is statutory, common law, or contained in a contract. Is the rule, whatever its origin, inconsistent with the recognition of the company's separate personality? As suggested, that is how the matter needs to be approached within company law as well. However, within company law the company lawyer can contribute effectively to the debate. Outside company law he or she normally has little to offer.

An example, from labour law, may help to make the point clear. One function of employment law is to help redress the balance of power between the employer and the dependent or subordinated worker by imposing mandatory standards below which the parties to the employment contract cannot agree to go. Suppose, however, the employer is a small company of which the worker, party to the employment contract with the company, is also the only shareholder and only director. Should the mandatory rules of labour law apply to such a contract? Is the worker here subordinated or, if one ignores the separate personality of the company, 'really' his or her own boss? The point is not always as easy to resolve as this way of putting it might suggest,[7] but my argument is that its resolution is a matter for employment lawyers and the vital interests of company law are not implicated, whichever way the decision turns out. The principal issue at stake in these cases is the scope of the protection to be afforded to the worker as against the employing company. However that question is answered, the shareholders of the employing company will not be made responsible for the company's obligations.

Thus, the upshot is that the company law aspects of piercing the corporate veil will be discussed in later chapters and the non-company law aspects will not be further discussed.

HOW DOES A COMPANY ACT AND KNOW?

Although the company may be a separate legal person, because it is an artificial person it is capable of acting and knowing only if the acts or knowledge of human beings are attributed to it. Thus, one needs to know whose actions or knowledge and in which situations shall be treated as the company's. This question arises in two principal situations. The first is where the question to be answered is whether a

---

[7] Cf. *Lee v Lee's Air Farming Ltd* [1961] AC 12, PC and *Connolly v Sellers Arenascene Ltd* [2001] I CR 760, CA.

company has entered into a transaction, typically a contract. The second is where the question to be answered is whether the company has committed a wrong, either civil or criminal. The answers are crucial for those involved with companies, whether internally or externally. Shareholders and managers need to know who can bind the company legally as to its future conduct or involve the company in legal responsibility for actions (in the sense that the company's assets are placed at risk for the satisfaction of the legal responsibility). Conversely, those seeking to deal with companies or affected by the actions of those operating within the corporate organization need to know whether their transaction with the company is secure or whether they can pursue a claim against the company's assets.

There is a broad spectrum of possible approaches to the issue of attribution, ranging from treating the acts and knowledge of all the agents and employees of the company, acting within the course of their agency or employment, as those of the company to confining the company's responsibility to the actions of its constitutional organs, that is, the board or the shareholders' meeting. As we shall see, British company law makes full use of the range of possible answers.

A related issue is to determine how, precisely, the process of attribution works. There are two broad approaches. One is to establish that an individual has incurred a liability and then to attribute that *liability* to the company because of the relationship that exists between the company and the individual and because there is a sufficiently close connection between that relationship and the circumstances in which the liability was incurred. The best known example is the rule of vicarious liability. For example, an employee commits a tort in the course of his or her employment and the employing company is held liable to the victim, not because it has committed the tort but because it is the employer of the tortfeasor.[8] The alternative is to treat the *acts or knowledge* of individuals as acts or knowledge of the company, on the basis of which the liability of the company is assessed. Here the company is the primary bearer of the liability; establishing whether the individuals have incurred the liability is not a necessary step in establishing the company's liability. For example, a statute may impose a duty only on employers. To decide whether an employing company has broken that duty it will be necessary to decide

---

[8] It may not be necessary under vicarious liability to show that a particular employee has committed a tort, provided it can be established that some employee of the company must have done so.

whose acts or knowledge (from among the individuals operating within the organization) should be attributed to the company, but those individuals will not themselves be in breach of duty because they are not employers.[9]

This second technique of attribution has a broader impact if it is combined with that of 'aggregation'. Here, the acts or knowledge of a number of individuals within the organization are attributed to the company, so as to make the company liable, even though no single individual has the combination of acts and knowledge which serve to make the company liable. By this technique, the company is put under legal pressure to have effective systems not only to monitor potential wrongdoing by its agents or employees, but also to distribute the knowledge of any one employee to all those within the organization for whom it may be relevant. However, in some cases aggregation defeats the purpose of the rule, which may be aimed at confining, not distributing, information within organizations. Here, companies need to be provided with a defence against aggregation. An example from the area of financial services is the oddly named 'Chinese wall'. If a conglomerate financial services company has effective barriers in place to prevent 'inside information' moving from one part of the company to another, its liability for insider dealing will be assessed on the basis of the compartmentalization produced by the barriers.[10]

As important as establishing the company's liability is knowing whether the persons whose actions brought about the change in the company's legal position will themselves be liable.[11] Under the first technique of attribution discussed above (vicarious liability), liability in the individual is a necessary part of the reasoning whereby the company is held liable. Under the second technique, however, the matter is left open and could be decided either way without affecting the company's liability. Where the individual actors are not liable but only the company, then the impact of the liability is borne mainly by the shareholders. If, for

---

[9] Though the individuals might incur various forms of secondary liability, such as aiding and abetting the company.

[10] Insider trading is trading in securities on the basis of price-sensitive information which is not publicly known. However, if an investment bank has effective barriers in place to prevent such information moving from, say, its corporate finance department to its dealing department, the liability of the dealers will be assessed on the basis of what is done and known in the dealing department alone. See FSA, Code of Market Conduct, 2001, paras 1.4.23–24.

[11] The discussion in the text assumes a liability; the same issue could be raised about entitlements.

example, the company has to pay out substantial damages to a claimant, the profits of the company will be reduced to that extent.

CONTRACTING

Primary rules of attribution

As far as contracting is concerned, the law displays two outstanding features. The first is that it allows a wide range of persons to commit the company to contracts, while giving the company control over the choice of those persons. The second is that it treats the resulting rights and duties as existing, normally, only between the third party and the company, and not also or instead between the third party and the person acting on behalf of the company.

The most obvious answer to the question of who can commit the company to contracts is that the company's constitutional decision-making bodies can do so. Lord Hoffmann recently referred to rules imposing liability upon a company in such a case as the 'primary rules of attribution'.[12] On this view, the actions of the board of directors or of the shareholders (normally acting by resolution passed at a meeting) will be treated as actions of the company. If the board approves a contract on the company's behalf, there is not usually any doubt that the company will be bound by the contract.

Even on this limited approach to attribution, however, the matter is not entirely free from difficulties. Take a person contracting with the board over a matter which the company's constitution says is one reserved for decision by the shareholders.[13] Is the company bound by the agreement? The modern tendency, as we shall see further below, is to treat the company's constitution as an essentially internal document and to relieve the third party of the need to concern itself with its provisions. Thus, s 35A of the Companies Act 1985 permits a good faith third party[14] to treat the board's power to bind the company as unlimited by

---

[12] *Meridian Global Funds Management Asia Ltd v Securities Commission* [1995] 3 All ER 918, 923, PC.

[13] Another risk for third parties is that the apparent directors have not been properly appointed under the procedure laid down in the company's articles. Section 285 of CA 1985 confers validity on directors' actions even if this is so, but the section protects a narrower range of third parties than does s 35A because it does not apply to those put on notice of the defect: *Morris v Kanssen* [1944] Ch 346, CA and [1946] AC 459, HL.

[14] A third party for this purpose does not include the directors themselves (contracting with the company) or those connected with them, who, the statute rightly states, ought to be aware of and to abide by the company's constitution. Transactions with such persons in breach of the constitution are voidable by the company: s 322A.

the constitution, and s 35A(2) and s 35B make bad faith so difficult to prove that very few third parties will fail to benefit from this provision. The CLR proposes to take the further step of abolishing the good faith requirement,[15] so that in all cases the validity of the transaction will be affected only by statutory or common law provisions which require certain classes of decision to be taken by the shareholders.[16] Thus, third parties dealing with the board normally do not need to concern themselves with constitutional restrictions on the board's powers. However, no similar protection exists for those contracting with the company by means of a shareholders' resolution (where the constitution gives contracting power to the board). This is perhaps to be explained on the grounds that, in all but the smallest companies, the advantages of centralized management[17] mean that the company's constitution routinely allocates contracting powers exclusively to the board,[18] so that third parties should have a very different set of expectations about the contracting powers of the board, on the one hand, and the shareholders' meeting, on the other. In very small companies a concerned third party can protect itself by obtaining the unanimous consent of all the shareholders.[19]

However, even with these problems solved, the primary rules of attribution are not enough. Any large company will find the primary rules of attribution inadequate, for their implication is that only contracts approved by the board will bind the company. That may suit our hypothetical small company, Smith & Jones (Decorators) Ltd,[20] but the board of any large company is likely to find its efficiency heavily diluted if it has to spend its time approving all the company's contracts rather than getting on with its main activity of setting and monitoring the company's business strategy.[21] An efficient legal system must provide a mechanism whereby those lower down the company's hierarchy can bind the

---

[15] *Final Report*, Vol II (July 2001), p. 375, Draft clause 16(2). This is less radical than it sounds, given the wide definition of good faith and the fact that, even on the CLR's approach, third parties who knowingly co-operate with directors acting in breach of their constitutional powers may be liable to the company as constructive trustees at common law: see p. 162 below.

[16] See p. 123 below.

[17] See Chapter 1, p. 13.

[18] In some cases the board's decision on a contract may need shareholder approval (see below, Chapter 5), but even in such a case the third party will be dealing with the board.

[19] The CLR proposes that it be made clear that the unanimous consent rule permits the shareholders to bind the company with regard to any matter within the capacity of the company, not just in relation to matters within the scope of the functions of the general meeting: *Final Report*, July 2001, vol. I, paras 2.14 and 7.17.

[20] Chapter 1, p. 25.   [21] See below, p. 157.

company contractually (at least in some cases). Thus, further (secondary) rules of attribution are needed. Here, however, company law has not developed its own comprehensive set of rules. Instead, it relies on the general rules of agency to define the legal position of both the company and those who act on its behalf. However, these rules apply to companies with certain special twists. The following briefly analyses the application of agency law to companies, with emphasis on the special twists.

Secondary rules of attribution: agency and authority

The rules of agency permit, but do not require, the company to disperse contract-making powers throughout the organization. Typically, in all but the smallest companies the company's constitution will empower the board to, and the board will, delegate contract-approval powers to senior managers, who are not directors, and they may be empowered to make a sub-delegation to more junior levels.[22] Only the good sense of the board and the senior management constrains the choice of the company as to whom it empowers to contract on its behalf and what limits it puts on their authority to contract.

Where a duly authorized agent of the company contracts on its behalf, the result is a contract between the third party and the company (the principal); the agent is normally not a party to the contract. This coincides with the expectations of those who work for companies, whether as directors or managers, and, it is suggested, of those who deal with companies. Both groups would be surprised if contracts made by managers in the course of their duties and on behalf of the company were to render the managers personally liable or entitled on the contracts, unless, of course, they and the third party chose to make the manager a party. Within company law the only significant exception to this position concerns contracts made on behalf of companies not formed at the time of the contract, typically a contract made with a third party by persons who are in the process of forming a company. In such a case s 36C of the CA 1985 treats the contract as one made with the persons purporting to act for the company, unless it is agreed that the agents shall not be liable.[23]

---

[22] See for example art 71 of Table A which contemplates the board having broad powers of delegation and sub-delegation.

[23] This is better than the common law result which was that, in many cases, there was no contract at all: not with the company, because it did not exist, and not with the agents because they did not purport to contract personally. Thus, the third party's expectations were entirely defeated. Even after the enactment of s 36C it would be an improvement to make it possible for the company, once formed, to ratify the contract and relieve the agent of responsibility.

In short, in this narrow situation the default rule that the agent is not party to the contract is reversed.

Agency is thus a highly flexible and efficient instrument for the allocation of contracting powers within the company. The main problems in agency law arise when the agent is not actually authorized by the principal to act on its behalf, but is believed by the third party to be so. This may arise because the so-called agent is not authorized to act at all on the principal's behalf or because, although the agent was authorized, the agent's authority was restricted in some way and the agent exceeded that authority. The starting point must be that the company (as any other principal) is not bound in such a situation. Unless this were so, the company would not be able to control the allocation of contracting power within its organization. Neither the third party's mistaken, even if honest, belief about the agent's authority nor the agent's mistaken, even if honest, belief about the scope of his or her authority should be permitted to impose on the company a contract to which it did not consent. However, it may be that the company has in some way misled the third party into thinking that the agent was authorized to act on behalf of the company. In such a case, the law protects the legitimate expectations of the third party by holding the company to a contract which it did not, in fact, authorize.

The typical way in which a company misleads a third party as to an agent's authority is by appointing the agent to a position, of which it can be said that persons in that position normally have a certain authority, but the company restricts the particular agent's power in some unusual way. In fact, as Lord Diplock pointed out some years ago, the doctrine of usual authority is even more important than this description might imply. Even where it is highly likely that the agent has actually been authorized to enter into the contract in question, the third party will probably not enquire whether this is so, but, in order to reduce transactions costs, will instead rely on the appearance of things.[24] The scope of the doctrine of usual authority thus defines the boundaries of efficient contracting.

The principle of usual authority is easy enough to state at a general level, though there may be factual arguments in particular cases as to what is the usual authority of a person holding a particular type of position.[25] For company lawyers it is important to note that the courts

---

[24] *Freeman & Lockyer v Buckhurst Park Properties (Mangal) Ltd* [1964] 2 QB 480, CA. The whole judgment is worth reading.

[25] A particularly thorny issue is whether an agent who does not have usual authority to contract can nevertheless bind the company on the grounds that he or she had usual

have been reluctant to accept that a single director has an extensive usual authority to contract on behalf of the company.[26] Directors are expected to discharge their duties at board meetings, that is, collectively, and so although the board may have very wide management powers,[27] these are not extended to the board members individually. This increasingly anachronistic doctrine, however, may be less important than it seems, because it contemplates a non-executive director. If the director holds in addition an executive position in the company, for example as managing director, the usual authority of that executive is what counts, not that of the associated directorship.

An alternative way in which the company[28] may hold out a person as having authority to contract is by representation to the third party, by words or conduct, that the agent does have authority (even though, as between the company and the agent, no such authority has been conferred). This is in fact simply a more generalized version of the principle of usual authority, where the holding out arises from the appointment of the agent to a particular position. It is common to use the term 'ostensible' authority to refer to both the particular and the general ways in which a holding out may be founded.

Restrictions in the company's constitution

This is general agency law. The particular issue which company law has contributed to this debate is the question of how far special rules should apply to attempts by the company to protect itself against third party claims through restrictions on agents' authority contained in its constitution (memorandum or articles of association). These restrictions may be of two kinds. First, the company's objects clause, contained in its memorandum of association, may limit the company's capacity to engage in

---

authority to convey to the third party the decision of the person within the company who does have power to contract: see *First Energy (UK) Ltd v Hungarian International Bank* [1993] BCLC 1409, CA.

[26] *Houghton & Co v Nothard, Lowe & Wills* [1927] 1 KB 246, CA. On the expanding usual authority of the company secretary see *Panorama Developments Ltd v Fidelis Furnishing Fabrics Ltd* [1971] 2 QB 711, CA.

[27] Cf. Table A, art 70, discussed further below at p. 115.

[28] But who is the company? Certainly someone with actual authority to make the representation, but there seems no reason why it should not be someone with ostensible authority to make the representation, provided the representor's ostensible authority can be properly founded. In theory, this could give rise to an infinite regression, but it is unlikely that more than two or three layers of authority would emerge in practical situations.

business to certain defined areas.[29] Although a third party's contractual rights are no longer at risk from this restriction on the company's capacity as such,[30] the restriction on capacity does spill over into the area of agent's authority. This is on the basis that an agent of the company cannot have actual authority to do that which the company does not have capacity to do.

Second, the constitution, normally the articles of association, may place restrictions on an agent's authority to act on behalf of the company, even in areas where there is no doubt about the company's capacity to act. Thus, the articles might say that no manager, without board approval, may enter into a contract on behalf of the company if the liability under it exceeds £50,000.

Company law has always shown some scepticism towards arguments that the company should be permitted to protect itself through provisions in its constitution against claims from third parties purporting to contract with it. Early on, it developed the 'indoor management rule'[31] to give some protection to third parties in such situations. However, that rule did not really do the job, partly because it operated against the background of doctrine of constructive notice (see below) and partly because it did not protect those who actually knew of the limitation in the constitution or knew enough facts to be put on enquiry as to whether there was a relevant limitation in the constitution. The risk that a court might, *ex post*, treat a third party as having known enough to have been put on enquiry meant that, for many third parties, the only safe course was to conduct, *ex ante*, that enquiry into the company's constitutional arrangements, thus providing certainty at the expense of higher transaction costs.

Moreover, the courts limited the potential of the rule by adopting the doctrine of 'constructive' notice. Because the memorandum and articles of the company are public documents, filed with the registrar of companies, the courts treated the public as knowing their contents, even if they had not read them. If a third party thus 'knew' from provisions in the constitution that the agent did not have the authority he or she claimed or appeared to have, the company could not be said to have misled the third party about the agent's authority by appointing him to a particular position or in some other way. Consequently, the company

---

[29] Typically, the company will list a wide set of objects or adopt a general commercial objects clause, as s 3A of the CA 1985 now permits. In either case the problem discussed in the text is reduced.

[30] CA 1985, s 35(1).

[31] Associated with the case of *Royal British Bank v Turquand* (1856) 6 El & Bl 327, HL.

could rely on the basic principle that an unauthorized agent cannot make a company liable contractually.[32] Constructive notice represented the triumph of formalism over commercial practice. Section 711A(1) of the CA 1985, added by the Companies Act 1989, abolishes the doctrine of constructive notice derived from public filing, but it has not yet been brought into force. It should be.

For many third parties, the security of their transactions with the company will be safeguarded by the abolition of the constructive notice doctrine arising out of public filing. However, its abolition will not solve all the problems of the interrelationship between authority and the provisions of the company's constitution. Some third parties, especially banks, may have been provided with a copy of the company's memorandum and articles of association before entering into the transaction in question. Should they be treated as knowing what they could have learned by reading those documents? The doctrine of constructive notice arising out of 'a failure to make such inquiries as ought reasonably to be made' is expressly preserved by CA 1985, s 711A(2). However, the trend in the current law and in reform proposals is to turn the company's constitution into an entirely internal document which has no impact upon the question of whether the third party may enforce its transaction with the company. In other words, the memorandum and articles are no longer seen as an appropriate way of conveying information about agents' authority to third parties contracting with the company. This is the exact opposite to the principle which underlay the idea of constructive notice arising from public filing. The company may still limit the authority of its agents as it wishes, provided it brings those limitations to the attention of third parties, but it cannot use the constitution to achieve the necessary notification.

The current law already goes a good way in this direction by virtue of ss 35A and 35B of the Act,[33] but does so effectively only for those third parties who contract with the company via the board, that is, those who

---

[32] Curiously, the courts were unwilling to allow the doctrine of constructive notice to benefit third parties, for example on the basis that a positive statement in the constitution about authority could be regarded as a misleading act by the company upon which the third party could rely: see the *Freeman & Lockyer* case, above, n. 24. This was on the argument that a person who did not actually know of a provision in the articles could not be said to have relied on it.

[33] See above, pp. 41–42. Within their scope of operation these sections also remove the doctrine of constructive notice, thus rendering the non-implementation of s 711A less significant.

rely on the primary rules of attribution.[34] As we have seen above, this is far too narrow a basis for the implementation of a policy that the third party should not have to peruse the company's constitution, even if it has a copy of it. The CLR has proposed going the whole way and suggests that the statute should straightforwardly provide that 'in determining any question whether a person has ostensible authority to exercise any of a company's powers in a given case, no reference may be made to the company's constitution'.[35] Thus, in relation to the secondary as well as the primary rules of attribution for contracting authority, the relevant rules would operate untrammelled by the provisions of the company's constitution,[36] and the policy of promoting security of transactions for third parties will be pressed home.

However, two points about these reforms need to be noted. First, in relation to the secondary rules of attribution, the proposed clause has a limited impact. It merely removes one argument (based on provisions contained in the constitution) which the company might have used to defeat the third party's otherwise successful argument that the agent had ostensible authority to contract on the company's behalf. However, it does not create such authority where there has been no misleading act by the company. Unless there is the basis for a finding of ostensible authority derived from some holding out by the company, the third party will not even get to the position where the new clause has to be considered. The 'self-created' agent would be no more a possibility under the reform than it is now. Second, although the company's constitution is being reduced in its external effects, it does not follow that breach of the constitution cannot have important internal effects, in the shape of actions by the company against the directors for breach of duty or by the shareholders for breach of contract against the company.[37]

---

[34] Although s 35A permits a third party to ignore any limitations in the constitution upon the board's powers to authorize others to bind the company, it is arguable that this does not cover a situation where the constitution limits the powers of the agents directly rather than via limitations on the board's powers to authorize agents. Thus, those dealing otherwise than directly with the board continue to run a risk that their transaction will not be upheld.

[35] CLR, *Final Report*, July 2001, vol. II, ch. 16, draft clause 16(7).

[36] The CLR also proposes that the company should have unlimited capacity, so that, presumably, objects clauses will in time cease to be a feature of most companies' constitutions. Even if that prediction is falsified, objects clauses would in any event be caught by draft clause 16(7).

[37] These are discussed below at pp. 160 and 243.

VICARIOUS LIABILITY AND TORT

At their core, contracts are voluntary legal instruments. It is consistent with this view that companies should be free to specify which persons shall be empowered to act as their agents for contracting purposes, that companies should be able effectively to limit the authority of those agents (provided the limitations are conveyed to third parties by an appropriate means), and that the resulting contractual rights and duties should exist only between company and third party. As we have seen, agency rules achieve this result in relation to the company's contracting powers. However, these are not necessarily an appropriate set of rules for the attribution of liability where the act done by the person is wrongful, either civilly (normally because it is a tort) or criminally. Here, one might expect the person who acts to be liable (even if the company is also liable) and for the rules which determine whether the company is also liable to attach less importance to the company's freedom to arrange its affairs so as to avoid liability. As we shall see, this is the pattern one finds in relation to tort liability as a result of the application of the doctrine of vicarious liability, whereas in relation to criminal liability, where the doctrine of vicarious liability is controversial, the law is currently in a state of development. Again, we shall see that the secondary rules of attribution in relation to wrongdoing are provided for companies by general legal doctrines, but these doctrines need to be examined in the particular context of company law in order to establish whether they help or hinder the implementation of the core features of our subject. We shall look first at tort law.

The doctrine of vicarious liability operates widely so as to make the company liable in tort. It applies to torts committed both by agents within the course of their agency and by employees within the course of their employment.[38] It makes the employer or principal (for our purposes, the company) liable to the victim for the tortfeasor's conduct. The employee or agent is the tortfeasor (and thus is liable to the victim of the tort) but, because of the relationship existing between the agent or employee and the company, the company is liable to the victim as well. In fact, company and individual are joint tortfeasors.[39] The nature of the doctrine of

[38] That the vicarious liability of principals for the acts of agents is as wide as that of employers for employees was asserted by the House of Lords in *Heatons Transport (St Helens) Ltd v TGWU* [1972] 3 All ER 101, 109. In the company context, the matter is less important than it might be, because nearly all those with authority to contract on behalf of the company will also be its employees.

[39] *New Zealand Guardian Trust Co Ltd v Brooks* [1995] 1 WLR 96, PC.

vicarious liability is such that it is not necessary to prove that 'the company' has committed a tort. What has to be shown is that the agent or employee committed the tort; the company then has liability for the tort attributed to it by the doctrine of vicarious liability provided the requisite relationship existed between the company and the tortfeasor and the tort was committed in the course of the agency or employment.

The doctrine of vicarious liability gives companies some control over their liabilities in tort: if employees or agents are not given certain functions, the scope of the company's vicarious liability is thereby reduced. However, if there is a business case for the company to engage in those functions, it is extremely difficult for the company to do so without accepting the associated risk of vicarious liability. In other words, the company does not enjoy the same freedom to fine-tune its vicarious liability in tort as it can the power of its agents to bind it contractually. In particular, an instruction given to an agent or employee not to engage in certain actions, even if that restriction is well publicized, will not necessarily operate to restrict the company's vicarious liability. In fact, a company can be held vicariously liable for intentional torts committed by employees or agents for the benefit of themselves, rather than of the company, involving the commission of acts which the company had expressly prohibited or to which it must have been clear to the employee or agent that the company did not consent.[40] Provided there is a sufficient connection between the functions the employee or agent is required to discharge and the tortious act, the company will be liable.[41]

Although vicarious liability involves imposing tortious liability on a person who is not the tortfeasor, it can be justified on the grounds of deterrence of tortious conduct and/or the internalization of costs. An employer is in principle in a good position to monitor its employees so as to prevent tortious conduct (for example by not hiring incompetent workers or by putting in place proper training programmes) or to sanction it (for example by disciplining workers who commit torts); or to design working practices which reduce the chances of wrongdoing. If none of these is possible in a particular case, then vicarious liability helps

---

[40] *Lloyd v Grace, Smith & Co* [1912] AC 716, HL (fraud committed on client by solicitors' clerk for his own benefit); *Morris v CW Martin & Sons Ltd* [1966] 1 QB 716, CA (theft of fur coat by employee of a cleaning company). Of course, there is no reason to treat the fraud as the fraud of the company if the company sues the agent in respect of the harm done to it by the fraud: *Re Hampshire Land Company* [1896] 2 Ch 743.

[41] Cf. *Lister v Hesley Hall Ltd* [2001] 2 All ER 769, HL. In determining the functions of an agent it will be necessary, of course, to come back to issues of actual and ostensible authority: see *Armagas Ltd v Mundogas SA* [1986] 1 AC 717, HL.

to ensure that the costs of engaging in a particular business are internalized within the business and then passed on to the consumers of the company's output through its pricing policy.[42]

Individual liability

Where the company's liability is based on vicarious liability, it is clear that the individual is liable as well. Indeed, without individual liability there will be nothing for which the company can be liable vicariously. Is this an appropriate rule where the individual has acted on behalf of a company? Would it be better to follow the agency pattern and treat the acts of the individual as the acts of the company alone, so that individual liability would not arise? Not surprisingly, the issue has emerged in recent years in that part of our law where the division between contract and tort is contestable. Where the rules of tort and contract overlap, it is not surprising that a major issue has arisen in respect of company agents as to whether the governing principle should be the contract/agency one of no personal liability or the opposite tort notion.

Take the area of negligent misstatements. If a director in pre-contractual negotiations makes a negligently false statement and that statement becomes (only) an implied term in the subsequent contract between the third party and the company, the company will be liable on the promise that the statement is true and the director, not being a party to the contract, will not. If, on the other hand, the negligent misstatement is regarded as a tort, the director will be liable as tortfeasor and the company will be vicariously liable for the director's tort. Indeed, the point applies more generally to the negligent provision of services under a contract with a company: if the action is brought in contract, the company will be the only available defendant; if in tort, the individual who has negligently provided the services on behalf of the company may be liable as well. This distinction matters little if the third party sues the company (which is liable on either analysis) but it does matter if the third party sues the director, as the third party may well wish to do if the company is insolvent. Thus, we need to see how the courts have handled the issue of the agent's personal liability.

The House of Lords has now held in *Williams v Natural Life Health*

---

[42] See R. Kraakman, 'Third-party liability' in P. Newman (ed.), *The New Palgrave Dictionary of Economics and the Law* (London: Macmillan, 1998), vol. 3, p. 583. These justifications also probably explain why vicarious liability is rarely imposed outside the employer/employee or principal/agent relationship, because in respect of non-tortfeasors other than employers and principals the deterrence and internalization arguments work much less well.

Foods Ltd[43] that the correct approach to the issue of liability of corporate agents in tort is to rely on a general requirement in the law of tort relating to negligent misstatements and the negligent supply of services. This is that a person must have assumed personal responsibility for the statement or services before liability in tort will be imposed. In the case of those acting on behalf of companies in the provision of services, such personal responsibility will not be taken to have been assumed unless the individual can be said to have conveyed to the third party, by words or conduct, that he or she was assuming personal responsibility. Merely to be the director or employee of a company is insufficient to lead to a finding of assumption of personal responsibility, even if that individual's expertise is the crucial resource available to the company for the effective delivery of the promised services.[44] The default rule is that the individual was assuming responsibility only on behalf of the company, so that the company can be sued as a primary tortfeasor because the individual's acts are attributed to it, but the individual cannot, because an essential ingredient for liability in these torts is missing.

Thus, in the case of torts arising out of the negotiation or performance of contracts on behalf of companies, the decision in *Williams v Natural Life Health Foods* amounts to saying that the appropriate distinction is not the formal one between liability in tort and liability in contract. Rather, the better distinction is between relationships voluntarily entered into by third parties with the company and obligations toward the whole world imposed by law upon everyone, including those acting on behalf of companies. In the former case, where the third party contracts with the company, the default rule should be that the person acting on behalf of the company is not liable, whether the cause of action is framed in contract or in tort. That default rule may be altered (where the company's agent accepts either contractual or tortious responsibility) but, unless the agent agrees to the contrary, the legal liabilities are those of the company alone. In the case of imposed obligations, say where the individual steals the third party's goods,[45] the individual will be liable in tort, whether he is acting on behalf of a company or not.

---

[43] [1998] 1 WLR 830, HL. The case concerned negligent advice given by the director of a franchising company about the likely success of a proposed franchised health food shop. This general issue emerged in recent years first in the New Zealand courts. For an excellent analysis of these New Zealand decisions see D. Goddard, 'Corporate Personality–Limited Recourse and its Limits' in R. Grantham and C. Rickett (eds), *Corporate Personality in the 20th Century* (Oxford: Hart Publishing, 1998), pp. 44–55.

[44] However, the test is an objective, not a subjective one, and so open to the influence of the courts' policy perceptions.

[45] See *Morris v CW Martin*, above, n. 40. And see n. 46 for the fraud exception.

In the *Williams* case, the House of Lords dealt with a company law problem without creating a specific company law rule but rather by relying on the general rules of tort law about assumption of responsibility.[46] Such an approach has one clear advantage. It enables all those acting on behalf of the company, whether directors or employees, to benefit from the protection of the rule. A situation where there is one rule for directors and officers and another for employees is thus avoided.[47] As with agency law, the same rules apply across the company's hierarchy of workers. On the other hand, the court's reasoning makes it clear that the conclusion in favour of the individual does depend upon the existence of another legal entity (the company) which can be said to have assumed responsibility for the services and upon which the third party can be said to have relied. If there is no other legal entity, as in the case of a partner in an ordinary partnership (at least in England and Wales), the individual who has provided the services negligently will be treated as assuming responsibility for them (if anyone has done so).[48] Thus, the *Williams* decision does constitute a consequence of, or at least build on, the doctrine of the separate legal personality of the company.

The *Williams* decision may also be seen as giving effect to another company law doctrine, that of limited liability, at least if one takes the broader view of limited liability discussed in Chapter 1.[49] On this broader view, limited liability means that the person dealing with the company is limited to the company's assets for the satisfaction of his or her claims. On this view of limited liability, the doctrine should protect the assets of those acting for companies as much as it protects shareholders' assets. From this perspective, to allow parties to contracts with the company to enforce their claims against the personal assets of agents or employees of

---

[46] For this reason, a director should be liable for fraudulent statements, because assumption of responsibility is not a requirement for this tort. See *Noel v Poland* [2001] 2 BCLC 645. This seems right: corporate personality should not be a shield for fraud.

[47] However, the courts have been reluctant to give immunity in negligence to professionally qualified employees working in organizations. See *Merrett v Babb* [2001] 3 WLR 1 (surveyor employed by a partnership) and *Phelps v Hillingdon BC* [2000] 3 WLR 776 (educational psychologist employed by LEA); cf. *Edgeworth Construction Ltd v M D Lea & Associates Ltd* [1993] 3 SCR 206 (Supreme Court of Canada)—individual engineers of an engineering company held not liable. Presumably, the same approach would be taken if the professionally qualified worker were a director of a company.

[48] The exposed position of individual partners as regards liability in negligence for services rendered generated a demand for a form of partnership with separate legal personality and limited liability (see below, p. 296). Despite government expectations to the contrary, it seems likely the courts will apply the *Williams* decision to members of limited liability partnerships.

[49] See p. 12.

the company is to permit them to escape from the terms of their bargain, just as much as is enforcement against the personal assets of the shareholders.[50] Clearly, the decision in *Williams* is a crucial element in the rules whereby British law provides this protection beyond shareholders. In particular, the *Williams* decision has provided comfort to those conducting business through small companies who may be, not only the company's dominant shareholder and director, but also its principal employee. To protect the personal assets of such people from contractual claims but not from tortious claims arising out of the same voluntary transactions would be to deprive them substantially of the benefits of operating through a company with limited liability. However, the comfort so provided does depend upon the view the courts take of the role of assumption of responsibility in the general law of tort relating to negligent statements or the negligent provision of services. It is always possible that general tort law will be pushed in a direction unfavourable to directors of companies without the impact of such a development on the doctrine of limited liability being uppermost in the judges' minds.

Tort liability and the primary rules of attribution

Given the width of vicarious liability in the law of tort, the primary rules of attribution for tort liability have received less attention from the courts, as indeed is also true of secondary rules based on some theory other than vicarious liability.[51] However, there seems to be no doubt that if the board of directors authorizes the commission of a tort on the company's behalf, the company will be treated as having committed that tort, as will the directors who authorized it.[52] The rule that the directors who authorize the tort are liable also gives the key to the problem of whether a director is liable in tort where the company is vicariously liable for a tort committed by an employee or agent other than the director. The answer is that he or she is not, unless he has authorized the tort.[53]

Even with the primary rules of attribution, however, the separate legal entity of the company may cause problems. Suppose the board decides not to honour a contract into which the company has entered. The

---

[50] Goddard, above, n. 43.

[51] P. S. Atiyah, *Vicarious Liability* (London: Butterworths, 1967), p. 383, but see n. 56 below.

[52] Those who authorize the commission of a tort are liable as secondary parties.

[53] *C Evans & Sons Ltd v Spritebrand Ltd* [1985] 1 WLR 317, CA. There is a risk that the courts could use the authorization argument to undermine the *Williams* rule. A director accepting responsibility on behalf of the company might be said to be authorizing the company to act negligently. Such an extension of the notion should be resisted.

company will be liable for breach of contract, but the directors will not (because they are not parties to it). However, can the directors be sued in tort by the other party to the contract for inducing breach by the company of its contract? A first instance judgment of some antiquity, *Said v Butt*,[54] suggests not. In principle, this seems correct and in line with the reasoning in *Williams*: the contracting party should be confined to the company's assets for the satisfaction of its claims. The agency principle thus applies as much in the performance of contracts as in their formation.

CRIMINAL LIABILITY

Legal systems differ in their approaches to the principles which determine the criminal liability of companies. Some (such as that of Germany) historically have treated guilt as something which can be attributed only to human beings, so that companies escaped criminal liability. At the other end of the spectrum, some (such as federal law in the United States) apply the principle of vicarious liability to crimes in much the same way as they have applied it to torts. Modern British law has no conceptual difficulty with the principle of corporate criminal liability, but, on the other hand, it has been unwilling to accept broad secondary rules of attribution in the criminal sphere. For example, vicarious liability, as we have seen, is a form of strict liability as far as the company is concerned. The common law, which has traditionally insisted upon a guilty mind as an essential element of crimes, has therefore been reluctant to find companies guilty, whether on the basis of vicarious liability or the attribution of mental states of individuals to the company.

However, criminal law in the UK is not just common law. Parliament has created many crimes, some based upon strict liability, and, where the statute has imposed strict liability, the courts have been willing to treat acts of employees and agents as acts of the company for the purposes of criminal liability. Crucially, this approach has extended to those crimes which impose strict liability but subject to a 'reasonably practicable' defence. This development is important, practically as well as theoretically, because one of the main sources of such 'hybrid' duties is the Health and Safety at Work etc. Act 1974, which imposes duties upon employers not to conduct their undertakings in such a way as to expose employees or members of the public to risks to their health and safety. If a corporate

---

[54] *Said v Butt* [1920] 3 KB 497. The case involves making an exception to the scope of the tort of inducing breach of contract, perhaps in all principal/agent situations.

employer, through its employees or agents, conducts its business in such a way as to create such a risk, then, subject to the reasonable practicality defence, it will be guilty of an offence, irrespective of whether any of its individual employees are guilty.[55] To hold otherwise, Steyn LJ thought, would be to allow corporate employers to escape liability where individual employers or partnerships would be liable.

None of this, however, provides any guidance for crimes requiring a particular mental state. However, some sixty years ago the British courts applied the doctrine of 'identification' to crimes of this type: where a person or persons who constitute the 'directing mind and will' of the company have committed a crime, the company will be treated as liable as well because such people 'are' the company.[56] It has remained rather unclear who can constitute the directing mind and will. Lord Diplock thought it was only those authorized by the company's constitution to exercise the company's powers: that is, that the doctrine provided only a set of primary rules of attribution for crimes involving a guilty mind.[57] This may still be the test for common law crimes, but it is now clear that in the case of statutory offences the question to be asked is who, for the purposes of the statute, is to be treated as the directing mind and will of the company.[58]

Despite these developments, the company is likely to escape criminal liability for serious common law crimes, unless the board or the shareholders have authorized the criminal conduct in question. This is widely regarded as unsatisfactory, especially in relation to serious accidents caused, it is alleged, by failures by companies to put in place and enforce proper supervisory systems. Under the identification doctrine, only if someone at a very senior level in the company can be shown to have committed the criminal offence will the company be liable as well. In particular, the limited scope of the doctrine of identification has made prosecutions of companies for involuntary manslaughter by gross

---

[55] *R v British Steel plc* [1995] 1 WLR 1356, CA: company guilty through the negligence (though probably not criminal negligence) of its employee.

[56] *R v ICR Haulage Ltd* [1944] KB 551, CCA. This was the application to the criminal law of a notion first developed in relation to civil statutes requiring 'actual fault or privity' on the part of a person: see *Lennard's Carrying Co Ltd v Asiatic Petroleum Co Ltd* [1915] AC 705, HL.

[57] *Tesco Supermarkets Ltd v Nattrass* [1972] AC 153, HL

[58] *Meridian Global Funds Management Asia Ltd v Securities Commission* [1995] 3 All ER 918, PC. In that case the acts of a senior investment manager, who was not a director, were attributed to the company. In *Re Supply of Ready Mixed Concrete (No 2)* [1995] 1 AC 456, HL, it was the acts of local managers, acting in defiance of express orders from senior management, whose actions were attributed to the company.

negligence[59] difficult to conduct, even though it is a common charge against individual defendants.[60]

Reform

There seem to be two ways forward from this unsatisfactory state of the law. One is to re-examine the arguments in favour of a general rule of vicarious liability for criminal offences. The deterrence and internalization of costs arguments, which we noted above in relation to vicarious liability in tort,[61] apply in principle to criminal liability as well. Indeed, if, as seems likely, the enforcement agencies of the state find it more difficult to detect and prove criminal wrongdoing within large organizations than do private claimants alleging tortious conduct, the argument in favour of vicarious liability is stronger in relation to crimes than torts. It is likely that the large company, through its internal disciplinary and monitoring techniques, is in a better position to deter criminal behaviour on the part of its employees than are the organs of the state, which may find it difficult to penetrate large organizations. Vicarious criminal liability could provide a powerful incentive to companies to make compliance with the criminal law a central goal of the company's overall strategy (a 'culture of compliance').[62]

However, there is a risk that vicarious criminal liability, just like vicarious tortious liability, could create perverse incentives. On the one hand, the company would have an incentive to detect criminal conduct, so that it could control it; on the other, detection of crimes would increase the risk that liability will be imposed on the company.[63] One way of counteracting these perverse incentives is for the courts to grant to those companies which do introduce effective compliance systems substantial discounts on the normal fine if, as will inevitably happen under even the

---

[59] It is actually rather odd that the identification doctrine has been applied to gross negligence manslaughter (as opposed to manslaughter based on recklessness) because negligence connotes, not a state of mind, but failure to observe a standard of conduct: *Attorney-General's Reference (No 2 of 1999)* [2000] QB 796, CA.

[60] See Home Office, *Reforming the Law on Involuntary Manslaughter: the Government's Proposals*, May 2000, para. 3.1.6: only three successful prosecutions, and all of small companies, where it is more likely that the person responsible at the operational level also holds a 'directing mind and will' position within the company.

[61] Above, p. 50.

[62] Indeed, failure to do so and the consequent exposure of the company to heavy fines could then become a breach of the duties which directors owe to the company: see the discussion in Chapter 6 of the duty of care and especially the discussion of the Turnbull Report.

[63] J. Arlen in P. Newman (ed.), above n. 42, vol. 1, p. 494.

best control systems, an employee does commit a criminal offence in the course of his or her duties, provided the company co-operates with the investigations by the public authorities. This is in essence the approach of the federal criminal law in the United States.[64]

An alternative approach, advocated by the English Law Commission,[65] is to build on the techniques of the Health and Safety at Work etc. Act and create criminal duties which apply to companies and the breach of which by the company can be demonstrated by attributing acts and omissions of relevant officers and employees to the company, whether or not those individuals are held to have committed a crime. Responding in particular to the difficulty of convicting a company of involuntary manslaughter, the Commission proposed the creation of a new offence of 'corporate killing'. In most cases, the immediate cause of the death would be the actions of the company's employees or agents, in the course of their employment, but this would not by itself be enough to make the company criminally liable for the new offence. To make the company liable it would have to be shown that 'management failure' on the part of the company contributed to the deaths, that is, that the risk to the health and safety of employees or others had been created by managerial conduct which fell far below the standard that which could reasonably be expected. Thus, organization failure becomes a basis for criminal liability.

Although the subject matter of the Law Commission's proposals, death arising out of the company's activities, is narrower than the US federal criminal law, which applies vicarious liability to a wide range of crimes, including fraud and money laundering, it is not clear that vicarious liability, in the abstract, is a wider principle of corporate liability than 'management failure' (which is undefined in the proposals). Vicarious liability, as we have explained, requires an individual to be identified who has committed the crime, for which the company is then held liable. It differs from the identification theory of current British law mainly by accepting a much wider range of subordinates whose liability is attributed to the company. However, if there is no crime by the individual, the company cannot be liable. Management failure, by contrast, could consist of the cumulative acts and omissions of a number of

[64] J. C. Coffee, 'Corporate Criminal Responsibility: an Introduction and Comparative Survey' in A. Eser, H. Heine, and B. Huber (eds), *Criminal Responsibility of Legal and Collective Entities* (Freiburg: Jus Crim, 1999). The Human Rights Act 1998 is likely to require such mitigation provisions: *International Transport Roth Gmb H v Secretary of State*, *The Times*, 22 February 2002, C.A.

[65] The Law Commission, *Legislating the Criminal Code: Involuntary Manslaughter*, Law Com No 237, 1996.

managers, none of whom individually could be said to be guilty of involuntary manslaughter.

By extension, to propose a new offence of corporate killing, based on management failure, invites the question of whether the individuals responsible for the management failure should not be brought within the scope of the new offence as well. Although the Law Commission recommended against,[66] the Government clearly felt the force of the argument that some penalty should be applied to those individuals who contributed to serious management failure, though they were undecided whether this should be a disqualification from engaging in business in the future or a criminal penalty.[67] Thus, the notion of management failure might lead to a broadening of the criminal law applicable to individuals (notably managers), whereas vicarious criminal liability of the company simply builds on, but does not require any extension of, the crimes which individuals may commit.

CONCLUSION

It is clear that the attribution rules for companies are complex, mainly because of the range of situations with which it is necessary to deal. However, they are fundamental. Whenever a statement is made about a company 'doing x' or 'deciding y', it is probable that there is an implicit reference to one or more of the rules of attribution. They form the bedrock of company law, even if their structure is still not fully defined. With hindsight, it can be seen that giving the company separate legal personality was the bold and imaginative but technically easy conceptual step. Giving that person the means of thought and action has proved a legally much more complex undertaking.

[66] Of course, if the individual has committed the offence of manslaughter by gross negligence, as it applies to individuals, he or she could be prosecuted as well as the company, but this would require a good deal more than proof of contribution to management failure. However, a bold court could use the Turnbull Report (see n. 62 above), with its stress on risk management by the board, to hold the directors guilty of manslaughter in the case of serious failures to spot and deal with safety risks, and the doctrine of identification could then operate to make the company liable as well.

[67] Above, n. 60, paras 3.4.7–3.4.13.

3

Limited Liability

Rationale and Creditor Self-Help

INTRODUCTION

Limited liability means that the claims of the company's creditors are confined to the assets of the company. In the previous chapter[1] we examined the rather insecure and partial way in which that doctrine is applied to the assets of the company's agents. In this chapter we shall examine the core function of the doctrine, which is its use to the personal assets of the company's shareholders. We saw in Chapter 1 that British company law achieves shareholder protection by a combination of the separate legal entity doctrine and the Insolvency Act (IA 1986) rules limiting the extent to which shareholders have to contribute to the company's assets upon its insolvency.[2] Limited liability for the company's shareholders is a universal feature of the company laws of advanced economies, though they vary to some extent in their willingness to depart from the principle in particular circumstances.

Nevertheless, limited liability is often regarded as a surprising doctrine, almost a departure from the normal order of things. Certainly, there is an apparently strong contrast between the position of the small entrepreneur who carries on business as a sole trader or through a traditional partnership, who does not have the benefit of limited liability, and one who uses the company vehicle to conduct the business. The privileged position of the user of the corporate form might thus be thought to need justification. Why should the user of the corporate form be able to shelter personal assets in a way the sole trader or partner may not? One might answer this point by saying that the law makes limited liability available to anyone who wants it, through the 'one person' company (recognized in practice for more than one hundred years)[3] or through the limited liability partnership introduced in 2000.[4] Nevertheless, since limited liability

---

[1] Above, p. 53. [2] Above, p. 10.
[3] Above, p. 28. [4] See Chapter 10, p. 295.

throws risks on to creditors which they otherwise would not have to carry, the question remains why the principle is so widespread and whether it ought to be so.

My view is that the grounds for disquiet about the limited liability rule arise not from this principle itself but from its combination with *control* of the company. If those who benefit from limited liability have direct control over the company, they face a strong temptation to use that control power in an opportunistic[5] fashion so as to benefit themselves as shareholders. At its simplest, they may shift assets into the company when they need to raise credit and out of the company when the time comes for repayment; but there are many other examples of opportunistic conduct. With regard to a passive shareholder, by contrast, there is little reason to be worried about such a person's exemption from responsibility for the company's liabilities, at least while we are prepared to accept that lenders of money to the company are not responsible for the company's liabilities.[6] The modern view that shareholders do not own the company, but only their shares, makes their limited liability a less surprising doctrine than it was previously thought to be (though that view does throw into contention their control rights).[7]

There are two paradigm cases of the combination of control and limited liability, though they are very different from one another. One is the small company where, at its extreme, the shareholders and the directors may be the same people, so that control of the company is directly in the hands of the beneficiaries of limited liability. Almost at the other end of the spectrum is the corporate group. No large business today is carried on through a single company. Rather a string of parent, subsidiary, sub-subsidiary, and associated companies exist behind a single name.[8] Even a quite modest business may be carried on through one or more linked companies. However, each of these companies is a separate legal person and its shareholders (i.e. one or more other companies in the group) benefit in principle from limited liability as much as individual

---

[5] This term is used to refer to self-interested behaviour which involves some element of deception, misrepresentation or bad faith. See O. Williamson, *The Economic Institutions of Capitalism* (London: Collier Macmillan, 1986). The term is not a legal term and the law may or may not characterize a particular example of opportunistic behaviour as illegal.

[6] Doctrinally, this is because lenders to the company do not become its members. If they do intervene substantially in the affairs of the company, they might attract liabilities towards other creditors as 'shadow directors' under the doctrine of wrongful trading (below, p. 104), though the courts are not astute to impose such liability.

[7] See Chapter 9.

[8] The composition of corporate groups is considered more fully at p. 102.

shareholders in a free-standing company do. Take a simple example of a parent company which holds all the shares of a subsidiary company. Parent and subsidiary are separate legal persons. The parent has complete control of the subsidiary: the directors of the subsidiary will be the nominees of the parent and may even be the same persons as the directors of the parent company, so that the subsidiary board has no independent business discretion. Yet, the parent in principle benefits from the doctrine of limited liability as against the creditors of the subsidiary. Again the combination of limited liability and control may lead to opportunistic behaviour on the part of the parent company, for example assigning risky activities to the subsidiary but not endowing it with adequate assets to carry those risks.

In the rest of this chapter we shall examine in more detail the operation of the limited liability doctrine in these two situations and some others. Assuming the risk of opportunistic behaviour on the part of those who have limited liability is thought to be significant, there are two obvious ways in which the law could seek directly to control such behaviour. On the one hand, it could simply remove limited liability from certain types of company; on the other, it could seek to identify and control certain types of opportunism. The former is a more radical approach because companies of a type where the risk of opportunism is judged to be high lose the benefits of limited liability entirely. Whether this is a wise course of action depends in part upon identifying the benefits of limited liability, the loss of which this first course of action will impose on the companies which are excluded from the doctrine. Consequently, the next section in this chapter will analyse the rationales for limited liability in order to establish what those benefits may be.

The second course of action might appear more attractive because it is precisely targeted at the mischief the limited liability rule has generated. However, it depends heavily upon the legislature being able to identify and keep up to date its list of unacceptable behaviour. Moreover, there is a third strategy which the law could adopt, replacing wholly or in part the second one. This is to permit broad access on the part of shareholders to the shelter of limited liability and then leave creditors to protect themselves, largely by contract, against the risks of opportunistic behaviour. In this strategy company law is not entirely without a role, because it could be used to place creditors in a position where they can bargain effectively with companies, for example by requiring disclosure of relevant information. However, the greater weight of the policy for dealing with opportunism in this strategy lies with private rather than public ordering. As we shall in this chapter and the next, British law traditionally has been reluctant to adopt the first strategy (exclusion of certain types of company from the doctrine of limited liability); has always leaned heavily on the third strategy (in effect, creditor self-help); but also has made some use of direct control of opportunistic behaviour, which use expanded significantly in the wake of the Report of the Cork Committee on Insolvency Law in 1982.[9]

THE RATIONALES FOR LIMITED LIABILITY

ENCOURAGEMENT OF PUBLIC INVESTMENT

Historically, the argument for limited liability which had the strongest impact upon the Victorian legislature was that, without it, companies would not be able to raise from the public the large amounts of capital needed for major projects, of which the paradigm example at that time was the construction and operation of a new railway line.[10] Unlimited liability throws upon investors in companies' shares the risk of the loss of the whole of their personal wealth if the company becomes insolvent. Potential investors might respond to that extra cost of investment in one of three ways, all of which, it was reasonable to think, would reduce the pool of risk capital available to companies. First, they might simply seek other forms of investment, say company bonds,[11] rather than their shares. As bondholders, the investors would merely be creditors of the company, rather than members of it. As creditors, they would not be liable for the company's debts; on the contrary, as creditors they might be in a position to apply the principle of unlimited liability against the company's shareholders for the satisfaction of their own claims. However, loans are a less flexible form of financing than share capital,[12] and so the effect of unlimited liability would be to decrease the amount of risk capital available to companies, even if the total amount of finance were not reduced.

Second, unlimited liability would increase the costs to investors of port-

---

[9] *Report of the Review Committee on Insolvency Law and Practice* (Chairman: Sir Kenneth Cork), Cmnd. 8558, 1982.

[10] Limited liability was made available in the Limited Liability Act 1855, some 11 years after the first modern companies Act, the Joint Stock Companies Act 1844 (see Chapter 1, p. 1). Thus, for 11 years there was a general system of incorporation by registration but without limited liability. This shows that the Parliament of the time was well aware that limited liability was not a necessary feature of incorporation.

[11] On the meaning of corporate bonds see above, p. 8.

[12] Mainly because the interest on loans is normally payable periodically, no matter how badly the company is doing, whereas ordinary shareholders are entitled only to such dividends as the directors declare. See p. 263.

folio diversification. Every investment in an additional company would increase the insolvency risk to the investor's wealth. Unlimited liability for shareholders would thus create an incentive for shareholders to concentrate, rather than diversify, their shareholdings, but such concentration would itself make it more difficult for investors to protect themselves against other sorts of risk. Risks that a particular company might turn out to have bad management or that some sectors of the economy might do better than others, for example, can best be met by sensible diversification of the investor's shareholdings across a number of companies. However, under unlimited liability the additional costs of diversification would reduce the incentives for risk-averse investors to buy shares in further companies.

Third, unlimited liability creates an incentive for shareholders to monitor closely the actions of the management of the company. If the whole of one's personal wealth is potentially at risk from the actions of the board, a review of the performance of the company at the annual general meeting of shareholders may seem inadequate. However, close monitoring of the board is both costly for individual shareholders (who may have other and more pressing calls on their time) and for the shareholders collectively, as it is likely to deprive the company of the benefits of centralized management.[13] Those not in a position to engage in close monitoring would thus be less willing to buy shares. One might say that, if limited liability with control generates the risk of opportunistic behaviour toward creditors, conversely unlimited liability without control creates unacceptable risks for investors.

It could be argued that this emphasis on the raising of capital from 'the public' is today misplaced, since the role of the individual shareholder has declined. It is true that the percentage of the ordinary shares of companies listed on the London Stock Exchange which were held by individuals fell from 54 per cent in 1963 to 16.5 per cent in 1997, while that held by pension funds, insurance companies, unit trusts, investment trusts, and other financial institutions (the 'institutional investors') rose from 29 per cent to 56 per cent,[14] and so it could be said that an increasing proportion of individual investment is channelled to the market via collective intermediaries. However, it is not clear how far this undercuts the arguments for limited liability. First, individual direct investment is still important and encouraged by governments (consider privatization

[13] See p. 13.
[14] Office for National Statistics, *Share Ownership* (London: The Stationery Office, 1999), Table A.

issues) and is also important outside the large listed companies (consider investment by wealthy individuals in medium-sized private companies). Second, unlimited liability for the institutions would reduce the returns to investment via intermediaries and thus provide an incentive for direct investment, which, in the case of small investors, makes portfolio diversification more difficult. In any event, in the worst case unlimited liability might still reach through the institution to the personal assets of the investor, say where the investor is a member of the institution, as in an investment trust, unless limited liability were reinstated at this point.[15]

FACILITATION OF PUBLIC MARKETS IN SHARES

We have already noted the important role that public share markets play in enabling companies to raise capital.[16] Such a market provides liquidity for the investor, while preserving the company's assets intact. Providing liquidity to the investor means providing a market on which at any time he or she can readily and cheaply sell his shares at a price (or within a narrow range of prices) that is publicly known. Under a regime of unlimited liability, however, the value of the shares would depend, not only on information about the company's performance, but also on the relative wealth of the shareholders. For example, if the shares over time traded into the hands of poor shareholders, the value of the shares to a wealthy shareholder would go down, because of the greater risk to his or her assets.[17] So, establishing the price of the shares would require the analysis of a whole new range of information and, in addition, that price would vary according to the shareholder's personal wealth. This would be likely to reduce the liquidity of the market.[18]

[15] However, institutions might choose to hold the shares of particularly risky companies through separate nominee companies, in an attempt to confine the insolvency risk. All this shows the insuperable problems involved in applying different rules on limited liability to institutional investors.

[16] Above, p. 22.

[17] This assumes that the shareholders are jointly and severally liable to the creditors, so that the creditor could sue the wealthiest shareholders for the total liability and the latter would then seek to recover a contribution from the poor shareholders, which might or might not prove feasible. On joint and several liability see DTI, *Feasibility Investigation of Joint and Several Liability by the Common Law Team of the Law Commission* (London, 1996), especially pp. 4–10. The result would be different under a regime of proportionate liability in which the shareholder was liable only for that proportion of the creditor's loss which his or her shareholding bore to the total equity capital.

[18] P. Halpern, M. Trebilcock, and T. Turnbull, 'An Economic Analysis of Limited Liability in Corporate Law' (1980) 30 *University of Toronto LJl* 117 seem to have been the first fully to articulate this particular argument. It is doubtful whether the Victorian legislature was much influenced by these securities market arguments.

It is clear that neither of the above arguments provides strong grounds for applying the limited liability doctrine to the whole range of companies. If a company does not have its shares listed on a public market, the second argument falls away. The first argument has a rather broader impact. It could be said to facilitate investment not only in companies which offer their shares to the public, but, by extension, in all companies which wish to have equity investors who are not closely involved in the management of the business. This would include many large private companies as well as public companies. Even so, the argument is inapplicable to the owner-managed company, where close involvement in the management of the company is not seen by the shareholder as a burden but as an entitlement. As we have seen, the Victorian legislature seems initially to have shared this view when it attempted to exclude small businesses (measured by the number of members) from the scope of the companies legislation.[19] The vestige of this policy lives on in the provision that the failure of a public company to maintain the minimum number of two members can result in unlimited liability for the remaining member.[20]

Nor do the arguments developed above have much application within corporate groups, unless they are very loosely structured. The arguments may support limited liability for the parent company (i.e. at the level of the group) but not *within* the group (i.e. as between one group company and another of which it is a shareholder). However, are there other arguments in favour of limited liability which might have a broader impact?

PARTITIONING OF ASSETS

Given the limited scope of the above two rationales for limited liability, it is not surprising that recent theoretical efforts have focused on trying to identify a broader rationale for limited liability. This is what the idea of a partitioning of assets attempts to provide.[21] It starts from the insight that corporate personality and limited liability do not function only so as to shelter the personal assets of the shareholders from the creditors of the company. They also function so as to shelter the assets of the company from the creditors of the shareholder. Thus, if a shareholder becomes insolvent, the personal creditors may seek to assert their claims against

---

[19] Above, p. 28.

[20] CA 1985, s 24. The rule serves no purpose today, other than as a trap for the unwary, and is ripe for abolition.

[21] H. Hansmann and R. Kraakman, 'The Essential Role of Organizational Law' (2000) 110 *Yale LJ* 387.

the insolvent person's shares but not against the assets of the company which issued the shares. In this way separate legal personality and limited liability permit a partitioning of a person's business assets (which are the assets of the company) and a person's non-business assets (which remain his own). These two classes of asset (held by separate legal persons) may then be used as security to raise finance from separate groups of creditors, the company's assets to raise finance for the business and the personal assets finance for the shareholder's other activities. The business creditors will face no competition from the personal creditors in relation to the company's assets; and the personal creditors will equally face no competition from the business creditors in relation to the non-business assets.[22] This result can be defended from an efficiency perspective. The business creditors need monitor only what the company does with its assets and the personal creditors need monitor only what the shareholders do with their personal assets.[23] Thus, the monitoring costs of the creditors are reduced.[24]

Equally, within the corporate group, limited liability permits the allocation of assets to legally separate companies and the pledging of those assets in support of particular business ventures to appropriately skilled creditors. Although creditors of a subsidiary might seem better off if they could claim on the assets of any of the companies in the group, they do in fact obtain a benefit from maintaining the separate legal entities of the companies. Excluding creditors of other group companies from claims on the assets of the subsidiary relieves creditors of that subsidiary of the need to monitor the activities of the group as a whole, and thus reduces monitoring costs.

It is to be noted that the above arguments assume that monitoring of corporate management is an activity engaged in by creditors and not only by shareholders. The creditors' monitoring role in companies is less widely recognized by company lawyers than the shareholders' role,

---

[22] This assumes that the company controllers cannot easily intermingle their business and personal assets by freely moving assets into or out of the company. Legal strategies to prevent such behaviour are analysed in Chapter 4.

[23] The force of this argument is not reduced if the same lender does both types of business; that merely means that the specialization occurs within a single organization.

[24] It is sometimes said that limited liability cheapens enforcement in a second way, namely, it means that the company's creditors do not have to face the prospect of obtaining enforcement against a large body of shareholders whose personal circumstances will vary. This seems a weak argument. Unlimited liability would not *require* the company's creditors to sue the shareholders, while the doctrine of joint and several liability (above, n. 17) allows the creditors, if they do sue, to pick out the wealthiest and make them liable for the whole of the debt.

because company law has designed institutional mechanisms which express the shareholders' monitoring function (annual reports by directors to shareholders, shareholders' meeting, duties owed by the board of directors), whereas the creditors' monitoring role is largely, if not wholly, expressed in the provisions of private contracts.[25] Nevertheless, it should not surprise us that creditors who have advanced large amounts to companies wish to be informed about and, in extreme cases, to control what the management of those companies do with the resources advanced and that they wish to put themselves in a position to take appropriate action if a substantial risk emerges that the loan may not be repaid.[26] In fact, in companies with dispersed shareholding bodies the creditors may be more effective monitors of management than the shareholders, and shareholders may then to some degree free-ride on the efforts of large creditors.[27]

CREDITOR SELF-HELP

LIMITED LIABILITY AS A DEFAULT RULE

Despite the robustness of the arguments in favour of the limited liability rule in companies where centralized management is practised, the arguments for extending the rule to all companies seem weaker. The Limited Liability Act 1855 accepted that the force of the argument for limited liability was stronger in relation to large companies by extending the principle only to joint stock companies above a certain size.[28] As we saw in

---

[25] However, the ingenuity of nineteenth-century practitioners in using freedom of contract to devise the floating charge has received statutory recognition, albeit in the IA 1986, Part III. The floating charge is considered further below.

[26] This will be the case even if the loan is secured on the assets of the company. It is likely to be cheaper for lenders to prevent the company from defaulting on the loan than to seek repayment after default. Going further, commercial law even knows various forms of 'non-recourse' lending, where a creditor really places no reliance for repayment purposes on the assets of the creditor. This is the essence of project finance, where the creditor places its main reliance on the income to be generated by the project, if it is successful, rather than on the assets of the borrower. In such cases lender monitoring of the borrower is particularly intense.

[27] See, for example, J. Drukarczyk and H. Schmidt, 'Lenders as a Force in Corporate Governance: Enabling Covenants and the Impact of Bankruptcy Law' in K. Hopt et al. (eds), *Comparative Corporate Governance* (Oxford: Clarendon Press, 1998).

[28] Section 1. To benefit from limited liability the company had to have at least 25 shareholders, the minimum nominal value of each share was £10 (a considerable amount at that time), and three-quarters of the company's authorized capital was required to have been issued and 20 per cent of the issued capital had to be paid up. However, this strict policy was soon relaxed. The Companies Act 1856 reduced the number of members required to seven where it remained, for public companies, until 1980. It is now two.

Chapter 1, however, when in the last decade of the nineteenth century the House of Lords in the *Salomon* case put its seal of approval on the practitioners' battle to give even the smallest businesses access to the corporate form and limited liability,[29] the legislature accepted its defeat. Thus, the policy of excluding whole categories of business from the shelter of limited liability ceased to be part of British law at an early stage. At European Community level, also, this policy has been rejected in the Twelfth Company Law Directive on one-person companies.[30] Such an approach certainly relieves the legislature of the difficult task of determining precisely which types of business shall have access to the company form or which types of company shall have access to limited liability. However, it is suggested that the main reason why it has become accepted that limited liability should apply across the whole spectrum of companies is that it is not a mandatory rule. Those who do not like its implications may seek to contract out of or around the rule. In other words, the question is not whether limited liability is the best policy but whether limited liability coupled with freedom of contract is the best policy.

The most dramatic demonstration of the default status[31] of the limited liability rule is freedom of parties to dispense with it entirely. The Act permits incorporators to establish companies which do not have limited liability,[32] and thus to opt out of limited liability across the board. In fact, this facility is little used. More significant in practice is opting out of the limited liability rule in particular transactions. Thus, in owner-managed companies, where the arguments for limited liability are perhaps least persuasive, limited liability is in practice often not available in respect of such companies' major liabilities. To revert to our small company, Smith & Jones (Decorators) Ltd,[33] the loan which that company raised from the local bank in order to begin business was likely to have been available only on the terms that Ms Smith and Mr Jones gave personal guarantees of the repayment of the loan by the company, which guarantees were secured on their personal assets, notably a charge on their dwellings.[34] In

---

[29] See p. 28.

[30] Council Directive 89/667/EEC, [1989] OJ L395/40, the Recitals to which include the following statement: 'Whereas it is important to provide a legal instrument allowing limitation of liability of the individual entrepreneur throughout the Community'.

[31] See Chapter 1, p. 7 n. 12.

[32] CA 1985, s 1(2)(c).

[33] See p. 25.

[34] Since the matrimonial home is often the most substantial personal asset an entrepreneur possesses, it is not surprising that the law reports now contain many cases dealing

this situation the bank has contracted out of limited liability: by contract, it has reinstated its right to assert its claim against the personal assets of the shareholders, should the assets of the company prove insufficient to satisfy the liability.

In fact, the choice between limited and unlimited liability is a choice between two default rules. Even if the legislature had never passed the Limited Liability Act 1855, it would have been possible for companies to contract in particular transactions on the basis that the creditor would not pursue the assets of the shareholders. So, the choice between limited and unlimited liability is a choice of starting points for private contracting. The basis of the choice should be the one which will most often suit the parties' needs *without* further substantial contracting, because in this way the costs of doing business are reduced. The standardization of modern economies on the limited liability rule suggests that the correct choice in this case is clear.

CONTRACTING AROUND THE CONSEQUENCES OF LIMITED LIABILITY

However, it would be wrong to see the role of private contracting as confined to opting out of limited liability. Contract has an equally important role in dealing with the *consequences* of transacting on the basis of limited liability. Most of these techniques are not specific to contracting with companies but rather are applicable to contracting with any counterparty whose solvency is in doubt.[35] In general, too, they are not techniques of company law but of commercial or property law, and so are excluded from most courses on company law. Nevertheless, they deserve to be mentioned briefly. A lender doubtful of the borrower's ability to repay may take security over some or all of the company's assets.[36] The latter course of action does not expand the pool of assets that the creditor can pursue (in the way that a personal guarantee does), but it does give the security-holder priority over other creditors in the event that the company's assets prove inadequate.

Alternatively or in addition, the lender may seek to control the actions

---

with the legal problems generated by entrepreneurs who have charged that home without obtaining the fully informed consent of their spouse. See, for the latest exposition of the law, *Royal Bank of Scotland v Etridge (No 2)* [2001] 4 All ER 449, HL.

[35] One should also avoid the fallacy of thinking that, absent limited liability, the creditors' problems would evaporate. There are plenty of devices whereby natural persons entering into contracts can seek to put their assets beyond the reach of their creditors.

[36] The floating charge, which is a technique of company law, is dealt with at p. 73.

of the corporate borrower by inserting provisions in the loan contract, requiring the lender's prior consent to certain courses of action which the lender judges might adversely affect the prospects of the loan being repaid. 'The theory is that a lender providing capital acquires an interest in the preservation of that capital, thereby conferring an entitlement to some voice, however muted, in the management of the business in order to protect that interest. Unlike equity shares, debt does not have a right to vote for management. That "vote" is conferred by covenants, the breach of which results in the sanction of an event of default, thereby encouraging compliance.'[37] The variety of protections for creditors that can be created in this way is large, and there is no need to explore them in detail here. Among the more common are restrictions upon the creation of security over the company's assets (the 'negative pledge' clause); restrictions on the borrower's disposing of its assets; and requirements that the company continue to meet certain financial tests relating to its liquidity, solvency, or capital adequacy.[38]

Finally, a supplier to a doubtfully solvent customer may refuse to give credit (by requiring cash against delivery); may contract only on the basis of a higher than normal interest rate; or may seek to retain title in the goods, even after delivery, until the point at which payment is made. Such action may be taken by an individual creditor but also by creditors collectively or, indirectly, by a credit rating agency on their behalf. Thus, if a major credit rating agency reduces the rating it gives to a large company's debt, that will have a major impact upon the cost to that company of raising debt; and the company's management can be expected to respond in an appropriate way.[39]

Thus, the scope for creditor self-help is wide. Nevertheless, three issues of principle arise. First, what can company law do to facilitate the processes of creditor self-help? Second, does creditor self-help, while solving some problems associated with the limited liability rule, generate any consequential problems for company law? Third, can creditor self-help deal with all the problems generated by the limited liability rule, that

---

[37] Philip R. Wood, *International Loans, Bonds and Securities Regulation* (London: Sweet & Maxwell, 1995), p. 31. 'Covenant' in this connection means simply an obligation in the loan agreement other than one relating to payment and not an undertaking under seal. Note that Wood is here using 'capital' in a more general sense than it is used in the phrase 'legal capital' which we explore below at p. 83.

[38] These are discussed in detail in Wood, loc. cit., ch. 3.

[39] 'Last week, Standard & Poor's cut BT's long-term credit rating by four levels from AA plus to A and warned that the rating would be cut again if asset sales were delayed': *Financial Times*, 28 August 2000.

is, can it be regarded as the sole solution? We will look in turn briefly at the first two issues in the remainder of this chapter and the third issue in the next one.

A ROLE FOR COMPANY LAW: FACILITATING CREDITOR SELF-HELP

The main contribution that company law makes to creditor self-help is in relation to disclosure of information. At a basic level, the Companies Acts have always attached great importance to the principle that a company with limited liability should signal this fact in a very public way to those who may deal with it. Thus, the Act requires limited companies to incorporate into their names the appropriate suffix ('plc' for public companies or 'ltd' for private ones or their Welsh equivalents), without which the Registrar will not incorporate the company;[40] it requires the company to give publicity to its name at all its places of business and on its correspondence;[41] and it prohibits the use of the term 'limited' by persons which are not limited liability companies.[42] The link between these provisions and the principle of limited liability is most forcefully demonstrated by the rule that failure to state the company's name properly in documents ordering goods or services for the company (or on negotiable instruments on which the company accepts liability) exposes the person signing the document, or authorizing its signature, to personal liability.[43] In the light of these provisions it is highly ironic to learn that many business people regard the acronyms 'plc' or 'ltd' as badges of respect rather than as warning signs.[44]

At a more fundamental level the Companies Acts require disclosure to the public of the company's annual financial statements. Achievement of this result has been a long haul since entrepreneurs initially resisted circulation of the accounts beyond the members, on the grounds that this wider disclosure would help competitors or just feed public inquisitiveness. Nevertheless, the principle of public disclosure (by filing of the accounts with the Registrar of Companies) gained ground during the first

[40] CA 1985, s 24. The limited exception to this requirement in s 30 for certain not-for-profit companies is discussed in Chapter 1 at p. 32.

[41] CA 1985, ss 348, 349, and 351.

[42] CA 1985, s 34.

[43] CA 1985, s 349(4). The section is, however, over-broad since it embraces any mis-description of the company's name, no matter how trivial and no matter whether any third party has been misled.

[44] J. Freedman, 'Businesses and the Corporate Form: Burden or Privilege' (1994) 57 MLR 555, 563–4.

half of the last century so that, by the time of the 1948 Act, the filing obligation was applied to the profit and loss account as well as to the balance sheet, both these documents had to be audited by external and professionally qualified persons, and the obligation to produce accounts was applied, in the case of corporate groups, to the group as a whole as well as to the individual companies within it.[45] In addition, the quantity and quality of the information contained in the accounts has been improved over time, notably by the development, largely by the accounting professions, of accounting standards, which both reduce the directors' discretion as to how transactions are presented in the accounts and promote comparability across companies.[46] Nevertheless, it can be argued that the information contained in the public accounts is often out of date,[47] and many large lenders no doubt require the production of more up-to-date information as part of the pre-contractual bargaining process.

THE FLOATING CHARGE

Moving beyond disclosure of information, we noted above that most of the legal techniques that creditors use to protect themselves against limited liability are not specific to company law. They are means of protection against debtors of uncertain financial status, whether that uncertainty derives from limited liability or some other source. However, there is one technique which was developed specifically in the company context. This is the floating charge.[48] This is a form of security which was developed by company practitioners in the nineteenth century and is available only to companies and, now, limited liability partnerships. It has a three-fold significance. First, it permits companies to give security over classes of asset which otherwise it would be difficult to pledge; second, it enables lenders to attach a significant additional sanction to the

---

[45] See now CA 1985, Part VII. The link between public filing and limited liability is demonstrated by the exemption of unlimited liability companies from the public filing requirement (s 254).

[46] Despite these developments the House of Lords has taken the narrow view that, in the structure of the Act, the accounts are addressed to the shareholders alone and indeed to them only in their monitoring capacity: *Caparo Industries plc v Dickman* [1990] 2 AC 605. The decision probably reflects worries about the scope of auditors' liability for negligence rather than a full analysis of the role of the financial statements in the modern world.

[47] CA 1985, s 244 gives private companies ten months from the end of the financial year, and public companies seven months, to file the accounts. For the CLR's proposed reforms, see below, p. 135.

[48] For a more detailed discussion than is possible here, especially on the distinction between fixed and floating charges, see E. Ferran, *Company Law and Corporate Finance* (Oxford: Oxford University Press, 1999), pp 507–33 and *Re Brumark Investments Ltd* [2001] BCC 259, PC.

restrictions a company may have accepted in the loan contract; third, through its enforcement mechanism it brings the charge-holder into the governance of the company.

On the first point, the difficulty with a fixed charge is that it requires lender assent to the disposal of the assets charged and thus is inappropriate for the charging of assets which are turned over in the course of a business. Thus, it is relatively easy to have a fixed charge on a factory but almost impossible to have one over the raw materials and half-finished products being worked on in that factory. A floating charge avoids these problems by not attaching to specific assets until some event occurs which causes the charge to 'crystallize'. Until that point the charge 'floats over' the assets charged and the company can deal freely with them, at least in the ordinary course of its business, as if they were unsecured. Of course, the floating charge is not as good a security from the creditor's point of view as the fixed charge, because the creditor runs the risk that the class of assets covered by the floating charge will prove to be less substantial at the point of crystallization than it was at the point of creation. Nevertheless, it has the undoubted merit of permitting the company to charge a type of asset which would otherwise have little value as security.

Second, English law now seems to have reached the position that the creditor has a very free hand to specify the events which will cause the charge to crystallize. It seems not to be necessary that the event be one which puts the repayment of the loan or the security in jeopardy; and the event may operate automatically so as to bring about crystallization. This puts the lender in a powerful position. It can attach the sanction of crystallization to the non-performance of any of the obligations which the loan contract lays upon the company as to the way in which it conducts its business. It is common for lenders to say that the loan becomes repayable if these restrictions are breached; it can now add the sanction of crystallization, which much increases the chances that the lender will in fact recover the money owing.[49]

Third, default has an impact, not only, via crystallization, on the property rights over the company's assets, but also upon the company's

---

[49] Cf. *Re Permanent House (Holdings) Ltd* [1988] BCLC 563, where the 'events of default' included 'the making by the [lender] at any time hereafter of a demand upon the Company for repayment of all or any of the monies hereby secured'. Note that, of course, the word 'default' is not used here in the same sense as in the phrase 'default rule'. In 'event of default' default means a failure to meet an obligation; a 'default rule' means the rule which applies in the absence of contrary choice, but there is no implication of an obligation to make an alternative choice.

governance. The existing board of directors is replaced by a receiver[50] appointed by the charge-holder, who henceforth runs the company. Consequently, once the receiver is appointed, the centralized management of the company is vested in him or her and the holder of that office becomes the focus of the rules relating to the conduct of the company's management.

For this reason, as well, the board has a strong incentive not to default on an obligation secured by a floating charge. However, the receiver procedure has been criticized on the basis that the appointee is under a duty to act only in the interests of the charge-holder. The Government has announced plans, accordingly, to replace the charge-holder's right to appoint a receiver with a right to apply to the court for the appointment of an administrator,[51] who would act in the interests of all the creditors, secured or unsecured, though the priority of the fixed charge holder over the unsecured creditors would not be disturbed. Such a revised procedure would also be likely to limit the situations in which a charge-holder could oust the board to those where the holder's security was genuinely at risk.[52]

CONTRACTING FOR GOVERNANCE RIGHTS

So far, we have looked at the ways in which company law facilitates creditor self-help in terms of mandatory disclosure of information and the floating charge. There is one other significant contribution by company law to creditor self-help. This is something we have remarked upon already, namely, the flexibility of the company's constitution.[53] This enables the creditor to secure representation within the governance organs of the company, even in advance of default by the company under a floating charge, if that seems to the creditor an appropriate course of action. Thus, by contract the lender may secure the right to nominate a director to the board. There is nothing in company law which requires directors to be selected by the shareholders. However, this is an area in which the law has not quite caught up with its own flexibility. Thus, the shareholders by ordinary majority can remove a director at any time, whether that director was appointed by them or not,[54] and the nominator

---

[50] Today termed an 'administrative receiver': IA 1986, s 29(2).

[51] Unsecured creditors can seek the appointment of an administrator under current law, but that process can be pre-empted by the appointment of a receiver under a floating charge: IA 1986, s 9.

[52] *Insolvency—A Second Chance*, Cm. 5234, 2001.

[53] See Chapter 1, p. 14.   [54] CA 1985, s 303. See below, p. 129.

has no redress other than that which it has stipulated for in the contract (which might include, of course, the right to call for repayment of the loan and to appoint a receiver). Equally, the courts have insisted that the nominee director owes duties to the company, in the same way as any other director, rather than to the nominator. They have not even, within that formula, accepted the proposition that the nominee director should be permitted to give special consideration to the interests of the nominator.[55] One wonders whether this injunction is observed in practice; even if it is, the nominee director may provide at least a useful channel of information to the nominator about the company's activities. Alternatively, if the lender wants up-to-date information, it can stipulate for it in the loan agreement.[56]

OPPORTUNISTIC BEHAVIOUR ON THE PART OF SECURED CREDITORS

Creditor self-help aims, largely by contract, to restrict the scope for opportunistic behaviour on the part of the controllers of companies which the limited liability doctrine permits. The very success of self-help, however, may generate consequential problems. First, the techniques of self-help may create scope for opportunism on the part of secured as against unsecured creditors. This was recognized by the legislature as an issue at an early stage, for the combination of the fixed and floating charge enables the secured creditor to scoop the pool of the company's assets, to the potential detriment of the unsecured creditors. Consequently, the legislature gave certain unsecured debts (mainly employees' claims to wages—to a modest extent—and certain claims of the public authorities) statutory priority over the floating, though not the fixed, charge.[57] The Cork Committee came close to recommending that 10 per cent of the company's assets should be set aside in any event for the unsecured creditors,[58] but the Government did not act.[59] In the same vein, the

---

[55] *Kuwait Asia Bank EC v National Mutual Life Nominees Ltd* [1991] 1 AC 187, PC.

[56] Cf. *New Zealand Guardian Trust Co Ltd v Brooks* [1995] 1 WLR 96, PC, where the directors of the borrowing company were required by the debenture trust deed to certify every three months to the trustee for the lenders that, they having made due enquiry, nothing had occurred which to their knowledge and belief adversely affected the interests of the lenders.

[57] See now IA 1986, ss 40 and 386 and Sch 6.

[58] Above, n. 9, paras 1523–49.

[59] The latest proposals from the Government (above, n. 52) resurrect this idea (see para. 2.19) and also would abolish the Crown preference in insolvency, thus further benefiting unsecured creditors.

Insolvency Act renders a floating charge invalid if it is created in the period shortly before insolvency, except to the extent that the charge-holder provides new consideration to the company. This prevents the powerful, but unsecured, creditor using the floating charge to elevate itself to the position of secured creditor when it sees that insolvency is probable, a particular risk if the creditor is closely connected with the management of the company.[60]

Second, the self-help possibilities, especially the floating charge and its associated enforcement mechanisms, have proved so effective that they can create the converse of the problem they aim to solve, namely, the potential for opportunistic conduct on the part of secured creditors as against the management of the company. This arises from the fact that the charge-holder may be able to use the contractually specified events of default to replace the existing board at a time when there is still a good chance that the company will be able to trade out of its difficulties.[61]

Thus far, we have looked at the considerable scope that creditors have for self-help and at the problems creditor self-help may cause. What we have not done is ask whether self-help can sensibly be relied upon to deal with all the problems that limited liability causes for creditors. We turn to this issue in the following chapter.

---

[60] IA 1986, s 245. The relevant period is normally one year before the insolvency, but *two* years if the creditor is connected with the company.

[61] For possible reform, see also text at n. 52 above.

4

Limited Liability
The Limits of Creditor Self-Help

THE CASE FOR MANDATORY RULES

In the previous chapter we discussed the role of self-help on the part of
creditors to protect themselves against the opportunistic behaviour by
controllers of companies which limited liability permits and even encourages. We saw that there was in fact considerable scope for such self-help
mechanisms and that, probably, the extension of the limited liability rule
to all companies, large and small, was rendered tolerable only because of
the availability of self-help. However, we now need to look at creditor self-
help more critically. Two questions need to be asked. Can we be confident
that self-help is in fact capable of addressing all forms of opportunistic
behaviour generated by limited liability, or is there a role for mandatory
rules to supplement self-help? Obviously, if self-help is ineffective in
relation to a particular problem, we may need to consider[1] whether mandatory legal rules could do the job instead. However, even if self-help is
capable of addressing a particular problem linked to limited liability, one
still needs to ask whether that problem can be regulated *more effectively*
by mandatory rules than by creditor self-help.

It is suggested that there are three arguments in favour of the law
making some use of mandatory rules against company opportunism. As
we shall see, these rationales for mandatory rules have been accepted to
some extent in British law, so that the picture of complete reliance on
creditor self-help to counter company opportunism is not an accurate
portrayal of that system. First, some creditors are not well placed to
protect themselves. The obvious example is those who had no prior relationship with the company before they became its creditors, into which

---

[1] It is illogical, of course, to argue that, if creditor self-help cannot work, therefore
mandatory rules will be effective. It is possible that some costs of limited liability are
unavoidable; in that case, the question is simply whether the benefits of the rule outweigh its
costs.

category fall many victims of torts committed by companies. A pedestrian knocked down by a company's vehicle, driven negligently, will not typically have had any prior opportunities to negotiate contractual protections with the company. Some other types of creditor are perceived as not able to contract effectively with the company on a self-help basis, for example individual employees injured by the company's negligent conduct of its business, despite apparent opportunities for *ex ante* bargaining. In short, one must not fall into the trap of thinking that all creditors have self-help remedies available to them; and such creditors must be candidates for protection through legal rules, if effective rules can be fashioned to meet their case.

Second, and most important in practice, it may be more efficient to use mandatory legal rules or to provide a mandatory framework for bargaining between company and creditors, even if such rules and procedures could be generated by private contracting. Where the legislature is able to predict in advance which particular rule or type of machinery will be effective in dealing with a particular form of opportunistic behaviour, it will be less costly for the legislature to specify it than for each set of contracting parties to have to grope their way, perhaps imperfectly, towards that solution. Thus, if the legislature thinks that creditor protection across the board requires that a particular level of resources should be kept in the company and not distributed to shareholders by way of dividend, it may so specify, and creditors who desire a higher level of protection may bargain for it. However, it is no easy task for the legislator to predict in advance that a particular legal rule will be the best way of dealing with a particular problem. Company law is full of examples of, or proposals for, over-broad rules, with adverse side-effects, to deal with problems that can best be solved in other ways.[2]

Third, some forms of opportunism generated by limited liability may involve conduct which, whether it occurs in the company context or not, is regarded as unlawful. A good example is fraud. Of course, the normal civil and criminal rules against fraud could simply be, and often are, applied to fraud in the conduct of the affairs of a company. However, it is possible that the efficiency of the criminal and civil law relating to fraud could be increased by the development of rules applying specifically to fraud in companies. These special rules can then be tailored to the particular features of company law, for example, so as to fit in with the processes for the liquidation of companies.

[2] See the discussion of minimum capital rules below, at p. 84.

GENERAL RULES AGAINST
DEBTOR OPPORTUNISM

Thus, there may well be a case for supplementing self-help with legal protection. Whether in any particular situation that case is made out will depend upon further analysis. Before engaging in such analysis there is one further preliminary point which needs to be made. In our discussion in the previous chapter[3] we have seen that many of the self-help techniques available to creditors can be used against all unreliable debtors, whether companies or not. Since this is a book on company law, however, we did not consider such general self-help techniques in detail. Equally, mandatory rules designed to deal with debtor opportunism may be aimed at all debtors, whether companies or not; and, similarly, the detail of these rules falls outside the scope of this book. Nevertheless, these other categories of rule deserve brief mention, if only to set the context in which company law operates. For example, we have just noted that self-help seems of limited value in relation to involuntary creditors, typically the victims of certain types of corporate torts, and it might be thought that there is a major role for mandatory rules of company law to protect involuntary creditors. Hansmann and Kraakman in the United States have accordingly proposed the abolition of limited liability and the reintroduction of personal liability for shareholders in such cases, albeit on the basis of proportionate liability.[4] In Britain, by contrast, the matter is hardly debated.[5]

This might be because tort judgments in the UK have not reached levels which threaten the viability of companies, unlike in the USA. Alternatively, it might be that the legislature has taken the view that the insolvency of tortfeasors is not just a problem of company tortfeasors but is one that applies across the board. It may be that in fact enforcing tort judgments against companies is not significantly more uncertain than enforcing them against individuals and partnerships. Limited liability may be a problem in relation to corporate tortfeasors but there may be

---

[3] Chapter 3, p. 70.

[4] H. Hansmann and R. Kraakman, 'Towards Unlimited Shareholder Liability for Corporate Torts' (1991) 100 *Yale LJ* 1879. On the difference between joint and several liability and proportionate liability see Chapter 3, n. 17.

[5] The CLR discussed the relationship between limited liability and torts only in the context of groups of companies and proposed no changes in the law: *Completing the Structure*, November 2000, paras 10.58–10.59. See also the discussion of the *Cape* case below at pp. 105–106.

significant, if different, problems of enforcement against personal defendants. If this is the case, then limited liability does not constitute the whole of the problem and removing it would be only a partial solution. Some other solution should be found which applies to all tortfeasors. This is indeed what one finds when the legislature requires potential tortfeasors to take out insurance. Two examples will suffice. The Employers' Liability (Compulsory Insurance) Act 1969 requires employers, whether corporate or not, to insure against liability for bodily injury or disease sustained by employees in the course of their employment.[6] A similar scheme operates in relation to third party liability for motor accidents, whether those responsible are companies or not.[7]

The problem of voluntary creditors who cannot bargain effectively can be dealt with in the same way. Thus, the issue of employees who have wages outstanding on the insolvency of their employer is a problem not confined to companies, and the relevant legislation, creating a fund from which unpaid employees are reimbursed, applies to all employers.[8] Nevertheless, this piece of labour law, as with the examples of compulsory insurance mentioned above, does in fact operate in the particular areas covered so as to mitigate for employees of corporate employers the incentives to opportunism which limited liability creates.

Coming closer to company law, the Insolvency Act 1986 aims to control the temptations which beset all debtors, whether corporate or otherwise, to put assets beyond the reach of their creditors in the period before insolvency supervenes. See for example the sections of that Act controlling transactions by debtors with their assets at an undervalue in the pre-insolvency period (a way of giving away assets to someone friendly to the debtor) or conferring a preference on one creditor (perhaps linked with the debtor) over the others.[9]

Our task, however, is to analyse the role of company law in providing mandatory rules to control company opportunism. Creditor protection issues can arise in many diverse contexts in company law. In this chapter

---

[6] See C. Parsons, 'Employers' Liability Insurance—How Secure is the System?' (1999) 28 ILJ 109. Since the amount of the compulsory cover is set at £5m., the legislature presumably viewed the problem as one linked to the size of the business rather than to its legal structure.

[7] Road Traffic Act 1988.

[8] Employment Rights Act 1996, Part XII. The coverage of the reimbursement right is rather limited, but the principle is there.

[9] On undervalue transactions and preferences see IA 1986, ss 238–41 (applying to companies) and ss. 339–42 (similar provisions for individuals); common remedial provisions are in ss 423–4.

we shall confine our attention to three sets of rules where creditor protection has traditionally been thought to be a primary concern of company law. The first set consists of those rules which either require a company to have a certain level of assets at its disposal before it commences business or restrict the ability of the company, after it has commenced business, to move assets out of the corporate 'box' and into the hands of the shareholders. These are generally referred to as the rules about a company's 'capital'. Since under a regime of limited liability the creditors' claims are confined to the *company's* assets, such rules have an intuitive plausibility about them, but we shall see on examination that they have their own costs as well. We look at the rules on corporate capital in the next section of this chapter.

The second set of rules are those which aim to reduce opportunism on the part of company controllers which takes the form of adding to the company's *liabilities* where there is little hope that there will be sufficient assets in the company's coffers to meet the creditors' claims when they fall due. The risks to creditors from such behaviour are clear; what is perhaps less clear is why company controllers should engage in such behaviour. We shall analyse the possible reasons and the law's response later in this chapter.

Finally, we look at the rules governing opportunism towards creditors within corporate groups and especially the position of involuntary creditors in such situations. Here we shall see a marked difference in the current stance of British law as compared with the two previous situations. British law does contain reasonably extensive rules governing capital, though rules that are not as protective of creditors as, say, those of German company law. Equally, there are extensive rules relating to the taking on by companies of liabilities which are unlikely to be met; and here the British rules in fact have been strengthened in recent times. This reform has perhaps occurred because this second form of opportunism is particularly prevalent in small companies where, as we have seen,[10] the arguments in favour of making limited liability available are least convincing. By contrast, comprehensive rules for the protection of creditors within corporate groups have never appealed to the British legislature, even though the standard arguments for limited liability apply more strongly as between the group and outsiders than within the group of companies.[11]

---

[10] Above, p. 66.   [11] Ibid.

CREDITOR PROTECTION AND COMPANY CAPITAL

WHAT IS LEGAL CAPITAL?

In this section we look at the rules on 'capital'. These appear to be, and indeed are, rather complex. However, the central thought which underlies them is simple, though it can be expressed in a number of different ways. It is that the law ought to regulate the freedom of companies to determine (and especially to reduce) the amount of assets deployed by the company in its business. It is clear that such restrictions could be embodied by creditors in their contracts with companies. However, mandatory company law rules in this area could be justified on the grounds that they reduce transaction costs, by specifying the regime which the parties to the contract would ultimately opt for after bargaining. Alternatively, it could be said that they protect those not able to bargain for themselves against some obvious forms of opportunism. We shall examine whether these rationales can be sustained after we have identified the main features of the rules on capital.

In company law, 'capital' is used in a restricted sense which does not coincide with the broader way in which it is used in ordinary speech or even by company financiers. My dictionary defines 'capital' (in the financial sense) as 'wealth available for or capable of use in the production of further wealth'.[12] For company lawyers, however, capital is a measure of value and what it values is *the consideration which the shareholders have provided to the company in exchange for their shares.* Thus, if the shareholders have contributed cash and other assets to the extent of £10,000 to the company in exchange for their shares, then £10,000 is the value of the company's capital. Of course, the company may have acquired a further £10,000 from some other source. A bank may have lent £10,000 to the company, but that money does not count as capital in the legal sense (even though it can well be said to be wealth available for the production of further wealth). Immediately after selling its shares and receiving the loan from the bank, the company may have £20,000 in its bank account, but only £10,000 counts as the company's capital.

The reason for restricting the legal definition of capital in this way reveals its creditor-protection function. Suppose the company becomes insolvent. The shareholders have no claim, on a winding-up, to the return of their contributions to the company until all the creditors' claims have

---

[12] *Collins English Dictionary* (1982).

been satisfied. This is the principle of 'shareholders last' which applies in a winding-up.[13] Therefore, it might be thought that, the greater the amount that the shareholders have contributed to the company in exchange for its shares, the more likely it is that the creditors will be repaid. As it is sometimes put, the shareholders' contributions constitute a 'cushion' for the creditors against the risk of default by the company. The bank, on the other hand, as a creditor, will have a claim on insolvency for the return of the £10,000 which will compete with the claims of other creditors,[14] and so its contribution should be excluded from the legal definition of capital.

There are three possible ways in which a legal system could use the concept of capital, as defined above, to protect creditors. The first is a way which would give the creditors a very high degree of protection, but at a cost to enterprise which is so great that no legal system adopts it. The second is a way which British law utilizes only grudgingly and partially, under pressure from EC law. The third has long been part of its thought patterns. The first two techniques are forms of minimum capital requirement; the third is referred to as 'capital maintenance'.

MINIMUM CAPITAL

The first protective technique for creditors would be to require companies, before commencing business, to raise a certain minimum amount of capital and to put that minimum amount on one side so that it can be made available to meet the claims of the creditors, should the company become insolvent.[15] Such a policy would genuinely turn capital into a fund for the protection of creditors. This would be all well and good if capital were an inexpensive commodity, but it is not. To require companies to raise, and pay for, but not to be able to deploy to profit-earning ends, a significant amount of capital would be to make the corporate form very unattractive for business. So, no legal system imposes this as a

---

[13] IA 1986, ss 107 and 143.

[14] Indeed, as we saw above (p. 73) the bank is likely to have secured its loan with a fixed and floating charge and thus repayment of its loan will be given priority over the claims of unsecured creditors. It is conceivable that the unsecured creditors would fare better in the liquidation if the company had never taken on the secured loan in the first place. See Chapter 3, p. 76.

[15] An alternative device might be to require the company to take out a bond (a form of insurance) to a certain amount, so that, upon insolvency, the guarantor of the bond would pay the prescribed amount to the creditors. This device is sometimes used in construction contracts to protect the client against the insolvency of the builder during the construction process. As such, it is an example of creditor self-help.

mandatory rule. Instead, the company is free, and expected, to deploy the consideration raised on the sale of its shares in the conduct of the company's business. Within a very short time, the £10,000 mentioned above will have been used to pay wages, rent premises, and buy equipment and raw materials and so on. Whether at the end of its first (or any subsequent) trading period the company's net assets (assets less liabilities) are worth more or less than its initial capital will depend, obviously, on how successfully the company has traded.

Nevertheless, there is a weaker form of this policy which could be implemented, and this constitutes the second policy. This would be to require a company to have received in exchange for its shares a certain minimum value (the 'minimum capital') before it commences business, but not to require this capital to be put on one side but instead to permit it to be used in the company's business. In Britain no such requirement is laid upon private companies. However, public companies, following the Second Company Law Directive,[16] must have allotted shares with a nominal value of at least £50,000, of which at least one-quarter must actually have been paid over to the company, before the company commences business.[17]

This weaker form of the policy may rescue the corporate form for business enterprise, but there are two good reasons for thinking that a minimum share capital requirement in this form does not do much to protect creditors. To start with, in economic terms the adequacy of the minimum capital figure must depend on the riskiness of the company's business, which varies from one company to another, so that in most cases a single figure will be either inappropriately high or inappropriately low. The latter gives creditors the illusion of protection; the former creates barriers to entry and thus restricts competition. The low figure stipulated by the legislature for public companies suggests that, given this choice, it will opt for illusion.

---

[16] Council Directive 77/91/EEC, [1977] OJ L26/1. This Directive applies only to public companies. The minimum capital requirement for public companies also necessitated the introduction of rules for valuing non-cash consideration and prohibiting certain speculative forms of consideration: see CA 1985, ss 102–111.

[17] CA 1985, s 117. The 'nominal' value of the share is the value attributed to it by the company when the class of shares of which it is part is created, for example, a £1 share or a 10p share. Shares may not be issued for less than their nominal value (a practice known as 'discounting': s 100) but may be issued for more. In the latter case, the additional amount received by the company is referred to as a 'premium' and is treated for almost all purposes as part of the company's capital. Since the nominal value need bear no relation to the consideration the company is likely to receive when it issues the shares (except that the former must be less than the latter), the whole system is rather confusing.

Further, the very fact that in this weaker form of the minimum capital policy the consideration received on the issue of the shares can be used in the company's business substantially undermines the creditor-protection rationale for the requirement. If all goes well, the net value of the company's assets will exceed the value represented by the consideration received for the shares. By contrast, if all goes badly and, by definition, if insolvency supervenes, all will have gone badly, the value of the company's actual assets will fall below the value of the consideration initially received. Thus, the minimum initial capital requirement does *not* guarantee that the company will have any particular amount of assets available to meet the claims of its creditors at any later period and in particular upon insolvency.[18] It would achieve that result only if it were combined with a requirement that the company cease trading if the net value of its assets fell below the capital value or some proportion of that value, but that might result in companies which were in fact viable being required to cease trading, to the detriment of their shareholders and employees, as well as possibly to the detriment of some of their creditors.[19]

CAPITAL MAINTENANCE

The third approach to the use of the concept of capital, and the one in fact long used by British law, is to leave companies free to raise what capital they will, both prior to commencing business and subsequently, but then to use the value of the capital *in fact* raised to control the freedom of the company's controllers to move assets out of the company.[20] This is the doctrine of 'capital maintenance'. Under this approach, the value of the capital in fact raised is used, not to regulate whether the company can commence or continue trading, but to determine the value of the assets which the company can distribute to its shareholders. More particularly, a public company cannot make a distribution of assets to its shareholders unless the value of the company's net

---

[18] So capital in a company limited by shares does not perform the function of the guarantee given by the members in a company limited by guarantee. See above, p. 31.

[19] Cf. CA 1985, s 142, which merely requires the directors of a public company to call a shareholders' meeting if the net value of its assets falls below *half* the value of its issued and paid-for capital. The Limited Liability Act 1855 reflected a stronger policy: a company which lost three-quarters of its initially issued capital had to cease trading and be wound up (s 13). However, s 142 could perform a valuable signalling function, by indicating publicly the state of the company's balance sheet, except that the secured creditors are likely to have intervened long before s 142 is triggered.

[20] This policy is now obviously subject to the minimum capital requirement for public companies.

assets (i.e. assets less liabilities) after the distribution has been made will exceed the value of the initial and subsequent capital contributions received from investors.[21] If a company cannot meet this requirement, it may make no distribution to its shareholders but the company is not prohibited simply for this reason from continuing to trade.

The capital maintenance rules thus restrict the freedom of the controllers of companies to move assets out of the company and into the hands of the shareholders, which policy, in a regime of limited liability, can plausibly be argued to protect creditors. In this way, the capital maintenance rules replicate for the company when it is a going concern the principles which apply on an insolvency: shareholders are entitled to payments only if the creditors' claims have been met (or 'shareholders last').[22] As near as can be with a going concern, that result is replicated by requiring that the company's net assets exceed the value of the shareholders' contributions before, and indeed immediately after, a distribution of assets is made to the shareholders.

Let us see how the principle, as embodied in the Companies Act, plays out in respect of some typical ways in which assets may be moved out of a company.

DIVIDENDS AND SHARE BUY-BACKS

First and obviously, the principle is applied to dividends declared by the company: their payment must not leave the company assets less than the value of its capital.[23] A dividend is a payment, usually in cash,[24] made by the company to its shareholders, in the case of listed companies usually twice a year,[25] the amount of the dividend being expressed as a percentage of the nominal value[26] of the shares. This makes the dividend sound like a payment of interest, but, at least for ordinary shares, the amount of the dividend is not fixed, as it would be on a loan, but is decided each year, in the light of the company's financial position, by the board,[27] and subject to the Act's capital maintenance rules.

---

[21] CA 1985, s 264. Private companies are treated slightly more generously: see s 263. This permits the company to distribute the full amount of its profits even though it has suffered an as yet unrealized loss, because only realized losses are set against gains (which also must be realized to count).

[22] See Chapter 9, p. 255.

[23] But see n. 21.

[24] Dividends in the form of shares in the company are possible, in which case they are called 'scrip' dividends.

[25] The so-called 'interim' and 'final' dividends.

[26] See n. 17 above.   [27] See below, p. 256.

The same principle is also applied to public companies in respect of the other main way for a company to return assets to its shareholders while it is a going concern, that is, by offering to buy back a proportion of its shares. Until relatively recently, it was thought to be inconsistent with the capital maintenance rules to permit a company to buy back its shares at all.[28] A shareholder who wished to liquidate his or her investment could do so only by finding another investor to step into his or her shoes. Hence the importance of the core feature of the free transferability of shares.[29] However, it has now been realized that capital maintenance does not require a complete ban on share buy-backs, which have in fact become a reasonably common way for companies to return unwanted assets to their shareholders or for implementing a scheme to replace equity finance by debt finance.

The law now recognizes that buy-backs can be funded in two ways which do not offend capital maintenance. First, they may be funded out of the proceeds of a fresh issue of shares, in which case the consideration received for the new shares simply replaces the repurchased shares in the company's legal capital. Here, one class of shares in effect replaces another. In practice, such buy-backs are relatively uncommon.

More radically, a company with unwanted assets may fund a buy-back, without a new share issue, out of distributable profits. Since the funds used for the buy-back could have been distributed to the shareholders, say by way of dividend, it might be thought that the creditors could have no objection to their use in this alternative way. However, there is a further argument. Once the shares have been bought back, the value of the consideration that the company then holds in exchange for its shares will have been reduced. In consequence, the freedom of the company to make distributions to its shareholders in the future, for example by way of dividend, will have been increased. This might be thought to represent a

---

[28] This general principle is still stated in CA 1985, s 143. Significantly, the section does not apply to companies with unlimited liability. It is now subject, however, to the buy-back rules discussed below. Moreover, British company law has also accepted the legality of redeemable shares. These are shares which are issued on the basis that either the company or the shareholder (or both) can require the shares to be bought back on certain terms at some date in the future. Unlike the buy-back provisions discussed below, the redemption of redeemable shares is contractually compulsory. From the creditors' point of view redeemable shares are less of a threat than re-purchases of shares because it is clear from the outset that redeemable shares may not be a permanent part of the company's capital (and the terms of the redemption are required to be publicly available: s 163(3)). They are not discussed further here because the rules on financing redemptions track those for buy-backs: see CA 1985, ss 159–60 and 171.

[29] See Chapter 1, p. 22.

threat to the creditors' interests. However, this point can be dealt with by requiring the value of the company's legal capital to be maintained at its pre-buy-back level, so that the company's freedom to make dividend payments in the future is not increased.[30] These are precisely the rules applied by the Act to buy-backs by public companies, and the creditors' consent to such action on the part of the company is not required.[31]

However, more lenient rules are applied to private companies. Take a private company built up by an entrepreneur who has now reached retirement age and wishes to sell his or her stake in the company to finance that retirement. If, as is likely, there is no public market in the shares, the other shareholders cannot personally afford to buy out the founder, and the company has insufficient undistributed profits to acquire the founder's stake, the only solution may be to sell control of the company to a larger, perhaps publicly traded, company or to a venture capitalist. In order to help such companies remain independent, the Act permits share re-purchases out of capital. Of course, on traditional thinking such a course of action is a threat to the creditors, since the net assets of the company will be reduced below the level of the company's capital, and for the future, once the shares have been bought back, the company's capital level will be set at a new and lower point. In order to protect creditors the Act deploys three devices.

1. The directors proposing a re-purchase out of capital must make a statutory declaration of solvency, stating that after due enquiry they are of the opinion that the company will be able to pay its debts as they fall due for at least a year after the re-purchase.

2. The directors' declaration must be approved by the company's auditors as reasonable.

3. Any creditor may apply to the court to have the re-purchase prohibited or approved subject to conditions aimed at protecting the position of the creditors.[32]

---

[30] Technically, this is done by requiring the company to create an undistributable reserve in its accounts. Thus, legal capital may consist of three things: the value received by a company corresponding to the nominal value of the shares; any additional consideration, which will be reflected in the share premium account (see n. 17 above); and a capital-redemption account used to maintain the capital yardstick if shares are re-purchased out of profits.

[31] CA 1985, ss 160, 162, and 170. A director who acts unreasonably in making the declaration commits a criminal offence. Whether directors or auditors who act unreasonably are civilly liable to the creditors is unclear.

[32] CA 1985, ss 173 and 175–7.

REDUCTION OF CAPITAL

It can be seen from the above discussion that the function of the capital-maintenance rules in controlling distributions to the shareholders depends upon the amount of the company's capital being a figure which is not subject to manipulation by the company, through either its board or the general meeting. If that amount could easily be reduced by the company, its constraining impact on distributions would vanish. However, there may be good reasons in particular cases for the company to 'reduce its capital'. In considering these reasons, it is important to be clear, at the outset, what a reduction of capital involves. It does not involve, necessarily, a reduction of the assets of the company by returning them to the shareholders, though that may be involved in particular cases. What is reduced in a reduction of capital is the value of the assets received by the company in exchange for its shares, as entered in the company's accounts. It is the figure for the share capital of the company which is reduced under this procedure.

Of course, the company may need to reduce this figure because it is proposing to return unwanted assets to its shareholders and does not have the necessary distributable profits to do so. On the other hand, it may have lost its assets in the course of normal trading and simply wish to bring the capital figure in its accounts into line with its actual position.[33] In this latter case, once the capital figure has been reduced, corporate assets which previously had to be maintained within the company may become available for distribution; or profits earned in the future, which would otherwise have had to be retained to build up the assets of the company to the level of the former capital 'cushion', may equally now be distributable on the basis of the lower level of protection. Indeed, this may be the very reason for the reduction: a rescuer may not be willing to inject fresh equity into the company unless any profits made thereafter are immediately distributable. However, it is the reduction of the figure for share capital which is the necessary pre-condition to these distributions and it is on the legality of the reduction, rather than the subsequent distribution, that the law concentrates.

The Act contains a procedure whereby the company can exceptionally reduce the amount of its capital.[34] Given the risks to the creditors of a

---

[33] These two examples are given in CA 1985, s 135, but that section permits a reduction of capital 'in any way'.

[34] CA 1985, s 135(1).

reduction of capital, the procedure is hedged about with protections for them. There are two main ones, which are rather different from, and much stronger than, those provided in the case of buy-backs. They are, first, that the scheme of reduction must be confirmed by the court before it is implemented, and, second, although the court retains a residual discretion in any event, a prima facie entitlement for an objecting creditor to have his or her claim paid off or secured.[35] Thus, present creditors are fully protected and future creditors will contract on the basis of knowledge of the company's new capital position.

CONCLUSION

Can the current capital-maintenance rules be defended on the grounds that they accurately predict the result the contracting parties would have arrived at and thus reduce transaction costs? Three criticisms can be made of the present rules, which are as follows in ascending order of gravity. It might be said that, even where the rules aim at the right targets and do so with appropriate techniques, they are not sufficiently flexible to produce the equivalent of bargained-out solutions. Thus, the rules prohibiting distributions where the distribution would bring the company's net assets below the capital figure probably do reflect what most creditors would bargain for, *except* that a creditor might well want to take as its base-line the position when it advanced credit to the company and not, as the Act stipulates, the position at the time the company was established or when it last raised fresh capital. For example, the Act permits a company which has distributable profits earned before the credit was advanced to pay them out after the advance, even if the company begins to make losses, so long as the losses have not wiped out the earlier profits.[36] However, it can be argued on the contrary that the law provides a minimum level of protection and creditors can bargain for greater protection, if they wish to have it.

Further, there is reason for thinking that, at least historically, the capital-maintenance rules have not aimed at reducing contracting costs but rather have reflected a more paternalist approach to the use of the law to regulate the affairs of companies. Thus, the historical prohibition on buy-backs seems an example of over-kill when viewed from a creditor-protection perspective, as the current law now recognizes. Again, the

---

[35] CA 1985, ss 136–7.

[36] This point is developed more fully by J. Armour, 'Share Capital and Creditor Protection: Efficient Rules for a Modern Company Law' (2000) 63 MLR 355, 373–7.

Company Law Review[37] has taken the view that the requirement of court confirmation and creditor guarantee, under the current capital reduction procedure, is both costly and overly protective of creditor interests. Instead, it proposes that the procedure for obtaining a reduction of capital be simplified by abolishing the requirement for court confirmation and substituting a declaration of solvency by the directors, coupled with an auditors' report where the company has auditors. Only for public companies, where the Second Company Law Directive requires this, would the right of creditor objection to the court be retained, but even this would not apply in the case of a reduction to write off losses. Where an objection was made by a creditor (and in its absence no court hearing would be required), the court would not be obliged to see that the company's liability to the creditor was secured, if it was of the opinion that the amount of the company's assets made this unnecessary.

In short, under these proposals court review in the interests of creditors is largely replaced by the solvency declaration delivered by the directors. The declaration may be of less value to the creditors than the near guarantee of payment which the current procedure provides, but it is arguable that it is more appropriate. A guarantee improves the position of the creditors (as compared with their pre-reduction position), whereas all a free negotiation is likely to have achieved is an assurance to the creditors that the reduction would not worsen their position, a result more nearly achieved by the declaration of solvency.

Finally, however, the work of the CLR raised doubts about how valuable creditors think the capital maintenance doctrine is. The relationship of the company's net assets to its legal capital is by no means the only way of measuring the creditworthiness of a company. The Company Law Review sought to establish its relative importance in the eyes of creditors (and investors) and concluded: 'The view of the substantial majority of consultees . . . was that a company's share capital is nowadays relatively unimportant as a measure of its ability to repay credit, and that other measures, including net assets, cash flow and interest cover are considerably more important.'[38] If empirical research reveals that financial ratios other than the relationship between the amount of the company's net assets and the consideration received for its shares are what creditors in fact rely on in assessing credit risks, then the whole policy of capital

---

[37] CLR, *Company Formation and Capital Maintenance*, October 1999, paras 3.27–3.35. In the light of this easing of the reduction procedure, it is proposed that the special provisions concerning buy-backs by private companies out of capital should be repealed.

[38] Ibid., para. 3.5.

maintenance is undermined. The capital rules may end up imposing restrictions on company management in return for benefits which creditors do not want.[39]

OPPORTUNISM AND INCREASES IN THE COMPANY'S LIABILITIES

WRONGFUL AND FRAUDULENT TRADING

In the previous section we examined rules which limit opportunistic behaviour on the part of companies by restricting the board's freedom to make distributions of assets to the shareholders. However, the controllers of a company may reduce the value of the company's net assets not only by shifting assets out of the corporate 'box', but also by taking on additional liabilities. Net assets equals assets less liabilities, so the net assets figure will decline if either the company's assets go down or its liabilities go up. To deal with an increase in liabilities a broader rule than one controlling distributions is needed.

There is, however, an initial puzzle here. One can see that shareholders may benefit if corporate assets are distributed to them, but how do they (or the directors) benefit from the company's taking on additional liabilities, if there is no concomitant distribution? The answer to the question can be found by considering the situation of a company which is nearing insolvency. By taking on extra liabilities (obtaining goods on credit or not paying money due to the Inland Revenue or to the company's pension fund, for example) the directors may put the company in a position where it is able to continue to function for a period of time. During that period it may be possible to extricate the company from its financial difficulties so that it returns to profit, thus preserving the directors' jobs, and is able to

[39] Similar doubts can be raised about the extension of the rule that a company may not purchase its own shares (s 143) to the proposition that a company may not give financial assistance to a third party which wishes to buy the company's shares (s 151). The latter course of action does not necessarily create risks for the company's creditors, depending on how the financial assistance is provided. Since inappropriate financial assistance can arguably be controlled by other rules and since the financial assistance rules themselves have become excessively complex in their attempt to distinguish between acceptable and unacceptable financial assistance, the CLR has proposed the abolition of the ban on financial assistance for private companies and its simplification for public companies, where the Second Directive requires its retention: ibid., paras 3.41–3.51. See E. Wymeersch, 'Article 23 of the second company law directive: the prohibition on financial assistance to acquire shares of the company' in J. Basedow, K. Hopt and H. Kötz (eds), *Festschrift für Ulrich Drobnig* (Tübingen: Mohr Siebeck, 1999).

pay dividends to its shareholders. On the other hand, if the period of continued trading does not resolve the company's difficulties and the company simply goes into insolvent liquidation, limited liability will ensure that it is the creditors rather than the shareholders who bear the downside risk of the decision to continue to trade.[40]

How should the law handle this situation? It is clear that the mere fact that the directors decide to continue trading and the company subsequently becomes insolvent is not in itself a good ground for imposing legal sanctions on them. Such 'strict liability' would be likely to render the directors strongly risk averse when taking the decision whether to continue to trade. Since continued trading where there is a realistic prospect of trading out of the difficulties benefits all concerned with the company (shareholders, employees, creditors), a legal regime which predisposes the directors against continuation in all cases seems undesirable. However, where the directors are also the major shareholders in the company (or are dependent upon it for employment), limited liability produces a structural bias in the directors' decision-making on this matter which the law ought to correct.

The bias arises from the fact that by the time things begin to go seriously wrong it is likely that the equity interest which the shareholder-directors have in the company will have all but vanished. In other words, the capital contributions which they have made to the company will have been used up and their shares will have lost their value. If, as directors, they decide to continue trading there is a prospect that the company will recover and, with it, the shares their value. If recovery does not come, the shareholder-directors will be no worse off (their shares will still be valueless) and the cost of the continued trading will fall on the creditors of the company. If, on the other hand, they decide to cease trading immediately, they lose the prospect, however slim, of recovery and with it the restoration of their position as shareholders. The same arguments apply, moreover, where the controlling directors' main interest lies not so much in the value of their shares as in the opportunities for gainful employment which the company provides for them.[41] In both cases, limited liability permits the director-shareholders to externalize the costs of continued

---

[40] The agency rules, discussed in Chapter 2 at p. 51 will similarly protect the directors from personal liability.

[41] As with our hypothetical case of Smith & Jones (Decorators) Ltd, see Chapter 1, p. 25. In a case where the shareholders have contributed no significant initial capital one might say that the danger of inappropriate trading decisions exists from the beginning and not just once the initial capital has been lost.

unsuccessful trading on to the creditors of the company, while permitting them to capture the benefits if the continued trading is successful. Hence, the structural bias in favour of continued trading.

Where the directors take on extra liabilities, knowing that the company will be unable to discharge them or acting recklessly in this regard, company law has long contained a mechanism for dealing with the situation. It prohibits conducting the affairs of a company with intent to defraud creditors (or indeed for any fraudulent purpose). Any person party to such conduct, whether or not a director of the company, commits a criminal offence[42] and can be made civilly liable.[43] The civil liability bites only if the company is wound up and takes the form of permitting the liquidator to apply to the court for an order that the parties to the fraudulent conduct make a contribution to the assets of the company, for the benefit of its creditors. The remedy is thus a collective one, by the liquidator on behalf of the creditors, not one vested in individual creditors. If the party to the fraudulent conduct is a shareholder of the company, such a court order thus involves removing the protection of the limited liability rule which would otherwise be applicable.[44]

However, fraud, because it involves dishonesty, is difficult to prove; and, even if it can be proved, covers only a small part of the opportunistic conduct against which it is arguable creditors deserve protection. Given the incentive structure outline above, the directors are likely to convince themselves that the continued trading will be successful and the creditors will be repaid, so that the problem is one of self-deception on the part of the directors rather than fraud committed on others. After the problem was revisited by the Cork Committee[45] the legislature enacted a rule which attempts to eliminate the structural bias identified above. It exposes the directors to the downside risks as well as to the upside benefits of their decision to continue trading.

The crucial conceptual shift made by s 214 of the IA 1986, as compared to the fraudulent trading provisions, is to create the potential of civil liability[46] for directors who *negligently* have decided to continue to trade. A director who *ought* to have realized that the company had no

---

[42] CA 1985, s 458.   [43] IA 1986, s 213.

[44] By virtue of IA 1986, s 74. See above, p. 12.

[45] *Report of the Review Committee on Insolvency Law and Practice*, Cmnd. 8558 (London: HMSO, 1982), ch. 44.

[46] Primarily by way of a liability to contribute to the assets of the company but also, where the director is in addition a creditor of the company, by subordinating his or her claim as creditor to the claims of all the other creditors of the company: IA 1986, s 215.

reasonable prospect of avoiding insolvent liquidation is liable to be ordered by the court to make a contribution to the assets of the company if the company does in fact go into insolvent liquidation, unless he or she 'took every step with a view to minimising the loss to the company's creditors as . . . he *ought* to have taken.' In short, the section imposes upon directors a duty of care, which is measured objectively and enforced by the liquidator on behalf of the creditors.

The choice by the legislature to review the directors' conduct by reference to a general standard of negligence was no doubt deliberate. The legislature did not wish to lay down precisely when a company should cease trading. Sometimes continued trading will be in the best interests of the creditors; sometimes not. That decision still has to be taken by the directors, and s 214 does not in terms mention ceasing to trade. The purpose of s 214 is to reverse the structural bias in favour of the shareholders by internalizing the risks of loss, as well as the chances of gain, in directors' decision-making processes when their company nears insolvency.[47] Unlike some of the rules analysed in the earlier section of this chapter on capital maintenance, here the legislature is not attempting to specify the substantive outcome but to restructure the decision-making process of the directors.

Whether s 214 will succeed will depend on two main things. The first is whether liquidators can raise the funds to enforce the wrongful trading liability. They are naturally reluctant to risk creditors' assets further on uncertain litigation, but there may be people willing to finance the litigation in return for a share of the proceeds. However, it is unclear how far the common law rules against champerty[48] restrict the liquidator's freedom to enter into agreements with such third parties for the financing of the litigation. The second is the ability of the courts to adjust the liability standard so that it neither discourages the directors of viable companies from continuing in business nor encourages those whose business is not viable to continue.

There is one final feature of the wrongful trading provisions which should be noted. Although the rule addresses opportunism generated by limited liability, s 214 operates to make the directors personally liable, not the shareholders. However, this should not surprise us. As we have

---

[47] In line with this, the court in *Re Produce Marketing (No 2)* [1989] BCLC 520 suggested that the maximum amount of the contribution the directors should be asked to make to the company's assets is the amount of the extra liability incurred by the company towards its creditors as compared with the position had the directors acted properly.

[48] Supporting litigation in which one has no interest and taking a share in the proceeds.

argued above,[49] the scope for opportunism arises most obviously where limited liability and control of the company are in the same hands, that is, where the directors are the shareholders (or the directors are effectively controlled by the shareholders).[50] In such a situation, the law can operate either by qualifying the shareholders' protection from limited liability or by qualifying the directors' powers of management. Since the opportunism normally expresses itself through managerial decisions, it is not surprising that s 214 focuses on what directors (or shadow directors) do.

Despite the innovations made by s 214 it is arguable that the section operates too late to provide complete protection for creditors' interests. The section applies only where the company has reached the position that there is no reasonable prospect that the company will avoid insolvent liquidation. It can be said that the directors may be tempted to take action which is adverse to the creditors' interests before that point is reached, for example, where it is likely that the company will become insolvent, even though it cannot be said that it has no reasonable prospect of avoiding this fate. There is in fact some authority to the effect that directors' fiduciary duties to act in the best interests of the company require them to balance the interests of shareholders and creditors in such a situation, and the Company Law Review has floated for discussion the idea that this duty should be part of the statutory statement of directors' duties.[51]

DISQUALIFICATION OF DIRECTORS

In terms of the design of its substantive provisions s 214 is much more convincing than many of the capital-maintenance rules. This is because of its procedural approach. Section 214 does not mandate any particular outcome in any specific case. Decision-making is left with the directors, but the environment in which they have to take the decisions is fundamentally altered. The section is thus much more flexible and closely attuned to the needs of particular companies than rules which specify one or a limited number of substantive results. However, it remains within the realm of private law, in particular with regard to the enforcement of the liabilities so created, which task rests with the liquidator on behalf of the creditors.

---

[49] Above, p. 61.

[50] Section 214 is not in terms so limited, because directors may have some incentive to act opportunistically towards creditors even when they have no shareholdings in the company, for example in order to preserve their jobs as full-time managers of the company. This provides another argument in favour of the law's focus on the directors' decision-making.

[51] See Chapter 9, p. 265.

Is there a case for conferring a role in this area upon the public author-ities, in order to protect the public from the activities of those who act inappropriately as directors? The law has long taken the view that certain types of financial behaviour ought to disqualify a person from being a director of a company (or otherwise involved in its management), so that undischarged bankrupts are prohibited from being directors of com-panies.[52] The Cork Committee[53] recommended a considerable strength-ening of the disqualification provisions, whose enforcement lies in the hands of the public authorities (in the shape of applications to the court by the Insolvency Service for disqualification orders against directors). These provisions may operate so as to restructure the decision-making processes of directors, even though they generate no monetary benefit for creditors, by holding out the threat of disqualification against directors who act improperly.

The Cork Committee concentrated in particular on the extension of the provisions for the disqualification of the directors of insolvent com-panies on grounds of 'unfitness'.[54] A disqualified director is prohibited from being involved in the management of companies, whether as a direc-tor or otherwise, unless the court consents, for a period of time, which in the case of unfitness disqualification is a minimum of two years and a maximum of 15. Infringement of the prohibition is a criminal offence, but it also renders the person personally liable for the debts of the company incurred during the period of infringement.[55] This is consistent with the fact that the disqualification order is not a ban on engaging in business but a ban on doing so through a company and with the benefit of limited liability. Unfitness, of course, is a very general term but for present pur-poses it is important to note that a major category of unfitness which the courts have identified is directors' attempting to trade out of difficulties on the backs of the creditors. Thus, in a leading case the Court of Appeal has affirmed that paying only those creditors who pressed for payment and taking advantage of those creditors who did not in order to provide the working capital which the company needed was a clear example of unfitness.[56]

---

[52] Company Directors Disqualification Act 1986, s 11 (hereafter 'CDDA').

[53] *Report . . . On Insolvency Law and Practice* (see n. 45 above), ch. 45.

[54] CDDA 1986, s 6. A court which declares that a director has engaged in wrongful or fraudulent trading may also disqualify that person for up to 15 years (s 10). No doubt, in most cases such a director could also be disqualified under s 6, but s 10 permits the court to disqualify without the intervention of the Insolvency Service.

[55] CDDA, 1986, ss 1, 2, and 15.

[56] *Re Sevenoaks Stationers (Retail) Ltd* [1991] Ch 164, CA.

PHOENIX COMPANIES

The point about effective enforcement of the wrongful trading and disqualification provisions is particularly important in relation to the 'Phoenix syndrome'. In the above account we have assumed that the opportunism of the company's controllers was displayed only in relation to a single company, but there is evidence of what one might call 'serial wrongful trading'. The Cork Committee quoted evidence from a Consumer Protection Officer about persons who set up companies with vestigial capital; immediately run up debts, often by taking deposits from consumers for goods or services which are never delivered; transfer the assets of the first company at an undervalue to a second company; allow the first company to cease trading, with its creditors confined to that company's inadequate assets; and then begin the process all over again with the second (or third or fourth) company.[57] So, like the Phoenix,[58] the second company rises from the ashes of the first. The Cork Committee hoped to combat such behaviour with the introduction of directors' liability for wrongful trading and speedy disqualification of directors on grounds of unfitness.[59] It also proposed one further reform (now ss 216–17 of the Insolvency Act 1986) designed to deprive such people of the freedom to use the same name to carry on the business of the second company as had been used for the first. Repeating the name across the successive companies is a common part of Phoenix schemes, designed to disguise, especially from the creditors of the second company, the insolvency of the first enterprise, so that they think they are dealing with the first, and still flourishing, company. A director of an insolvent company is now prohibited from carrying on the second business under the name used for or by the first company, unless the court consents, and such an act both constitutes a criminal offence and renders the director personally liable for the second company's debts (though the second company is not liable for the first company's debts).

The Company Law Review found that, despite these reforms, the problem of the Phoenix company persisted. The problem seemed to be mainly one of enforcement of the existing law, rather than its reform. If

---

[57] Above, n. 45 at para. 1741.

[58] A legendary Arabian bird said to set fire to itself and rise anew from its ashes every 500 years. The comparison is inapt only to the extent that the average Phoenix company is likely to last 500 days rather than 500 years.

[59] And also through the introduction of regulation of the profession of insolvency practitioner, since the effective implementation of a transfer of assets to the new company requires the consent of the liquidator of the old one.

the assets of the first company were meagre, the liquidator would not have the resources to embark on wrongful trading litigation or even to investigate the affairs of the company in any depth. Without investigation by the liquidator no information was likely to emerge upon which the Insolvency Service could base disqualification proceedings.[60] It was equally difficult for the Registrar or the Insolvency Service to monitor breaches of the names provisions, if the second company was formed with a different name from that of the first but in fact traded under a similar name.[61]

CONCLUSIONS

What conclusions can be drawn from these three examples of the use of mandatory rules to control fraudulent or quasi-fraudulent conduct on the part of the controllers of companies, stemming from the doctrine of limited liability? First, it is suggested that they confirm the suggestion made in the previous chapter[62] that the risks of opportunistic behaviour are particularly strong when limited liability is combined with control of the company. Wrongful trading, conduct rendering directors unfit to continue in that role, and the Phoenix syndrome are predominantly problems of small companies, where the directors of the company are also those who are in a position to take the lion's share of the company's economic success (whether by way of dividends as shareholders or fees as directors or salary as employees of the company). Such company controllers have the strongest incentive to exploit whatever advantages limited liability gives them as against the creditors of the company, if the company falls into financial difficulties.

---

[60] Liquidators (and others dealing with insolvent companies) are obliged to report matters coming to their attention which suggest unfitness to the Service: CDDA s 7(3) and (4) (and Regulations made thereunder), but since the Service does not pay for the liquidator's services, it cannot ask him or her to investigate matters which it is not in the financial interests of the creditors to have investigated. In any event, in some cases of Phoenix companies it is not in any creditor's interest even to secure the appointment of a liquidator, and so all that happens is that eventually the company is struck off the Register of Companies by the Registrar, usually for non-compliance with the Act's reporting requirements, without any investigation of the company's affairs: see CA 1985, s 652.

[61] CLR, *Completing the Framework*, November 2000, para. 13.104. A company need not trade under the name with which it is formed and there may be legitimate reasons for not doing so. Section 216 in fact applies to trading as well as registered names, but it is very difficult for the public authorities to detect whether a company is using a trading name which is different from its registered name. The Insolvency Service reported knowledge of 134 breaches of s 216 in 1999/2000, which led to nine convictions. Invocation of personal liability under s 217 seems very rare.

[62] See p. 61.

Second, the creditors likely to get hurt in the case of such small companies include those who are financially unsophisticated and incapable or unable to take advantage of the self-help remedies outlined in the previous chapter.[63] The use of mandatory rules of company law to protect them can thus be justified under the first rationale identified at the beginning of this chapter.[64]

Third, in terms of civil liability the design of an appropriate set of rules to make the directors personally liable to the creditors collectively is relatively straightforward, as we have seen with the wrongful trading provisions. The difficulty is ensuring that such liabilities are meaningful in practice, for liquidators have no public funds to pursue wrongful trading actions. They can use only the assets of the company which would otherwise be available for distribution to the creditors, and will naturally be reluctant to divert them towards litigation except when they can be sure that the result will be to enhance the financial position of the creditors they serve. The most promising course of action for liquidators is often to assign the cause of action, in exchange for a share of the eventual proceeds, if any, to a specialist claims agency which can spread the risks of non-success over a portfolio of similar claims from other companies.[65]

Fourth, the difficulties of private enforcement give scope for public law controls in relation to fraudulent and quasi-fraudulent behaviour. However, effective enforcement is not guaranteed simply through the involvement of the public authorities. Although the Insolvency Service is now better resourced than it was and, for example, secured the disqualification on grounds of unfitness of over 3,000 directors in the two years ending March 2001,[66] it is beyond its capacity to police continuously the 70 per cent of all companies which have only one or two shareholders, at least at the level of official monitoring of business activities which society thinks tolerable. Since the chances of detection are only moderate, it is probably right to deploy fairly substantial sanctions against those who are caught. In this way one can justify the possibility of imposing disqualification for periods of up to 15 years[67] and the threat of custodial criminal sanctions against those who breach the disqualification orders.

Fifth and finally, some emphasis on the effectiveness in practice of the wrongful trading and disqualification provisions is in order because they may be regarded, functionally, as a substitute for the minimum capital

---

[63] See p. 70.   [64] See p. 78.   [65] But see n. 48 above.

[66] Insolvency Service, *Annual Report and Accounts 2000–2001* (London, 2001), p. 17.

[67] In fact in all but 2.5 per cent of cases the period of disqualification was 10 years or less, and half the disqualifications fell within the range of 2 to 5 years: ibid.

rules which British law lacks, at least for private companies.[68] In Britain companies may be established on the basis that the shareholders have contributed no substantial assets to the company, as we saw with the example of Smith & Jones (Decorators) Ltd.[69] All the financing for the company's business in such a situation comes in one way or another from the company's creditors, by way of bank loans, goods and services supplied on credit, facilities taken on lease rather than outright purchase, and so on. If the business does not prosper, the creditors' interests will be threatened immediately.[70] A minimum initial capital requirement could operate to insert *ex ante* a 'cushion of protection' for the creditors into the company's financial structure, but with the costs noted above. The wrongful trading and disqualification provisions take a different tack and operate *ex post*. Companies are permitted to adopt what might be thought to be, from the creditors' perspective, more risky financial structures, but those risks are then moderated by the imposition of a legal duty on the directors towards the creditors and the threat of future exclusion from use of the corporate form. *Ex post* control is less of a drag on enterprise but requires effective enforcement of the rules if opportunism is to be controlled.[71]

GROUPS OF COMPANIES

As we saw when we explored the rationales for limited liability at the beginning of the previous chapter, those based on encouraging investment in shares or on facilitating the operation of public markets in shares do not explain why company law permits the operation of the limited liability principle within groups rather than simply as between the group as a whole and the outside world. However, the rationale based on the partitioning of assets is applicable within groups. Thus, the main policy questions are questions such as whether the law should permit the assignment of perhaps risky activities to a particular company in a group

---

[68] Above, p. 85.   [69] Chapter 1, p. 25.

[70] In fact, a company with no legal capital probably becomes insolvent on a 'balance sheet' test (are assets more than liabilities?) the moment it begins to trade, unless it is very lucky, which is no doubt why the statutory test for compulsory winding-up is the 'going concern' test, i.e. whether the company can meet its debts as they fall due: IA 1986, ss 122(1)(f) and 123(1)(e). A company whose assets are less than its liabilities may nevertheless have plenty of cash with which to discharge the immediate claims on it.

[71] For an energetic argument that *ex post* controls cannot do the whole job and that access to the corporate form with limited liability should be made more difficult see A. Hicks, *Disqualification of Directors: No Hiding Place for the Unfit?*, Association of Chartered Certified Accountants, Research Report 59 (London, 1998).

in such a way as to confine the claims of the creditors to the assets of that particular company and so as to deny them recourse to the assets of other companies in the group. Alternatively, should the group be permitted to allocate a particularly valuable asset to a non-trading subsidiary, thus shielding it from the creditors of the trading companies in the group? The asset-partitioning argument, and its associated incentives for creditor monitoring, would suggest that in principle such segregation of assets and liabilities should be permitted. As ever, creditors who were uncomfortable with this situation would be free to negotiate contractual protections from other companies in the group, in particular from the parent company.[72]

The essence of the idea of a group of companies is that two or more companies, although separate legal entities, are managed as a single unit. Within the single managerial or economic unit, however, the legal structure of the group may display enormous variations. In particular, the parent company may control the subsidiary on the basis of holding all the subsidiary's shares (a 'wholly owned' subsidiary) or simply a majority of them or it may even be able to control the decisions of the subsidiary without holding a majority of its shares.[73] In the latter cases the law needs to think about the position of the 'outside' shareholders in the subsidiary as well as the subsidiary's creditors.[74] Further, parent (or 'holding') companies may spawn strings of subsidiaries, as where P has a subsidiary S1 which has its own subsidiary SS1, which thus becomes an 'indirect' subsidiary of P. If P has another direct subsidiary, S2, which also has its own subsidiary SS2, one may need to think also, for example, about the relations between S1 and S2 or between SS2 and S1. In short, group structures provide company lawyers with the most complex factual situations to analyse.

However, two things are clear about the British law relating to groups. The first is that the issue of liability within groups is not addressed

---

[72] Cf. *Re Polly Peck International plc (in administration)* [1996] 2 All ER 433, where a Cayman Islands subsidiary company without significant assets was formed and issued bonds to the amount of 700m. Swiss francs, in order to avoid the costs of listing the bonds in London, a situation which was acceptable to the purchasers of the bonds only because the parent company, then a substantial company, guaranteed the obligations of the subsidiary. But courts are not astute to treat statements by parents to creditors of subsidiaries as contractual promises: *Kleinwort Benson Ltd v Malaysia Mining Corp Bhd* [1989] 1 All ER 785, CA ('letter of comfort' treated as being a statement of present fact, not a promise about future conduct).

[73] For example, where a substantial but minority corporate shareholder has the right to appoint the majority of the subsidiary's board.

[74] See Chapter 8.

specifically in the companies legislation. The second is that the courts have allowed the separate legal personality doctrine of the *Salomon* case[75] to operate within the group structure, so that in general the partitioning of assets and liabilities to particular subsidiary companies is permitted— and, indeed, frequently done. On the first point, it is sometimes suggested that the legislation has not addressed the issue specifically because British company law lacks the necessary conceptual apparatus. This is clearly not the case. Where the Act wishes to impose rules on groups of companies, it is fully able to do so. We have already noted the obligation imposed on groups by the middle of the last century to produce group accounts[76] and to that end the Act contains a detailed definition of parent and subsidiary undertakings. Again, a number of the duties imposed by statute on directors are extended to 'shadow directors', defined as 'those in accordance with whose directions or instructions the directors of a company are accustomed to act'.[77] This definition embraces a wide range of persons who exercise control within a company without themselves acting as directors. Among such persons may be a parent company that instructs the directors of a subsidiary how they shall conduct the business of the subsidiary.[78]

The shadow director example is particularly important in the context of British law, because among the statutory provisions extended to shadow directors are those relating to wrongful trading, discussed in the previous section of this chapter.[79] Thus, s 214 may operate to impose liability upon a parent company to the creditors of the subsidiary. One can see that the Companies Act has no difficulty with the idea that, exceptionally, parent companies should be liable for the debts of their subsidiaries. What the wrongful trading provisions do not create is a routine liability of this type, flowing simply from the fact of the existence

---

[75] See Chapter 1, p. 10.

[76] Above, p. 73. The definition of parent and subsidiary for accounts purposes is set out in CA 1985, s 258. A rather different definition for non-accounts purposes is set out in s 736 and 736A.

[77] S 741.

[78] See *Re Hydrodam (Corby) Ltd* [1994] 2 BCLC 180, where the judge was prepared to view a company as the shadow director of an indirect subsidiary. This was on the basis that the parent could be shown in fact to give the indirect subsidiary the instructions the section requires. However, the judge was not prepared to hold that the directors of the parent became shadow directors on the basis of instructions given in the course of their functions as directors of the parent: they were protected from this liability because they acted as the parent's agents in giving the instructions. Cf. above, p. 51.

[79] The provisions relating to disqualification on grounds of unfitness are also extended in this way.

of a parent and subsidiary relationship. Something more is required, and in the case of s 214 that additional thing is the failure of the parent company to treat the management of the subsidiary as having an independent existence, plus negligent disregard by the parent of the interests of the subsidiary's creditors in the period before insolvency.

A similar conclusion flows from an analysis of the common law rules which sometimes permit the courts to ignore the separate legal personality of the subsidiary. We have already encountered the common law doctrine of 'piercing the veil'.[80] We noted that this doctrine is particularly important when it operates to remove the protection of limited liability, because one of the primary functions of separate legal personality doctrine within company law is precisely to facilitate the implementation of limited liability. As far as groups are concerned, the courts have varied somewhat over time in their willingness to pierce the veil, but the latest authority is quite restrictive. The leading modern authority is *Adams v Cape Industries*,[81] a particularly important case because it involved the failure of an attempt to pierce the veil on the part of *involuntary* creditors of the subsidiary.[82] The claimants were allegedly the victims of asbestos-related diseases which had been caused by the products put into circulation by the subsidiary.

In a robust judgment the court was clear that the fact that a group was in fact conducted as a single economic entity did not mean that the normal operation of the principles of separate legal personality and limited liability were to be set aside. Cape was not to be exposed to liability on the grounds that it 'ran a single integrated mining division with little regard to corporate formalities as between members of the group'. So, the parent company could make the other members in the group dance to its tune without losing the benefits of limited liability as against those companies. Moreover, a questionable motive did not deprive Cape of these benefits: it retained them even if 'the purpose of the operation was in substance that Cape would have the practical benefit of the group's asbestos trade in the United States, without the risk of tortious liability'. It was, the court thought, a legitimate use of the group structure to bring this result about.

Cape was at risk of being held liable for the actions of a subsidiary only

---

[80] See p. 37.   [81] [1990] Ch 433, CA.

[82] In fact, the central company in the case (CPC) was not a subsidiary of the defendant, since its shares were held by an independent third party, though CPC was closely associated with Cape and the discussion in the case proceeded on the basis that the rules applicable to subsidiaries proper were the relevant ones.

if the group arrangements were a 'façade'. The tests to be passed for this conclusion to be reached were not explored in detail, but they seemed to involve a complete abandonment of the formalities of company law *vis-à-vis* the subsidiary. As we have seen, the fact that Cape controlled the business policy of a subsidiary would not turn it into a façade in the sense meant by the court. Cape would have to go well beyond that, as it had with a Liechtenstein subsidiary, which was 'no more than a corporate name', having no employees or officers of its own but using those of other group companies. Thus, at common law the requirements for piercing the veil seem even more demanding than the statutory definition of a shadow director. Whereas domination of the subsidiary's board is likely to trigger the statutory definition of a shadow director, the common law seems to regard a separate if compliant board as sufficient to maintain the separate legal personality of the dominated company.

However, even at common law the claimants' position may be stronger if the control exercised by the parent over the activities of the subsidiary can be argued, not to make the parent liable for the debts of the subsidiary, but to create a direct duty (in tort) owed by the parent towards the claimants. Thus, it has been argued that where a parent company prescribes the health and safety policies of its subsidiaries, it comes under a duty of care in tort towards the employees of the subsidiary and local inhabitants to take reasonable care to protect them in respect of their health and safety. In such a case the common law of tort acts in a way which is parallel to s 214, as extended by the shadow director provision.[83]

It is clear that British law is at one end of the spectrum as far as the regulation of liability within groups is concerned. Other countries, as different as Germany and New Zealand, have specifically addressed the group issue in legislation. If such legislation were to be introduced in Britain, a large number of policy choices would have to be made.[84] The legal techniques for modifying limited liability are not confined to making the parent liable for the debts of its subsidiary. In some cases it might be more appropriate to confine the creditors' claims to the assets of the subsidiary but to make the parent liable to the subsidiary for harm caused

---

[83] See *Connelly v RTZ Corporation plc* [1998] AC 854 and *Lubbe v Cape plc* [2000] 1 WLR 1545, both decisions of the House of Lords, which decided, however, only the question whether the claims should be heard in the English courts and not the existence or breach of the tortious duty. The second case involved the same company as in the *Adams* case, but the facts related to its South African subsidiaries.

[84] For a recent discussion of these issues, see Corporate Governance Forum, *Corporate Group Law for Europe* (Stockholm, 2000).

by it to the subsidiary's financial interests or to protect the subsidiary's creditors by restricting the freedom of the parent to shift assets out of the subsidiary into the hands of the parent, say, by way of dividend.[85]

A further set of choices relates to whether the group law would be mandatory or optional. It might seem odd to make liability towards a subsidiary optional for a parent company. Why should the parent ever choose it? However, separate legal personality has some costs for the management of corporate groups, as well as for group creditors. In particular, the fact that the duties of the directors of each group company are owed in principle to that company and not to the group as a whole may restrict the flexibility of group management. Thus, there might be some scope for a 'deal' whereby the parent benefited from the removal of some or all of the legal obstacles to running the group on an integrated basis in exchange for undertaking certain obligations towards the creditors of subsidiaries. The CLR proposed a modest version of such a policy towards groups. In exchange for a guarantee given by the parent to the creditors of a wholly owned and controlled subsidiary, the subsidiary would be relieved of the obligation to produce annual accounts, so that the only public financial statements would be the accounts for the group as a whole.[86]

Finally, there would be a choice between making the modification of limited liability a permanent feature of group law or something which cuts in only upon the insolvency of a group company. The New Zealand legislation operates on the latter basis, giving the court a wide 'just and equitable' discretion to make a solvent group company liable for the debts of another insolvent group member or to require the liquidation of two or more group companies to be consolidated.[87]

At present such discussion is not well developed in the UK, at least at the level of policy-makers. The British legislature has yet to be convinced that the problems of limited liability within groups cannot be solved by a combination of creditor self-help, general company law strategies such as s 214 or the unfair prejudice remedy,[88] and targeted statutory interventions, such as the requirement for group accounts.

---

[85] All these techniques can be found in the German *Konzernrecht*, introduced in 1965.

[86] CLR, *Completing the Structure*, November 2000, paras 10.19–10.57. Without this scheme both individual company and group accounts would have to be produced, but in the end the CLR decided not to proceed with it: *Final Report*, July 2001, vol. I, paras 8.23–8.28.

[87] Companies Act 1993 (NZ), ss 271 and 272, a solution supported by R. Austin, 'Corporate Groups' in R. Grantham and C. Rickett (eds), *Corporate Personality in the 20th Century* (Oxford: Hart Publishing, 1998).

[88] See Chapter 8.

CONCLUSIONS

It may be helpful to draw together at this point some threads of the law discussed in this and the previous chapter.

First, we have seen that British law extends the protection of limited liability to all companies incorporated under the Companies Act, and permits even the smallest business to incorporate.[89] This is despite the fact that the traditional rationales for limited liability apply only weakly to small companies. In going in this direction, however, British law follows a common, if not universal, trend in the development of the company laws of other comparable states.[90] Yet, in comparative terms one feature of the British response to the danger of excessively risky behaviour in small companies, created by the broad acceptance of limited liability, does stand out. The traditional response to this danger in the Germano-Latin legal systems has been to insist on a minimum legal capital for all companies. By contrast, common law systems have always been sceptical of the advantages of a minimum legal capital.[91] However, British company law has not ignored the perverse incentives which limited liability, coupled with control of the company, may create. Rather, it has sought to combat them through the *ex post* rules relating to wrongful trading and disqualification of directors.

Second, the other area where the traditional arguments in favour of limited liability seem weakly applicable is that of groups of companies and where, equally, a danger of excessively risky behaviour arises through the assignment of high-risk activities to under-capitalized subsidiaries. However, in rejecting the general proposition that a company is liable for the obligations of another company which it controls and in failing to develop a comprehensive set of rules to regulate such liability within groups, British law does not depart from the pattern to be found elsewhere. Very few countries have followed the German lead and legislated for such a code.[92] This is probably because group structures and

---

[89] De facto since the decision in *Salomon v Salomon* [1897] AC 22; de jure since the transposition of the Twelfth EC Company Law Directive (see above, p. 69).

[90] M. Lutter, 'Business and Private Organisations' in *International Encyclopedia of Comparative Law*, vol. XIII, ch 2 (Tübingen: Mohr Siebeck and Dordrecht: Martinus Nijhoff, 1998), pp. 25–9.

[91] Ibid. p. 33, and especially the table on p. 9 suggesting that all the EC countries except the UK and Ireland have minimum capital rules for all companies and that no common law-influenced country does.

[92] U. Immenga, 'Company Systems and Affiliation' in *International Encyclopedia of Comparative Law*, above n. 90, vol. xiii, ch. 7.

relationships within groups are highly variable and the appropriate general rules are accordingly difficult to identify.[93] Nevertheless, the result is that group problems are addressed in British law in a rather piecemeal fashion, as the courts struggle to apply general statutory or common law rules in a group context. Without further research it is difficult to assess whether the resulting set of rules addresses the risks of opportunistic behaviour within groups in an efficient way.

Third, like all company laws the British system relies predominantly upon self-help by creditors (usually via contract) to protect themselves against company opportunism generated by limited liability. This is an efficient solution, because, even in the absence of limited liability, large lenders and other creditors will want to secure contractual protections against debtor opportunism.[94] Thus, additional contractual protections to deal with the risks generated by limited liability can easily be added to the creditor/debtor contract. A contractual relationship does not have to be created in order to deal with opportunism generated by limited liability; an existing contractual structure has simply to be extended. This argument assumes, of course, an existing and effective bargaining relationship. Where that does not exist, the tendency of British company law, as elsewhere in Europe, is to deal with the resulting problems outside company law, through, for example, compulsory insurance.[95] Assuming that the insurance requirements are appropriately widespread and the premiums sensitive to the risks generated by each company, both of which are empirical questions, this system can operate to internalize into the company's decision-making processes the costs of its activities for involuntary creditors. What is more remarkable, in comparative European terms, is the way in which British law currently permits, via the floating charge,[96] self-help by one group of creditors (the secured) to operate so extensively as virtually to exclude the unsecured creditors from access to the company's assets. In some other European countries, it is the very fact that the company, which has granted a floating charge, is able to continue to deal with its current assets (and in particular to acquire further goods on credit) as if they were unencumbered which renders the device

---

[93] Cf. the New Zealand solution mentioned above (p. 107) which involves giving the court a broad discretion at the point of liquidation.

[94] For example, if I personally (and so without limited liability) borrow money from a bank or building society ostensibly to buy a house, the loan being secured on the house, the lender will take steps to ensure that that is what I actually use the money for and require me to insure the house under an approved policy.

[95] Above, p. 81.

[96] Above, p. 73. But see there the discussion of the Government's proposed reforms.

suspect as a fraud on the unsecured creditors.[97] To date, however, the resistance of banks lending to companies, which naturally find the floating charge attractive, has prevented significant reform.

---

[97] The Cork Committee (above, n. 45) commented at p. 33: 'The matter for wonder is that such a device should ever have been invented by a Court of Equity. It is not easy to discern on what principle of equity the holder of a floating charge should obtain security over goods for which his money has not paid, in priority to the claim of the unpaid supplier of goods.' The floating charge must be registered (CA 1985, Pt XII) but this is unlikely to help the small creditor.

5

Centralized Management I

Empowering Shareholders in Widely Held Companies

THE LEGAL BASIS OF CENTRALIZED MANAGEMENT

In all but the smallest companies one finds that the function of managing the company has become to some degree specialized and separated from that of providing risk capital to companies. The former task is lodged by the law and the company's constitution in the hands of the board of directors, while the latter is the function of the shareholders. Of course, in the largest companies there will develop an elaborate hierarchy of managers, only the most senior of whom will be members of the board of directors. The top executive in a big company—the managing director in British parlance or the chief executive officer (CEO) in US and, increasingly, international parlance—may become much better known publicly than even the largest shareholders in the company. The identification of centralized management as a distinct phenomenon was made as long ago as the 1930s by two US scholars, A. Berle and G. Means, in what must be the most famous English-language company law book ever written, *The Modern Corporation and Private Property*.[1] Their thesis was that, with the fragmentation of shareholdings in large companies, the development of centralized management had caused shareholders to lose control over the company. To what extent this is an accurate picture of the relationship between shareholders and the board in large companies has been a question which has dominated company law scholarship, at least in the USA and the UK, ever since. This chapter and the following ones analyse the

---

[1] New York: Harcourt Brace and World, revised edn, 1968. Berle and Means did not use the term 'centralized management' but rather 'the separation of ownership from control'. The former term is preferred here as leaving open the question how far this development means that shareholders no longer control the company.

extent to which the law can effectively maintain shareholder control in
large companies.

In Chapter 1 we suggested reasons for the development of centralized
management.[2] In sum, these reasons were that, in big companies, with a
large and fluctuating body of shareholders, decision-making by shareholders was likely to inefficient. Decision-making would be slow, if it
routinely required the convocation of a large number of people to take
management decisions. It might be inexpert because there is no reason to
suppose that those who are skilled in investing money are the best people
to manage the enterprises in which the money is invested. Management
and investment are not the same thing, though they are obviously related.
Finally, decision-making might be uncommitted. In a large decision-
making body, where no one has a large financial stake in the common
enterprise, the incentive to free-ride, rather than invest substantial time
and effort in working out what is the best course of action for the
company, is likely to be strong.

What needs to made clear at this point is some assumptions that lie
behind this picture of tardy, incompetent, and detached management of
the company by the shareholders. It is premised upon the company in
question having a large body of shareholders. Where the shareholding
body is small, the first and third objections to shareholder management
are very much lessened, though the second may still prevail. Thus, where
the shareholder body is small, the pressures to centralize management
may not operate with the same force.[3] Furthermore, the arguments in
favour of centralized management assume that none of the large body of
shareholders has a sufficiently big shareholding to give him or her
even factual control of the company.[4] If there is a controlling shareholder,
the third argument against shareholder decision-making (lack of commitment) is much less likely to hold, and the first argument (slow

[2] See Chapter 1, p. 13.

[3] Note that a small number of shareholders is not necessarily to be equated with an
economically small company. Consider the joint venture between three multinational oil
companies (so only three shareholders) which was the subject of litigation in *Multinational
Gas and Petroleum Co v Multinational Gas and Petroleum Services Ltd* [1983] 1 Ch 258, CA,
which ultimately became insolvent with a deficiency of £113 million (in 1977 prices).

[4] 'Legal control' of the company is a holding of shares which carry 50 per cent or more of
the voting rights in the company, i.e. a proportion sufficient to secure the passage of an
ordinary resolution by the shareholders. However, a much smaller shareholding may in fact
be enough to secure the passing of an ordinary resolution, because not all shareholders
bother to vote on any resolution and some can be persuaded to vote with the block-holder.
Take-over regulation often regards one-third of the voting rights as sufficient to provide
factual control.

decision-making) may not apply either. This is because the controlling shareholder can use its votes to appoint its nominees to the board and thus shift decision-making from the large body of shareholders to the small board. Although the board is the locus of decision-making when this happens, this is not a true example of centralized management, as the term is used in this book, because the board is not in this case an expression of specialized management separate from the shareholders but rather has become an expression of the will of the controlling shareholder.

It is not my purpose to argue that companies with small bodies of shareholders, or with large bodies which nevertheless contain a controlling shareholder, do not pose important questions for the law arising out of the location of management decision-making. Rather, my argument is that the legal policy issues become clearer if the analysis proceeds in stages. Consequently, we shall analyse in this chapter and the next two the legal issues which arise in companies with large bodies of shareholders where, however, no single shareholder (or associated group of shareholders) has sufficient shares to constitute a controlling block. Here, the arguments for centralized management are the strongest. We shall examine that situation before, in the later chapters, going on to an analysis of the situations where there is a controlling shareholder and, afterwards, to situations where the company has only a small number of shareholders.

In Britain, centralized management in large companies with dispersed shareholdings has developed on a rather slender legal foundation. Certainly, the Act provides for meetings of the members (shareholders) of the company and requires companies to have directors.[5] To this extent the Act supports the creation of the two constitutional decision-making bodies of the company, the shareholders meeting and the board of directors, to which we have frequently referred so far. However, even public companies are required to have only two directors, and the Act makes no distinction between executive and non-executive directors, says nothing about the possible functions of the chair of the board, does not mention committees of the board, nor does it stipulate whether the chair of the board should be a different person from the CEO. Moreover, the Act says very little about the managerial functions of the board, although certain administrative and reporting tasks are laid by the Act upon the board, or

---

[5] CA 1985, s 282, though there seems to be no legal sanction on the company simply for not having directors nor any statutory mechanism to ensure they are appointed.

about the division of managerial functions between the board itself and the senior management of the company.

How different is all this from, for example, the provisions of German company law about the board structure of public companies (*Aktiengesellschaften*). For a start, the German Act requires the company to have two boards to which different functions are attributed: the managing board (*Vorstand*) and the supervisory board (*Aufsichtsrat*). The composition and functions of those boards are specified and, as well, a certain amount of detail on their methods of operation is laid down in the relevant legislation (the *Aktiengesetz*). The equivalent rules for British companies are located not in the (mandatory) provisions of the legislation but in the company's own constitution. The contents of the articles of association are for each company to decide on, but the importance of the articles in conferring powers on the board is shown by the fact that some 30 (out of 118) regulations in the statutory model articles (Table A) are devoted to the board.[6]

Why should so much more be left to private ordering in the UK than in Germany? Partly, it is because the UK uses a single Act to regulate all companies, whereas Germany, in line with most continental European countries, has separate legislation for public and private companies. The German legislation for private companies (the *GmbHGesetz*) gives much more flexibility to private companies as to their internal division of powers and in this respect much more resembles the British Act. This supports the argument we made above to the effect that board decision-making is a universal feature of large companies, whether or not the company is dominated by a large shareholder, but with smaller companies the extent to which decision-making by the board is the efficient regime will vary from case to case. The consequence is that a single statute on the UK model cannot sensibly mandate a unique model of board functioning for all the companies it covers.

However, the reluctance in the UK to give official guidance on how even large companies should be managed goes deeper than this. The legislature could have developed different sets of model articles for different sizes of company or for companies with different shareholding patterns or, at least, for public and private companies, but in fact there is at present only one model for all companies limited by shares (the well-

---

[6] Arts 64 to 98 in the 1985 version of Table A (SI 1985 No. 805). Table A is the model set of articles produced by Parliament to guide companies that do not wish to go to the bother of generating their own articles.

known Table A).[7] In consequence, even the statutory model articles, despite the number of provisions about directors, provide little guidance on the crucial issues of board composition, structure, and function, where they are either silent or naive. Thus, art 70 says that 'the business of the companies shall be managed by the directors', which in the case of large companies is impossible. Only a part of the management of the large company can be carried on by the board, and modern business-school consensus is to the effect that the relevant part is setting, and monitoring the execution of, the company's overall strategy, concepts with which Table A is unfamiliar. It is only when one moves beyond Table A to the corporate governance codes, which have become a feature of the British scene since the Report of the Cadbury Committee in 1992,[8] that one has the sense that one is reading a set of rules which bear a substantial relation to what boards of large companies do in fact. However, the distinguishing feature of such codes, the contents of which we shall discuss in the course of this chapter and the next two, is that they are the result of City, professional, and industrial, rather than of governmental, wisdom, even if state rules may be used to some degree to enforce them.

Despite the frugality of the legal rules in this area, medium-sized and large British companies have developed sophisticated management structures, albeit around the single board required by British law rather than the two-tier structure of the *Aktiengesetz*. This has been largely the result of practice rather than law. Company law's contribution to the development has been significant in only one area, where the judiciary engaged in some necessary ground-clearing. The judges contributed to the recognition of management as a separate function by abandoning at the beginning of the twentieth century the view that the directors were the agents of the shareholders (who could instruct the board by ordinary majority vote at any time what to do or not to do) and adopted instead a constitutional view of the board.[9] The articles of association were now regarded as dividing up the powers of the company as between the shareholders'

---

[7] Somewhat bizarrely, for the rare cases of companies not limited by shares or unlimited companies, separate models are provided: s 8. The CLR recommended the adoption of a model set of articles specifically for private companies limited by shares, and produced a draft set: *Final Report* (2001), vol. II, ch. 17.

[8] *Report of the Committee on the Financial Aspects of Corporate Governance* (London: Gee, 1992). And the picture the codes provide of how the boards of large companies should function is much closer, though not identical, to that found in the German legislation. See P. Davies, 'Board Structures in the UK and Germany: Convergence or Continuing Divergence?' (2000) 2 *International and Comparative Corporate Law Journal* 435.

[9] *Automatic Self-Cleansing Filter Syndicate Co v Cuninghame* [1906] 2 Ch 34, CA.

meeting and the board, each body being supreme in its own sphere, so that the shareholders by ordinary resolution could not impugn the constitutional position of the board. The board cannot interfere with the shareholders' meeting nor the shareholders' meeting with the board so long as they are exercising their respective powers conferred upon them by the articles. To allow this, as Lord Wilberforce once said, would be to permit either board or shareholders' meeting 'to interfere with that element of the company's constitution which is separate from and set against their powers'.[10]

Thus, directors became the agents of the company, not of the shareholders. However, the significance of the point should not be exaggerated, since the shareholders retain control of the articles of association and so can instruct the directors by special resolution (requiring a three-quarters majority in favour), because such a resolution is equivalent to a decision to change the articles. Thus, it is plausible to view the directors' powers under British company law as still deriving from a delegation to them from the shareholders, even if that delegation is now of a formal and constitutional nature.[11]

The theoretical position of the shareholders as the ultimate source of authority in the company will be reinforced if the CLR's proposals for the codification of the unanimous consent rule are implemented. It has long been clear that the shareholders, if unanimous, can take certain decisions on behalf of the company, even though they come to that unanimous decision in an entirely informal manner, for example without a meeting being called. This is a particularly useful device in small companies where the directors and the shareholders are the same people, as we shall see in Chapter 10. However, it has been unclear in case law whether this doctrine applied only to decisions which the constitution of the company had allocated to the shareholders. The CLR proposes[12] to adopt the view that the unanimous consent of the shareholders will bind the company, no matter that the company's constitution has allocated the decision in question elsewhere. In other words, the unanimous consent of the shareholders will override the constitution. Thus, the unanimous consent doctrine is not just a rule permitting informal decision-making by

---

[10] *Howard Smith Ltd v Ampol Petroleum Ltd* [1974] 1 All ER 1126, 1136, PC.

[11] See CA 1985, s 9 and Table A, art 70. See also the discussion below at p. 128 on the shareholders' powers to remove the directors by ordinary resolution under s 303. For a contrary view see R. Grantham, 'The Doctrinal Basis of the Rights of Company Shareholders' (1998) 57 CLJ 554.

[12] *Final Report* (2001), vol. I, paras 7.17–7.26.

shareholders, but constitutes also an expression of the shareholders' control of the company, whether they act formally or informally. A company can take decisions either through the body to which that decision has been allocated by the company's constitution or by unanimous agreement among the shareholders. The rule is a startling expression of shareholder supremacy, even if, no doubt, a rather theoretical event in the large companies we consider in this chapter.

CENTRALIZED MANAGEMENT AND PRINCIPAL/AGENT PROBLEMS

Historically, centralized management emerged as a form of specialization. It was more efficient for shareholders to hire managers to fulfil that function than for shareholders to do the job themselves, at least outside small companies. As has been said, hired managers were likely to be more expert, more rapid in their decision-taking, and more committed than a large and fluctuating body of shareholders holding only small stakes in the company. Yet, centralized management was not without its danger for shareholders. The managers might begin to exercise their powers in a way which was, predominantly, in the managers' interests rather than the shareholders' interests. At worst, they might divert corporate assets to themselves or, more likely, set out to achieve goals which were more closely aligned to the promotion of their own interests rather than those of the shareholders. For example, they might seek to maximize the size of the company, because managerial remuneration is, or was, often linked to the size of the company, rather than its profitability.[13] Or the managers might simply shirk. In short, the shareholders could not simply delegate management powers without engaging in some monitoring of how those powers were exercised. On the other hand, if the costs of monitoring exceeded the benefits of centralized management, the whole institution of centralized management would be called into question. A surprisingly large part of company law can be seen as addressing this problem by providing a series of legal strategies whereby the costs to shareholders of monitoring management are reduced. These strategies are the subject matter of this and the following chapters.

Economists have made a very substantial contribution to the analysis of the benefits of delegation and the costs of monitoring. Less helpful is the phrase they use to characterize the relationships they are analysing:

---

[13] R. Marris, *Managerial Capitalism in Retrospect* (Basingstoke: Macmillan, 1998).

principal/agent relations. The phrase is unhelpful for lawyers because, as
we have seen in Chapter 2, the legal analysis of the principal/agent relationship is one where the agent has authority from the principal to act on
the principal's behalf, usually authority to alter the principal's legal
position. For the economist, a principal/agent relationship arises out of a
purely factual dependency. If the furtherance of A's interests depends
upon the actions of B, then A is the principal and B is the agent. In this
situation A has an incentive to take steps to secure that B acts in a way
which is favourable to A. The economist's conception of a principal/
agent relationship is thus very much wider than that of the lawyer.

The legal and economic concepts may coincide exactly, as they did in
the nineteenth-century view of the directors as agents of the shareholders. They may coincide substantially, as in the more modern view of
the directors as the agents of the company but receiving their powers by
virtue of the company's constitution, which is controlled by the shareholders. However, in many cases the two ideas seem at odds with one
another, as where, for economists, minority shareholders are the principal
and a majority shareholder the agent in respect of decisions taken in
shareholders' meetings. The minority shareholders may be factually
dependent upon the views of a majority shareholder, but it is far-fetched
to describe the minority shareholders as having conferred any authority
on the majority shareholder to act on their behalf. Given these differences
in approach between economists and lawyers, why do company lawyers
pay so much attention to the economists' views? A large part of the
answer is that situations of factual dependency are much more widespread within companies than true agency relationships, and the
regulation of these situations of factual dependency is a major task for
company law and for which the economists' analysis may be helpful.

A TYPOLOGY OF LEGAL STRATEGIES

It might be objected that there is no need for any legal strategies, beyond
freedom of contract, to deal with the principal/agent relationship
between shareholders and managers. The shareholders may negotiate
with management what constraints they will when they delegate power to
the directors via the constitution. However, it is doubtful whether simple
contractual solutions are available. It is highly unlikely that shareholders,
when deciding the terms of delegation of power to directors, will be able
to foresee all the situations which will arise in the management of the
company's future business and which will call for an exercise of discre-

tion and thus to identify the full range of situations in which rules will be required. This is the so-called problem of bounded rationality. Even if these situations could be foreseen, the costs of working out an appropriate solution to each one would be high, especially in lawyers' time. This is an example of the problem of transaction costs. So, any contract initially agreed by the shareholders with the board is likely to be incomplete, and to need to be supplemented at a later date. Thus what is required is one or more legal devices that will steer the parties towards an appropriate solution *ex post*, even if the *ex ante* bargaining between shareholders and management has not identified one.

Of course, the fact that long-term relationships require governance structures does not mean the law has to provide them; the parties could design the structures that fit their own situation best. We examined a similar claim in relation to creditors' claims against the company. We saw there,[14] however, that there were arguments for state-provided default solutions, so that each set of contracting parties did not have to re-invent the wheel. We also saw that in some situations the parties might not be able to contract for their best solution, for example because on the shareholders' side there was such a degree of fragmentation of shareholdings that they were unable to co-ordinate their positions. Thus, relying wholly on private contracting to produce governance mechanisms is unrealistic, but, equally, the statutory mechanisms need to be adaptable and flexible.

On examination, it turns out that there is quite a wide range of strategies available to the law to deal with principal/agent problems. A basic division is between strategies which focus on enhancing the control of the principal over the agent (then leaving the principal to exercise his or her enhanced control over the agent) and those which seek to influence directly the exercise by the agent of his or her discretion. Even this banality, however, is enough to demonstrate that the relevant legal strategies go beyond the obvious one of laying down, for example, the requirement that 'agents shall not treat principals unfairly'. That would be an example of a legal strategy constraining the discretion of agents, but it is by no means the only legal strategy available. An example of another and very different strategy, focusing on the power of the principal, would be to make it easy for the principal to dismiss an unsatisfactory agent.

In fact, as Figure 1 suggests, five pairs of strategies are available for the regulation of agency relationships, of which two focus on agents and

---

[14] Chapter 4, p. 78.

three on principals.[15] This analysis of legal strategies for regulating principal/agent relations is not confined to shareholder/management relations (therefore, we shall use it in later chapters as well) or even to company law, though of course some types of principal/agent relationship may respond better to some legal strategies than to others. We shall say a little about each of the strategies now and then look at each in more detail in this and the next two chapters.

Proceeding from right to left across the diagram, we look first at the agent-focused strategies and the use of rules or standards. To a lawyer, this is perhaps the most obvious legal strategy to use to reduce agency costs, for it involves the stipulation of norms which directly constrain the exercise by the agent of his or her discretion. However, these norms fall into two categories. They may be precise rules or they may be general standards.[16] An example of a rule would be that all shareholders (of the same class) must be paid dividends pro rata to their shareholdings. Such a rule clearly prevents the directors favouring one group of shareholders over another, but only in the matter of dividend payments. A standard would be that the directors must treat all shareholders of the same class fairly. Such a standard catches a much wider range of directorial activity, but is much less clear about what behaviour is required of directors and

Enhancing the principal's control			Structuring the agent's decisions	
Affiliation rights	Appointment rights	Decision rights	Setting agent incentives	Constraining agent decisions
Entry	Selection	Initiation	Trusteeship	Rules
Exit	Removal	Veto	Rewards	Standards

Figure 1 Legal Strategies for the Regulation of Principal/Agent Relationships

[15] This figure is an earlier version of what now appears in H. Hansmann and R. Kraakman, 'Agency Problems and Legal Strategies' in R. Kraakman, P. Davies, H. Hansman, G. Hertig, K. J. Kopt, K. Kanda, and E. B. Rock (eds), *The Anatomy of Corporate Law: A Comparative and Functional Approach* (forthcoming).

[16] On this distinction see L. Kaplow, 'Rules versus Standards: an Economic Analysis' (1992) 42 *Duke LR* 557.

requires an expert judiciary for its effective application. With a standard the legislature is, in effect, sharing the law-making process with the judiciary: the standard is a grant of power by the legislature to the courts to be exercised on a case-by-case basis, because the legislature cannot predict in advance what the proper outcome of those cases should be.

The second pair of agent-constraining strategies addresses itself, not to controlling the external manifestations of the conflicts of interest between agents and principals, but to moderating the underlying conflicts of interest and so reducing the incidence of self-interested behaviour. One strategy would be to give the decision to an agent who is not exposed to the temptation of self-interest (though such an agent may be hard to find). Alternatively, the strategy might seek to align the self-interest of the agent with the self-interest of the principal, most obviously by tying the agent's remuneration to the successful achievement of the principal's goals. The first version of this strategy has been called, albeit at the risk of further terminological confusion, a 'trusteeship' strategy and the second version a 'reward' strategy.

Turning to the three left-hand pairs of strategies, which are based on the idea of empowering the principal, an obvious approach is to give the principal a greater input into the decision-making of the agent. At one extreme the decision-making function could be transferred wholly to the principal, that is, the agency relationship could be terminated. However, this is a drastic solution since, in our context, it would deprive the share-holders entirely of the benefits of centralized management. A less extreme form of the strategy would be to leave the initiation of decisions with the agent but require at least certain classes of those decisions to be approved by the principal, thus giving the latter a veto power. These are the two versions of the 'decision rights strategy'.

The other two strategies for empowering principals are closely related. One is to give the principal easily exercised powers in relation to the selection or removal of the agent (the appointment rights strategy), so that the agent will know that divergence from the interests of the princi-pal is likely to lead to swift dismissal and difficulty in obtaining a similar position for the future. A linked strategy is to make it easy for the princi-pal to enter or leave agency relationships of a particular type (not just with a particular agent)—the affiliation rights strategy. In company law terms this means making it easy for shareholders to enter or exit com-panies. Transferability of shares, for example, promotes this last pair of strategies, allowing dissatisfied shareholders to leave the company, while facilitating the entry of, say, a take-over bidder who will shake up or even replace the existing management.

The aim of the rest of this chapter and the following two is to analyse the five strategies discussed above in the context of centralized management in companies with dispersed shareholdings.

DISCLOSURE OF INFORMATION

Before doing this, however, it is important to deal with an immediate objection to the above typology of legal strategies, which is that it is not clear where mandatory disclosure of information fits in, even though a great deal of company law is concerned with precisely this topic. We have already seen the importance of corporate financial reporting in facilitating creditor self-help. Disclosure is equally important for shareholders. Indeed, as we have already noted in Chapter 3,[17] mandatory and regular reporting by directors to shareholders has generally been less controversial with business people than mandatory public filing of those reports, thus making them available to investors and creditors at large (but also to competitors and the public authorities). Further, the current stance of the common law of negligence is that the primary purpose of financial reporting is to aid shareholders in the exercise of their governance rights.[18] Thus, it might be asked why disclosure of information is not separately mentioned in the above typology.

The answer, it is suggested, is not that disclosure of information is not important but that it is so important that it is relevant to all the above legal strategies. It is difficult to imagine that any of these strategies can operate effectively in the absence of accurate and up-to-date information about the performance of the company. Provisions on disclosure of information thus constitute a method of implementing the above strategies and one that is so important that it plays an over-arching role. One consequence of the centrality of information disclosure in company law is that economies of scale are generated: a single set of effective disclosure provisions may facilitate the implementation of a number of (probably all) the above strategies. Perhaps for this reason, information disclosure takes on the appearance of a distinct strategy, but it is suggested that, functionally, it is simply a way of implementing the strategies identified above.

---

[17] See Chapter 3, p. 72.   [18] *Caparo Industries v Dickman* [1990] 2 AC 605, HL.

SHAREHOLDER INVOLVEMENT IN DECISION-MAKING

We shall devote the remainder of this chapter to an analysis of the legal strategies which address the shareholders' agency problems by aiming to enhance the principal's control. This is the left-hand side of Figure 1. In the following chapters we shall analyse the strategies which aim to structure the agents' decisions, that is, the right-hand side of the Figure.

We begin our analysis of the strategies which aim at enhancing the principal's control with what we have termed the 'decision rights' strategy. As already noted, as between directors and shareholders as a class, a strategy of shifting decisions into the hands of the shareholders is very effective at dealing with principal/agent problems but comes with the high price that shareholders are substantially deprived of the benefits of centralized management. Thus, it is not surprising that company law, in the main, leaves it to shareholders themselves to determine, via the articles, the distribution of decision-making powers as between the board and the shareholders in general meeting. Nevertheless, there are some instances where the Companies Act requires a shareholder input into the decision, either by way of approval of the directors' proposal or even by way of initiative from the shareholders themselves.

How does this strategy protect shareholders? Where shareholders as a whole take the decision, it may seem obvious that they can shape it so that it furthers their interests. Where they have merely the right to veto the directors' proposal, their position appears less strong, for they will have to engage in bargaining with the directors in order to get the latter to produce a proposal of which the shareholders do approve. However, even where the shareholders have an initiation right, their reliance upon the directors for management skills to set and implement strategy will in fact often require them to bargain with the directors. This is perhaps why the Act often does not make it clear whether it is conferring a veto or an initiation right on the shareholders. In any event, we may expect that both initiation and veto rights for shareholders will generate bargaining between shareholders and directors, unless the directors regard the costs of securing shareholder consent as so high that they seek to avoid decisions which require shareholder input.[19]

---

[19] For an analysis along these lines in the context of Part X of the Act see S. Deakin and A. Hughes, 'Economic Efficiency and the Proceduralisation of Company Law' (1999) 3 CFILR 169, especially at 184–8.

As indicated, the number of cases in which the Act qualifies central-ized management by requiring a shareholder input into decision-making is small, though the shareholders remain free, through the articles, to add to that number. Although few, the mandatory cases are instructive. They seem to share one or more of the following characteristics:

- The decision is likely to be an infrequent one (so that the general run of management decisions in the company is not affected).

- The decision is one which the shareholders are likely to be as good at taking as the directors (for example, the decision is as akin to an investment as to a management decision).

- The decision is sufficiently important to the shareholders that they are likely to devote appropriate resources to taking it.

- The decision is one where there is a high degree of conflict between the interests of the directors and those of the shareholders, so that leaving the decision entirely to the board is particularly risky from the share-holders' point of view.

In other words, the cases where the legislature feels confident enough to insist on shareholder input into decision-making involve decisions which display the converse of the features which argue in favour of centralized management as the normal rule.[20]

Even when based on these general criteria, any attempt to identify the decisions which should require an explicit shareholder input is likely to be contestable. To require shareholder consent only of decisions which meet all four criteria identified in the previous paragraph would mean very few decisions were subject to this requirement; to require it where only one criterion is met would be to impose shareholder decision-making on a wide scale. Company laws in different countries differ somewhat, though not enormously, in their choice of decisions to be subject to this control. In the UK the main corporate decisions which the Act subjects to shareholder approval are:

- alterations to the company's constitution;[21]

- change in the type of company (for example, from private to public or vice versa);[22]

---

[20] See above, p. 13.

[21] The most important are probably alteration of the articles (CA 1985, s 9) and of the objects clause (s 4).

[22] And a variety of other change of type decisions: CA 1985, Part II.

- decisions to wind the company up voluntarily;[23]

- decisions by companies to issue or re-purchase shares, to alter their legal capital, or (in the case of private companies) to give financial assistance for the purchase of their own shares;[24]

- appointment of the company's auditors, whose duty is to verify the financial statements which the company presents annually to the shareholders;[25]

- approval of 'schemes of arrangement'[26] between a company and its shareholders or creditors (a bland name for a useful procedure which can be used for many things, ranging from a merger between two companies to a scaling down of creditors' rights on an insolvency);

- approval of certain transactions involving a strong conflict of interest.[27]

This is a relatively short list of instances where the Act deploys the decision rights strategy. The shortness of the list should not surprise us: the legislature will use this technique only where it is convinced that it is appropriate for all companies, despite the loss of the advantages of centralized management which is potentially incurred. However, under the British approach to the conferment of authority on the board, the shareholders may choose to treat the above list as only a minimum statement of their decision-making rights. Since authority is conferred on the board, in the main, by way of the articles of association (under the control of the shareholders) rather than directly by the Act, the shareholders may always add to the instances in which their consent is required, through appropriate provisions in the company's constitution. The imperatives of centralized management, however, mean that in large companies this is done only sparingly.

In addition, regulators sometimes insist on shareholder consent for particular corporate actions. As we shall see below, the City Panel on Take-overs and Mergers does so in order to promote the affiliation rights strategy.[28] The rules applying to companies listed on the London Stock Exchange add a more general example. The Listing Rules, formerly

---

[23] IA 1986, s 84.
[24] CA 1985, ss 80–96 and Part V, chs IV, VI, and VII. The provisions on reduction of capital and re-purchase of shares are discussed in a little more detail in Chapter 4 above at pp. 83–91.
[25] CA 1985, s 384.
[26] CA 1985, ss 425 ff.
[27] CA 1985, Part X, discussed in Chapter 6 in connection with directors' duties (at p. 176).
[28] See pp. 144–149 below.

issued by the Exchange itself, have traditionally operated as an expression of shareholder and investor concerns, a situation which will probably continue even though the Listing Rules are now issued by the FSA.[29] The Listing Rules extend the principle of shareholder approval to transactions which the company is contemplating simply because of the size of those transactions.[30] Provided the contemplated transaction has a size equivalent to at least 25 per cent of the company's current assets, profits, turnover, market value, or gross capital (the so-called Class 1 transactions), prior approval of the shareholders is required. This rule is imposed on the basis that it is likely that a transaction of this size will significantly alter the nature of the company and it thus is as much an investment as a managerial decision.[31]

However, the question of whether to include a particular type of decision within the category of those requiring shareholder approval is unlikely ever to be settled to everyone's satisfaction. An issue of great controversy in recent years has been the level of directors' remuneration, at least in listed companies, and in that context it has been debated whether shareholder approval should be required either of individual directors' remuneration packages or, more feasibly, of the company's remuneration policy towards directors. At the time of writing, however, both the Act[32] and the Listing Rules[33] impose reasonably extensive disclosure requirements in relation to remuneration, and the Listing Rules require shareholder approval of incentive schemes.[34] Otherwise, decision-making on remuneration under the articles of most companies is left with the board itself. The government has floated the idea of shareholder approval of remuneration policies and has committed itself to introducing an advisory shareholder vote on the matter.[35]

Does directors' remuneration meet any of the criteria identified above

---

[29] In its capacity as UK Listing Authority under the provisions of Art 105 of what is now Directive 2001/34/EC on the admission of securities to official stock exchange listing and on information to be published on those securities (OJ L184/1, 6.7.01).

[30] Listing Rules, ch. 10.

[31] The CLR considered extending the Class 1 requirement to all public companies, but eventually left it with the Listing Rules: *Final Report*, vol. I, para. 5.61.

[32] Section 318 and Sch 6.

[33] Para. 12.43A(c). The disclosure requirements of the Listing Rules are more extensive than those of the Act.

[34] See Chapter 7, pp. 208–209.

[35] DTI, *Directors' Remuneration: A Consultative Document*, 1999 (URN 99/923); DTI, Directors' Remuneration—A Consultative Document, 2001 (URN 01/1400). Since the Government had the matter of directors' remuneration under review during the period the CLR was considering the reform of company law, the latter was in effect excluded from looking at the matter.

for allocating a role in such decisions to shareholders? One can usually see a conflict of interest if decision-making on remuneration is left to the board itself, even when remuneration is handled by a remuneration committee consisting of non-executive directors.[36] It is less clear that any of the other criteria are routinely met. It may be significant that evidence from the United States, where shareholder voting on remuneration matters is available on a more widespread basis, suggests that voting has its greatest impact where what is being proposed by way of remuneration constitutes a significant departure from the norm, and that otherwise remuneration is regarded by the shareholders as a matter of business policy.[37] Thus, shareholder voting may fail to exert any general downward pressure on directors' remuneration, but may subject to shareholder scrutiny step-changes in remuneration patterns. In an area where effective regulatory intervention has proved elusive, this might be thought to be a not inconsiderable achievement.

Of course, a law involving shareholders in decision-making does not guarantee that the shareholders are in a position effectively to exercise their decision-making rights. We shall turn to that issue as part of the discussion in the next section of shareholders' appointment rights, since a similar issue arises in relation to that strategy.

APPOINTMENT RIGHTS

In the previous section we saw that involving shareholders in corporate decision-making can constitute a way of addressing their agency problems, but only at the potential cost of depriving the shareholders of the benefits of centralized management, which depend upon the exclusion of shareholders from that process. Not surprisingly, therefore, company law uses this strategy sparingly, at least on a mandatory basis. More promising, it might be thought, is the strategy of giving the shareholders strong legal rights in relation to the appointment or removal of the directors. This strategy does not involve the shareholders in decision-making on matters of management, but could allow the shareholders to choose the best people to lead the company and to remove them if their performance fell below what was expected of them. We shall look briefly at the scope of

---

[36] See Chapter 7, p. 208 (the non-executive directors are often executive directors of other companies).

[37] See B. Cheffins and R. Thomas, 'Should Shareholders Have a Greater Say over Executive Pay? Learning from the US Experience' (2001) 1 *Journal of Corporate Studies* 277.

the shareholders' appointment and removal rights and then consider the problems which arise when shareholders seek to use those rights.

Contrary to popular perception, company law does not insist that the directors be elected by the shareholders or that they be periodically re-elected by them. Partly, this is because there may be good reasons for giving other groups (for example, creditors) the right to appoint a director in order to protect their interests. Whether appointment rights shall be distributed more widely is a matter for the company, but a mandatory company law rule requiring shareholder appointment only might stand in the way of such broader distribution.[38] However, the absence of a mandatory rule requiring appointment or periodic reappointment by shareholders may simply operate so as to facilitate the entrenchment of incumbent management.

Not only does the company (usually through its articles) decide on the necessity for shareholder appointment and reappointment, but it also regulates the details of the appointment and reappointment processes.[39] Although it must be borne in mind that this is a matter of practice rather than of mandatory law, it can be said that a typical pattern of directorial appointment in large companies is as follows. New directors are approved by the shareholders, either by being elected at an annual general meeting of the shareholders or by being approved at the first AGM after their appointment by the board to fill a vacancy which has occurred in between AGMs. They are then subject to re-election by the shareholders every three years, that is, the normal term of appointment is such a period. However, it is also usual for the articles to make it difficult for shareholders to appoint their own nominees to the board, as opposed to accepting or rejecting the proposals of the existing board. For example, the articles may require significant prior notice to be given to the board of shareholder proposals for board membership. In practice, what the articles give the shareholders is a veto right, rather than an initiation right, over board appointments.

However, the appointment and reappointment rules rather fall into insignificance in the light of the rules on removal of directors. Here, British law contains an apparently tough mandatory rule: the

---

[38] Equally, though it is rarely done, the company could give appointment rights to its employees.

[39] The only significant mandatory rule contributed by the Companies Act is that the appointment or reappointment of directors must be voted on individually (s 292), so that a director who has incurred shareholder disapproval cannot be protected by bundling up his reappointment with that of a director of whom the shareholders think well.

shareholders, by ordinary resolution, can at any time remove any director (or, indeed, all of them) without having to assign a reason for so
doing.[40] This power overrides anything to the contrary in the company's
articles or in any contract between the company and the director, and so
removal may occur at any time and not just when the director comes
up for reappointment at the end of his or her term of office. The rule
applies even to directors not appointed by the shareholders, though if
a director appointed by the creditors is removed, that may put the
company in breach of its loan covenants and so removal in that case
may carry undesirable consequences for the company. Other company
law systems also adopt this tough rule, but it is far from universal.
German law, for example limits the circumstances in which a director can
be removed before the expiry of the term of office and US state laws
generally permit companies to contract out of the rule of removal at any
time by shareholder vote, for example, by a provision in the articles that
the directors shall be removable only for cause. However, unlike UK
law, they often put a mandatory limit on the length of the director's
term.[41]

The next question we have to ask is whether s 303 is as effective in
practice as it appears at first sight to be. Broadly, the question is whether
the incentives for shareholders to use s 303 outweigh the disincentives.
Two categories of disincentive can be identified: first, steps taken by
directors to counteract s 303; second, more general problems which
shareholders have in invoking the internal governance machinery of the
company, usually referred to as their 'collective action' problems.

DEFENSIVE STEPS BY DIRECTORS

Section 303(5) specifically preserves for the dismissed director the right
to 'compensation or damages payable to him in respect of the termination
of his appointment as director or of any appointment terminating with
that as director'. This clearly permits an executive director, who has a
service contract with the company, to claim any sums payable to him or
her under or by virtue of the contract if dismissed by the shareholders

---

[40] CA 1985, s 303. However, it seems that a director could contract with the shareholders
not to exercise their right to remove him and such a contract could be enforced by injunction if the director acted quickly enough: *Walker v Standard Chartered Bank plc* [1992]
BCLC 535, CA.

[41] For Germany, *Aktiengesetz*, art 84; for the United States, see, for example, the Model
Business Corporation Act, ss 8.05–8.08. US laws also provide for the 'staggering' of the
terms of the members of the board, so that they do not all expire in the same year; rather, it
may take two or three AGMs to remove the whole of an existing board.

under their s 303 powers.[42] The newspapers are full of reports of dismissed directors receiving sums running into several million pounds as compensation for loss of office, even where the cause of their removal seems to have been the poor performance of the company. Whether such payments do in fact chill the shareholders' s 303 powers, in the case of companies with multi-billion pound turnovers, is not clear. Often, the objection is to the inappropriateness of failed directors receiving large rewards, an issue which relates more to the incentive strategy, which is discussed below, than to the appointment rights strategy which is under consideration here. Nevertheless, there are some rules which potentially constrain the amounts of compensation payable to directors who are removed from office.

Most executive directors are employed on fixed-term service contracts. The longer the length of the term at the point of removal, the greater the damages payable for breach of contract. So executive directors could protect themselves against the operation of s 303 by entering into contracts with long contractual terms. Alternatively, whether or not the contract is for a fixed term, it might be expressed to be terminable only after a long notice period, thus enhancing the director's claim for payment in lieu of notice. Both devices are even more effective from the director's point of view if these provisions are asymmetrical, that is, they do not apply (or apply in full) where the director seeks to terminate the contract. The Act responds to these contractual arrangements in two ways. Section 318 requires the terms[43] of directors' contracts of service[44] to be available for inspection by the members of the company, so that the contractual terms are transparent. Section 319, using the strategy of shareholder involvement in decision-making, requires shareholder approval for directors' service contracts which are not lawfully terminable by the company within a five-year period. This approval must be given in each specific case; the board cannot be given a general permission in advance to exceed the five-year limit in the contracts it enters into with individual directors. A term incorporated into a service contract without shareholder approval is statutorily modified so as to reduce the term of the contract (or period of notice) to five years.

However, the effectiveness of s 319 is open to question. Five years is still a long time, especially since directors (or, rather, their legal advisers)

---

[42] It is normal to provide in the service contract that the executive position will terminate if the manager is removed from the board.

[43] All the terms; not just the term as to length.

[44] Though not, apparently, contracts for services.

responded to that section with 'five-year rollers', that is, contracts structured in such a way that the five-year period is always still to run whenever the contract is terminated. In any event, large payments can be granted by including within the contract explicit entitlements to payments upon termination, rather than leaving the matter to be handled by way of claims for breach of contract.

A somewhat more robust line, however, than is evident in s 319 is taken in relation to listed companies by the Combined Code on corporate governance, which is the result of the efforts of three main committees set up in the 1990s,[45] established by business and professional bodies with interests in the governance of large companies. Although these committees were supported by the Government, because they were formally the product of a private rather than a governmental initiative, the recommendations they produced led, not to legislation, but to a private Code of Practice. However, this Code of Practice does not lack entirely an enforcement mechanism. It is annexed to the Listing Rules now propounded by the FSA, and all listed companies must state in their annual reports whether they have complied with the Code during the preceding year and, if not, why not. This is the so-called principle of 'comply or explain'. However, it is important to note that any action subsequent upon non-compliance is for the shareholders to take, not the London Stock Exchange or the FSA. The latter is involved only if the company does not make the requisite statement about the extent of its compliance.

The Combined Code[46] states that 'there is a strong case for setting notice or contract periods at, or reducing them to, one year or less'. It also recommends that there be explicit agreement in the contract on any compensation to be paid upon removal from office. The CLR[47] proposed that the statutory provisions, which apply to all companies, should be brought closer to the Combined Code, which would continue to apply to listed companies. The five-year period should be reduced to three. Further, in many cases the maximum period after which shareholder approval was required would be reduced to one year. However, the lower limit would not apply on the first appointment of a director, and shareholders would be able to give their approval to exceed the one-year limit

---

[45] *The Financial Aspects of Corporate Governance* (London: Gee, 1992) (the 'Cadbury' Committee); *Report of the Study Group on Directors' Remuneration* (London: Gee, 1995) (the 'Greenbury' Committee); *Final Report of the Committee on Corporate Governance* (London: Gee, 1998) (the 'Hampel' Committee). See further Chapter 7, p. 200.
[46] At paras B.1.7 and B.1.9 of its Code of Best Practice.
[47] *Final Report* (2001), vol. I, paras 6.10–6.14.

in advance of the appointment of any particular director, by means of a special resolution which could be valid for up to five years. The shift to prior general approval for breaches of the one-year limit constitutes a significant weakening of the proposal. Explicit compensation payments would be void to the extent that they provided for more compensation than was payable, under the above provisions, for breach of contract.

An alternative avoidance strategy for directors is to concentrate, not on the terms of their service contracts, but upon the vote which shareholders have to take when a removal resolution is put forward. In *Bushell v Faith*[48] the articles provided that on such a resolution the shares of the director proposed to be removed should carry, on that occasion only, enough shares to outvote all the other shareholders. Thus, through the device of 'weighted voting' any director, acting as shareholder, could veto his own removal. Somewhat surprisingly, the House of Lords upheld this arrangement, even though s 303 is expressed to override contrary provisions in the articles. However, that scheme is likely to be agreed to by the shareholders only in a small company and where the directors have a substantial shareholding, notably where, as in the case itself, the shareholders and the directors are the same people. In such a case, the weighted voting provision is functionally equivalent to the default rule in partnerships that a partner cannot be expelled without his agreement.[49] Section 303 is really aimed at the type of company under consideration in this chapter, where shareholders and directors are different groups of people; and it is far from clear that the courts would give effect to a *Bushell v Faith* clause in such a company's articles, should any public company have the gall to adopt it.

Even in the absence of avoiding action on the part of directors, s 303 deals with only part of the process of the removal of directors. It deals, in essence, with the voting level needed to adopt a removal resolution and the effect of such a resolution. However, s 303 says nothing about the procedures and processes as a result of which the shareholders come to be assembled at a meeting to consider a removal resolution. For that, one has to look elsewhere. However, unless that prior process works effectively, s 303 will be a dead letter. A shareholder, contemplating summoning a shareholders' meeting to consider a removal resolution, needs three things. The first is reliable information about the company on the basis of which he can decide whether it is in his or her interests to try and

---

[48] [1970] AC 1099, HL.
[49] The general issue of the special adaptations that company law needs to make for 'owner-managed' companies is considered in Chapter 10 below.

persuade fellow shareholders to remove one or more directors. The second is the legal power to summon a meeting of the shareholders. The third is the support of a sufficient proportion of those fellow shareholders to secure the passage of the resolution. Let us look at what company law says about each of these matters. It should be noted that these issues are not specific to removal resolutions. They arise generally, no matter what the issue is on which the shareholder wishes to take a collective decision, and thus they are relevant as well to the decision rights strategy discussed in the previous section.[50]

PROVISION OF INFORMATION TO SHAREHOLDERS

The information rights of individual shareholders as against the company are extremely limited. The Act confers no general entitlement upon individual shareholders to access the information held by the company, and art 109 of Table A explicitly provides that the individual shareholder has no right to inspect the company's records, unless the directors or the shareholders by ordinary resolution have conferred such a right. Even at a general meeting of the shareholders, an individual member has no right to expect an answer to a question which is not related to an item on the agenda for the meeting. However, most listed companies do in practice afford some opportunity for those present at annual general meetings to ask unrelated questions.

The information rights of shareholders under the Act are collective, and fall into two main categories. First, where a resolution is proposed for adoption by the shareholders, the proposers (usually, but not necessarily, the directors) will be obliged in law and practice to provide an accompanying circular to the shareholders which sets out the reasons in favour of the adoption of the resolution. That circular will generally reveal a certain amount of information about the company. If the information given is misleading, the resolution will be invalid.[51] However, this is of little comfort to the shareholder contemplating use of the s 303 powers, since he or she is the proposer in such a case and, thus, he or she has to provide, rather than receive, information. However, the shareholder may have gleaned relevant information from previous resolutions on other topics proposed by the board.

---

[50] Where the shareholders have a veto right, of course, they need not concern themselves with the summoning of the meeting (the board will take care of that) but the information and support problems remain.

[51] See *Tiessen v Henderson* [1899] 1 Ch 861, on both the obligation on the proposers to provide information and the legal consequences of failing to provide it fully.

The other source of collective information under the Act is the periodic reporting which the board is obliged to make to its shareholders, whether or not any resolution is proposed for adoption by the shareholders. It is the annual responsibility of the directors to prepare, send to the shareholders individually, lay before a meeting of the shareholders, and file with the Registrar of Companies a set of accounts consisting of a balance sheet and a profit and loss account.[52] In the case of groups of companies, there must normally also be provided a set of accounts relating to the group as a whole. The balance sheet provides a snapshot of the company's assets and liabilities at the end of the financial year; the profit and loss account a statement of the company's income and expenditure during the year. In addition, the directors must add a report from themselves to the shareholders, dealing with the development of the company's business during the financial year.

In addition to requiring the publication of accounts, the Act says something about the format in which they should be produced,[53] in order to enable investors to compare companies' accounts more easily. However, much of the learning about how different types of transaction should be reflected in the accounts is embodied, not in the law, but rather in accounting standards, produced largely by the accounting profession under the auspices of the Accounting Standards Board. The CLR endorsed, and proposed to extend, the principle of delegation to expert bodies of standard setting in this field, but also proposed that compliance with the accounting standards should be made mandatory for companies, which at present it formally is not.[54] Finally, the Act does something to provide assurance about the accuracy of the accounts by requiring that they be checked by an independent and professional person (the auditor).[55] Here all we need note is that it is a common misconception that the auditor is responsible for the accounts, whereas it is the directors who carry that responsibility. The auditor has a checking function. However, if the auditors fall down on that checking function, they are, like other professional people, potentially liable in the tort of negligence, and there is no doubt that the shareholder, contemplating

---

[52] CA 1985, ss 226, 233, and 238. Small companies may dispense themselves from the meeting requirement: see Chapter 10.

[53] Sch 4 and Sch 4A.

[54] *Final Report*, vol. I, para. 5.47. CA 1985, Sch 4, para 36A requires the accounts to disclose and justify material departures from the applicable accounting standards. For multinational companies the appropriate accounting standards will increasingly be set by international bodies.

[55] CA 1985, s 235. Small companies are exempt from this requirement. See Chapter 10.

exercising his or her internal governance rights, is owed a duty of care by the auditors.[56]

Thus, a significant part of the Companies Act is devoted to providing shareholders, collectively and on an annual basis, with historical, financial information which follows a standard format and which has been checked by an outsider. However, that information may not be provided very quickly. A public company has seven months and a private company 10 months from the end of the financial year before the accounts have to be filed with the Registrar (and thus are in the public domain). The CLR has recommended that these periods be reduced to, roughly, four months for public companies (and involve publication on a web site as well as filing with the Registrar) and seven months for private companies.[57] More important, the shareholder may wish to have forward-looking or 'soft' information as well as hard, historical financial data. Some large companies already provide this via the so-called operating and financial review (OFR), which the CLR has recommended should be made mandatory for large companies.[58] The OFR constitutes an expanded directors' report, which it would replace for the relevant class of company, and its function is to 'provide a review of the business, its performance, plans and prospects. It would include information on direction, performance, and dynamics (capital projects, risks, etc) and on all other aspects which the directors judge necessary to an understanding of the business, such as key relationships and environmental and social impacts.'[59]

The CLR recommendations are for the future. However, in the case of companies quoted on the main market of the London Stock Exchange ('LSE') the Listing Rules of the FSA already go beyond the Companies Act reporting requirements. Listed companies must produce six-monthly reports (sometimes called 'interim accounts') to supplement the Act's annual reports and do so within 90 days of the end of the relevant half-year.[60] In addition, a preliminary statement of the company's full annual results must be made available within 120 days of the year end.[61] As we have already noted in relation to disclosure of information about

---

[56] *Caparo Industries plc v Dickman* [1990] 2 AC 605, though that duty will not normally extend to acts done by the shareholder in any other capacity, such as investing in further purchases of the company's shares.

[57] *Final Report* vol. I, paras 4.39–4.42 and 8.80–8.110.

[58] Ibid., paras 3.33–3.45 and 8.29–8.71.

[59] Ibid. para. 3.34. See further Chapter 9, p. 279.

[60] Listing Rules, paras 12.46–12.59. The six-monthly reports are distributed through the Exchange's dissemination mechanisms. They are less detailed than the full annual reports.

[61] Ibid., para. 12.40.

directors' remuneration, the Listing Rules require more detail on certain topics than does the statute.[62] Finally, the Listing Rules contain a third trigger for disclosure (in addition to proposed resolutions and periodic financial reporting). This is the occurrence of major new developments which are likely to have, when made public, a substantial impact on the price of the company's shares.[63] Although these additional disclosure requirements may be motivated primarily by the FSA's desire to ensure accurate pricing by the market of the securities traded on it, individual shareholders can also take advantage of the disclosure for the purposes of exercising their internal governance rights.

CONVENING MEETINGS

Although the absence of an individual right to have access to the company's information may sometimes prevent a shareholder from knowing whether it is appropriate to attempt to invoke s 303, in one way or another a considerable amount of information about public companies is available, especially if they are also listed companies. In particular, the obligation upon a listed company under the 'major new developments' rule of the FSA to issue a 'profits warning' if the directors form the view that the company's profits at the yearly or half-yearly stage are likely to be significantly less than the market had expected, may galvanize the shareholders into action. But what action and how easy is it to take the action?

Clearly, if the shareholders are to adopt a removal resolution under s 303, a meeting of the shareholders must be convened; equally clearly, the board of the company are unlikely to summon one themselves for this purpose, if they can avoid it. The Act gives the shareholder two possibilities for laying a removal resolution before a meeting of the shareholders in the face of an uncooperative board. The first involves 'piggybacking' on the AGM which the directors are obliged to summon once in each calendar year and with a gap of not more than 15 months between AGMs.[64] The second consists of the shareholders requisitioning an extraordinary general meeting (an EGM being any meeting of the shareholders which is not an AGM).

The Act empowers shareholders holding 5 per cent or more of the

---

[62] Listening Rules, paras 12.41–12.44 and above, p. 126.

[63] Ibid., paras 9.1–9.9; and for companies whose securities are traded on a public market other than the main market of the LSE see the Traded Securities (Disclosure Regulations) 1994 (SI 1994 No 188).

[64] Section 366. If the board does not convene an AGM, the Secretary of State for Trade and Industry will do so, on the application of any member: s 367.

company's voting rights (or 100 or more shareholders each holding shares whose paid-up value is at least £100) to require the company to add to the AGM agenda any resolution which may properly be moved there, together with a circular of not more than 1,000 words in support of the resolution.[65] Unless the company determines otherwise, the requisitionists will have to pay the costs of the circulation, but these should not be large if the resolution goes out with the AGM papers which the company has to mail in any event to those entitled to attend. However, it is also required that the shareholders lodge the proposed resolution at the company's registered office at least six weeks before the AGM. Since, however, an AGM requires only three weeks' notice,[66] though the company might opt to give longer notice or otherwise indicate at an earlier stage when its AGM is likely to be held, this puts the shareholders in a bind. They may have to choose either to put in a requisition before the AGM papers are sent out and before the contents of the directors' report and the accounts are known[67] or wait until that information has been circulated, by which time it may be too late to requisition a resolution. Of course, if the provisions in the statute and the company's articles as to the length of notice for resolutions permit, the shareholders might circulate their fellow members directly, after the company sends out the AGM papers, rather than go through the company. However, this certainly is an expensive operation, in the case of a large company, and for a removal resolution seems to be foreclosed by the Act's requirement that 'special notice' (i.e. 28 days) be given of any resolution to remove a director.[68]

In short, the 'piggybacking' procedure, although at first sight helpful to shareholders, is pretty much a dead letter. However, the CLR has proposed a better integration of the rules on requisitioning resolutions and the timetable for the company's annual report, at least for public companies.[69] As we have seen, such companies would have to publish their annual report and accounts (including on a web site) within 120 days of the end of the financial year. There would then be a compulsory 'holding' period of 15 days before any notice of the AGM could be sent out, during which period the company would be obliged to accept members' resolutions for circulation at the *company's* expense, provided the thresholds of shareholder support set out above were met. This set of

---

[65] Sections 376–7. A resolution under s 303 would clearly count as a proper resolution.
[66] Section 369.
[67] The company need not file these documents with the Registrar until the point at which they are circulated to the members.
[68] Sections 303(2) and 379.   [69] *Final Report*, vol. I, paras 8.83 and 8.86.

rules would apply to all appropriate resolutions from members, including removal resolutions.

This reform may breathe some life into the procedure for adding resolutions to the AGM agenda. However, the triggering event for the shareholders' decision to take action may be something other than the contents of the AGM papers. As we have seen, for listed companies a preliminary announcement of the company's results appears long before the AGM. Again, the last straw for the shareholders may be something in a listed company's half-yearly report or in a 'major new developments' statement. In other words, waiting for the AGM may seem an unattractive option for the shareholders who do not want to sit idly by while the company continues its decline. Section 368 offers a solution by permitting shareholders having 10 per cent of the voting rights to requisition an extraordinary meeting of the shareholders to consider a resolution they wish to put before it, which may include a removal resolution. Thus, requisitioning a meeting requires a higher level of shareholder support than adding a resolution to the AGM, but the costs of holding the meeting fall on the company. The 10 per cent threshold may seem high, but, in the case of a removal resolution, shareholders who cannot get 10 per cent support for the meeting are unlikely to get 50 per cent support for the resolution.[70]

Our interest in shareholders' powers to require resolutions to be put before meetings of shareholders arose out of our discussion of removal resolutions, though we have noted that these provisions are by no means confined to removal resolutions. The resolution might contain, instead, an instruction as to how the directors should conduct the affairs of the company. In terms of the categorization of legal strategies set out in Figure 1, however, such a resolution would not constitute an example of the appointments right strategy, but of the decision rights strategy discussed earlier in this chapter. In fact, it would be an example of the stronger form of the decision rights strategy: the shareholders by their resolution initiate a corporate decision. It could thus be said that the statutory provisions on resolutions facilitate, even if they do not require, the deployment of the decision rights strategy.

However, there is a difficulty here. How is a shareholder instruction to the directors about how they should exercise their managerial powers consistent with the constitutional view of the company which, as we saw in the first section of this chapter, divides the company's powers up

---

[70] Though, of course, these are percentages of different things: 10 per cent of the total voting rights; 50 per cent of the votes represented at the meeting.

between the board and the shareholders? How can the shareholders by resolution give a binding instruction to the board on how the latter should exercise their powers, if the articles have taken those powers away from the shareholders?[71] We have seen that s 303 states that removal resolutions override anything in the articles, but that statutory rule is not applied generally to resolutions of the shareholders.

At one level, the issue is simply one of the construction of the articles of any particular company. Where has *that* set of articles placed the boundaries of the exclusive powers of the board? However, in governance terms the issue is an important one and it has generated much controversy among commentators, because earlier versions of Table A were unclear on the point. However, art 70 of the current version of Table A is clear: the general grant of management powers to the board can be overridden only by a special resolution of the shareholders, that is, one requiring a three-quarters majority vote of the shareholders, the same resolution as is needed for the shareholders to change the articles.[72] Thus, shareholders may take the initiative on any matter of corporate policy, but, in relation to matters within the exclusive powers of the board, only if there is shareholder support equivalent to that needed to change the constitutional division of powers.

COLLECTIVE ACTION PROBLEMS

On the face of it, the statutory provisions about removing directors and summoning an EGM to do so look rather strong. It seems to be mainly on the basis of these sections that Bob Monks, vice chairman of Hermes Lens asset managers, has characterized the UK as 'easily the world leader' in the accountability of management to investors.[73] However, it may still be that shareholders prefer not to use the mechanisms for internal governance provided by company law and instead to sell their shares if they are dissatisfied with the performance of the board, at least where there is an available market in the company's securities. Why

---

[71] Shareholders might try to avoid the problem by adopting a 'precatory' resolution, one merely requesting the board to consider a particular course of action—though such resolutions are open to the response by the board that it has considered the option and rejected it!

[72] For the definition of a special and an extraordinary resolution see s 378. A special resolution also requires 21 days' notice to the shareholders, and in this respect differs from an extraordinary resolution to which the normal notice periods apply but which does require a three-quarters majority. It is necessary to distinguish a special resolution from an ordinary resolution, such as a removal resolution, requiring special (i.e. 28 days') notice: s 379. For the debate about earlier versions of Table A, see *Gower*, 6th edn, 1997, pp. 183–7.

[73] *Financial Times*, 17 February 2000, p. 18.

should this be? The answer is to be found, once again, in the extent to which the shareholdings in a particular company are concentrated. We have already stipulated that, for the purposes of this chapter, the companies we are considering do not have one or a small number of shareholders acting in concert who have a sufficient block of shares to control the company. So we are assuming there is no block-holder with, say, 50 per cent or even 30 per cent of the shares carrying voting rights in the company. But even where that is not the case, the pattern of shareholding may vary in the extent to which it is dispersed.

Let us assume, first, a pattern of highly dispersed shareholdings, for example no single shareholder has more than 1 per cent of the voting shares in the company and many have very much smaller shareholdings than that. So, one has a large body of shareholders, perhaps tens of thousands, each with very small holdings. The incentives in such a situation for any one shareholder to seek to put forward a removal resolution against, let us further assume, a determined incumbent board, are weak. That shareholder will have to spend many resources contacting fellow shareholders and persuading them to his or her view of the company, before there is any question of requisitioning an EGM on the basis of 10 per cent support or passing a removal resolution. Those are costs which are certain to be incurred if the shareholder goes down the removal route. The countervailing benefits may be none, as where the activist shareholder fails to secure enough support to pass the resolution or where the new directors prove to be as ineffective as the previous ones. Or they may be very limited: the incumbent board is replaced, the new board does much better and the company's share price and dividend levels improve, but our activist shareholder will benefit only to the extent of 1 per cent of those improvements. Even worse, other shareholders have an incentive not to join in with the activist. If they do, they share the costs but for the same limited benefits. If they do not, they obtain their share of the benefits without incurring any costs. So, they have an incentive to 'free-ride'.[74]

The above situation may be said to demonstrate what is normally called the 'collective action' problems of shareholders, that is, the difficulties that a large body of people face in adopting and sticking to a common position, in the absence of a strong incentive for one of their number to take an organizing role or, alternatively, in the absence of reliable knowledge as to how one's fellow shareholders will act in the future. During

---

[74] It is true that, by not joining in, they reduce the chances of the activists succeeding, but any individual shareholder will calculate that the increased chances of benefiting do not outweigh the certain costs of joining the activists.

the 1950s the shareholding structure of many large British companies seems to have been of this highly dispersed kind and shareholders' use of the internal governance system was at its lowest. The incentives on shareholders in such companies were always to take what the Americans graphically call the 'Wall Street walk', that is, to sell the shares, if dissatisfied with the board's performance, and invest elsewhere.

However, since then a limited re-concentration of shareholdings has occurred, not a re-concentration into the hands of personal shareholders but into the hands of what is collectively referred to as the 'institutional shareholders': unit trusts (and similar forms of collective saving scheme), pension funds, and insurance companies. It is clear that the biggest driver behind this growth in institutional shareholding has been the desire of reasonably well-off people to make financial provisions for their retirement (beyond the state provision), and to do so in a way which spread their risks across many types of share (not just one or two companies) and which left the choice of the range of companies to expert fund managers. Indeed, fund management has become an international business, with British investors putting some of their money into shares elsewhere in Europe, in the United States, and Asia; equally, investors elsewhere in the world put some of their money into the shares of UK companies.

All this may not be very apparent to the individuals in the UK who simply wish to provide themselves with an income when they cease to work. For example, all they may have done is join an occupational pension scheme to which they and their employer make a contribution or buy an

Table 1 Ownership of Listed UK Equities

Beneficial owner	1963	1969	1975	1981	1989	1993	1997
Individuals	54	47.4	37.5	28.2	20.6	17.7	16.5
Insurance companies	10	12.2	15.9	20.5	18.6	20	23.5
Pension funds	6.4	9	16.8	26.7	30.6	31.3	22.1
Collective investment schemes	1.3	2.9	4.1	3.6	7.5	9.1	8.6
Banks	1.3	1.7	0.7	0.3	0.7	0.6	0.1
Others*	27	26.8	25	20.7	22	21.3	29.2

* In recent years this consists mainly of the category 'Rest of World' (in 1997: 24%). Unfortunately, this category is not broken down further.

Source: Office for National Statistics, *Share Ownership: A Report on the Ownership of Shares at 31 December 1997* (London: The Stationery Office, 1999), p. 8. Reproduced with permission.

insurance policy or personal pension plan which pays out many years in the future. However, as Table 1 demonstrates, the effect of channelling savings into the securities markets in this way over a number of decades has been to produce a remarkable concentration of shareholdings in the market as a whole in the hands of institutional shareholders. The proportion of shares in companies listed on the LSE which is held by individuals fell to less than one-third of its 1963 level by 1997, while that of pension funds and insurance companies together increased nearly three-fold in the same period. If anything, the table underestimates the position of institutional shareholders because much of the 'others' category represents overseas institutions: the CLR stated that 'more than 80% of quoted shares in British companies are controlled by institutional investors'.[75]

Concentration at the level of the market does not mean that at the level of individual companies a single institutional shareholder can be found holding a majority of the company's shares. However, it is often the case that, except in the largest quoted companies, a coalition of five or six institutional shareholders or of fund managers acting on their behalf, if they could bring themselves to act together, might well control about a quarter of the voting rights.[76] They would therefore easily be able to summon an EGM under the statutory provisions discussed above, and would stand a good chance of being able to get through a removal resolution (or some other resolution which they thought appropriate). On the other side, a large shareholder may find it difficult to exit the company without driving the share price down to unacceptable levels. In fact, it is clear that there is considerably more institutional shareholder activism in relation to the internal governance of companies today than, say, a quarter of a century ago.

Two points need to made about this activism, however. First, to the dismay of the journalistic press, a great deal of the exercise by shareholders of their statutory powers takes place behind closed doors and so is not visible to the outside observer. Shareholders in a position to make a credible threat that they will remove one or more directors are likely to raise the issue first of all with the existing board in a private meeting. If the shareholders can secure a change of policy or a re-constitution of the board through agreement in private with the incumbent board, that has the major advantage that they achieve their objectives without a public

---

[75] See n. 69 at para. 6.22.

[76] Some illuminating factual data on the UK situation is to be found in G. P. Stapledon, *Institutional Shareholders and Corporate Governance* (Oxford: Clarendon Press, 1996), Parts I and II.

row which is likely, in one way or another, to cause damage to the company.

Second, and more important, it is likely, nevertheless, that the level of usage by institutional shareholders of their statutory powers is suboptimal because of competition among institutional shareholders or fund managers and because of conflicts of interest within them.[77] Competition among institutional shareholders and their managers means that there is always a temptation for any one shareholder to seek to free-ride on the efforts of the others. Conflicts of interest can occur where the fund manager is part of a financial conglomerate which carries on a variety of financial businesses in addition to fund management, for example providing corporate finance services to companies. The corporate finance arm of a large investment bank may not be best pleased if the fund management arm of the bank is attempting to unseat a board of directors with whom the corporate finance people are doing lucrative business. The CLR was impressed with the evidence it acquired about potential conflicts of interest, but could think of no more effective a solution than to require quoted companies to disclose in their annual reports the identity of their major suppliers of financial services, so that potential conflicts of interest would be revealed.[78] It also proposed that institutional shareholders should disclose to their clients on demand (and possibly to the public) their voting record, which might also discourage them from caving into conflicts of interest. Furthermore, the Myners Report has suggested that institutional shareholders should be placed under a duty to give proper consideration to the exercise of their voting rights.[79] The latter proposal would also do something to address a problem, which is not directly a problem of company law, but is crucial for the governance of companies, namely, the accountability of institutional investors to those who give their money to them for investment.[80]

---

[77] Analyses of this issue can be found in Stapledon, n. 76 above, Parts II and IV and in B. Black and J. Coffee, 'Hail Britannia? Institutional Investor Behavior under Limited Regulation' (1994) 92 *Michigan LR* 1997.

[78] *Final Report*, vol. I, paras 6.22–6.40.

[79] P. Myners, *Institutional Investment in the United Kingdom* (London: HM Treasury, 2001).

[80] There is a great deal of statutory and common law on the accountability of pension fund trustees to the beneficiaries of the pension fund: see R. Nobles, *Pensions, Employment, and the Law* (Oxford: Clarendon Press, 1993). But, as the Equitable Life affair demonstrated, the law on the equivalent relationship between insurance companies and policy-holders is much less developed and is founded mainly in contract. For reform proposals, see FSA, *Governance of With-Profits Funds and the Future Role of the Appointed Actuary* (London, 2002).

Even if the competition and conflicts problems of institutional shareholders could be overcome, it by no means follows that they would choose to exercise their governance powers in all situations where they were in fact able to do so. They might regard it as more attractive, at least in some cases, to sell their shares and invest the money elsewhere. As we shall see in the next section, the law does promote 'affiliation' strategies which facilitate a shareholder's leaving the company. So, one might say that the removal right and the affiliation right give the shareholder, whether institutional or otherwise, a choice between 'voice' and 'exit'. The conflicts of interest which may make the levels of institutional intervention into companies to remove failing management less than optimal by the same token may increase the willingness of institutional shareholders and fund managers to accept take-over bids. Some influential voices have urged institutional shareholders to make more use of voice and less of exit.[81] However, even if free of conflicts of interest, fund managers might well conclude that in some cases the certainties of sale would promote the interests of their clients more effectively than the uncertainties of battle with incumbent management.[82]

AFFILIATION RIGHTS

Affiliation rights constitute a means of empowering shareholders as against the board by enabling them to exit the company by selling their shares and thus substituting new members in their place. Here, the law revolves around that core characteristic of company law which we identified in Chapter 1 as the free transferability of shares.[83] We noted that, from the company's point of view, free transferability is provided by the doctrine of separate corporate personality: the shares in the company can be transferred without any impact on the ownership of the business assets, which remains vested in the company. By contrast, we saw that, from the shareholders' point of view, free transferability is legally much less secure. Company law embodies a presumption that shares may be transferred from one investor to another without another's consent, but the articles of a company may alter that position, for example by requiring board consent to transfers or by giving the board or the other shareholders a right to buy the shares at a price which is fixed or can be

---

[81] See especially J. Charkham, *Corporate Governance and the Market for Companies: Aspects of the Shareholders' Role*, Bank of England Discussion Paper, No 44, 1989.

[82] See Stapledon, above, n. 76, ch. 10.

[83] See p. 21.

ascertained (a 'pre-emption' right). Such provisions are common in small companies,[84] but for companies whose securities are traded on a public market, the rules of the market will insist that the shares be freely tradable.[85] In this instance, capital markets law makes up for a deficiency in company law.

However, none of this guarantees that a purchaser will be available to buy the shares of a dissatisfied shareholder at an attractive price. On the one hand, this is hardly surprising: the law cannot act as a market-maker. On the other hand, unless such purchasers are available, the exit right as such is not much protection for the dissatisfied shareholder. A mere right of exit is of value only to the highly prescient shareholder, one who can predict the unlawful or unwise conduct of the board before it occurs and, just as important, before the rest of the market realizes what is about to happen. In the more likely situation where the shareholder detects the objectionable conduct only after it has happened and has become apparent to the market, the price of the share will now reflect the harm which has been done to the company and, moreover, the risk that the harmful conduct will continue. In this circumstance, selling the shares may provide the former shareholder with some psychological relief, but not with effective protection against the loss which he or she has suffered.

What, then, can the law do to facilitate the availability of not just a purchaser for the shares (that is the function of a liquid stock market) but a purchaser who will offer a price above the market price which reflects the depredations of the incumbent board? The standard answer to this question is that the law should facilitate take-over bids, that is, offers by an investor, usually another company, made to the shareholders of a company (the target) to acquire all the shares of the target at a price above the prevailing market price. The consideration offered may be cash or may be shares in the offeror company (or a mixture of the two). From the point of view of shareholders, not just in target companies but more generally, the take-over offer has major advantages. Under a legal regime which facilitates take-overs, the threat of the take-over will be a constant pressure on the boards of all companies quoted on public markets to keep the interests of the shareholders centre-stage. Indeed, the threat of the take-over is one of the main drivers behind the currently fashionable concern for 'share-

---

[84] See Chapter 10.
[85] In the case of listed companies free transferability is a requirement of EU law. See Council Directive 2001/34/EC, Art 46. This rule can cause problems for 'golden shares' retained by governments after privatizations.

holder value'.[86] Yet, from the shareholders' point of view, the take-over threat requires no input of resources, unlike both the legal strategies discussed earlier in this chapter. On the other hand, if the board does not respond appropriately to this pressure and the shareholders' interests are neglected, the advent of the take-over will enable the shareholders to exit the company at a premium to the (admittedly depressed) market price.

Why should the take-over bidder be prepared to pay a higher price for the shares of the target company than other investors in the market? The answer is that, once the bidder has obtained control, it will be able to replace the board of the target (using the ss 303 and 368 powers discussed above) and install a new board which is more responsive to the shareholder interests. The bidder will be willing to share part of the expected benefits of this course of action with the existing shareholders of the target, in exchange for the opportunity to implement its plan.[87] The precise split between the bidder and the existing shareholders of the target will depend on a number of factors, in particular upon whether a competing bidder for the target company emerges.

Since the transaction in a take-over occurs between the offeror and the target shareholders, it may seem that the law has to do nothing more than make available the normal rules of contract law in order to facilitate the take-over process. It is in fact quite clear that the take-over cannot succeed if a sufficient proportion of the target shareholders are not prepared to accept the offer, so that they have at a minimum a veto right over the transaction. However, it is also possible for the incumbent board to prevent or discourage an offer being put to the shareholders, or being persisted with, even if the shareholders might well accept it. Indeed, the board has a strong incentive to do so, since they are likely to lose their positions if the offer is successful. The directors' conflict between their personal interests and their duty to promote the interests of the shareholders may reveal itself in a number of ways, for example by seeking to issue new shares to shareholders who will support the incumbent board or by putting prized assets of the company out of the reach of the bidder, even if it does achieve control.[88]

---

[86] Davies, 'Shareholder Value, Company Law and Securities Markets Law' in E. Wymeersch (ed.), *Company Law and Financial Markets* (Oxford: OUP, 2002).

[87] Take-overs may also be motivated by the prospect of economies of scale or scope, a reason which is not dependent upon any shortcomings on the part of the board of the target. However, this motivation does provide an additional argument in favour of facilitating take-overs.

[88] For an example of the former see *Hogg v Cramphorn* [1967] Ch 254 and of the latter L. Gower, 'Corporate Control: The Battle for the Berkeley' (1955) 68 *Harvard LR* 1176.

The obvious legal response to this problem is to side-line the board of the company in the decision-making over the take-over bid. The transaction is made one wholly between the bidder and the shareholders of the target. In terms of the decision rights strategy, used earlier in the chapter, the decision is allocated compulsorily and entirely to the shareholders of the target. This is in fact the strategy adopted in the UK in the City Code on Take-overs and Mergers, drawn up and enforced under the auspices of the City Panel on Take-overs and Mergers. The City Panel is an increasingly anomalous part of the regulatory structure in the UK for companies and securities markets. Sir John Donaldson MR memorably described it as follows: 'Perched on the 20th floor of the Stock Exchange building in the City of London, both literally and metaphorically it oversees and regulates a very important part of the United Kingdom financial market. Yet it performs this function without visible means of legal support.'[89] In truth, the Panel was put together by a group of financial institutions, led by the Bank of England, in the late 1960s, in order to ward off the threat of legislation to regulate take-overs, and it is the continuing nature of that threat which largely explains why its decisions are accepted by the parties to take-overs despite the lack of 'visible means of legal support'.[90]

From the beginning the Panel, through the Code, has endorsed the principle of side-lining incumbent management in take-over bids. That policy is now enshrined in General Principle 7 of the City Code,[91] which prohibits 'any action to be taken by the board of the offeree company in relation of the affairs of the offeree company, without the approval of the shareholders in general meeting, which could effectively result in any bona fide offer being frustrated or in the shareholders being denied an opportunity to decide on its merits'. Thus, management cannot act unilaterally to defeat a bidder. The rule does not prohibit corporate action which has a frustrating effect on the bid but it does require that such action be approved by the shareholders at a general meeting and, crucially, that that approval be given in the face of the bid. Thus, we can see that the City Code facilitates an exit right for the shareholders at an

---

[89] *R v Panel on Take-overs and Mergers, ex parte Datafin Ltd* [1987] QB 815, CA. This decision contributes to the maintenance of this situation by subjecting the Panel's decisions to only the lightest form of judicial review.

[90] Though now those who need the authorization of the FSA to carry on investment business risk the loss of that authorization if they flout the Panel's decisions, a potentially important legal sanction against investment banks which are the major advisers (and fee earners) in bids. See Financial Services and Markets Act 2000, s 143.

[91] 6th edn, 2000, as amended.

attractive price, but does so mainly by removing the constraints that target management might place on the offeror's entry rights.

Two arguments might be mounted against the blunt rule embodied in General Principle 7 of the City Code. The first is that, while side-lining management deals effectively with the board's conflicts of interest, it also leaves the dispersed shareholders without any help from the board in dealing with the offeror, who may thus be able to exploit the collective action problems which the shareholders have as against the offeror as much as they have against the board of their company. Thus, the offeror may be able to structure the offer in such a way as to pressurize the target shareholders into accepting it, even though they think it is sub-optimal. If the board could play a role in take-overs, it could exclude such opportunistic offers. If the board is side-lined by the take-over rules, however, this cannot occur, and so the rules must go on and address directly the agency problems of the target shareholders as against the offer, principally by insisting upon a rule of equal treatment of shareholders in take-overs.[92]

The second argument, or rather group of arguments, raises objections of a more fundamental kind to take-overs. One form of this objection is that take-overs are driven, not by the gains to be made by addressing the shareholders' agency costs, but by the possibilities take-overs open up for offerors to transfer wealth from stakeholders such as employees or creditors. Another form of objection denies the proposition that financial markets price companies' securities accurately. If this is so, transactions based on market prices are not necessarily efficient. Finally, it could be argued that take-overs constitute a demonstration, not of the agency problems of the target, but of the agency problems of the bidder. Bidders embark on take-overs which are not wealth maximizing from the point of view of the *bidder's* shareholders because they fit the interests of the bidder's management, for example by promoting the aggrandizement of the latter.

We cannot explore the arguments for and against take-overs in this book.[93] What should be pointed out, however, is that the affiliation rights strategy, embodied in General Principle 7 of the City Code, is in consequence of the debate about the desirability of encouraging take-overs, a

[92] There is not space to consider the nature of these problems and the possible regulatory responses, but see P. Davies and K. Hopt, 'Control Transactions' in R. Kraakman et al. (eds), above, n. 15.

[93] For a dispassionate analysis which is sceptical about the second group of objections to take-overs, see R. Romano, 'A Guide to Takeovers: Theory, Evidence and Regulation' in K. Hopt and E. Wymeersch (eds), *European Takeovers: Law and Practice* (London: Butterworths, 1992).

highly contested rule. Most take-over codes in Europe have adopted it, but the new German code does not,[94] and this was one of the main points of disagreement which led to the failure of the EC to adopt a directive on take-overs in 2001.

CONCLUSION

In this chapter we have looked at three legal strategies for empowering shareholders in companies where there is no controlling shareholder: the decision rights strategy, the appointment rights strategy, and the affiliation rights strategy. Both the first and the third strategy can be used only sparingly. This is true of the decision rights strategy, which turns on involving the shareholders as a body in corporate decision-making, because it is a cure which, if used in relation to a wide range of managerial decisions, may turn out to be worse that the disease. Shifting decision-making into the hands of the shareholders risks making the corporate decision-making process inefficient, even if it protects the shareholders against self-interested behaviour on the part of the board. The third strategy can be used only sparingly as well, but for a very different reason. As noted, an exit right for the shareholders is not as such much protection. They need to be able to sell at an attractive price. As between the board and the shareholders as a class, the law can hardly impose an obligation upon the directors of public companies to buy at a fair price the shares of all the shareholders who have suffered from managerial shirking or self-seeking, or at least it cannot do so without the risk of severely curtailing the supply of businesspeople willing to act as directors of such companies.[95] This strategy emerges as a feasible one only in relation to the facilitation of take-over offers.

By contrast, the second strategy—appointment rights—can be applied generally by company law. Its impact may be lessened, however, by the inability of highly dispersed shareholding bodies to make much use of it. The partial re-concentration of shareholdings into the hands of institutional shareholders in the UK in recent decades may have lessened, but it has not removed, this problem. This is an area where the context very

---

[94] WpÜG, art 33 which crucially permits shareholders to authorize the board to take frustrating action by resolution adopted before the emergence of the offer, and permits the supervisory board to give permission for frustrating action in the face of the bid.

[95] By contrast, within small companies and as between controlling and non-controlling shareholders, an obligation on the former to buy the shares of the latter at a fair price may be a feasible remedy. See Chapter 8.

much affects the practical impact of the legal rule. Enough has been said to demonstrate, it is hoped, that our enquiry into the legal strategies for controlling principal/agent problems as between board and shareholders as a class cannot stop at the strategies for empowering shareholders. We must look, as well, at strategies for constraining directors, and this we do in the next chapter.

6

Centralized Management II
Constraining the Board

THE CONSTRAINTS STRATEGY: INTRODUCTION

In this chapter we continue our analysis of the legal strategies available for the reduction of agency costs as between shareholders and the board where there is no controlling shareholder and so de facto control lies with the board. In the previous chapter we examined three legal strategies which might be used by the law in this situation to strengthen the hand of the shareholders as a group against the board. These were the decision rights, the appointment rights, and the affiliation rights strategies. See Figure 1 on p. 120. However, we also saw that only the second of these could be deployed other than in rather special situations, and even the appointment rights strategy is highly dependent upon the ability of shareholders to overcome their collective action problems. Consequently, it is not surprising that company law has deployed strategies aimed at affecting directly the actions of management, and has not confined itself to strategies which facilitate the imposition of constraints by the shareholders.

In this chapter and the next we analyse the strategies that structure the decisions of agents, that is, the right-hand side of Figure 1 on p. 120. There are two sets of strategies here, which we have termed the 'constraining' strategy and the 'incentive' strategy. We intend to devote this chapter to the constraining strategy, which involves either specifying rules for decision-making by the board or laying down standards by which board decisions can be reviewed. Rules and standards constitute, of course, the most obvious use of the law to address the agency problems of shareholders. Indeed, most company law courses, rightly, assign a substantial proportion of the curriculum to the analysis of the duties imposed in this way on directors, which is why we shall spend this chapter analysing this strategy.

At present, the fundamental propositions relating to directors' duties are to be found in the common law, in cases going back to the middle of the nineteenth century, and in some eyes, at least, the examination of these authorities constitutes a welcome break from, and even a higher form of scholarly activity than, the pursuit of the meaning of sometimes rebarbative statutory provisions. However, such attitudes are short-sighted, at least in an extreme form. At a purely positive level, both the Law Commissions and the Company Law Review[1] have recommended that there should be a statutory statement of the main duties imposed upon directors by company law, in the interests of clarity and the better understanding by directors of what is required of them. This statement would replace the common law, though, since it would be phrased at a fairly high level of generality, there would still be scope for debate about the application of its principles. Moreover, in so far as the statement adopted the prior common law, reference to the pre-statement cases would be useful in some instances. The CLR *Final Report* helpfully con-tains a trial draft of the 'General Principles by which Directors are Bound' and a commentary upon it,[2] and that will be referred to at various points in this chapter. Thus, the law on directors' duties may become less case law based than it currently is.[3]

Even more questionable, however, is the proposition which is some-times implicit in the importance attached to the study of the law on directors' duties, namely, that it is the most effective of the legal strat-egies for dealing with shareholders' agency problems. To deduce this from the fact that the law on directors' duties generates a certain level of litigation would be to adopt too court-centred a view of the impact of law. The relative importance of the different legal strategies discussed in this chapter and the previous one is in fact a question for empirical investigation, conclusive findings from which do not exist at the moment. However, we should at least keep our minds open to the possi-bility that a quiet word behind closed doors with incumbent manage-ment by shareholders who have the power to remove that management is likely to be more effective in changing behaviour than the uncertainties of litigation.

It is conventional to divide the rules and standards contained in the

---

[1] Law Commission and Scottish Law Commission, *Company Directors: Regulating Con-flicts of Interest and Formulating a Statement of Duties*, Cm. 4436, 1999; CLR, *Final Report*, vol. I, paras 3.5–3.27 and Annex C.

[2] Ibid., Annex C.

[3] Even at present statutory law plays an important part, as we shall see below, in shaping the rules that govern directors' conflicts of interest.

constraints strategy into two broad groups. The first imposes on directors a duty of competence; the second and larger group a duty of loyalty. It can be remarked at the outset that the common law starting points for these sets of duties seem to embody a model of the director as a gentlemanly amateur: a low level of competence was required, but a high level of loyalty, at least in the avoidance of conflicts of interest. Under developments in society and in the law generally, both these starting points have been left behind to some degree.

Both sets of duties are owed to 'the company'. As we noted in Chapter 2, this is a meaningless statement unless we go on to specify which groups of persons constitute the company. For the purposes of this chapter we shall adopt the traditional view that the company is the shareholders, both present and future. We shall examine in Chapter 9 the arguments for and against a broader specification of the company. For the moment, the importance of the fact that the duty is owed to the company (i.e. the shareholders collectively) is the negative consequence that the duties are not owed to shareholders individually.[4] Therefore, the shareholders as a whole should normally decide by ordinary resolution whether to enforce the duties of the directors.[5]

The duties considered in this chapter are owed by directors. This obviously includes those regularly appointed to the board, but the common law duties probably attach also to those who act as directors in fact, whether regularly appointed to that position or not; and some of the duties extend downwards to senior but non-board managers. In modern times, the legislature has explicitly brought within the legislation applying to directors a further group of persons. It has identified the 'shadow' director, that is, a person in accordance with whose instructions or directions the directors of the company are accustomed to act.[6] Such a person is subjected to a number of the provisions of the Act, notably the more modern provisions of Part X, discussed at pp. 176–183 below, though only where the shadow director is a natural person and not another company. The CLR has proposed that its statutory statement of duties should apply to both de facto and shadow directors.[7] Some older statutory provi-

---

[4] This means that directors, simply because they are directors, do not owe duties to the shareholders individually. In special circumstances, however, the directors may come under duties owed to individual shareholders: *Peskin v Anderson* [2001] 1 BCLC 372, CA.

[5] See the section on forgiveness and enforcement later in this chapter (pp. 191–195).

[6] CA 1985, s 741(1). Note that the majority of the board must be accustomed so to act, not just an individual director. On the distinction between de facto and shadow directors, see *Re Hydrodam (Corby) Ltd* [1994] 2 BCLC 180.

[7] CLR, *Completing the Structure*, November 2000, paras 4.6–4.7.

sions apply to 'officers' of the company, a word whose exact scope is unclear, but it certainly includes directors.[8]

Following our division in Figure 1 on p. 120 we shall look first at the standards and then at the rules which constrain agents' behaviour in company law. There are two principal standards which we need to analyse, one relating to competence and the other to loyalty.

THE DUTY OF CARE

OBJECTIVE VERSUS SUBJECTIVE STANDARDS OF CARE

The common law of tort imposes on directors a duty to take care in the exercise of their functions as directors. As with the other duties considered in this chapter, this formulation is wide enough to catch what the directors do individually in the exercise of their duties, as well as what they do as a board. Failure to comply with this duty renders the director liable to compensate the company in damages for the loss which it has suffered in consequence. This may seem very familiar, since the law of negligence imposes such duties across an extremely wide range of activities which go on in society, both within and outside the business world. However, until at least recently, the accepted view was that the duty imposed upon directors displayed the unusual characteristic that only a very low standard of care was required. Unlike professional groups involved in the company's affairs, such as accountants, who are subject to an objective standard of care (the reasonable person test), directors were required by the law of tort to comply only with a subjective standard. Directors were required to display in relation to the conduct of the affairs of the company only such competence as they themselves were capable of. Thus, an innately incompetent director was not in breach of duty if he did his (limited) best. Shareholders were expected to protect their interests through the effective exercise of their *ex ante* appointment rights, screening out the incompetent, rather than by suing the incompetent director *ex post*. Whether the common law definition of the standard of care was always wholly subjective can be debated.[9] However that may be, some of the old cases seem to show directors being held not negligent in remarkable circumstances.

---

[8] CA 1985, s 744.

[9] The classic decision is *Re City Equitable Fire Insurance Co Ltd* [1925] Ch 407. This decision of Romer J can be read as not adopting a wholly subjective view in relation to care and diligence (as opposed to skill).

One such case might be thought to be *Re Cardiff Savings Bank*,[10] where the Marquis of Bute was held not to have fallen below the required standard of care even though he had attended only one board meeting of the company in his whole life.[11] But, perhaps the result was not so remarkable. The bank had appointed the Marquis president of the bank when he was a mere six months old. This hardly suggests that the bank expected sage business advice from its new, and indeed leading, board member, but rather wanted him merely as a figurehead. It was the bank, therefore, which by subsequently suing the Marquis sought to depart from the expectations embodied in the appointment. The court may have thought that the bank could hardly complain if one appointed *infans* failed to speak.

Although figurehead directors are not unknown today in British companies, they are much less common. As we have noted several times already, a proportion of the members of the boards of large companies are likely to be full-time managers of the company as well, who have spent their careers working their way up the managerial hierarchy of that or other companies until they reach board level.[12] This gives rise to the somewhat neglected possibility of the company suing incompetent directors on the basis of the implied duty of care in their service contracts, but that is a matter of employment rather than of company law. Nevertheless, the change over time in the type of person appointed to the board has also led to a shift of view within company law about the appropriate standard of care for directors. We noted in Chapter 4 that s 214 of the Insolvency Act 1986 imposes upon directors an objective standard of care, albeit one limited by the scope of the functions entrusted to the director in the particular company,[13] in favour of creditors of the company, when a company nears insolvent liquidation. The actual abilities of a particular director may raise the required standard above that level, but

---

[10] [1892] 2 Ch 100.

[11] Even if the Marquis had been held to be negligent, the claimants would have faced formidable causation problems: the bank had collapsed, but could it be shown that the Marquis's diligent attendance would have prevented this event? If the modern trend towards an objective standard of care continues (see below), causation issues will become more pressing. See *Cohen v Selby* [2001] 1 BCLC 176, CA.

[12] In the discussion of the trusteeship strategy in the next chapter we shall examine the problems that might be thought to arise from having too many executive directors on the board.

[13] IA 1986, s 214(4): 'a reasonably diligent person having . . . the general knowledge, skill and experience that may reasonably be expected of a person carrying out the same functions as are carried out by the director in relation to the company'. Functions include those entrusted to the director, whether he carries them out or not (s 214(5)).

the objective standard remains the minimum even if a particular director cannot reach it. A small group of authorities take the view that this statutory formulation now constitutes the common law standard required of directors generally in the performance of their functions, not just during the period preceding insolvency. In any event, both the Law Commissions[14] and the CLR[15] have recommended that this ought to be the law. This change perhaps constitutes a recognition that, at least in large companies, shareholders' selection rights over directors are limited and their removal rights fall to be exercised only after the damage has been done.[16]

JUDICIAL RESTRAINT AND THE OBJECTIVE STANDARD

Although a move to an objective standard of care is in line with developments generally in the law of negligence, it is in functional terms a potentially significant change for company law. There is a danger that *ex post* review by courts of directors' decisions on negligence grounds will, unless carefully handled, slow down the process of decision-making on the part of boards and lead them in the direction of excessive risk avoidance. It is much easier to mount a legal challenge to board decisions to take up business opportunities, which turn out badly, than to decisions to turn down opportunities, except perhaps in those rare cases where the opportunity was virtually riskless. The standard method adopted to avoid this danger in those jurisdictions which use objective standards of care is to limit court review to the procedural aspects of the board's decision-making process, an approach formalized in many US states in the 'business judgement rule'. Under this approach, the court's review of the substantive merits of the decision is limited to the need to show that there was a rational relationship between the decision and the best interests of the company. In order to escape liability the directors do not have to show that the decision taken was the best way of advancing the company's interests, still less that the court itself would have taken the same decision.[17] The primary focus of the law's scrutiny is on whether the board

---

[14] Above, n. 1, Part 5.

[15] Above, n. 1, Annex C at pp. 346 (Principle 4) and 353.

[16] See Chapter 5, pp. 127–129. It is significant that, in relation to partnerships, where the selection rights of partners are often more effective, the Law Commissions have proposed that the objective standard of care should be formulated by reference to skill and care which the partner either actually has or purports to have, not that of the reasonable person: *Partnership Law—A Joint Consultation Paper* (Law Commission No 159; Scottish Law Commission No 111, 2000), pp. 185–92.

[17] American Law Institute (hereafter 'ALI'), *Principles of Corporate Governance*, 1994, para. 4.01.

took reasonable steps to inform itself before it took the decision in question and not on whether the substantive decision taken was reasonable.

DELEGATION AND THE DUTY OF CARE

This emphasis on procedural reasonableness can be applied not only to the taking of business decisions but also to their subsequent implementation. This fits in well with the modern view from the business school that the role of the boards of large companies is to set and monitor the execution of the company's business strategy, not to take every business decision needed to implement that strategy. As is obvious, in any large company considerable areas of management responsibility will have to be delegated to sub-board managers. However, the postulate that the board should monitor the execution of business strategy immediately raises the question of what the board's responsibility is for areas of management which have been delegated. The Report of the Turnbull Committee,[18] one of the committees whose output contributed to the Combined Code attached to the Listing Rules,[19] gives extensive guidance on what is required to meet the Code's requirements. Paragraph D.2.2 of the Code states that 'the board should maintain a sound system of internal control to safeguard shareholders' investment and the company's assets'. Listed companies must explain their internal control systems as part of their obligation to comply with the Combined Code.

As far as legal liability on the part of the board for delegated decisions is concerned, the question was considered about a century ago in relation to directors' common law duties of skill and care,[20] but, again, the modern debate in the UK has occurred in an area of law which borders the division between company law and insolvency law. Under s 6 of the Company Directors Disqualification Act 1986 the court is under a duty to disqualify for a period a director of a company which has become insolvent if, on the application of the Secretary of State or his appointee, the court finds the director's conduct in the past renders him 'unfit' to be concerned in the management of a company.[21] The courts have

---

[18] The Institute of Chartered Accountants, *Internal Control: Guidance for Directors on the Combined Code* (London: Accountancy Books, 1999).

[19] Below, p. 200.

[20] *Dovey v Corey* [1901] AC 477, HL. For an updating of the common law principles in the context of delegated decisions see the decision of the Court of Appeal of New South Wales in *Daniels v Anderson* (1995) 16 ACSR 607.

[21] See Chapter 4, p. 97.

interpreted unfitness widely enough to embrace incompetence, and it is perhaps not fanciful to detect the influence of the thinking which underlies the Turnbull Report in the recent decisions of the courts applying the concept of unfitness to directors' responsibility for delegated decision-making. The current position appears to be that the board may delegate substantial management powers to one of their number, but even non-executive directors must keep themselves informed of the true financial position of the company so as to be able to check whether the delegated powers have been properly exercised.[22] Boards as a whole may delegate managerial authority to non-board managers, even junior ones, but only on condition that they understand the risks involved in the business so delegated, have in place systems designed to reveal whether the risks involved have materialized, and respond appropriately to warnings thrown up by those internal control systems.[23]

Despite the impeccably procedural language of Turnbull and the courts applying s 6 of the CDDA 1986, the risk remains that, in time, the courts might become unduly attached to their procedural requirements or, worse, substitute their view of the directors' substantive decision under the guise of procedural considerations. The classic example of this type of error is the decision of the Delaware Supreme Court in *Smith v Van Gorkam*,[24] where some procedural shortcuts on the part of the board seemed to lead to liability being imposed on the directors for taking a substantively acceptable decision. In other words, the proper application of an objective standard of care requires a clear understanding on the part of the courts about the appropriate limits to intervention. However, the objective standard of care is not unique in this respect. Several important recent innovations in company law have already put the courts in this position, including s 6 itself, s 214 of the Insolvency Act 1986, and s 459 of the Companies Act 1985. It is probably more productive to analyse the courts' discharge of their new interventionist powers than to attempt to put the clock back.[25]

---

[22] *Re Westmid Packing Services Ltd* [1998] 2 All ER 124, CA.

[23] *Re Barings plc (No 5)* [1999] 1 BCLC 433, approved on appeal: [2000] 1 BCLC 523. In this case none of these conditions was met and so a major investment bank was driven into insolvency through the unauthorized derivatives-trading of a young employee in a foreign branch of the bank.

[24] 488 A 2d 858 (1985)—a decision made in a jurisdiction containing an express business judgement rule, which neither the Law Commissions nor the CLR recommend.

[25] See pp. 93–98 above on CDDA 1986, s 6 and IA 1986, s 214 and p. 236 below on CA 1985, s 459.

THE DUTY TO ACT BONA FIDE IN THE BEST INTERESTS OF THE COMPANY

The second broad standard, which we now need to examine, promotes the directors' duty of loyalty. We saw at the beginning of the previous chapter[26] that the law has always regarded the directors as agents, first of the shareholders, now of the company. In that situation it has seemed to judges appropriate to apply to directors the set of rules developed in the courts of equity for fiduciaries. Fiduciaries, of whom the paradigm case is the trustee, are those who undertake to act for another party in circumstances which give rise to a relationship of trust and confidence between the parties. As between directors and shareholders, as we have remarked before, the economists' and the lawyers' concepts of agency are largely congruent, and equity has readily supplied a standard and a set of rules by which the director is encouraged to place the interests of the company at the centre of his or her concerns when exercising the discretionary powers vested in him or her.

Let us look first at the standard. This requires the director, when exercising discretion, to act bona fide in what he or she thinks is the best interests of the company (which, for the time being, we are equating with the best interests of the shareholders). Although this standard has been the subject of much debate, which we examine in Chapter 8, it is doubtful whether in practice it has much impact, by itself, upon directors' decision-making. This is because it is so subjectively worded. The directors' duty is, said Lord Greene MR in 1942, to act 'in what they may consider—not what a court may consider—to be the best interests of the company'.[27] Consequently, no matter how eccentric the directors' decision may appear to a court, assessing it from the shareholders' point of view, that eccentricity does not amount to conclusive proof of a breach of duty on the part of the directors but is, at most, evidence that the directors did not think the decision was in the best interests of the company.[28] Only the careless or naive director[29] is likely to leave direct evidence that he or she did not consider the interests of the company (shareholders).

---

[26] See p. 115.

[27] *Re Smith & Fawcett* [1942] Ch 302, 304, CA.

[28] See, for example, *Regentcrest plc v Cohen* [2001] 2 BCLC 80 where a director was a party to a decision, shortly before the company's liquidation, to release his company's claim for £1.5m. against another company, in which fellow members of the board had an interest, in return for a speculative consideration. The judge refused to find that he had not acted bona fide.

[29] Or their legal advisers, as in *Re W & M Roith* [1967] 1 All ER 427.

Functionally, the traditional subjective formulation of the directors' duty of care and the equally subjective formulation of the duty to act in the best interests of the company fulfil a common purpose. They significantly reduce the chances of a court reviewing the substantive merits of the directors' decision, on the grounds that either a competent board or a board with the company's interests to the fore would have reached a different decision. However, whereas the modern pressures, as we have seen, are to inject an objective element into the duty of care, the loyalty duty remains subjective, perhaps because an objective element is injected in a different way. Thus, the CLR proposes that the duty should be formulated as one 'to act in the way [that the director] decides, in good faith, would be most likely to promote the success of the company for the benefit of its members as a whole'.[30]

OBEYING THE CONSTITUTION

If the only contribution of equity to the duty of loyalty were the subjective standard considered in the previous section, one could say that the duty of loyalty was a very weak reed. However, the subjective standard is supplemented by some additional equitable rules, which are objectively based and increase the impact of the law in this area. The rest of this chapter will be largely devoted to an analysis of these rules. Yet, the formulation of effective rules also faces a fundamental difficulty. Just as shareholders find it difficult to design contracts which specify in advance how the board is to act in the many different situations it may face,[31] so also do law-makers (whether judges or legislators) find the task of *ex ante* specification daunting. In fact, for the law-maker the task is worse, since it has to lay down rules for classes of company, not just a particular one. The judges in particular have traditionally sought to avoid the creation of rules which would permit controversies about the ordinary management of companies to be litigated in the courts. As Lord Eldon famously protested at the beginning of the nineteenth century, 'This court is not to be required on every occasion to take the management of every playhouse and brewhouse in the kingdom'.[32] Thus, it is rare for rules to indicate too closely how the directors should exercise the discretion conferred upon them.

Where the rule-maker does embark on the task of placing specific,

---

[30] Above, n. 1 at p. 345 (Principle 2(a)). However, the CLR does impose a significant objective duty to take certain factors into account in reaching the good faith view. See Principle 2(b) and below, p. 279.

[31] See p. 118.   [32] (1812) 1 Ves & B 154, 158.

substantive limits on the ways in which managerial discretion should be exercised, the results are sometimes questionable. For example, s 311 of the CA 1985 prohibits a company from agreeing to pay a director's remuneration on a tax-free basis. Since a company cannot in fact exempt a director from the exactions of the Inland Revenue, the purpose of the section seems to be to avoid the shareholders being misled about the gross level of the directors' remuneration, which objective is achieved, however, by other disclosure provisions in the Act.[33] Nevertheless, the existence of this rule in the Act is significant. It suggests that rules may be resorted to where the particular area of company law is publicly controversial, as is the topic of the setting of directors' remuneration. Thus, we noted in the previous chapter[34] the Combined Code rule that normally the length of a director's service contract should not exceed one year. Rules provide a more hard-edged expression than standards[35] of the principle that directors should be appropriately compensated. By the same token, however, through their lack of flexibility, rules may, on the one hand, make it harder for some companies to engage the board-level talent they need[36] and, on the other, not catch all manifestations of undesirable conduct.

As a general matter, however, it was not likely that the judges would develop common law rules which contained explicit guidance on how directors should exercise their discretion in substantive terms. Where else, then, could the judges turn, if they wanted to move beyond the subjective bona fides rule? Within the strategy of constraining agents' decisions, the approach which emerged was to base the rules on the company's constitution (principally, its articles and memorandum of association). This had the advantage that the constitution is an example of private ordering, so that building directors' duties on that basis was not open to the objection that inexpert judges were imposing rules from outside; on the contrary, the courts could claim to be reinforcing the rules adopted by the shareholders themselves. Thus developed the general notion that the directors have an obligation to act in accordance with the company's constitution (and, further, to abide by decisions taken by shareholders where, under the decision rights strategy discussed in the

---

[33] The Law Commissions have recommended accordingly the repeal of the section: above, n. 1 at p. 82.

[34] See p. 131.

[35] A standard might be: 'Directors should be paid at a fair or reasonable level.'

[36] The Combined Code rule is probably not open to this objection because (a) it is formulated flexibly and (b) the Code is subject to the 'comply or explain' principle. See above, p. 131.

previous chapter, the shareholders have an initiation or veto right over a particular decision). Even if the directors believe that action contrary to the constitution would be in the best interests of the company, they are not free to take it. The constitution thus provides the framework within which the directors are required to confine the exercise of their discretion rather than simply an element which they are obliged to take into account. 'Obeying the constitution and other lawful decisions' thus appears as the first principle in the CLR's draft statement of principles applying to directors.[37]

ACTIONS LACKING AUTHORITY

What concretely might such a duty entail and what might be the consequences of breaking it? The obvious deduction is that directors cannot exercise a power which the constitution does not give them. They may not have the power because it has not been allocated to the particular directors who have sought to exercise it, because it has not been allocated to the directors at all but has been reserved by the constitution to another body (normally the shareholders in general meeting) or because it falls outside the powers of the company, no matter who purports to exercise the power on behalf of the company. If, nevertheless, the directors do purport to exercise a power they do not have, their decision at common law is legally ineffective. Any contract purported to be made is void and any disposition of property of the company without authority is regarded as involving a breach of trust on the part of the directors (so that, subject to defences, the director or any third party into whose hands the property comes holds it on trust for the company).[38] Thus, in *Hogg v Cramphorn*[39] the directors of a company formed the view that its best interests would be promoted by defeating a take-over bid for the company. They accordingly issued some new shares to a trust which supported the directors and attached ten votes to each share. The judge held that the proper construction of the company's articles was that the company did not have the power to attach more than one vote to each share, and so the attempt to attach ten votes was ineffective.[40] In *Guinness v Saunders*[41] a committee

---

[37] Above, n. 1 at p. 345.

[38] *Rolled Steel Products (Holdings) v British Steel Corporation* [1986] Ch 246, CA.

[39] [1967] Ch 254. The events at issue in this case occurred before the institution of the 'no frustration' rule by the City Code in the late 1960s (see above, p. 147).

[40] The allottees could elect to keep the shares but only on the basis that they carried one vote each.

[41] [1990] 2 AC 663, HL.

of the board purported to enter into a contract to make a substantial payment to a director (in excess of £5m.), if a particular take-over bid succeeded, in circumstances where the constitution authorized only the full board to make such a contract. The contract was held to be void and the director was obliged to repay the money.[42]

This approach may seem pretty tough on outsiders dealing with the company, especially if they did not know or have the means of knowing of the directors' lack of authority. As we saw in Chapter 2,[43] the modern tendency is to protect genuine outsiders[44] from having to concern themselves with the minutiae of the company's constitution and that policy is now reflected in ss 35 and 35A of the Companies Act. However, the rule that the decision does not bind the company, if made without authority, may still be applied if third party rights have not intervened, so that, for example, a shareholder can obtain an injunction in such a case to restrain the board from implementing a decision they do not have the authority to take.[45]

More realistically, perhaps, the directors can be regarded as making themselves liable to the company for taking a decision they had no authority to take, a liability which the statutory provisions protecting third parties specifically preserve.[46] Indeed, with the transaction now more likely to be enforceable by the third party, despite the provisions in the constitution, the directors' potential liability to the company acquires an added significance. The directors will be liable for the loss caused to the company for acting without authority, though it is not clear whether the directors will be liable to the company for any gains made by them by so acting.

ACTIONS IN ABUSE OF AUTHORITY

The above cases involved directors purporting to exercise powers that the constitution of the company had not conferred upon them. However, the principle of the directors' duty to abide by the constitution has been extended to embrace situations where the constitution has conferred the relevant power on the directors, but the directors can be said to have

---

[42] Either on the grounds of a total failure of consideration or because he had received the money as constructive trustee for the company.

[43] See p. 47.

[44] And so a director of the company, as in the *Guinness* case, would not benefit from this protection: see CA 1985, s 322A.

[45] As CA 1985, ss 35(2) and 35A(4) recognize.   [46] CA 1985, ss 35(3) and 35A(5).

abused that power.[47] This is illustrated by the second part of the decision in *Hogg v Cramphorn*. The judge went on to hold that the directors had no power to issue the shares in question, even with one vote per share attached. At first sight, this seems incomprehensible since the articles of association clearly empowered the directors to issue new shares with voting rights. The judge's objection was to the purpose of the issue—to defeat a take-over bidder—which he held to be outside the range of purposes for which the directors of the company were empowered to issue shares.[48] Thus, he drew a distinction between proper and improper purposes for which shares could be issued—a distinction in principle applicable to all powers conferred upon directors under the articles.

The remedies for directors' abuse of the powers conferred upon them under the articles are more sensitive to the interests of outsiders dealing with the company than is the common law rule on lack of authority, the transaction entered into in abuse of duty being, apparently, voidable only against an outsider who knew of the breach of duty.[49] More important, however, as where the directors act without authority, a decision taken by the directors for an improper purpose will not bind the company internally and so can be challenged by an individual shareholder seeking to restrain the company from acting on the decision;[50] and a director who through such a decision causes harm to the company will be liable to reimburse the company for any loss caused to it.[51]

THE SCOPE OF THE 'PROPER PURPOSES' DOCTRINE

Despite the conceptual elegance and policy utility of tying rules constraining directors' exercise of their discretion to the provisions of the

[47] I gratefully adopt the distinction between lack of power and abuse of power from Sarah Worthington, 'Corporate Governance: Remedying and Ratifying Directors' Breaches' (2000) 116 LQR 638, on which I have drawn generally for this chapter—which is not to say that she agrees with what I say. The 'proper purposes' doctrine is also recognized in the CLR's first principle: see n. 30 above.

[48] Thus, in effect anticipating the City Code. See n. 39. It is important to note that there is likely to be a range of purposes contemplated in the constitution for the exercise of any power conferred on the directors rather than just a single purpose. Also, if, as is not unlikely, more than one purpose actuated the directors and only one of those purposes was improper, the 'proper purposes' test is applied to the predominant purpose: *Howard Smith Ltd v Ampol Petroleum* [1974] AC 821, PC.

[49] *Rolled Steel Products v BSC*, above, n. 38. There is considerable debate about what kind of 'knowledge' counts.

[50] *Gaiman v National Association for Mental Health* [1971] Ch 317, where, however, the directors were held not to have acted for an improper purpose. Of course, the injunction will not be available if it will defeat the rights of bona fide third parties.

[51] *Bishopsgate Investment Management Ltd v Maxwell (No 2)* [1994] 1 All ER 261, CA.

company's constitution, it must be doubted whether the principle discussed above imposes wide-ranging constraints upon the board. The rule based on directors' lack of power bites only if the power in question has not been conferred, either on the directors or on the company. However, such limitations of the company's or the directors' powers carry costs for the shareholders. Setting up a company with only limited capacity reduces its ability to respond flexibly to unforeseen developments in its business environment. In practice, therefore, most companies will adopt widely drawn objects clauses, giving the company capacity to do all the things it anticipates doing and many things it does not.[52] Alternatively, conferring broad capacity on the company, but then limiting the powers which the directors are given to pursue the company's business objectives, risks depriving the shareholders of the benefits of centralized management.[53] In fact, as we have noted several times already, the articles of companies other than the smallest will normally contain a broad and general delegation of management powers to the board.[54] Perhaps the most useful function of the 'absence of power' rule is that, as in *Guinness*, it encourages respect for the structure of further delegation within the board to board committees.

The 'abuse of power' rule is also open to a version of the same criticism, because it is not usual for companies' articles, when conferring powers on the directors, to indicate for which purposes it is intended those powers should be used. Since the shareholders cannot foresee the future, they are reluctant to tie the directors' hands. Thus, the difficulty here is to know how one draws the line between proper and improper exercises by directors of their powers, whilst remaining faithful to the idea that the improper purposes rule is grounded in the company's constitution. If judges are given (or arrogate to themselves) a free hand to determine what is proper and what is improper, the rule would no doubt have an important impact, but that would also be to encounter the very problem which basing the rule on the constitution is designed to avoid. The judges would be determining from outside how managerial discretion is exercised rather than confining themselves to reinforcing the distribution of functions decided on by the shareholders. How have the judges dealt with this problem?

---

[52] See Chapter 2, p. 46. The legislature facilitates this approach through CA 1985, s 3A, which permits companies to adopt a general commercial objects clause. The CLR proposes to set aside the whole issue by stipulating that companies shall have unlimited capacity: *Company Formation and Capital Maintenance*, October 1999, para. 2.35.

[53] See Chapter 5, p. 123. [54] Table A, art 70 (SI 1985 No 805).

In *Hogg v Cramphorn* it was relatively easy to find criteria within the company's constitution on the basis of which it was possible to conclude that the issuance of shares to defeat a take-over bidder was improper. The judge drew on earlier authority to the effect that the integrity of the division of powers within a company between directors and shareholders, which is to be found in the articles of large companies, would be undermined if the directors could 'pack' the shareholding body with their supporters so as to achieve the result they desired.[55] However, in the area of share issues to defeat bidders subsequent developments, sometimes based on different legal strategies, have rendered the improper purposes rule less important. As we have seen, in the case of post-bid issues, as in *Hogg*, the City Code now implements directly an affiliation rights strategy by sidelining target management and requiring shareholder approval of defensive measures.[56] In relation to share issues generally, whether pre- or post-bid, the Act, under the influence of EU law,[57] now requires shareholder authorization for the issuance of new shares by public companies (a decision rights strategy). The Second Directive also requires new shares issued for cash to be offered on a 'rights' basis, that is, pro rata to existing shareholders (a sharing strategy).[58]

Outside the area of upholding the division of powers between shareholders and the board, does the improper purposes doctrine have a role to play? It is rather infrequently raised in litigation, and even less frequently with success. It has been suggested that the only way to give the doctrine greater bite would be to abandon the principle that it is there to implement the decisions of the shareholders, expressed through the articles, and to treat it as giving the courts power to review directorial exercise of discretion by reference to the 'standards expected of a fiduciary office holder'.[59] Even this proposal, however, is a limited one, for it would confine judicial review to the internal aspects of the exercise of directors' discretion (i.e. the impact of the decision upon distributional issues as between groups of shareholders), where it is suggested that court

---

[55] See also the subsequent elegant analysis by Lord Wilberforce in *Howard Smith Ltd v Ampol Petroleum* [1974] AC 821, PC, discussed above at p. 116.

[56] Above, pp. 147–149.

[57] Second Company Law Directive 77/91/EEC, [1977] OJ L26/1, Arts 25 and 29.

[58] CA 1985, ss 80 (shareholder authorization) and 89 (pre-emption rights). Both these requirements of the Act can be waived by prior shareholder agreement, but, even so, the statute and the Code between them seem to have made share issues to defeat actual or potential bidders uncommon.

[59] R. Nolan, 'The Proper Purpose Doctrine and Company Directors' in B. Rider (ed.), *The Realm of Company Law* (London: Kluwer Law International, 1998), pp. 19 ff.

intervention would be more expert and more acceptable than in the case of the external aspects of the exercise of discretion, which are more intimately connected with the execution of business policy. We shall return to judicial review for the purpose of protecting non-controlling shareholders in Chapter 8.

DELEGATION AND FETTERING DISCRETION

DELEGATION OF DECISION-MAKING

In this section we discuss two further equitable rules, which the courts have developed for fiduciaries and which they have applied to directors. In their differing ways, they are both troublesome. The first is encapsulated in the Latin tag: *delegatus non potest delegare*. Persons to whom powers have been delegated may not delegate them further. In company law terms, this means that the directors, as persons to whom powers have been delegated from the shareholders, normally by means of the company's constitution, may not further delegate those powers. The rule, fortunately, is only a default rule, for otherwise there would be few takers for non-executive directorships. In fact, the articles of large companies normally grant the board a plenary power to engage in further delegation, either to committees of the board, as argued in the *Guinness* case, or to executive directors.

Note that what delegation is about in this context is entitlement to take part in decisions which are properly to be taken at director level: is the decision-maker *at this level* the board as a whole, a committee of the board, or an individual executive director? Of course, delegation has another meaning, which is how far directors are permitted to rely on non-directors for the development and implementation of the company's business policies. This, more important, form of delegation is regulated by company law under the heading of the directors' duty of care and has been so discussed above.[60] Granted the narrow meaning of delegation in this context and the fact that it is a default rule, the non-delegation rule is nevertheless a rather odd one to apply to boards of directors. In order to minimize transaction costs a default rule ought to reflect the rule which most parties subject to it would choose. However, most companies in fact reverse the no-delegation rule in their articles, and indeed Table A, which

---

[60] See p. 157. We also saw there that the law requires directors to keep themselves informed as to the company's overall position, even if certain functions have been delegated (in the narrower sense) to a particular director.

is itself a set of default rules, reverses the common law position.[61] An equitable default rule which is reversed by a statutory default rule seems unnecessarily complicated. It might be better not to apply this equitable rule to boards and leave those companies that want all directors to be involved in all director-level decisions to stipulate for this in their articles. However, the rule still appears in the CLR's draft.[62]

FETTERING OF DISCRETION

The second rule for consideration is the one which forbids a director to fetter his discretion or, to put it positively, requires him or her to maintain herself in a position where she can exercise independence of judgement on what the best interests of the company require.[63] This rule is applied even to directors who are appointed to represent particular interests, such as those of a large shareholder or creditor. Such 'nominee' directors are obliged to ignore the interests and wishes of their appointer, in so far as these diverge from what is in the interests of the company as a whole.[64] They certainly may not agree to take instructions from the nominator. One may speculate how far this rule is observed in practice by nominee directors.[65]

Unlike the 'no delegation' rule, the prohibition on fettering is obviously sensible. It is a corollary to the directors' duty to act in the best interests of the company: the director cannot contract to act in a different way. The difficulty with the 'no fettering' rule is to work out its limits. It should not prevent directors, who have committed the company in good faith to a transaction and who have undertaken, as part of that contract, to exercise their discretionary powers in a particular way in the future, from acting in accordance with the contract. The company should not be able to escape from its contractual commitments nor should the directors be regarded as in breach of duty if they act so as to fulfil those commitments, just because circumstances change after the contract has been entered into and it becomes clear that it would have been better for the company never to have entered into the agreement. If the law did sanction such behaviour, either third parties would be less willing to contract with

---

[61] Art 72. See Chapter 1 at p. 16 on the default status of Table A.

[62] Above, n. 1, at p. 346 (Principle 3(a)).

[63] This is how the matter is put in the CLR draft: Principle 3(b).

[64] *Kuwait Asia Bank EC v National Mutual Life Nominees Ltd* [1991] 1 AC 187, PC. In return, the nominator is not liable for the negligence or other breach of duty of the nominee.

[65] In particular, there is a good argument for explicitly permitting nominee directors to transmit to their appointers certain types of information which is confidential to the company.

companies or directors would be less willing to commit themselves to doing the things necessary to carry out the contract on the company's behalf. The 'no fettering' rule would become, in that situation, a fetter on corporate contracting. Not surprisingly, the judges have not interpreted the 'no fettering' rule so as to permit companies to escape from their contracts or to penalize directors for sticking to them.[66]

However, it is arguable that this robust approach should be applied only where the decision falls within the directors' powers under the principle of centralized management. If under the decisions rights strategy, discussed in the previous chapter,[67] the consent of the shareholders also is needed to commit the company to a particular transaction, then a more nuanced approach may be called for and, in fact, seems to have been accepted by the courts. In a couple of cases, involving the sale of substantial assets by a company, where the Listing Rules required shareholder approval for the deal,[68] the courts have refused to allow directors to agree with the proposed purchaser that the directors will recommend the sale to the shareholders, even if a better offer should emerge before the shareholder meeting called to consider the matter.[69]

These decisions can be explained on the basis that, until and unless the shareholders give their consent, the company is not bound by the contract and, further, that the rationality of the shareholders' part in this process depends heavily upon their being given reliable advice by their directors. Consequently, the directors may not contract out of their duty to give that advice in the way that best promotes the interests of the shareholders, as the directors view them at the time the advice is given. It must be admitted that even this rule may chill transactions with the company: some third parties who cannot reduce the risk of the shareholders' rejecting the deal by signing up the directors to recommend it, come what may, may react by being unwilling to make a proposal to the directors in the first place. However, some risk of this nature is inherent in the strategy of involving the shareholders, in addition to the directors, in the corporate decision. Accordingly, it is appropriate for the courts to prefer the policy of promoting the integrity of the shareholders' role in decision-making. If this argument is accepted, it can be said to apply a fortiori where the

---

[66] *Fulham Football Club Ltd v Cabra Estates plc* [1994] 1 BCLC 363, CA.
[67] Chapter 5, p. 123.
[68] Above, p. 126.
[69] *Rackham v Peek Food Ltd* [1990] BCLC 895; *John Crowther Group plc v Carpets International plc* [1990] BCLC 460.

third party's transaction is not with the company at all but with the shareholders individually, as in a take-over offer.[70]

CONFLICTS OF INTEREST: SELF-DEALING TRANSACTIONS

With the rules governing conflicts of interest we reach the heart of what shareholders may fear when they delegate powers to the board: the directors may exercise their discretion so as to promote their own interests rather than those of the company (shareholders).[71] The risks of such behaviour are at their greatest in two situations, upon which we shall focus in this section. These are where the director contracts with his or her company and where the company enters into a contract with a third party in which the director has an interest, for example because the third party is a company in which the director has a major shareholding or is a partnership of which the director is a member. These can be referred to as 'self-dealing' transactions.[72]

POSSIBLE APPROACHES

There are four approaches which the law might take to the regulation of self-dealing transactions. The first would be simply to prohibit contracting in the situations described above. Although relatively simple to operate, such a rule might be regarded as an example of overkill. A self-dealing transaction is not in itself objectionable: only if the presence of the director on both sides of the bargaining leads to a deal which is less favourable to the company than an arm's length negotiation would have produced can the shareholders be said to have suffered harm. Moreover, a prohibition might impose more costs on the shareholders than benefits. This is because the director or the third party in which the director is interested might be the best source for the company of the service or good which the company is seeking to acquire. Such a rule would mean, for example, that a director could never enter into a service contract under which he agreed to work for the company full-time and be remunerated for his work. Thus, either the top managers of a company

---

[70] *Dawson International plc v Coats Patons plc* [1990] BCLC 560, Inner House.

[71] The rules considered here also apply, in principle, in the less likely case of the director being under two conflicting duties. However, the law evidently does not apply the principle so rigorously as to prevent a person from acting as director of two competing companies.

[72] For a stimulating comparative analysis, see L. Enriques, 'The Law on Company Directors' Self-Dealing' (2000) 2 ICCLQ 297.

would have to remain off the board or, on becoming members of the board, they would have to give up their full-time managerial roles. Neither rule is likely to be conducive to the efficient running of the company.

Thus, banning contracting is not likely to be a generally acceptable solution to the self-dealings problem, though it could be used in particular situations where the utility to the company of a particular type of transaction is low and the risk of self-interested behaviour on the part of the director high. Seemingly, it is on this basis that the Act prohibits loans to a director from his or her company (and related transactions): experience has shown that directors often abuse the facility to receive loans from their company, while if a director is a good risk for a loan, there is no reason why he or she should not get it in the normal way from sources other than the company.[73]

The second approach is to subject contracts with directors to review by the courts by reference to some standard such as fairness or reasonableness. On this approach, companies are permitted to contract with directors or third parties in which directors are interested, but the risk arising from the fact that the director appears, so to speak, on both sides of the bargaining table is controlled by giving the court the power to take appropriate steps if that risk, in a particular case, has resulted in contract terms different from what arm's length bargaining would have produced. As with all standards, it is an approach which is dependent upon the existence of an expert judiciary to apply them. In the United States, where some use is made of this strategy,[74] there has always been greater confidence in the skills of the judiciary in this regard than in the UK. In consequence, judicial assessment of the fairness of self-dealing transactions has not been a significant part of British law.[75]

If prohibiting contracting (at least across the board) and review by reference to fairness are not part of British law, what other approaches are there? The obvious ones are to subject the self-dealing transaction to approval by either the board or the shareholders in general meeting. These are the third and fourth approaches to the problem. The latter

---

[73] CA 1985, ss 330–44. Where there is a good reason for requiring the director to take the loan from the company, for example in the case of a director of a bank, the statute creates an exception to the prohibition. See s 338.

[74] R. C. Clark, *Corporate Law* (Boston: Little, Brown, 1986), pp. 160–1. Even so, under the ALI principles (above, n. 17, para. 5.02) substantive fairness is only one of four possible gateways to legality, the others being procedural.

[75] Even in relation to remuneration, where the director faces strong conflicts of interest, the courts will not review the fairness of the payment, though they may intervene if the alleged remuneration is a sham: *Re Halt Garage (1964) Ltd* [1982] 3 All ER 1016.

appears at first sight to be the main technique in the UK for dealing with self-dealing transactions, but it is suggested that, on further analysis, it can be seen that it is the former which prevails.

SHAREHOLDER APPROVAL OR BOARD APPROVAL?

The rule of equity is normally stated to be that directors, as fiduciaries, must not put themselves in a position where their personal interest and their duty to promote the best interests of the company conflict. However, this appears to be little different from a prohibition on contracting: the most obvious way for directors not to put themselves in this position is not to contract and in some cases, as with the negotiation of service contracts, any alternative course of action may be difficult to discern. However, the 'no conflict' rule is subject to an important rider: conflicted contracting (contracting where there is a conflict of interest) is permitted provided the conflict of interest is disclosed in advance to the shareholders and the shareholders nevertheless approve the contract. This rider in part expresses the principle that, because the 'no conflict' rule is there to protect the company, the company is free to waive compliance with it if, after full disclosure of the facts, it thinks it is in the best interests of the company to do so. However, it is important to stress that 'the company' in the eyes of the common law means the shareholders in general meeting and not, for example, the uninvolved members of the board. This is because of the common law principle that the company is entitled to the unbiased advice of all its directors and, if that is not available because one or more of them is interested in the transaction in question, then the decision reverts to the shareholders in general meeting.[76]

This rider demonstrates that the equitable rule is not a prohibition on contracting, but it still does not explain why it is appropriate to deal with the rule in this chapter. The rider, one can argue, turns the 'no conflict' rule into an example of the decision rights strategy: the shareholders are given a veto over contracts and other decisions where one or more members of the board is subject to a conflict of interest. In that light, we should have discussed the rule in the previous chapter when we analysed the decision rights strategy. If there were nothing more to be said about the 'no conflict' rule, the argument that its analysis in this chapter is misplaced would be a strong one. However, there is more to be said.

Since one of the purposes of the 'no conflict' rule is to relieve the

---

[76] *Imperial Mercantile Credit Association v Coleman* (1871) LR 6 Ch App 558, 567–8; *Movitex v Bulfield* [1988] BCLC 104.

courts of the task of assessing the merits of self-dealing transactions, it operates to shift the risky transactions into the category of those needing shareholder approval without the court having to assess whether the risk of unfair treatment of the company has in fact materialized in any particular case. Two points in particular about the scope of the rule illustrate this. First, the requirement of shareholder approval exists without its being necessary to show that there was an actual conflict of interest between the director and the company. It is enough if there was a real potential for conflict, that is, the rule will apply provided the alleged conflict is more than fanciful. Second, it is not necessary to show that the conflict had an impact upon the terms of the transaction. Even if the self-dealing transaction appears eminently fair on its face, it will still need shareholder approval.

Both these facets of the rule reduce the judicial role to a minimum, but they also mean that, under the equitable rule, a large number of transactions into which a company may want to enter will need shareholder approval; and obtaining shareholder approval, in a large company, slows down decision-making, makes it more unpredictable (as we saw above in the discussion of delegation), and is costly. However, a remedy was at hand, once the courts accepted, as they did in the nineteenth century, that prior shareholder approval could be given generally and not only in the face of a specific transaction which was put to the shareholders for their consideration. General prior approval for categories of conflicted transactions could then be provided through the articles of association which constitute a contract between the company and each shareholder[77] and thus provided a means for the giving of general prior consent to conflicted transactions. Thus, provisions began to appear in the articles permitting the board to contract on behalf of the company, in the normal way, even though some of its members were interested in the decision in question. In fact, arts 84 and 85 of Table A authorize contracts between a company and the director or the company and a third party in which the director is interested on a very wide scale, which shows how common such provisions had become.

Thus, our analysis so far shows that, by virtue of provisions in the articles, the consent of shareholders to specific self-dealing transactions is not usually required. The board takes these decisions, and does so pretty much in the same way as it would if no conflict of interest were involved,[78] or indeed the decision may be taken at sub-board level. This is the

---

[77] CA 1985, s 14.   [78] See n. 82 below.

justification for not treating the 'no conflict' rule in the previous chapter as an example of the decision rights strategy, which is where the common law would seem to place the rule. However, this justification seems to go too far in the opposite direction and, in effect, to assert that the 'no conflict' rule normally has no impact. What else can one conclude if the board takes both conflicted decisions and non-conflicted ones as part of its powers of central management? However, here we have to add a third ingredient to our analysis, in addition to the equitable starting point and such provisions as the company may have decided to include in its constitution so as to modify the equitable principle. That third ingredient is the Companies Act 1985, consolidating earlier statutory provisions. The Act limits the extent to which the articles of association can write out the 'no conflict' rule. The law in this area is thus a highly complex mixture of judge-made law, private ordering through the company's constitution, and legislation.

MANDATORY DISCLOSURE TO THE BOARD

The Act limits private ordering in relation to self-dealing transactions in two ways, one of which applies to all self-dealing transactions, the other of which applies only to certain categories of self-dealing transactions. We shall look first at the general restriction which is to be found in s 317 of the Act and which is normally also incorporated into the provisions in the company's articles which write out the common law requirement of shareholder approval. Section 317, introduced in 1929 but expanded in scope since then, is built on the premise that the articles may operate effectively to cancel the need for shareholder approval, and it concentrates instead on regulating board-level procedures for the taking of self-dealing decisions. The section requires a director to disclose his or her interests to the board in relation to proposed transactions,[79] so that at least the board is informed about the conflict when the company decides whether to enter into the transaction. Without this section, the director's conflict of interest might remain wholly hidden and the company could proceed with a transaction in complete ignorance of it. However, it does not prohibit the interested director from voting on the transaction in which he or she is interested. Where the company's articles make compliance with s 317 a condition for writing out or modifying the equitable

---

[79] It also requires the disclosure of interests which arise after a transaction has been entered into by the company, which might be relevant to the company's decision to enforce its contractual rights or to renew the contract.

rule, then, if the interest is not disclosed in accordance with the section, the board's approval of the transaction will be ineffective, whether the concealment was intentional or not. This is because failure to comply with s 317 constitutes in this case also a failure to comply with the method for giving general prior consent to conflicted transactions, to which the shareholders have consented in the articles, and so the basic equitable rule requiring shareholder approval of the specific transaction revives.[80]

Having looked at the equitable rule, provisions in articles, and s 317 of the Act, we are finally in a position to formulate the general 'no conflict' rule as it appears in practice in British company law. It is, normally, that a director may not enter into a transaction with his or her company or authorize[81] the company to enter into a transaction in which he or she is interested unless there has been compliance with the relevant disclosure provisions of the Act. This is how the CLR proposes the 'no conflict' rule should be reformulated.[82] The result would be a simpler way of stating the effect of the present three tiers of rules. The basic equitable principle, requiring shareholder approval, would no longer be applied to companies and so there would be no need for provisions in the articles to write it out. Instead, the only general control over conflicts of interest would be the requirement of appropriate disclosure to the board. This simplification of the law would make it clear what is already normally the case: the general rule for dealing with self-dealing transactions in the UK is approval by the board after full disclosure.

However, there is perhaps one surprising feature of the CLR's proposals. They do not formally exclude the interested director from voting on the transaction in question.[83] Although this reflects the current law,[84] the failure to exclude interested directors from voting in all cases means

[80] Where the articles do not refer to CA 1985, s 317, the impact of a failure to comply with it on the validity of the conflicted transaction is at present obscure. See for an analysis of the now rather complex case law, *Gower*, 6th edn, 1997, pp. 612–15.

[81] In fact, CA 1985, s 317 requires disclosure by the director, where he or she is not party to the transaction, whether he played any part in taking the decision to enter into the transaction or not, but the CLR proposes to restrict the section in the way stated in the text: *Developing the Framework*, March 2000, para. 3.62.

[82] Above, n. 1 at pp. 346 (Principle 5) and 353. However, the CLR formulation does make it clear that disclosure to the board is an integral part of the directors' duty in a self-dealing situation. See n. 80 above.

[83] The CLR appears to leave it to the articles or, in the absence of such provision, to the bona fides test to determine whether the interested director can vote: *Completing the Structure*, November 2000, para. 3.25.

[84] Table A (see arts 94 and 95) does not normally permit an interested director to vote on the transaction or to be counted in the quorum for that decision, but the articles of particular companies can, and do, permit both these things.

that the level of protection is less than that provided by the ALI's *Principles of Corporate Governance* in the United States[85] in such a case and, perhaps more important, is less than that proposed by the CLR for board approval of the taking of corporate opportunities, as we shall see later in this chapter.

PART X OF THE ACT

The CLR's proposed redrafting of the 'no conflict' rule has the merit of revealing, rather starkly, how limited is the control over such transactions offered by British law. The disclosure rule does not offer judicial review on grounds of unfairness nor scrutiny by the body of shareholders which, in the type of company under consideration in this chapter, is independent of the board. Instead, the rule relies heavily on fellow directors to act appropriately in response to the conflicts of interest which are brought to their attention. How strong a check this is likely to be one can assess only after looking at the rules on board composition, considered in Chapter 7, but even at this stage it is clear what the risks of the strategy are. The uninvolved directors may fail to act effectively because of what the Americans graphically, if somewhat disconcertingly, term 'mutual back-scratching', that is, the uninvolved directors may fail to scrutinize closely a particular self-dealing transaction, in the expectation of similar treatment when theirs is the conflict under consideration at some later date. Or, in the face of a dominant chief executive, the uninvolved directors may simply opt for a quiet life. Both courses of action will probably amount to breaches of duty on the part of the uninvolved directors, but the weak *ex post* threat of suit for breach of duty by the company[86] may be far less protection for the shareholders than a requirement for their *ex ante* approval.

That such risks are not merely fanciful and that there is merit in the common law principle of shareholder approval is shown by two sets of rules. First, the Listing Rules, which are now in the custody of the Financial Services Authority (FSA) in its capacity as the UK Listing Authority, in fact reinstate a general requirement for shareholder approval in listed companies. Chapter 11 of the Listing Rules, subject to certain exceptions, requires full disclosure to the shareholders and their

---

[85] Above, n. 17 at para. 5.02(2)(B).
[86] On the question of who might seek to enforce the company's rights, see the discussion later in this chapter on forgiveness and enforcement.

approval for what it calls 'related party' transactions, which category includes transactions between the company (or any of its subsidiaries) and a director or associate[87] of the director and also certain transactions under which the company and the director or associate engage in joint financing activities. Thus, for the largest companies the company law principle of disclosure to the board for self-dealing transactions is in fact overtaken by a more rigorous requirement to be found in the Listing Rules.

Second, even for non-listed companies, the Act requires shareholder approval for certain classes of self-dealing transaction. Experience, often in the form of reports from inspectors appointed by the Department of Trade and Industry to investigate the affairs of companies, has shown that some classes of transaction are particularly open to abuse. We have already noted the statutory prohibition on loans to directors which Part X of the Act contains.[88] Three other types of transaction are dealt with by special rules in Part X,[89] but in these cases the statutory technique falls short of prohibition. Instead, the Act reintroduces the equitable rule of shareholder approval. In other words, in relation to these three classes of transaction, the strategy used by British law to deal with self-dealing transactions is, indeed, the decision rights strategy. The CLR proposes to retain these provisions.[90]

TERMINATION PAYMENTS AND LONG-SERVICE CONTRACTS

The first, and oldest, set of rules deals with 'end game' situations, where the imminent departure of all or most of the members of the board weakens their incentives to put the shareholders' interests first. In particular, where a third party is acquiring the bulk of the company's assets or of its shares, there is a strong temptation for the third party to divert to the directors (and for the directors to accept) part of the consideration which would otherwise go to the company (for the assets) or to the

---

[87] See rule 11.1(d) for the definition of an associate. It bears some relation to s 346 of CA 1985, mentioned in n. 98 below.

[88] Above, p. 171.

[89] These transactions must also be disclosed in the company's annual financial report (CA 1985, Sch 6), which requirement has the advantage that the threat of audit is likely to reduce the incentive of directors just to keep quiet about self-dealing transactions.

[90] Part XA, introduced by the Political Parties, Elections and Referendums Act 2000, applies the principle of shareholder approval to political donations and related matters, but this Part is as much driven by constitutional considerations as by concerns limited to company law and is not further considered here.

shareholders (for their shares), in exchange for the existing members of the board facilitating the transaction. Consequently, the Act[91] requires shareholder approval for payments to the directors for or in connection with their loss of office in such situations, whether the payment is made by the third party or the company itself. Unapproved payments made to the directors are held on trust for the company (in the case of asset sales) or for the selling shareholders (in the case of share sales).

The Act[92] also applies the shareholder approval rule to payments in connection with loss of office made to individual directors by their company at any time, whether in connection with an assets or share sale or not. At first sight, this section might appear to contain at least a partial answer to the question of whether directors' remuneration packages should require shareholder approval (approval is required by s 312 only for termination payments and not, for example, for ordinary salary). However, this rule is substantially undermined by the fact that it does not catch payments which the director is entitled to under his service contract or by reason of its breach.[93] In other words, the section applies only to gratuitous payments to directors and probably not even to gratuitous payments by way of pension provision.[94] Therefore, it is perhaps not surprising that the Act goes on, in a second provision, to require shareholder approval of directors' service contracts, but at the moment it does so only in respect of a very limited sub-set of such contracts. We analysed these provisions when we looked at the removal rights strategy in the previous chapter and saw that the Act's requirement for shareholder approval extends only to contracts not terminable without cost to the company within a five-year period.[95]

Shareholder approval is not required for the level of remuneration and other benefits which directors may be entitled to under their service contracts. This has proved to be a major issue of public concern in recent years, as the salaries of senior managers have increased much more rapidly than those of members of other sections of society and without, often, any obvious link to the performance of the company. This might not be a cause for concern if it were possible to credit the standard justification that such levels of remuneration are simply a response to the (international) market for executive services, where talent is scarce and

---

[91] CA 1985, ss 313–16.   [92] CA 1985, s 312.

[93] *Taupo Totara Timber v Rowe* [1978] AC 537, PC, where an express contractual entitlement for the managing director to resign upon a change of control of the company and receive five times his gross annual salary was held to fall outside CA 1985, ss 314–16.

[94] CA 1985, s 316(3).   [95] Chapter 5, p. 130.

prices correspondingly high. However, it is at least possible that directors' remuneration represents a situation of market failure. If the 'market' rate consists of the average of the decisions taken by companies, and decision-making by companies on the matter of remuneration is dominated by the very executives whose remuneration is at issue, there is no reason to suppose that, in such a 'rigged' market, the price represents a true reflection of supply and demand. One solution to this problem of conflict of interest would be to inject a substantial element of shareholder approval into company decision-making on this matter.[96]

SUBSTANTIAL PROPERTY TRANSACTIONS AND REMEDIES

As the law stands at the moment, perhaps the most significant area where shareholder approval is required is the third: substantial[97] property dealings between a director (or those 'connected with' him) and the company (or its holding company).[98] Selling assets to the company at an overvalue or acquiring assets from the company at an undervalue is an easy way for a director to expropriate value from the shareholders, since the transaction may appear to be a normal commercial one and the defect in it is revealed only if the values of the respective considerations are investigated. Requiring the director to take the initiative to seek prior shareholder approval of the transaction thus prevents him or her from taking the benefit of shareholder inertia. A particular additional interest of these provisions is that they provide a reasonably elaborate set of remedies for breaches of the statute.[99] The company is provided with the following choices.

  1. The transaction entered into in breach of the provisions is voidable and so, in principle, may be either affirmed or rescinded (reversed) by the company.[100] The company may affirm, for example where it approves of the transaction in principle but objects to its terms (where one of the remedies listed below may be adequate for its purposes). It will want to

---

[96] See also the discussion in Chapter 5 (p. 126).

[97] Normally, and subject to a *de minimis* exception, transactions of a value exceeding 10 per cent of the company's net assets. 'Property' includes any non-cash asset.

[98] CA 1985, ss 320–2. Section 346, containing a definition of 'connected persons', is a good example of the complications which the drafter of the Act has to deal with, if a director is not simply to avoid the rule by dealing with the company through another person or business entity, rather than directly.

[99] CA 1985, s 322. Section 341 does the same thing for the prohibition on loans.

[100] Affirmation requires a resolution of the company in general meeting (i.e. it replaces the prior shareholder authorization which should have been obtained). The decision to reverse the transaction can presumably be taken by either board or general meeting.

rescind where it wishes to return to the situation which obtained before the transaction was entered into and, thus, recover the assets disposed of or the price paid for the assets acquired. The company is permitted to reverse the transaction only provided it can restore what it received under the transaction to the other party. Further, the director or connected person may have disposed of the property to a third party before the issue of lack of shareholder consent is raised. This does not constitute a complete bar to reversal (which would now occur as against the third party), but a broad category of third parties is protected against reversal. These are those third parties who have acquired rights in good faith, for value, and without actual notice of the contravention of the statute (that is, innocent third parties who have paid for what they hold). Oddly, the fact that the party to the transaction with the company has acted in good faith, for value, and without notice of the breach is not a bar to rescission. It is unlikely that a director party to the transaction with the company could fall into this category, but a person 'connected with' the director might do so.[101]

2. Whether or not the company avoids the transaction, it may recover from the director any gain made by him 'directly or indirectly' on the transaction. Thus, if the company wishes to keep the property it has purchased from the director, it can affirm the transaction and sue the director for any gain made.[102] However, the company may sue for profit made even if the transaction has been reversed. Suppose the director buys an asset for $£x$, sells it to a connected company for $£3x$, which then sells it to the claimant company for $£5x$. Reversal of the transaction will give the company its $£5x$ back, but it appears the company could recover $£2x$ from the director as a profit made 'directly or indirectly' out of the transaction, at least where the two sales were in contemplation by the director from the beginning, and provided the reversal of the sale by the company does not permit the connected company to reverse its transaction with the director. The only defence made available to the director in this situation is that he took all reasonable steps to ensure compliance with the section by his or her company. The company is thus better off than it would have been, had the director committed no breach of the

---

[101] To take a far-fetched example, where the contracting party is a company of which a trust holds 20 per cent of the shares (but as a passive investment) and of the 30 beneficiaries of the trust one is the estranged son of the director by a previous marriage. See CA 1985, s 346(2)(c) and (4).

[102] Query whether that gain should be assessed by reference to the market price of the asset at the time of its purchase by the company or by reference to the price paid for it by the director.

statutory provisions. This shows that the section puts a higher value on extracting an undeserved profit from the director than on exact compensation for the company. This is the so-called 'prophylactic' (or deterrent) aim of the law, though it should be noted that, even when stripped of the profit, the director is financially no worse off than before the transaction was entered into.

Any profit made directly or indirectly by the connected person may also be recovered by the company. So also may the profit be recovered which was made by any other director of the company who authorized the transaction, whether or not he or she was party to it. Both such groups may benefit from the defence that they did not know of the relevant circumstances constituting the contravention, but this will not help them if they knew the facts but failed to draw the conclusion that shareholder consent was needed. This potential liability of co-directors supports the monitoring obligation which the courts have drawn out of the duty of care and the disqualification provisions, discussed above.[103]

3. Finally, the section provides for the company to seek an indemnity from the director for loss or damage resulting from the breach of the statutory provisions. However, if there has been full indemnification of the company (from whatever source), the company loses its right to rescission. It seems that causation rules are applied in assessing losses which are favourable to the company. Suppose a company buys property from another company in which a director of the first company is interested, but, by the time this connection comes to light, the property market has collapsed and the company disposes of the property for less than it paid for it. Having disposed of the property, the company cannot reverse the transaction (because it can no longer give the property back), but it can recover from the director the difference between the prices paid on acquisition and sale.[104] The company's right to seek an indemnity is in addition to its right to seek an account of profit from a director or connected person. However, it is presumably the case that, often, an account of profits will reduce or even extinguish the company's loss; and that a payment by way of indemnity will reduce the director's gain. The duty to indemnify may also be asserted against those connected with the director and any director who authorized the transaction, subject to the defences described in the previous paragraph.

*

[103] See p. 157.
[104] *Re Duckwari plc* [1999] Ch 253, CA, shows that the company can recover for the consequential loss arising out of the fall in the property market.

The remedies available to the company against the directors and associated parties in the case of substantial property transactions entered into without shareholder consent have been set out in a little detail, partly for their intrinsic interest and partly because it has been proposed that s 322 should be used as a model for developing a single set of statutory remedies for breaches of the fiduciary duties. The CLR proposes that the remedies should be codified, as well as the duties, though it was unable to produce a draft of remedies to complement its proposed statement of duties.[105] Such a step would simplify the law and also clarify it, because in many cases it is not obvious what the remedies are which the common law provides for breaches of the duty of loyalty.[106] In addition, rendering the transaction which the company has entered into as a result of the breach of duty voidable, but subject to bars to reversal (rather than void, which is sometimes the result under the current law)[107] would be more in line with modern policies of protecting innocent third parties contracting with the company.

However, one major issue that would need to be addressed, if remedies were to be codified, would be the extent to which proprietary remedies as well as personal remedies should be made available. At present, s 322 creates only personal remedies, whereas the English common law, as we have seen, sometimes creates proprietary ones because it treats the director's breach of duty as a breach of trust.[108] The main point about a proprietary remedy is that it enables a claimant to say that particular assets belong to it, not simply that the defendant is obligated to transfer a certain value to it. This is particularly important if the director is bankrupt because, by asserting its proprietary claim, the company can take the assets in question out of the director's bankruptcy and thus prevent other creditors claiming any share of them. By contrast, if a director who is accountable under s 322 for profits made becomes bankrupt, the company's claim against him has no higher priority than that of any other unsecured creditor. Again, rescission (reversal) under s 322 appears not to

---

[105] See CLR, *Final Report*, July 2001, vol. I, para. 15.28 and R. Nolan, 'Enacting Civil Remedies in Company Law', paper produced for the CLR and now published in (2001) 1 JCLS 245.

[106] For example, it is not clear in what circumstances a company, acquiring property from a director in breach of the self-dealing rules, is restricted at common law to the remedy of rescission: *Erlanger v New Sombrero Phosphate Co* (1878) 3 App Cas 1218.

[107] See p. 162.

[108] Ibid. The reason s 322 does not create proprietary remedies appears to be that it applies also to Scotland, and Scottish law has been reluctant to create proprietary remedies in this class of situation.

revest any proprietary title to the assets in the company, whereas rescission in equity does. In the case of rescission, the argument for a proprietary claim seems high, because what the company is trying to do is recover corporate assets disposed of in breach of duty by the directors. Third party interests are appropriately protected by the bars to rescission. In the case of simple profits made by a director out of a breach of duty, however, it is less clear in policy terms whether the company's claims should prevail over those of the director's other creditors.

CORPORATE OPPORTUNITIES AND SECRET PROFITS

THE NATURE OF THE PROBLEM

We have assumed in the previous two sections that the director's conflict of interest has taken the form of a dealing with the company, either directly or indirectly through another entity in which the director has an interest or another person with whom the director is connected. However, the director's self-interest need not show itself in a manner which involves the company in the transaction. Indeed, the self-interest of the director may lead him or her to *exclude* the company from the transaction. Suppose, for example, that a director learns of a lucrative business opportunity which the company could exploit. Instead of offering the opportunity to the company, in which the director has only a limited shareholding, the director chooses instead to develop it through a new company wholly owned by her, so that she can capture the whole of the profits arising out of the opportunity. Here the self-interest of the director leads to the exclusion of the company from the opportunity.

However, it is highly unlikely that it would be efficient to prevent all directors from exploiting personally all business opportunities which they come across while they are directors of a company. Such a rule would certainly reduce the number of people prepared to take on non-executive directorships, for non-executives are expected to devote only a part of their time to the company. What has engendered much debate is how to identify the set of rules which best distinguishes those opportunities which the director may exploit personally from those in which the company has a legitimate interest.

The traditional approach of British law has been to use in this situation the rule against secret profits, which is applied by equity to all those in a fiduciary position. Thus, the director must not make a profit arising out of or in the course of his office as director without that profit having been disclosed in advance to the shareholders and approved by them. The rule is obviously sound as far as it goes. If directors could make profits out of third parties without the shareholders' approval, they would have a substantial incentive to conduct the business of the company so as to maximize those personal profits rather than the profits of the company. In terms of our typology of legal strategies, it amounts, once again, to a decision rights strategy: the transaction which yields the profit must be approved by the shareholders (though it should be noted that what the shareholders are approving here is a transaction which the director intends to enter into personally, not a decision on behalf of the company).

THE ARTICLES, SECTION 310, AND BOARD APPROVAL

Unlike with self-dealing transactions, it is apparently much less common to write out the 'no profit' rule by means of appropriate provisions in the company's articles. Table A provides only one example of approval of an otherwise secret profit, which appears to have been inspired by a desire to reverse the result of the decision of the House of Lords in *Regal (Hastings) Ltd v Gulliver*.[109] In that case the directors, who were also the majority shareholders, invested in a subsidiary which the company was establishing, and later sold their shares in the subsidiary at a profit. The House of Lords held that the opportunity to invest in the subsidiary had arisen out of and in the course of the discharge of their duties as directors of the parent, and so they were accountable for the profit made to the parent, which was now controlled, in fact, by a new set of shareholders. Article 85 of Table A permits a director, who has disclosed to the board the nature and extent of his interest, to be 'interested in any body corporate promoted by the company' and provides that he shall not be accountable to the company for any profit made as a result of the interest.[110]

There are two possible explanations of this reticence in the articles about corporate opportunities, one legal, the other functional. The functional explanation is that, unlike in contracts with the company, where, as explained above, the shareholders may have an interest in facilitating such transactions, the shareholders have no interest in facilitating the taking up of corporate opportunities by directors, and so they are unwilling to adopt articles under which they forgo their approval role. The alternative explanation is that the articles normally reflect the views of the boards of

---

[109] [1942] 1 All ER 378, HL.
[110] Article 85(b) and (c), building on Table A of 1948, art 78, which made it clear that 'interest' includes interest as a shareholder in the promoted company.

companies and directors ideally would want to write out the 'no profit' rule, just as the articles normally write out the 'no conflict' rule. What prevents them from doing this is the provisions of s 310 of the Act, which prohibits companies from exempting directors from liability for breach of duty or of trust (or indeed from liability for negligence) via provisions in the articles or otherwise.

The puzzle with the second explanation, which had exercised commentators for decades, is not so much how s 310 prevents exclusion of the 'no profit' rule, but rather how the regular exclusion by the articles of the 'no conflict' rule, which we noted in the discussion of conflicts of interest earlier in this chapter, is compatible with the provisions of the section. The most convincing solution of this conundrum is that provided by Vinelott J in *Movitex v Bulfield*,[111] where he treats the 'no conflict' rule, not as one which imposes a duty on the director to avoid conflict situations, but as one which disables the director from contracting with the company if he or she is in a conflicted position. The extent of the director's disability may be modified by the articles, precisely because no breach of duty is involved. Of course, this explanation makes the reversal by Table A of the result in *Regal (Hastings)* of doubtful validity, unless the 'no profit' rule can be seen as a disability as well.

If the CLR's proposals in this area are implemented, it may be that we shall be enlightened as to which of the two explanations for the absence of exclusionary provisions in the articles (in relation to corporate opportunities) is correct. The CLR contemplates the significant step of adding prior board approval to prior shareholder approval of the use by directors of corporate opportunities (and, indeed, any other property or information of the company). In the case of private companies, board approval will be available unless the company in its articles opts out of this possibility; in the case of public companies the articles will need to opt for board approval for that mechanism to be available.[112] In either case, however, board approval of the taking of a specific opportunity will become a way of renouncing the corporate interest in the opportunity, which arguably it is not at present.[113] However, in contrast to Principle 5 on self-dealing transactions, Principle 6 on corporate opportunities proposes to exclude

---

[111] [1988] BCLC 104.

[112] Above, n. 1 at p. 346—Principle 6 (Personal use of the company's property, information and opportunity).

[113] It will not be possible for the board to approve in advance the taking of categories of opportunity, but only specific opportunities: CLR, above, n. 1 at para. 3.25.

interested directors from voting on the resolution to approve the taking of a particular opportunity.[114]

At the same time, the s 310 issue will be solved. Where the statutory statement, or the articles of a particular company adopting provisions as envisaged by the statutory statement of directors' duties, permit board authorization, these will override s 310. On the other hand, s 310 will otherwise apply fully to the statement of directors' duties. This means that, for example, prior board authorization will be the only way of escape from the 'no profit' rule, other than by prior shareholder approval. The articles will not be able to provide alternative escape routes, based, for example, on mere disclosure, as Table A arguably now seeks to do in the *Regal* situation.[115] Overall, prior board approval for the taking of corporate opportunities will be available to all companies, and no section of the Act will cast a cloud over this approval mechanism. If, despite this change, board-level approval provisions are not adopted by the articles of public companies or are excluded by private companies, that will tell us quite a lot about the influence of shareholders over directors in modern companies—and vice versa if board approval of the taking of corporate opportunities becomes the norm.

The addition to the CLR's draft statement of duties of prior disinterested board approval for releasing the company's interest in corporate opportunities might seem only a minor change, as compared with the way in which that statement recasts the self-dealing rule. However, as we have seen,[116] the recasting of the self-dealing rule does nothing more than reflect the way in which that rule operates in practice, whereas the addition of board approval for corporate opportunities arguably involves downgrading the role of the shareholders in this area. If the proposal is implemented, it will be clear that the law no longer insists on a decision rights strategy with respect to the authorization of the taking of corporate opportunities; such takings will be capable of being approved by the disinterested members of the board. This is, in fact, a trusteeship strategy, which we examine more generally in the next chapter.

It is precisely the disadvantages of the decision rights strategy to which the CLR points in support of its proposal: it 'is impractical and onerous, is inconsistent with the principle that it is for the board to make

---

[114] Note 1 to Principle 6.

[115] Above, n. 1 at para. 3.26. Having thus dealt with the s 310 problem, the CLR is also free to treat the 'no conflict' rule as imposing a duty, not a mere disability, and this is how its statement of duties appears to be formulated: above, n. 1, at p. 346.

[116] See p. 175.

business assessments, and stifles entrepreneurial activity'.[117] The CLR might have pointed to Commonwealth authority which, in one way or another, can be read as empowering the board to release the company's interest in an opportunity.[118] In any event, what is clear is that under the proposed rule, the impact of the law will depend heavily upon the integrity of the decision-making of the non-involved members of the board and upon their ability to avoid self-interested decisions and pressure from those seeking approval. No doubt, an approval decision taken by the board other than in good faith in the interests of the company can be challenged, but will the courts be able to spot such decisions?[119]

CRITERIA FOR IDENTIFYING CORPORATE OPPORTUNITIES

Irrespective of how the issue of shareholder only versus shareholder-or-board approval is ultimately resolved, it will be necessary in any event to have robust criteria for distinguishing corporate from non-corporate opportunities. For the latter, no one's approval will be needed for the director to exploit them personally. We have noted the traditional test in the *Regal* case of liability for opportunities arising 'by reason and in the course of' the directorship, but it can be argued that this criterion is too narrow.[120] The decision in *Industrial Development Consultants v Cooley*[121] is instructive. The defendant managing director had obtained a substantial professional reputation as an architect, principally as chief architect of the West Midlands Gas Board. He was hired as managing director of the claimant in order to obtain public sector work for the company, which previously had operated mainly in the private sector of the economy. The Eastern Gas Board was contemplating suitable work, but had decided against using the company because they disliked its organization. However, the Board, which knew and trusted Cooley because of his previous public sector experience, were prepared to give Cooley the work personally, provided he could extricate himself from his contract with the

---

[117] Above, n. 1, at para. 3.23.

[118] *New Zealand Netherlands Society 'Oranje' Inc v Kuys* [1973] 1 WLR 1126, PC; *Queensland Mines Ltd v Hudson* (1978) 18 ALR 1, PC; and *Peso-Silver Mines Ltd v Cropper* (1966) 58 DLR (2d) 1 (Supreme Court of Canada), though the first two cases can be read as instances where the approval was in fact given by the members of the company.

[119] In this respect, the devastating critique of the court's analysis of the board's decision in *Peso* by S. Beck, 'The Saga of *Peso Silver Mines*: Corporate Opportunity Reconsidered' (1971) 49 *Can B Rev* 80, is instructive.

[120] In other cases the mere fact that the opportunity arose out of the directorship may be too broad a criterion for liability: see n. 123 below.

[121] [1972] 1 WLR 443.

company. Cooley did so (though without revealing why he wished to depart) and contracted with the Board for the work.

The company sought an account of the profit Cooley had made on the contract, but was faced with the difficulty that, if ever there was one, this was a case where the director has obtained the opportunity in spite of, not because of, his directorship. To avoid this problem, the judge put his decision in favour of the company on the broader basis of a conflict of interest: as managing director it was his duty to promote the interests of the company, whereas, in the last few months of his directorship, Cooley had spent his time mainly promoting his personal interests. On this basis he was accountable for the profit made, even though he had signed the contract only after resigning his directorship. The duty to put the company's interest first had attached to a course of conduct which he had put in train while a director and his resignation did not operate to relieve him of that duty.[122]

The broader basis of conflict of duty and interest provides a convincing rationale for the decision in *Cooley*, though it does seem to depend heavily upon the precise opportunity which the director subsequently took up being one he was obliged to secure for his company.[123] A number of similar cases are to be found in the books, often involving, unlike *Cooley*, the additional element of the use by the directors of substantial corporate assets so as to put themselves in a position where they could take the opportunity personally and where, therefore, the *Regal* rationale is equally applicable.[124] However, the conflict rationale for the imposition of liability for corporate opportunities requires further specification if it is to answer all the questions likely to be posed in this area. While the personal interest of the director is clear in all cases (it is the interest in taking up the opportunity for him- or herself), the scope of the conflicting duty (to offer the opportunity to the company) is not. *Cooley* was in this respect an easy case, which is why the judge did not need to elaborate on the scope of the duty: the director had been hired to obtain for the company precisely the type of opportunity he diverted to himself. However, far less obvious cases can be imagined.

---

[122] The CLR draft makes the point clear by applying the rules on corporate opportunities to former as well as current directors.

[123] Otherwise, any director who spent the last months of his office setting up his next directorship might be thought to hold the profits of the resulting office on behalf of his former company, a result the courts have rejected: *Framlington Group plc v Anderson* [1995] 1 BCLC 475.

[124] *Cook v Deeks* [1916] 1 AC 554, PC; *Canadian Aero Services v O'Malley* (1973) 40 DLR (3d) 371 (Supreme Court of Canada).

Suppose X, the non-executive director of a company, is offered a business opportunity by his golfing partner, who is unaware of X's directorship. The opportunity does not relate to any area of activity which the company either is currently pursuing or has decided to embark on, but it does fit easily with a business which X already carries on as a sole trader, with the full knowledge and consent of the company. It is difficult to imagine that any modern system of company law would make the exploitation of that opportunity by X subject to the approval of the company, whether through its board or its shareholders. Where, however, between this hypothetical case and the facts of *Cooley* should the line be drawn, in other words, what are the boundaries of the director's duty to prefer the interests of the company over personal interests? It is the prime advantage of the so-called corporate opportunity doctrine, as it has been developed in the United States, that it seeks to give a coherent answer to this question.[125] It seeks to define the nature of the corporate interest in the opportunity, thus requiring more than just the existence of a profitable opportunity in the hands of someone who happens to be a director. In essence, two main identifiers of the corporate interest are put forward in the US cases: the opportunity should be either one falling within the company's existing line of business or one of a type which the company has decided to pursue (whether successfully or not).[126] In these cases, the company holds a veto over personal exploitation of the opportunity by the director, but normally not otherwise. Whether the British courts will go down a similar route remains to be seen, but it can at least be said that the CLR's draft statement of principles permits its adoption and certainly requires an answer to the question: how does one distinguish a corporate from a non-corporate opportunity?[127]

Assuming a corporate opportunity and the absence of approval from the company, what are the company's remedies? The primary one is

---

[125] See Note, (1961) 74 *Harv LR* 765 and J. Lowry and R. Edmonds, 'The No Conflict—No Profit Rules and the Corporate Fiduciary: Challenging the Orthodoxy of Absolutism' [2000] JBL 122.

[126] The ALI Principles (above, n. 17, para. 5.05 (b)) require the opportunity to meet either these tests or a version of the *Regal* (see n. 109) test.

[127] The draft of Principle 6 requires that the director must have become aware of the opportunity 'in the performance of his functions as director', but this is likely to prove less helpful to the courts than it might since it is not clear when the functions of directors are to be performed. It is probably too narrow to say, for example, that non-executive directors perform their functions only at board meetings or when reading the papers preparatory to the meeting, since many non-executives are appointed precisely because of the contacts they have in the wider world.

likely to be an accounting by the director for the profits made out of the personal exploitation, though in some cases the company's interest might be satisfied by a simple injunction preventing further personal exploitation. As *Cooley* shows, it is no bar to the recovery of the profit by the company that it could not, or was unlikely to, make the profit itself. The aim is to deprive the director of any incentive to put the company's interests second. On the other hand, the courts have been less certain whether the same policy should lead them, when calculating the profit, to make the director no allowance for the skill and time devoted to achieving the profit.[128] In a number of cases, the courts have been led to treat the corporate opportunity as the property of the company, from which it is easy to reason that personal exploitation of the opportunity amounts to misapplication by the director of corporate assets. On this basis, the director is under not just a personal liability to account for the profit made to the company; he holds that profit (or the assets representing it) as a constructive trustee for the company.[129]

Alternatively, but not additionally (here s 322 is more favourable to the company), the company can sue for damages. These may well be less than the profit made, as where the company could not easily have obtained or exploited the opportunity itself. Equally, there might also be cases where the damages were greater than the profit made by the director, as where the director was incompetent and the company well placed to exploit the opportunity (though, even so, the director might have no assets out of which to reimburse the company). There is no case for rescission of contract by the company, since in the case we are considering the company has been excluded from the opportunity.

BRIBES

One final word on the rule against 'secret' profits. We have seen that this rule can be used as a rationale for the law dealing with corporate opportunities, though we have argued that it needs to supplemented. However that may be, the scope of the secret profit rule is not exhausted by corporate opportunities. It may extend to any profit made by a director out of his office, even if this profit does not arise from the exploitation of a business opportunity. As the CLR Draft puts it, a director 'must not accept any benefit which is conferred because of the powers he has as director or by way of reward for any exercise of the powers he has as such'.[130] This

---

[128] Contrast the *Guinness* case, see n. 41 and *Phipps v Boardman* [1967] 2 AC 46, HL.
[129] See *Cook v Deeks*, above, n. 124.   [130] Above, n. 1, at p. 347 (Principle 7).

is separately stated from the duty not to make personal use of the company's property, information, or opportunity, if only because the rule against personal benefits is subject only to prior approval by the shareholders, whereas, as we have seen, corporate opportunities, and so on, it is proposed, may be authorized by independent members of the board as well.

The classic example of personal benefits, outside the corporate opportunity area, is what are usually called 'bribes', though in fact the term covers any payment made by a third party to a director, whom the third party knows to be a director, which payment has not been disclosed to the shareholders. A corrupt motive is not required to turn the secret payment into a bribe. The full range of remedies is available to the company: the transaction to which the secret payment was linked may be rescinded by the company; and the director and the payer are liable, jointly and severally, in damages to the company or to account for the amount of the bribe. Finally, it seems that the liability to account is not just a personal one; the amount of the bribe is held on a constructive trust for the company.[131]

FORGIVENESS AND ENFORCEMENT

THE NATURE OF THE DECISIONS TO BE TAKEN

Assuming the company thinks one or more directors have acted in breach of duty, should it initiate legal action against them and which body within the company should be allocated that decision? It is important to see that taking legal action is not necessarily the correct thing to do from the perspective of the best interests of the company. The company's argument may not stand up in court; even if it does, the directors may not have the assets with which to meet the court's judgment; the litigation may divert the time of management away from other, more valuable projects; or the company, even if it wins the litigation, may suffer harm to its public reputation which damages its business. As in other walks of life, it is not necessarily wise to enforce one's legal rights. On the other hand, there is no doubt that the company ought to give proper consideration to the matter and that in some substantial number of cases litigation, or the threat of it, will be the appropriate response in the best interests of the company.

If the company's view is in the direction of taking legal action, then the

---

[131] *Attorney-General for Hong Kong v Reid* [1994] 1 AC 324, PC.

nature of the decision which it has to take is clear enough, though there is an important issue, which we address below, about which body within the company is vested with the power to take this particular decision. On the other hand, if the company is leaning in the direction of not taking legal action, that decision might express itself in a number of different ways, with different legal consequences. The company might take no decision at all, simply failing to enforce its legal rights, or it might go a little further and take a formal decision not to initiate litigation. In either case it would seem that the company, in principle, could later change its mind and initiate litigation (subject to the applicable limitation periods and subject to the company not dealing with the potential defendants in such a way as to give them a contractual or other entitlement that the company stick by its first decision). However, the company might want to go even further and, so to speak, legitimate the breach of duty and, in so doing, deprive itself of the power in the future to bring litigation and give the potential defendants the comfort of knowing that their apparently wrongful conduct had been approved.

Legitimization, usually called 'ratification' in this context, can have two aspects. As we have seen, one consequence of a breach of directors' duty is often that the associated transaction is one which is not binding on the company. However, apart from the breach of duty, the company may regard the transaction as one which is in the company's interest and so it may wish to adopt it and so make it binding on the company. By this aspect of ratification the company is depriving itself of the legal power to escape from the transaction. Second, a breach of duty usually generates some liability on the part of the director towards the company, for example to indemnify it against losses or to account for a profit made. A second type of ratification, and the more controversial one, involves releasing the director from this liability. Ratification here has the effect of expunging the wrong that the director has committed. Sometimes these two forms of ratification are expressly distinguished, as is s 35 of the Act, which deals with directors exceeding the limitations contained in the company's objects clause. Separate resolutions of the shareholders are required, to make the transaction entered into in excess of authority binding upon the company (as against dissenting shareholders),[132] and to relieve the directors of liability to the company. The shareholders could decide to pass either, neither, or both of these resolutions. At common

---

[132] The transaction, as we have seen, is binding as between the company and third parties in any event: above, p. 46.

law, ratification resolutions seem to have both effects, though presumably the resolution could be expressly confined to one or other of them.

WHO DECIDES?

In relation to both the litigation and the non-litigation decisions, the crucial questions become: who has the power to take these decisions and what, if any, limitations should be placed on their powers? Thus, we are in large part back in the territory of the decision rights strategy, which we discussed in the previous chapter,[133] but the consideration of which in relation to the enforcement of directors' duties needed to be postponed until those duties themselves had been analysed. We turn first to the decision to litigate, and there seems no reason not to permit the board to decide in favour of litigation, if that would normally fall within its grant of management powers. One might be sceptical about how often a board will decide to sue one of its fellows, but that is no reason to prevent it from litigating, if it chooses to do so.[134] In any event, the board which decides to sue may no longer contain the wrongdoing directors because there has been a change of management, as in the *Regal* case.[135] More likely, perhaps, the management of the company may have passed upon insolvency into the hands of a liquidator, who decides to sue the former directors.[136]

More problematic are decisions by the board not to sue the wrong-doers. The presence of the wrongdoing director on the board, even if he does not vote on the issue, casts a cloud over any such decision by the board. Here, the common law rule, which we have already mentioned, that the company has the right to the unbiased advice of all its directors,[137] seems to express itself in the proposition that the shareholders in general meeting have a power, by rule of law, which is parallel to that of the board, to initiate litigation against the wrongdoing directors, even though there

---

[133] Chapter 5, p. 123.

[134] *John Shaw & Son (Salford) Ltd v Shaw* [1935] 2 KB 113, CA, where this principle was accepted, provides an example: the management of the company had been vested by the articles in a sub-set of independent directors, who initiated the litigation against the wrong-doers. And see Chapter 7 where trusteeship in relation to non-executive directors and disinterested directors is discussed.

[135] See p. 184.

[136] The special position of the liquidator is recognized in s 212 of the Insolvency Act 1986. He or she can initiate a summary procedure by which the court inquires into the alleged breaches of duty by directors of the company and orders them to restore property or make payments to the company.

[137] Above, text at n. 76.

is a general and exclusive grant of management powers to the board in the articles.[138]

As to ratification, the common law rule about unbiased advice of the directors again puts that decision into the hands of the shareholders and companies' articles do not in practice purport to allocate the decision elsewhere. The CLR does not propose to alter the common law rule on ratification, even though, as noted above, it proposes to confirm the current rule that the board can give prior approval in self-dealing transactions and to extend that rule to prior approval of the taking of corporate opportunities. Thus, if the director does act in breach of duty, whether in relation to self-dealing transactions or corporate opportunities or otherwise, the body with the power to ratify the breach subsequently is the shareholders' meeting, not the board, and the CLR proposes that this should remain the position. Overall, therefore, in relation both to the decision to sue and to the decision to ratify, the shareholders' meeting is a crucial centre of decision-making power.

ENFORCEMENT AND SHAREHOLDERS' COLLECTIVE ACTION PROBLEMS

Is that a sensible allocation of decision-making powers over the ratification/litigation decision? One objection to the decision rights strategy is that it may achieve very little if the directors as shareholders control the shareholders' meeting. The conflicts of interest are thus simply transferred from board to general meeting. This is a serious point and the responses to it are considered further in Chapter 8, where we deal with majority/minority shareholder conflicts. In this chapter, however, we have adopted the hypothesis that there is no controlling shareholder, whether that shareholder is the wrongdoing director or not. On the other hand, we have also hypothesized that the company is a large one, and that it has a large body of shareholders. Is it likely that the collective action problems, which large bodies of people experience,[139] will prevent effective exercise by the shareholders of their ratification/litigation decision-making powers? This requires some analysis here.

As far as ratification is concerned, collective action problems are not

---

[138] The point is not entirely clear (see *Gower*, 6th edn, 1997 pp. 187–8), but unless the proposition is accepted the 'rule in *Foss v Harbottle*' ((1843) 2 Hare 461; see Chapter 8) does not make much sense, for that rule says that the individual should not normally be permitted to enforce the company's rights but should ask the shareholders collectively whether they wish to do so.

[139] Above, p. 139.

likely to be much of a hurdle, because in practice the burden of initiating the ratification process lies with the wrongdoing directors. They must summon the shareholders' meeting to consider the ratification resolution and disclose to that meeting the information necessary for the shareholders to make an informed decision.[140] More difficult is the situation where the shareholders' power to initiate litigation is at issue. The directors may simply sit quiet, not seeking ratification nor in any other way to put the issue before the shareholders in general meeting. In so doing, the directors run the risk that they may subsequently lose control of the company or it may fall into insolvency, so that a subsequent board or a liquidator may sue them, but they may prefer that to putting the issue explicitly before the current shareholders. Or they may simply take the view that they have committed no wrong. In this situation, the burden of convening a meeting falls on the shareholders. We saw in the previous chapter that here the collective action problems of the shareholders are serious.[141] The CLR's proposals to better align the annual reporting and requisitioning timetables may help, for example where the accounts reveal self-dealing transactions which have not been properly authorized,[142] but the difficulties encountered by a large body of shareholders wishing to initiate a meeting should not be underestimated.

In short, the risk is that, in a substantial number of cases, the company will never give proper consideration to the question whether the wrong-doing directors should be sued, because they control the board and the shareholders' meeting, in practice, cannot be convened. There are two techniques which the law could, and to some extent does, use to address this problem. One is to allocate the decision to a sub-set of the shareholders, perhaps even to the individual shareholder; the other is to give the decision to a 'trustee'. However, these techniques are better discussed in the following chapters as part of a more general analysis of the strategies involved.[143]

INSURANCE AND RELIEF

There are two final matters to be mentioned in relation to enforcement and ratification. Even if the company does not ratify a director's breach of duty subsequent to the breach, the director may face the prospect of litigation with at least financial equanimity because the company has, at an earlier stage, bought him or her insurance against liability for breach

---

[140] See Chapter 5, n. 51, *Tiessen v Henderson* [1899] 1 Ch 861.
[141] See Chapter 5, pp. 136–144.
[142] See Chapter 5, n. 32.   [143] See pp. 224 and 249 below.

of duty. In 1989 s 310 of the Act[144] was amended so as to permit such insurance to be purchased at the company's expense and for the benefit of the director. Taking out such insurance will normally be a decision for the board. Although such insurance has the unattractive feature of shareholders paying to protect their representatives against the consequences of wrongs done by those representatives to the shareholders, it is likely that insurance is not in fact available in respect of wrongdoing intentionally aimed at the company and that such insurance is in fact unlawful as contrary to public policy. Outside the area of intentional wrongdoing, the board might well take the view that, without such insurance, senior persons might be unwilling to come forward for directorships or would require even higher remuneration so that they could purchase their own insurance. The downside of such insurance, both for the director and the company, is that the presence of insurance may actually encourage litigation. As well as or instead of buying insurance for the director, s 310 permits the company, on a particular occasion, to indemnify the director against the costs of defending an action for breach of duty, but only if the director is found not liable.

Second, even if the shareholders do not ratify the director's wrongdoing and in fact initiate litigation, CA 1985, s 727 gives the court a discretion to relieve a director who has acted 'honestly and reasonably' from liability for breach of the above duties, either wholly or in part. This section protects the honest director against swingeing liabilities for what might appear to be largely technical breaches of the above duties, but it has not been used by the courts in an expansive way so as to undermine the substance of the law set out above.

CONCLUSION

As is conventional, in this chapter we divided the discussion of the duties of directors into two categories, duties of competence and duties of loyalty, and we have seen that the latter have received a much larger elaboration by the law. We also suggested that the nineteenth-century starting point was one which displayed the director as a 'gentlemanly amateur', not expected to be very skilled but expected to observe the highest punctilio of honour, especially in avoiding apparent conflicts of interest. By the end of the chapter, we can see that this initial starting position has almost been stood on its head. Over the past twenty years or so the courts have

---

[144] Above, p. 184.

begun to demand standards of skill and care of directors which are much more closely attuned to those required of people in other walks of life, a development which has been driven as much by the new statutory provisions dealing with wrongful trading and disqualification of directors as by changes in the common law. On the other hand, from the very beginning, those responsible for drafting articles of association tried to modify the inconveniences of the more demanding duties of loyalty, notably the need for prior shareholder approval, and, as we have seen, the CLR proposes both to endorse and to extend that tendency. Only in a limited class of cases will the full force of the common law be insisted upon.

What has probably driven these developments is the changing role of the director, at least in large companies. No longer a set of figureheads, the board claims its legitimacy, not only as against the shareholders but also as against other stakeholders in the company, on the basis of expertise, which, indeed, can be studied and enhanced in the business schools of the universities. This greater emphasis on the managerial qualities of the board makes the undemanding competence standard an anachronism, but it also, and with opposite consequences for the common law, tends to enhance the claims made for centralized management as against the involvement of shareholders in corporate decision-making. This has proved a difficult development for the common law on self-dealing transactions and corporate opportunities, which depends heavily on the involvement of shareholders in the approval of conflicted transactions.

Theoretically, it would have been possible to retain the rigour of the fiduciary requirements by replacing shareholder approval with court scrutiny of conflicted decisions on grounds of fairness, but this strategy has not proved attractive to the courts, which have been unwilling to fashion for themselves objective grounds of intervention which departed very far from the company's own constitution. In any event, court approval is likely to suffer as much, if not more, from the perceived defects of shareholder decision-making in this area. In consequence, once the CLR's proposals are implemented, if the directors stay within the (broad) powers conferred upon them by the company's constitution and disclose conflicts of interests to the board and obtain prior board approval for corporate opportunities, it will be difficult to find grounds within the law on directors' duties on which to challenge them. This conclusion makes analysis of the ways in which the law can structure the incentives which drive board-level decisions of the greatest importance, a matter to which we turn in the next chapter.

7

Centralized Management III
Setting the Board's Incentives

In this chapter we conclude our analysis of the legal strategies available to reduce the agency costs as between shareholders and the board in large companies with no controlling shareholder. In the previous chapter we considered the strategy of constraining agent decisions (that is, the fifth column in Figure 1 on p. 120), a strategy to which, as we saw, company law has devoted considerable attention. In this chapter we analyse the other strategy for directly structuring agents' decisions, which appears in the fourth column of the Figure under the heading 'Setting agent incentives'. Of course, in a broad sense the legal standards and rules considered in the previous chapter set incentives for directors. For example, the prospect of liability, so far as it exists, will give directors an incentive to abide by the law relating to directors' duties. However, what we cover in this chapter is those incentives, provided by the law, which encourage directors to act in the best interests of the shareholders, whether or not any legal sanctions are attached to their not so doing. With this strategy, the interests of the shareholders are internalized, so to speak, by the directors, not imposed on directors from outside, by way of the threat of legal sanctions.

The incentive setting strategy takes two, rather different, forms. It may operate negatively, by reducing or removing the self-interest of the directors, so that the competition between that self-interest and the interests of the shareholders is mitigated or even eliminated. This we have called 'trusteeship'. Alternatively, the self-interest of the directors may be given free rein, but the shareholders benefit from this because that self-interest is aligned with the interests of the shareholders. By benefiting themselves the directors benefit the shareholders. This is the rewards strategy. As applied to any one director, these strategies are mutually exclusive, though both could be, and normally are, applied to the board, non-executive directors being subject to the former and executive directors to the latter strategy. We shall look at each strategy in turn.

TRUSTEESHIP AND NON-EXECUTIVE DIRECTORS

THE NATURE OF 'TRUSTEESHIP' ON THE BOARD

The 'trusteeship' strategy has been a central element of the reforms which have resulted from the modern 'corporate governance' debate.[1] These reforms are based on the insight that the most powerful incentives to self-interested behaviour on the part of directors stem, not so much from holding a directorship, but from holding a directorship in conjunction with a full-time executive position in the company as a senior manager, especially as CEO. Such a person not only has an obvious interest in raising his or her reward package to the highest levels possible, but also may be able to exercise his managerial powers in a wide variety of other ways so as to confer private benefits which do not advance the interests of the shareholders, such as private or doubtfully business-related use of a private jet. However, the distorting private interests of full-time executive directors may not be primarily financial. A leadership position in a large company gives frequent opportunities for the exercise of power or for public display, which do not clearly advance the interests of the shareholders. A dominant chief executive may wish, for example, to launch a take-over offer which will expand her business empire, but, because she overpays for the target company, the profitability of the combined enterprise suffers. Or he may give lavish support from the company's coffers for a sport which he personally enjoys, even where market research suggests that equally effective promotion of the company's image could be obtained much more cheaply by other means.

So long as the company is a going concern, it may be difficult to demonstrate from outside that the company could have been run differently and better from the point of view of the shareholders. Indeed, some non-shareholder stakeholders in the company may benefit from a partial setting aside of the shareholders' interests, as where the enlarged company increases employment. However, in the late 1980s a number of sudden corporate failures occurred which seemed to be in part attributable to the CEO of the company being insufficiently accountable to his or her board of directors, those collapses hitting hard at the interests of all the stakeholders in the company and not just the shareholders. The remedy, it was proposed, was to increase the number of, and the importance

[1] See Chapter 5, p. 115.

of the roles performed by, non-executive directors (NEDs) and, in particular, by *independent* NEDs, that is, those not otherwise currently or recently connected with the company. Such directors have only their directorships and thus no managerial positions in the company; are part-time and so their lives are not wholly bound up in the company; and are modestly remunerated, at least by corporate standards. While one may accept that such directors are not subject to the high-powered incentives of executive directors to put self-interest above shareholder interest, one might wonder what incentives they have to act as a check on those directors who are subject to the high-powered incentives of self-interest. The answer which is given is that they are motivated by low-powered reputational incentives to do a good job of controlling headstrong executive directors. Those seen to have acted as effective non-executives will enjoy the public esteem of being so regarded and, of course, will be more in demand in this role for other companies. It has to be said that, at present, the jury is still out on the empirical question of whether low-powered reputational incentives can act as an effective counterweight to self-interested executives.

THE ORIGINS AND CONTENT OF COMBINED CODE

Although the appropriate role for NEDs on the board has been much discussed publicly in recent years, this debate has rather passed by general company law. As far as the Companies Act is concerned, it is perfectly proper for all the directors to be executives or none or some of them. When the modern corporate governance debate was launched in the United Kingdom in the early 1990s, that occurred through a business initiative, albeit with governmental support, rather than through proposals for legislation. It seems that the Government thought the whole issue too much of a 'hot potato' for legislation, but wanted to have some influence on how this important public policy matter was handled. The result was business-sponsored committees, but serviced by civil servants. The public policy arguments in favour of NEDs will always be associated with the Report of the Cadbury Committee.[2] That Committee set out the basic arguments in favour of increasing the number and importance of NEDs. Their ideas were refined, though not fundamentally altered, in the subsequent Greenbury Committee[3] and Hampel Committee[4] Reports.

---

[2] *The Financial Aspects of Corporate Governance* (London: Gee, 1992). See p. 131.
[3] *Report of the Study Group on Directors' Remuneration* (London: Gee, 1995).
[4] *Final Report of the Committee on Corporate Governance* (London: Gee, 1998).

Because these Committees, at least formally, were private-sector initiatives, their output was not legislation but codes of practice, which have now been brought together in a single Combined Code. However, as we pointed out in Chapter 5,[5] the Code is not entirely lacking in binding force as far as publicly traded companies are concerned. UK-incorporated companies, which are listed, are required to state in their annual report to shareholders whether they have complied with the provisions of the Combined Code and to explain any examples of non-compliance ('comply or explain').[6] The fact that this rule applies only to UK-incorporated companies (and not to foreign companies which have listed their securities on the LSE) shows perhaps that the Combined Code has more to do with company law (where the conflicts of law rule is that the company is governed by the law of the country of incorporation or of the country where its headquarters are situated)[7] than with securities markets law. If the Combined Code were primarily a securities market matter, one would expect it to be applied to all companies whose securities are listed on the LSE, no matter their place of incorporation.

The argument for applying the Code only to listed companies is largely pragmatic, namely that listing happens to identify the sub-set of public companies for which the Code rules are appropriate. The CLR largely accepted this argument, though it proposed to extend the Combined Code to all companies whose securities are publicly traded, whether or not they are listed.[8] It also sought to emphasize the company law aspects of the Code by proposing that responsibility for keeping the contents of the Code under review should pass to the proposed Companies Commission.[9]

---

[5] Chapter 5, p. 131.

[6] Listing Rules, r 12.43A. The Combined Code is set out as an Annex to the Listing Rules.

[7] These are obviously two different conflicts rules and the choice between them is highly important in terms of fostering competition among jurisdictions. See B. Cheffins, *Company Law: Theory, Structure and Operation* (Oxford: Clarendon Press, 1997), ch. 9 and Case C-212/97, *Centros* [2000] All ER (EC) 481 (ECJ). However, the point in the text stands whichever conflicts of law rule is chosen.

[8] CLR, *Completing the Structure*, November 2000, para. 4.44. Listed companies are a sub-set of publicly traded companies and consist of those companies with sufficient track record to meet the listing requirements of the UK Listing Authority (which requirements are now derived substantially, though not wholly, from EC law). The main market of the LSE consists only of listed companies. However, the LSE also runs a junior market, the Alternative Investment Market (AIM), for which the admission requirements are less demanding than those for listing. Other bodies may also organize markets for either listed or non-listed securities.

[9] CLR, *Final Report*, 2001, vol. I, paras 3.62–3.64.

What, concretely, does the Combined Code require in the way of board structure? Its requirements can be summarized as follows.[10]

- The board has a dual function, both to 'lead' and to 'control' the company.

- At least one-third of the board as a whole should be NEDs, most of whom should be independent. Independent means 'independent of management and free from any business or other relationship with the company which could materially interfere with the exercise of their independent judgement'. As with the board as a whole the NEDs have a role both in setting the company's strategy ('leading') and in 'controlling' it. In the case of the NEDs, however, 'controlling' includes monitoring the performance of the company's executive directors.

- There should be introduced committees of the board to deal with certain specific matters on which the NEDs should be the only or the majority of the members. These are the audit, remuneration, and appointment committees.

- In principle, the CEO and the chair of the board should not be the same person. However, the chair of the board need not be an NED, still less an independent NED, so that the chair of the board may be a former CEO of the company. Whether the roles are combined or not, however, there should also be an identified senior independent NED on the board with whom the shareholders can liaise.

- There should be a formal statement of the matters on which the board's decision is necessary.

- The NEDs should have access to appropriate outside professional advice and to internal information from the company.

This account of the requirements of the Combined Code in the area of board structure makes clear the importance of the 'trusteeship' strategy in its approach to this issue. NEDs (and especially independent NEDs) are to be a significant part of the board as a whole and dominant on the committees where the conflicts of interest of the executive directors might be expected to be most prominent: the remuneration, audit, and appointment committees. Trusteeship is not the only policy: the chair of the board, who should normally be someone other than the CEO, need

---

[10] This section draws heavily on P. Davies, 'Board Structure in the UK and Germany: Convergence or Continuing Divergence' (2000) 2 *International and Comparative Corporate Law Journal* 435.

not be an NED, so that strategy here is a simple division of powers. Nevertheless, trusteeship through independent NEDs is a, if not the, main strategy of the Code in relation to the structure of the board.

THE IMPACT OF THE COMBINED CODE

The effect of implementing a trusteeship strategy is to move the board of listed UK companies rather decisively in a two-tier direction. NEDs, besides participating in the general board task of setting and monitoring the execution of the company's business strategy, also have the role of monitoring the performance of the executive directors and the senior non-board managers of the company. The non-executives are thus potentially in a slightly uncomfortable position: they are both responsible for the company's business strategy (with the executive directors) and responsible (against the executive directors) for assessing the performance of the executives in setting and implementing that strategy. This might be thought to be an argument in favour of institutionalizing the two functions, by creating a supervisory board (consisting wholly of non-executives) and a management board (consisting of executives).[11] The contrary argument is that the discomfort of the non-executives on a unitary board is a price worth paying for the better access to information that membership of the single board gives to the non-executives. Nevertheless, British company law does not prohibit the creation, de facto, of a two-tier board and the CLR found evidence that some large companies were creating informal management boards beneath the formal board on which the non-executives were represented.[12]

What has been the impact of the Combined Code's recommendations? In terms of their acceptance by listed companies, the level of compliance with the Code is high, though the separation of the positions of CEO and chair of the board has often been controversial.[13] Nevertheless, research done for the CLR shows that listed companies have largely complied with

---

[11] In the Netherlands, under the 'structure' regime for large domestic companies, the theory of trusteeship has been taken a step further, because the (non-executive) members of the supervisory board are appointed by the board itself, with the shareholders (and the employees via the works council) having only weak veto rights over the proposals made by the largely self-perpetuating supervisory board.

[12] CLR, *Developing the Framework*, March 2000, para. 3.152: 'the practice of delegating day to day management and major operational questions to a "management board" is becoming increasingly common in this country'. And it adds: 'It is, of course, perfectly legal and gives many of the advantages of the two-tier board.'

[13] At the end of 2000 it was said that 20 or more companies among the 350 largest listed companies had the same person as CEO and chair of the board, including Marks and Spencer and Powergen: *Financial Times*, 10 October 2000.

the Code's provisions, though the level of compliance falls off a bit among the smallest listed companies.[14] This level of compliance seems to have been in large part due to the support given to the Combined Code by the institutional investors,[15] some of whom have produced their own codes which go beyond what the Combined Code requires. At the level of the impact of the Combined Code on the business success of companies, it is much more difficult to be sure what the effect of the Code has been. On the basis of its consultations the CLR concluded: 'The general response was that the Code had been generally beneficial, perhaps more by preventing value destruction by ineffectively managed and monitored businesses and by creating a climate of openness and accountability, with consequent beneficial market effects, than by directly and beneficially influencing management of corporate resources'.[16] The truth is, perhaps, that the economic climate was benign for many years after the Code was introduced and that evidence of its effectiveness will become clear only as the economy turns down and it becomes apparent, for example, whether during the good times dominant entrepreneurs had been pursuing their own aggrandizement rather than shareholder value.

In one area, however, that of directors' remuneration, there is already evidence to suggest that the Code has not been successful, at least if the test in this area is the exertion of a downward pressure on executive salaries. If anything, implementation of the Code seems to have been associated with the upward rise of remuneration packages. The explanation for this state of affairs appears to be that the main source of NEDs is executive directors of other companies. Although independent of the company of which they are non-executives, they are likely to share a 'high compensation' culture with the executives of that company because of their executive positions elsewhere. This analysis, if it is correct, indicates the problems with implementing a trusteeship strategy, namely, the difficulty of finding NEDs who are both effective (which will necessarily involve business experience) and free across the whole range of issues of the self-interest to which the executive directors are prone. Indeed, it points to a fundamental problem with the strategy: executive directors may favour non-executives who are not interventionist and may carry that disposition over into the discharge of their duties as non-executives of other companies, not only in relation to remuneration questions but in relation to all matters coming before the board.

---

[14] Pensions and Investment Research Consultants Ltd, *Compliance with the Combined Code*, September 1999, available on the CLR web site: **www.dti.gov.uk/cld/review.htm**.
[15] See p. 141.   [16] Above, n. 9, at para. 4.44.

The problem was pointed up some time ago by Professors Gilson and Kraakman,[17] writing from a US perspective, where the drive for NEDs has been taken much further, to the point where they usually constitute the overwhelming majority of members of the board.[18] They suggest that the crucial step is not to make the non-executives independent of the company but dependent upon the shareholders, that is, that the appointments rights strategy is likely to be more effective than the trusteeship strategy. On the supply side, this would involve creating a cadre of persons whose activities as directors would consist only of being NEDs of companies (though they would probably have other non-directorial but business-related activities as well). On the demand side, institutional investors would involve themselves in appointing and liaising with such NEDs.

We have noted that the institutional investors in the UK have embraced with enthusiasm the provisions of the Combined Code on NEDs, but they have not sought to become closely involved in their appointment. In fact, NEDs are appointed in the usual way, which, as we saw in Chapter 5,[19] is board nomination and ratification of that choice by the shareholders. The Cadbury Committee itself rejected a proposal for closer shareholder involvement in the selection of non-executives,[20] probably because it did not want to alienate management from its proposals, but it is less clear why institutional investors have not pressed for it. The answer may be found in the conflicts of interest which face institutional investors or, more likely, in an unwillingness to accept the legal and, more important, the political risks associated with appearing to become the monitors of British industry.[21]

Whatever the true explanation may be, the trusteeship strategy has clearly not dealt with the issue of directors' remuneration to the satisfac-

---

[17] R. Gilson and R. Kraakman, 'Reinventing the Outside Director: an Agenda for Institutional Investors' (1991) 43 *Stanford Law Review* 863.

[18] See D. DeMott, 'The Figures in the Landscape: A Comparative Sketch of Directors' Self-Interested Transactions' (1999) 3 *Company, Financial and Insolvency Law Review* 190, 194: the average US board had 'two "inside" (or executive) directors and nine "outside" directors'.

[19] See Chapter 5, p. 128.

[20] Above, n. 2, paras 5.9–5.12.

[21] See Davies, n. 10 above, at pp. 444–6 and CLR, n. 9 above, at paras 6.22–6.39. The Mynors Report (*Institutional Investment in the United Kingdom: A Review*, HM Treasury, 2001) illustrates the pressures pension funds are already under to be active investors, ostensibly in the interests of the beneficiaries of the fund, but in the Government's eyes partly in the public interest.

tion of the Government and, as we saw in Chapter 5, it has been edging its way towards supplementing the trusteeship strategy with a more developed decision rights strategy, by requiring a shareholder vote on companies' remuneration policies. Whether the experience with remuneration reflects a more deep-seated weakness in the trusteeship strategy remains to be seen. Significantly, in 2002 the Government announced an independent review of the role and effectiveness of non-executive directors in the UK.[22]

NON–EXECUTIVE DIRECTORS AND DISINTERESTED DIRECTORS

There is one final, but important, issue to be considered here, which is the interrelationship between independent NEDs and the exclusion of 'interested' directors from voting on the approval of the taking of corporate opportunities, etc. by directors, as discussed in Chapter 6.[23] The two things are clearly not the same. For the purposes of the corporate opportunity doctrine an independent NED might be an 'interested' director, as where it is he or she who has come across and wishes to exploit personally the opportunity in which the company has a legitimate interest. Equally, an executive director who is not involved in the proposed exploitation of the opportunity is not 'interested' as far as the law on directors' duties is concerned.

Nevertheless, the theory underlying the Combined Code's recommendations on NEDs and the CLR's use of disinterested directors seems similar: in both cases decision-making is said to be transferred to a sub-group of directors who are not tempted to prioritize self-interest over the interests of the shareholders. In the narrow sense of interest in the particular decision in mind, the argument is undoubtedly right. However, as with independent NEDs, so also with disinterested directors, it is less clear that they are free of self-interest when the broader decision-making context is examined. Just as independent NEDs may have an interest in high levels of executive remuneration because they are executive directors of other companies, disinterested directors may support a relaxed attitude to board approval of the taking of corporate opportunities because they may benefit from that policy in the future when they are the interested directors.

[22] DTI, Press Release P/2002/128, February 2002.
[23] Chapter 6, p. 185. The point is made clear in note (1) to Principle 6 of the CLR's draft Statement of Principles: 'In this paragraph, "the board" means the board of directors acting without the participation of any interested director.'

OTHER TYPES OF TRUSTEE

In the above section we have considered only directors as trustees. There is no reason why the relevant disinterested person should not be found elsewhere within the company or, indeed, outside it. We saw in Chapter 5 that the auditors perform a trusteeship role in relation to the company's financial statements. The Act seeks to ensure the independence of the auditors by requiring that they be appointed by the general meeting. However, the possibility for accountancy firms to earn large sums from the provision of non-audit services to the company may compromise the independence of the auditor.[24] Or a court may be able to perform a trusteeship role in some cases. We find examples of this technique in the law dealing with majority/minority shareholder conflicts and we shall examine it in Chapter 8.

THE REWARD STRATEGY

The reward strategy has an entirely different point of departure from the trusteeship strategy. The self-interest of the director is accepted as a powerful motivator of his or her behaviour, but the attempt is made to align that self-interest with the interests of the shareholders. Normally, this is done by tying a significant part of the director's earnings from the company to the advancement of the shareholders' interest. In principle, this strategy seems to have significant potential, not least because it does not need an elaborate legal framework for its implementation. The incentives for the directors are normally embodied simply in a contract between him or her and the company. The strategy suffers, however, from two drawbacks.

The first is the difficulty of identifying an appropriate indicator of the shareholders' welfare to which the directors' remuneration can be attached. A traditional mechanism is the share option scheme, whereby the director is given an option to subscribe for a certain number of shares in the company at some point in the future (normally three years or more) at the market price prevailing at the time the option is granted. If over the three-year period the shares do well, the director will exercise his or her option at the relevant time, probably sell the shares immediately, and pocket the difference between the option price and the market price prevailing when the option is exercised. It is said that the shareholders

---

[24] CA 1985, ss 385, 390A–B; CLR, *Final Report*, 2001, Vol. I, paras 8.124–8.126; DTI Press Release, P/2002/128, February 2002.

should be pleased about this because their shares will have increased in value over the period as well.

However, a thoughtful shareholder might wonder about this argument. If the market for shares as a whole increases in value over the period in question, because it is a period of economic boom, the value added to the company's shares might not be attributable at all to the efforts of the directors, so that it is unclear why they should be especially rewarded for it. Equally troubling to the thoughtful shareholder may be the insight that, if over the period the market as a whole declines, the directors will receive no reward, even though they have worked especially hard and have taken some astute business decisions. Of course, there are ways around this problem. The rewards of the directors may be attached to the relative performance of their company as against appropriate comparator companies, so that the directors are rewarded if they do better than the comparators, whether the market as a whole is going up or down. Such schemes may involve a move away from share options towards other forms of long-term incentive plans (LTIPs). Considerable ingenuity has been devoted by the business schools and by remuneration consultants to the invention of appropriate schemes.

The second disadvantage takes us back to territory we have already covered. Directors have traditionally had a considerable input into the design of their remuneration packages. It is likely that they still do, even in listed companies where the remuneration committee is dominated by NEDs. There is therefore a risk that LTIPs will operate, not as a method of aligning directors' and shareholders' interests, but as an expression of the self-interest of the directors. The crucial factor, for distinguishing an LTIP which performs the task of alignment effectively from one which is simply a mechanism whereby the director extracts an even higher level of remuneration from the company than is represented by his salary and other benefits, is the rigour of the performance criteria which trigger the reward. The Combined Code is clear that these should be demanding. Schedule A to the Code provides: 'Payouts or grants under all incentive schemes, including new grants under existing share option schemes, should be subject to challenging performance criteria reflecting the company's objectives.'

It is easier to state this principle than to ensure that it is applied in practice. In recent times the financial press has contained complaints from institutional shareholders that a number of companies were proposing to adopt LTIPs with undemanding performance criteria. Here, however, even in advance of governmental implementation of the principle of shareholder approval of the company's remuneration policy, the shareholders have a hook on which to hang their complaints, at least in listed companies. In the case of UK-incorporated companies, the Listing Rules[25] require shareholder approval by ordinary resolution of all LTIPs for directors. Although no company seems to have been defeated on a vote over an incentive scheme, some have found it politic to abandon certain features of proposed schemes in advance of the vote or to give undertakings about future conduct.[26] It is unclear at the moment whether alignment of interests or simple enhancement of remuneration is the predominant effect of LTIPs, that is, whether such schemes reduce or enhance the agency costs of shareholders.

Perhaps because the advantages of LTIPs are so unclear, British company law, like probably all other company law systems, does not insist upon use of the reward strategy. However, it should be noted that it is conventional wisdom in business circles to favour incentive schemes, and the Combined Code states that 'the performance-related elements of remuneration should form a significant proportion of the total remuneration package of executive directors'.[27] Thus, for better or worse, the reward strategy is in fact embedded in the remuneration policies of large British companies, even though company law may not require it. Company law does not even need to do much in the way of facilitating incentivized remuneration, since, as we have noted, that is based mainly in private contract law. The main facilitation for LTIPs comes probably from tax law, rather than company law.

CONCLUSIONS ON BOARD/ SHAREHOLDER STRATEGIES

In this chapter and the previous two we have examined the application of the strategies, set out in Figure 1 on p. 120 for the regulation of principal/ agent problems in general, to relations between shareholders and the board. That Figure identified three strategies for empowering shareholders as against directors (the decision rights, appointment rights, and affiliation rights strategies) and two strategies for directly structuring agents' decisions (the constraining and the incentive strategies). What

---

[25] Para. 13.13(b). This implements a recommendation of the Greenbury Committee, above n. 3, para. 6.33.

[26] Among the companies which faced revolts at shareholder meetings over incentive plans or bonus payments in the first seven months of 2001 were Billiton, Cable & Wireless, Marconi, Reuters, Royal Bank of Scotland, United Business Media, and Vodafone.

[27] Combined Code, para. B.1.4. It goes on to say that such elements 'should be designed to align their interests with those of shareholders.'

these chapters have shown is that British company law makes use of all five strategies to reduce shareholders' agency costs. This is perhaps not surprising. None of the five strategies is obviously effective on its own, and all have costs as well as benefits, so that it would probably be unwise for the law to put reliance on only one of them. Is it possible to go beyond the statement that British company law make some use of all these strategies?

One thing that seems clear is that British company law does not make equal use of all the strategies. At least in terms of the formal rules, the British system seems more wholeheartedly committed to the appointment rights and affiliation rights strategies (both considered in Chapter 5) than any of the others. The shareholders' removal rights as against directors are strongly formulated: only an ordinary resolution is required and there is no need to wait until the end of the director's term of office.[28] As for affiliation rights, we have seen that the City Code is firmly committed to the sidelining of incumbent management during take-over bids and placing the decision on the offer in the hands of shareholders of the target company, thus promoting both the exit rights of existing shareholders and the entry rights of the bidder.[29]

By contrast and despite the weight of legal analysis which it is necessary to undertake in order to understand the law on directors' duties (considered in Chapter 6), it is doubtful whether that law operated during most of the last century so as to impose significant constraints on directors' conduct. The directors' duty of competence was highly subjectively formulated, whilst self-dealing was something the board (dominated by executive directors) could sort out among themselves and the law on corporate opportunities was conceptually underdeveloped.[30] No doubt, the law was effective to pick up the egregious cases of conflict of interest, but it probably achieved no more than that. The law relating to directors' competence may be about to break out of its constricting mould, though as much through the impact of insolvency-related law on company law as through the innate force of the common law itself.[31] In particular, state enforcement of the rules on disqualification of directors helps to redress what has been a weak point of the common law of directors' duties: the difficulty facing minority shareholders who wish to enforce those duties.[32]

As for the two, very different, aspects of the incentives strategy (considered in this chapter), they are relative newcomers to the regulation of boards and on neither of them does company law actually insist. Board

[28] See p. 128.   [29] See p. 147.   [30] See pp. 154, 175 and 187.
[31] See p. 157.   [32] See above p. 194 and below p. 225.

structure is a matter for the Combined Code and thus only (at present) for listed companies, the boards of which in any event formally comply with the Code simply by explaining why they have not adopted its recommendations,[33] while the adoption of reward strategies is a matter entirely for the company, as far as the Companies Act is concerned. The tentativeness of the law towards this strategy is understandable for it has yet to prove itself. There is some evidence that splitting the roles of the CEO and the chair of the board is associated with replacement of the former in underperforming companies,[34] but the role of the NED has yet to be conclusively assessed, while there are grounds for suspicion about the effectiveness of the reward strategy.[35]

Finally, the decision rights strategy (the first strategy we considered, in Chapter 5)[36] has turned out to play a curious role. As a general strategy, it is clearly hopeless, because it involves solving the agency problem by ending the agency relationship. However, as a solution to particular problems it has an enduring role to play and, as we saw, it kept on emerging as a possible solution for dealing with the difficulties which the other strategies encounter in coping with conflicts of interest. The attraction of involving the shareholders, compulsorily, in the decision-making process is that the law thereby insists upon a procedure in which the shareholders have a good chance of protecting themselves, without the law having to determine, substantively, the point at issue. That was the approach of the common law to self-dealing transactions (before the drafters of articles excluded the principle in the managerial interest)[37] and its enduring value is shown by its partial reinstatement by Part X of the Companies Act;[38] the adherence to it by such modern codes as the Listing Rules (for related-party transactions)[39] and the Combined Code (for long-term incentive schemes);[40] and now, it seems, its adoption by the Government as a solution to one of the most intractable of company law issues (companies' remuneration policies).[41]

However, analysing the formal rules and assessing which of the five strategies they seem to favour is only part of the task. There remains the difficult issue of determining whether the strategies the law favours (above all, the appointment rights and the affiliation rights strategies)

---

[33] See p. 131.
[34] J. Franks and C. Mayer, 'Governance as a Source of Managerial Discipline', p. 17, paper prepared for the CLR and available on the CLR web site: **www.dti.gov.uk/cld/review.htm**.
[35] See p. 208. [36] See p. 123. [37] See p. 172. [38] See p. 177.
[39] See p. 176. [40] See p. 208. [41] See p. 126.

are effective in practice. As to the former we have noted that there is reason to think that shareholders still face collective action problems in companies without a controlling shareholder over the use of their removal rights. Even if shareholders' traditional collective action problems have been mitigated in recent decades with the rise of institutional shareholders, there remain the conflicts of interest among institutional shareholders which are likely to reduce the level of their intervention below what is optimal.[42]

As for the disciplinary effects of take-overs, the latest evidence for the UK suggests that take-overs do operate so as to change the management of badly performing companies, but that, across the board, take-over targets are not noticeably badly performing companies.[43] This suggests that take-overs are more often motivated by synergistic than disciplinary reasons,[44] but this fact is not necessarily conclusive in an assessment of the disciplinary impact of take-overs, which relies as much on the threat of the bid as on the actual bid. However, this evidence is consistent with the view that the threat of a take-over provides an incentive to the boards of companies to avoid only the worst levels of performance and not to maximize shareholder utility. In other words, the take-over threat may put a floor under board performance but may not do much to influence the level of performance above that floor.

The five strategies discussed above all focus on the shareholder/director relationship and aim either to enhance the shareholders' control or to structure the board's behaviour. However, it is possible that the shareholders may also benefit, indirectly, from strategies whose ostensible aim (and, indeed, effect) is to advance the interests, as against the board, of principals other than the shareholders. We noted in Chapter 4 that large lenders have an incentive to establish contractual mechanisms which permit them to monitor the performance of the boards of companies to which they lend money and to intervene to replace the management of the company in extreme cases. Particularly in companies with highly geared capital structures (that is, a high proportion of debt to equity), the shareholders may well benefit from the monitoring activities of the lenders. Although, logically, the lenders are interested solely in the company generating enough cash to pay the interest due on the loans and to repay the capital and do not care whether there is anything left over after that for the shareholders, it may in fact be difficult for the creditors to monitor

---

[42] See p. 143.   [43] Franks and Mayer, above, n. 34 at pp. 12 ff.
[44] See p. 146.

the board with that degree of precision and so the shareholders benefit indirectly from the creditors' activities.[45] This reverses the traditional argument[46] that, so long as the company is a going concern, the creditors do not need to be involved directly in the monitoring of boards, because monitoring in the interests of the shareholders will indirectly protect the creditors. It is the high degree of risk for lenders in highly leveraged capital structures which leads to this reversal, and there is, indeed, some empirical evidence that replacement of boards is associated in the UK with high levels of leverage.[47]

Finally, the shareholders may be protected by markets, rather than by legal strategies, and again this protection may be provided directly or indirectly. Indirect protection for shareholders may arise out of, for example, strongly competitive product markets. If the markets into which the company sells its products are competitive, at least some forms of board disregard of shareholder interests (for example shirking) will carry major penalties for the board itself, which may see the company driven into insolvency or become a take-over target (with the consequent loss of the directors' jobs) if the company does not operate effectively so as to meet the interests of its customers. More direct protection for shareholders may arise in the case of a company which needs regular access to the capital markets for fresh injections of equity finance. Investors may be reluctant to provide additional funding for the company if the board's record is one of disregard of the existing shareholders' interests; and the board, anticipating this, will give the shareholders' interests a high priority.

The impact of the capital market as a check on board performance is strengthened in the UK by the rule that new equity capital, issued for cash, must normally be raised on a 'rights' basis, that is, the new shares must first be offered pro rata to the existing shareholders.[48] This reduces the risk that the board will do an implicit deal with the new investors, whereby the board issues new shares at a substantial discount to the current market price in exchange for the support of the new shareholders against the existing shareholders, who are the ones who sustain the loss inherent in the dilution of the company's capital through the new issue at

---

[45] J. Drukarczyk and H. Schmidt, 'Lenders as a Force in Corporate Governance: Enabling Covenants and the Impact of Bankruptcy Law' in K. Hopt et al. (eds), *Comparative Corporate Governance* (Oxford: Clarendon Press, 1998), ch. 10.

[46] See below, p. 264.   [47] Franks and Mayer, above, n. 34, pp. 15 ff.

[48] CA 1985, s 89, see p. 253.

less than the current market price.[49] The importance attached by institutional shareholders to their pre-emption rights is demonstrated by the supplementary rules, which they have sponsored, applying to such issues. Although the Act permits the pre-emption rights of the shareholders to be disapplied by the articles or a shareholder vote for periods of up to five years, the Pre-Emption Guidelines indicate the limited circumstances in which the institutional shareholders will support such resolutions. The Pre-Emption Group Guidelines, which are essentially the result of bargaining between the institutional shareholders and companies and their advisers, under the aegis of the Exchange, indicate that institutional shareholders will accept waiver of their statutory rights if the company (a) restricts the new shares to be issued for cash to 5 per cent of the issued ordinary shares in any one year and 7.5 per cent over any rolling period of three years, and (b) restricts the discount on any issue to 5 per cent.[50]

Thus, we can see that overall the agency problems of the shareholders (as a class) as against the board are addressed through a portfolio of legal strategies as well as through the operation of markets, whose effectiveness is sometimes supported by company law rules, such as that on pre-emptive rights. Given the variety of circumstances in which those problems can arise and the lack of conclusive empirical data about which strategies are most effective, having a range of approaches seems a wise approach for the law. The balance among the strategies, however, will always be a matter for public policy debate and something which is likely to be subject to change.

---

[49] The CLR accordingly recommended the retention of the pre-emption rule, despite arguments that it increases companies' cost of capital: CLR, *Developing the Framework*, March 2000, para. 3.160.

[50] The Guidelines are conveniently set out in Appendix 3.1 of Monopolies and Mergers Commission, *Underwriting services for share offers* (London: The Stationery Office, Cm. 4168, 1999).

8

Majority and Minority Shareholders

In the previous three chapters we analysed the legal strategies available for dealing with the agency problems of the shareholders as a class as against the board of directors. That analysis assumed a shareholding structure in which the shareholders were a group of people effectively separate from the board. Although as a result of the reward strategy, discussed in Chapter 7,[1] the directors might hold some shares in the company, their holdings were insignificant as compared with the total issued capital of the company. We also assumed that we were dealing with companies where the shareholding body was a large one and subject to collective action problems if it sought to act in a co-ordinated way. It is time now to relax both those assumptions and to analyse the problems which result. That is the task for this chapter.

Control of a company by a majority shareholder or small group of shareholders is not common in the largest listed British companies, though it is not unknown at this level. This is one of the contrasts between the shareholding structures of British and US companies, on the one hand, and the structures of large companies in most other parts of the world, especially continental Europe,[2] where a controlling block-holder is common even in the largest listed companies. However, such control certainly becomes more common in the UK when one examines the smaller, publicly traded companies, public companies whose securities are not traded, and, especially, private companies. Thus, the problems generated by majority/minority shareholder relationships constitute a widespread set of problems, even in British companies, and company law must address them if it is to provide an effective regulatory framework for the full range of companies.

---

[1] See p. 207.

[2] M. Becht and A. Röell, 'Blockholdings in Europe: An International Comparison' (1999) 43 *European Economic Review* 1049; F. Barca and M. Becht (eds), *The Control of Corporate Europe* (Oxford: OUP, 2001). For an analysis of the implications for comparative company law scholarship see B. Cheffins, 'Current Trends in Corporate Governance: Going from London to Milan via Toronto' (2000) 10 *Duke Journal of Comparative & International Law* 5.

However, what are those problems? Where there is a controlling shareholder in a company, by which we mean one or a small, semi-permanent
group of shareholders who can command at least half of the votes likely
to be cast at a meeting of the shareholders,[3] there is little difficulty in
resolving the agency problems of the majority as against the board.
Under British company law, where, as we saw in Chapter 5,[4] the shareholders have strong removal rights over the board, the majority should
have little difficulty in securing board adherence to the majority's view as
to how the company should be run. The majority may appoint themselves
to the board and, whether they do or not, the directors are likely to be the
majority's nominees. The main problem which majority control generates
is the risk that the company will be run exclusively in the interests of the
majority shareholder and the interests of the minority shareholders will
be either ignored or not fully recognized.

  This is obviously a matter of concern to investors thinking of taking
stakes in majority-controlled companies, but it is also a matter of concern
for public policy and majority shareholders. If investors are not protected
against such risks (through self-help, markets, or the law), they will
demand financial compensation for running the risks. Most likely, this
will express itself in the price investors are prepared to pay for the company's securities. In other words, lack of effective minority protection is
likely to increase controlled companies' cost of capital. Thus, both majority shareholders and public policy have an interest in minority shareholders being given effective guarantees against opportunistic conduct on
the part of the majority after investors have committed themselves to the
company by purchasing its shares. Those guarantees need not come from
the law, but it is likely that the law does have a significant role to play in
this area. Unlike large lenders, for whom self-help is a promising strategy,[5] almost by definition minority shareholders will not be able to use
that strategy effectively (though they may be protected to some degree by
markets).[6]

  The relationship between majority and minority shareholders can be
conceptualized in terms of the economists' view of principal/agent
relationships, which, as we have seen,[7] turns on the factual dependence
of the principal upon the agent. Thus, in this situation, the minority

---

[3] As we pointed out above at p. 112, n. 4, factual control of a majority of the votes may
well be achievable with ownership of less than half of the voting shares, depending on the
dispersion of the shareholdings in the company.

[4] See p. 128.   [5] See Chapter 3, p. 68.

[6] See p. 213.   [7] See p. 117.

shareholders are the principal and the majority shareholder the agent. Unlike the principal/agent relationship between shareholders (as a class) and the board, there is obviously a much less good fit in this situation between the lawyers' view and the economists' view of the principal/ agent relationship. There will be few situations where it can truly be said that the minority shareholders have *authorized* the majority to act on their behalf. Nevertheless, the legal strategies, set out in Figure 1 (see p. 120), for dealing with situations of factual dependency apply to minority/ majority shareholder relationships as much as they do to shareholder/ board relationships. They are strategies for regulating principal/agent relationships in general, no matter who is the principal and who the agent.

In this chapter we shall analyse those strategies as they apply as between minority and majority shareholders, and will go through the strategies in the same order as the one we adopted in Chapters 5 to 7 for the analysis of shareholder/board relationships. As we shall see, however, there are differences in the balance among the strategies in this area, in contrast to the shareholder/board relationship. It is important to note that, as well, the legal analysis needs to be more complex in the context of the minority/majority shareholder relationship than in the shareholder/board relationship. In the latter case, the risk to the share-holders arises from the way in which the board or individual directors exercise the discretion conferred upon them. In the former case, however, the majority may override the minority's interests either through decisions of the board (controlled by the majority) or through decisions of the shareholders' meeting (equally controlled by the majority). So effective legal protection for the minority has to be capable of operating at both levels. For this reason, we shall often refer to the majority share-holders in this chapter as the 'controllers', so as to take account of the fact that the majority shareholders may express their power either as shareholders or through the board.

DECISION RIGHTS

With regard to shareholder/board relationships, we saw in Chapters 5 and 6 that the decision rights strategy could not be one of general applica-tion because, by ending the principal/agent relationship, it deprived the shareholders of the benefits of centralized management.[8] On the other

---

[8] See p. 123.

hand, it had continuing attractions in certain areas, notably for dealing with conflicts of interest.[9] A somewhat similar pattern emerges in respect of minority/majority relationships, though for rather different reasons.

DECISION-MAKING BY MINORITY SHAREHOLDERS AS A GROUP

The risk for minority shareholders in the area of shareholder decision-making arises out of the basic proposition that decisions at shareholders' meetings bind the company (and thus the minority) where a simple majority of the voting shares represented[10] at the meeting and voting on the matter support the decision.[11] The decision rights strategy might take the form of protecting minority shareholders either by shifting the decision entirely into the hands of the minority (the initiation version of this strategy) or by requiring minority shareholder approval of the decision taken by the meeting as a whole (the veto version of this strategy). In fact, company law makes no general use of either version of this strategy. Apart from the difficulty of defining who is in the majority and who is in the minority in any particular case, there is the principled objection that giving the minority initiation or veto rights simply solves one principal/agent problem at the cost of creating another. Minority consent to majority decisions may protect the minority against opportunistic conduct on the part of the majority, but in turn exposes the majority to opportunistic conduct on the part of the minority. In particular, the minority may exercise the 'hold up' right which the law would give them under this strategy to extract private benefits for their consent to decisions which are clearly in the interests of the shareholders as a whole.

Judicial creativity

Thus, under the current law decision rights are given to minority shareholders only in circumscribed situations, which are usually the result of judicial creativity rather than explicit legislative policy. Two examples can be given. In *Re Hellenic and General Trust*[12] the court interpreted a statutory requirement for shareholder approval (in this case of a proposed

---

[9] See p. 176.

[10] Shareholders may be present either in person or by proxy. Most voters attend by proxy, usually appointing the chair of the meeting as their proxy, and thus have indicated to the proxy in advance of the debate at the meeting how they wish the proxy to vote on the matter.

[11] We assume here that the matter is one for the shareholders. The principles upon which the division of power between shareholders and the board is based are discussed above at p. 111.

[12] [1976] 1 WLR 123.

'scheme of arrangement'[13]) as requiring the separate consent of the minority shareholders, who were thus given a veto over the scheme. In effect, the scheme in this case amounted to a take-over offer for the company by an offeror which already controlled 53 per cent of the shares of the target company. In order to preserve the integrity of the requirement of approval of the proposed scheme by the target company's shareholders, the judge treated the non-controlling shareholders as a separate 'class' of shareholders (even though their shares were identical to those held by the majority) and thus required the consent of the (majority of the) minority to the take-over.

A second and more complex, but also more important, example is provided by the decision of Knox J in *Smith v Croft (No 2)*,[14] a case concerning the enforcement of the duties owed by directors to the company. As we have seen, the decision whether to sue normally falls to be taken by the shareholders as a whole.[15] However, in the case of breaches of duty which cannot be ratified (forgiven) by the shareholders by ordinary resolution,[16] there is obviously a difficulty about leaving the decision whether to sue with the shareholders if the alleged wrongdoers control the general meeting. To do so may be to allow the wrongdoers, by deciding not to sue, to thereby achieve a large part of what they would get by ratifying the wrong. Traditionally, in this restricted situation the law has permitted the individual shareholder to sue to enforce the company's rights for the company's benefit (the so-called 'derivative' action) and, indeed, it will normally require the company to pay for the litigation, whether it is successful or not.[17] In *Smith v Croft (No 2)* Knox J added the significant extra restriction on the individual's right to sue, namely, that individual suit would not be permitted if the majority of the shareholders not involved in the wrongdoing were opposed to the litigation. In the case, therefore, where the alleged wrongdoers are the controlling shareholders, the minority has a veto right over the decision to sue, albeit as a result of a rather complex analysis which first sees the decision transferred from the shareholders as a whole to the individual shareholder.[18]

---

[13] See p. 125.   [14] [1988] Ch 114.   [15] See p. 193.   [16] See p. 192.

[17] *Wallersteiner v Moir (No 2)* [1975] QB 373, CA and Civil Procedure Rules, r 19.9(7). The extent of the power conferred upon the individual shareholder is considered further below at p. 225.

[18] An intermediate solution, adopted in Part XA of the CA 1985, introduced by the Political Parties, Elections and Referendums Act 2000 for breaches of the duties laid by that Act upon directors in respect of the use of company funds for political purposes, is to give the right of suit to any group of shareholders representing 5 per cent or more of the

No general principle

In both *Re Hellenic and General Trust* and *Smith v Croft (No 2)* it could be argued that what happened was that decision-making was transferred from the shareholders as a whole to a sub-set of the shareholders by excluding from voting those shareholders who had a personal interest in the outcome of the vote. It might be argued further, by analogy with directors, that these cases should form the basis of a more general principle that interested shareholders should be excluded from voting on shareholder resolutions. However, the law does not accept this as a general proposition, because there is a fundamental difference in the law's analysis of the legal position of the shareholders and that of the board. The law perceives directors' powers as fiduciary, that is, conferred upon the directors in order to promote the interests of the company (the shareholders).[19] The discretionary powers of shareholders, in particular their voting powers, however, are not perceived as conferred upon them to be exercised for the benefit of others. There is therefore no general obligation upon shareholders not to place themselves in a position where they have a conflict of interest. This was graphically illustrated many years ago in a case where a director proposed to vote as a shareholder to approve a self-dealing transaction involving him as director. In *North-West Transportation Co Ltd v Beatty*[20] the Privy Council said: 'every shareholder has a perfect right to vote upon any such question, although he may have a personal interest in the subject-matter opposed to, or different from, the general or particular interests of the company'.

In fact, the analogy to which the courts often resort when analysing the shareholders' right to vote is that of a property right, no doubt because the share is the property of its holder. Of course, the days are long past when the acceptance of a right as a property right means that its holder can do whatever it likes with the right. Property rights are regulated in the public interest. Nevertheless, the property rights analysis (of shareholders' powers) and the fiduciary analysis (of directors' powers) do illustrate forcefully the different starting points of the law in relation to the discretion vested in the two primary organs of the company. Directors' powers are in principle to be exercised to promote the interests of others; shareholders' powers are in principle to be exercised in their own interests, so that shareholder decisions emerge through the interplay of those

company's issued capital, irrespective of the majority's view. This is an approach to the allocation of litigation rights which is used in German law, but it is unusual in British law.

[19] See p. 153.   [20] (1887) 12 App Cas 589, PC.

interests, though the law does set some limits, as we shall see,[21] on the expression of self-interest.

However, the CLR has made one important proposal to shift decision-making into the hands of the minority shareholders because of a conflict of interest on the part of the majority. It proposes that any decision by the shareholders to ratify a breach of duty to the company by the directors or any decision by the shareholders whether to sue the directors should be taken on the basis that the votes of the wrongdoers 'or of those who are substantially under their influence' should be excluded.[22] Thus, if the alleged wrongdoing directors controlled the company, the decision whether to ratify the wrong or to sue the directors would become a matter for the non-controlling shareholders. Such a reform would not constitute a general implementation of the decision rights strategy where majority shareholders face a conflict of interest, but it would reverse the decision in *North-West Transportation* and deal with one of the major weaknesses in the rules relating to the enforcement of directors' duties.[23]

Contracting for decision rights

Nevertheless, although the law may not insist upon minority shareholder decision-making in a wide range of situations, it is open to minority shareholders to contract for decision-making rights, where they have sufficient bargaining power. There are a number of ways in which this can be done. The current shareholders may enter into an agreement amongst themselves, outside the articles, in which they agree that the consent of some of them or of a majority of some sub-group of shareholders shall be necessary for the taking of certain decisions. Such shareholder agreements are enforceable by injunction.[24] This is the simplest solution if the shareholder body is a stable one, but making the agreement part of the articles has the advantage that new shareholders will be bound automatically by it. On the other hand, the articles can be altered by majority vote of the shareholders, in which those shareholders who do not benefit

---

[21] See p. 231.

[22] CLR, *Completing the Structure*, November 2000, paras 5.85–5.86. On ratification and decisions not to sue, see Chapter 6, p. 191.

[23] See Chapter 6, p. 194.

[24] There may be a difficulty if the company is made party to the agreement and the decisions subject to it include proposed alterations of the articles, because a company cannot contract out of its power to alter the articles: *Russell v Northern Bank Development Corpn Ltd* [1992] 1 WLR 588, HL. However, if all the shareholders are party to the agreement, the exclusion of the company causes few problems, since all those who are in a position to act as the company are covered by the agreement.

from the agreement may be entitled to participate (whereas amendment of a shareholders' agreement in principle requires the consent of each shareholder party to it). An intermediate solution is to issue to the shareholders whose consent is to be required a separate class of shares, identical in economic terms to the other shares issued by the company but carrying in addition the consent requirement for the relevant group of decisions. Under the statutory class rights provisions, the consent requirement will not normally be removable without the agreement of the class of shareholders who benefit from it.[25]

ALTERING THE SIZE OF THE MAJORITY FOR DECISION-MAKING BY SHAREHOLDERS AS A WHOLE

If giving the minority shareholders an initiation or veto rights over shareholders' decisions is not a widely used technique, because of the 'hold-up' risk, what other techniques are available for implementation of the decision rights strategy? One is to leave the decision with the shareholders as a whole but to move from a simple majority requirement for shareholder decisions to some form of 'supermajority' rule. This technique is in fact widely adopted by the Companies Act, which often imposes a requirement for the consent of three-quarters of the shares present and voting at a meeting. Such resolutions are termed 'extraordinary' resolutions by the Act or 'special' resolutions if, in addition to the supermajority requirement, at least 21 days' notice of the intention to move the resolution has to be given to the shareholders.[26] By expanding the size of the majority required to adopt a particular decision the Act requires more attention to be paid to the views of non-controlling shareholders than under a simple majority rule, because at least some of the non-controlling shareholders will need to be persuaded to support the resolution.

The approval of three-quarters of those shareholders present and voting tends to be required by the Act where the rights of the shareholders are potentially at risk of alteration. Thus, looking again at the list, given on p. 124, of decisions the Act requires to be taken by the shareholders, one sees that the Act requires supermajority consent in the cases of

---

[25] CA 1985, ss 125–9, especially s 125(1) and (2). The recent tendency has been for the courts to extend the statutory protection also to rights embodied in the articles and linked to shareholdings, even though there has been no formal issue of a separate class of shares: *Cumbrian Newspaper Group Ltd v Cumberland and Westmoreland Herald Newspaper and Printing Co Ltd* [1987] Ch 1.

[26] CA 1985, s 378.

changes to the company's constitution, alterations in the form of the company, decisions to wind the company up, and schemes of arrangement. In other situations, it is risk of opportunistic treatment which seems to drive the requirement for supermajority consent. Thus, in relation to share re-purchases by a company,[27] a re-purchase effected on the market requires only simple majority consent of the shareholders, whereas an 'off-market' re-purchase requires a special resolution.[28] This appears to be because, in a re-purchase effected through the market, the board of the company does not have the same freedom to choose the persons whose shares are to be re-purchased or to set the terms of the re-purchase.

A supermajority requirement is obviously helpful to non-controlling shareholders, but, equally obviously, does not guarantee their protection against opportunistic conduct on the part of the controlling shareholders. Whatever the size of the majority required, there will always be a minority who do not need to be brought within the consensus and whose interests therefore are at risk. A supermajority requirement in fact benefits most obviously the large minority shareholder (controlling 25 per cent or more of the shares likely to be cast at a meeting) and requires a controlling shareholder with just a bare majority to incorporate the large minority shareholder in the taking of fundamental decisions about the company's future. This involves giving the minority shareholder a hold-up right, but since the minority's stake is large, it can perhaps be argued that the risk of the minority exercising its veto for non-company-related reasons is reduced.

As far as small minority shareholders are concerned, the legislator might seek to effect protection by tinkering with the supermajority requirement in various ways. The 'three-quarters' rule adopted by the Companies Act does not represent the only level at which a supermajority requirement could be pitched. However, the truth of the matter is that any majority requirement short of unanimity carries the potential to leave some minority shareholders exposed. Yet, the objections to a unanimity rule for shareholder decision-making are overwhelming. It would create a hold-up problem even more severe than would arise if decision-making were given to the non-controlling shareholders as a group. However, there may be occasional situations in which unanimity is appropriate. Thus, the Act requires the consent of all the members of the company

---

[27] Share re-purchases are discussed in Chapter 4 at p. 88.
[28] CA 1985, ss 164(2) and 166.

(and not just of those entitled to vote at a shareholders' meeting) for a decision to re-register a limited company as an unlimited one.[29] Here, it is appropriate that an individual shareholder should be able to veto a company decision, even if it is supported by all other shareholders, because of the impact of the decision on the shareholder's personal liabilities and creditworthiness.

However, moving from limited to unlimited liability is a rare step for a company to take. In fact, the most significant area where unanimity of shareholders is required is where they take decisions other than through a meeting. We have already noted the common law rule that a company is bound by the informal but unanimous decisions of its members.[30] As we shall see in Chapter 10, shareholders may also resolve unanimously to dispense with some meetings which they would otherwise be required to hold and they may take decisions by written resolution without a meeting on a unanimous basis. However, the CLR has proposed a substantial move away from the statutory unanimity requirements in this area.

An alternative technique for preventing the overreaching of minorities on shareholder votes is to cap the percentage of the votes that any one shareholder and its associates may cast. For example, the rule might be that no one shareholder may cast more than 5 per cent of the votes, no matter how large its shareholding. The articles of companies may impose such a cap and it was not uncommon to do so in the nineteenth century. However, voting caps are not required by law and are in fact uncommon in practice today, perhaps because their impact is unpredictable and perhaps because they may well exacerbate the agency problems as between the board and the shareholders as a class.[31]

ALLOCATING THE DECISION TO THE INDIVIDUAL SHAREHOLDER

Alternatively, the decision may be allocated to any individual member of the company. Of course, the objections to allocating decisions in this way as a matter of general practice are very strong, because individual shareholder decision-making involves a denial of the collective nature of the corporate enterprise. If any individual member is given a veto right over the decision, the hold-up problem, noted above, would be very strong indeed. However, assume, as is more likely, that we are contemplating

---

[29] CA 1985, s 49(8). On unlimited liability companies see p. 69.
[30] See Chapter 5, p. 116.
[31] Precisely for this reason they are popular in some continental European systems, as a defence against the take-over bid.

giving any individual member an initiation right, so that the hold-up problem virtually disappears, because there would be so many possible decision-makers. Nevertheless, a serious problem emerges, because a broadly distributed initiation right generates an incentive to take decisions which are not in the best interests of the company. Such decision-making permits a single shareholder, holding only a proportion, perhaps a very small proportion, of the equity of the company and therefore entitled to only a proportion of the return (or subject to only a proportion of the loss) on any corporate venture, to commit the resources of the company as a whole to a course of action. The risk is that he or she will take the decision not in order to advance the interests of the shareholders as a whole but in order to advance an objective personal to the shareholder. In other words, individual decision-making permits a misalignment of risk and return.

Derivative actions

However, there is one area where the common law of companies, reluctantly, has traditionally permitted individual decision-making. Analysis of the relevant common law takes us back to the topic of the enforcement of directors' duties. As we have seen,[32] the duties of directors are owed to the company and the company, acting by ordinary resolution of the shareholders, can normally forgive the directors their transgressions. However, the traditional view is that some types of breach of duty are not ratifiable by the shareholders. It is far from clear what the boundaries of these non-ratifiable wrongs are. It is likely that they embrace situations where the directors have acted dishonestly or where the wrong involves the misappropriation of company property,[33] but 'property' is such an elastic concept that these broad statements give little guidance about the range of non-ratifiable wrongs. Granted, however, that there is such a category of non-ratifiable wrongs, the common law accepted that where the wrongdoers were in control of the company, the individual shareholder should be able to commence litigation on behalf of the company. To leave it to the shareholders as a whole to decide whether to sue in such a case would be to enable them, by deciding not to sue, to secure part of the benefit of (prohibited) ratification.

This is not a set of rules which pleases anyone. Those concerned to promote the enforcement of directors' duties regret the absence of individual shareholder powers of enforcement of breaches of duty which are

---

[32] See Chapter 6, p. 191.   [33] *Cook v Deeks* [1916] 1 AC 554, PC.

ratifiable. The risk here is that breaches of such duties will be neither ratified nor enforced.[34] Those concerned to promote the corporate nature of the litigation decision are reluctant to accept individual rights to sue at all. So far, the latter concern has been addressed through the decision in *Smith v Croft (No 2)*, discussed above at p. 219, in which the majority of the disinterested shareholders seem to have been given at least a veto over individual shareholder decisions to initiate litigation on behalf of the company. After this decision, it is arguable that there is no longer a right for individual shareholders to take the litigation decision.

More fundamental change may come from the CLR's recommendation, also discussed above in this section, that the votes of interested directors be disregarded on ratification decisions and decisions whether to sue directors for breach of duty. If this rule were adopted, it might be thought no longer necessary to maintain the distinction between ratifiable and non-ratifiable wrongs, for there is some evidence that the category of non-ratifiable wrongs was developed by the courts in response to the proposition that interested directors may normally vote on ratification resolutions.[35] If all wrongs were ratifiable, but with interested directors excluded from voting, then the basis for individual suit to enforce breaches of directors' duties would have to be re-considered. It would no longer be possible to attach individual suit to a category of non-ratifiable wrongs, which would have disappeared. This issue is explored further under the heading of Trusteeship later in this chapter.

APPOINTMENT RIGHTS

In Chapter 5[36] we saw that British company law attaches great weight to appointment rights, especially to removal rights, as a strategy for dealing with the agency problems of the shareholders as a class as against the board. It would be possible to extend this strategy so as to use it to deal with minority/majority agency problems, by ensuring that minority shareholders were able to have one or more representatives on the board. In this way, the board would be prevented from becoming simply the expression of the powers of the controlling shareholder; the minority shareholders would have access to more, and more current, information about the way the company's business was being conducted; and the

---

[34] See p. 195.

[35] With regard to the CLR's recommendation in relation to the votes of interested directors, see p. 219.

[36] See p. 127.

minority might be able to influence the substantive decisions taken by the board. In short, minority shareholders would have access to centralized management.

It is always open to minority shareholders to contract for such representation. Indeed, in practice the notion that a large minority shareholder should be afforded some level of board representation seems reasonably widely accepted. Going beyond practice, it would be possible formally to contract for an entitlement to board representation in a number of ways, for example by issuing a class of shares carrying the entitlement to appoint one or more directors. However, British company law has never insisted upon such rules, in contrast to US state laws, which, at one stage, imposed the principle of 'cumulative voting' on a reasonably wide scale. The essence of cumulative voting is that, on the election of the directors, each voting share is allocated a number of votes equivalent to the number of directors to be elected. Those votes may be allocated by the shareholder in any way he or she wishes across the directors to be elected, but a sufficiently large minority shareholder, by concentrating her votes on one or a small number of directors, will be able to ensure that her candidates are elected.[37]

Cumulative voting could be said to represent the application to the company of the principle of proportional representation which is often urged in the political sphere. However, this may be the very reason why it has fallen out of favour even in the United States, where today only a very small number of economically unimportant states insist on it. It can be argued that the board is not the place for the expression of competing interests among the shareholders or, at least, if it does become so, its effectiveness in setting and monitoring the company's business strategy is likely to be impaired. It is therefore unlikely that British company law will adopt mandatory cumulative voting, even though the partial reconcentration of shareholdings amongst institutional shareholders in recent years has provided a situation in which cumulative voting could work effectively.[38]

---

[37] The mathematics of this process are rather complicated and need not detain us here, except to note that in the United States formulae were worked out which indicated to minority shareholders of different sizes how they should allocate their votes for maximum effect.

[38] See J. Gordon, 'Institutions as Relational Investors: A New Look at Cumulative Voting' (1994) 94 *Columbia LR* 124. This article contains much interesting material on the rise and fall of cumulative voting in the USA. On the likely reluctance of British institutions to make use of cumulative voting, were it introduced, see Chapter 7, p. 205.

AFFILIATION RIGHTS

EXIT RIGHTS

When in Chapter 5[39] we looked at affiliation rights in companies with dispersed shareholding patterns we saw that a mere exit right gives little protection to shareholders. What is needed is a right to exit at a 'fair' price, not at the current market price which may reflect, for example, the results of the majority's disregard of the interests of the minority shareholders. In companies with dispersed shareholdings the right to exit at a fair price is provided, functionally, by the possibility of a take-over bid. Where there is a controlling shareholder, however, no bid will be forthcoming unless it has the consent of that shareholder, and so the take-over is unlikely to provide effective redress for minority shareholders' agency problems since this mechanism is dependent upon the consent of the agent.

An alternative way of implementing an effective exit right would be to give the minority a legal right to have their shares purchased at a 'fair' price, either by the majority or by the company. However, the arguments against giving minority shareholders a unilateral exit right of this type are extremely strong. Requiring the company to purchase the minority's shares whenever the minority wanted this would be to go against the fundamental rule we examined in Chapter 1,[40] that share capital is in principle a permanent contribution to the company's finances (until the company is wound up) and that the normal method for a shareholder to liquidate his or her investment is by sale to another investor. In certain circumstances, examined in Chapter 4,[41] a going concern company may choose to buy back its shares but it cannot be forced to do so. The principle is obviously functional: a unilateral exit right might undermine the company's business activities by requiring it to pay out cash from the business (to the minority shareholders) at an inappropriate time, for example when it was needed to expand the company's business. Alternatively, it might threaten the interests of the company's creditors by reducing the company's legal capital.[42] Requiring purchase of the minority's shares by the majority shareholder avoids some of these problems, but is hardly more functional. Controlling shareholders would be less willing to invite minority investment in the companies they controlled for fear that they might be required in the future to increase their commitment to the

---

[39] See p. 145.   [40] See p. 22.   [41] See p. 88.
[42] See Chapter 4, p. 88.

company, again at a time which, from the point of view of the majority, was inappropriate.

Of course, the minority shareholders may contract for such a unilateral exit right, for example by incorporating it in the articles of association. Indeed, the majority may be willing to concede such a right in order to prevent the admission to the company of shareholders of whom they disapprove. This is especially likely in small companies, though the majority may prefer to achieve this object by simply making any transfer of shares subject to the veto of the board, without any offer to buy the shares in question.[43] However, the CLR declined to proceed with a proposal to draft a model exit article for small companies to adopt, if they wished, on the grounds that it would be impossible to design a single model which would suit all companies, even if the model was confined to private companies.[44]

More promising is the use of the right to exit at a fair price as a *remedy* where the majority have infringed some rule or standard which the law has laid down to regulate their conduct. In fact, the exit right is used extensively in this way in British company law where the majority have been found to have acted in a way which is 'unfairly prejudicial' to the minority under s 459 of the Act. We shall examine this remedy further when we consider rules and standards later in this chapter, in our consideration of statutory constraints on company controllers.

APPRAISAL RIGHTS

Lying in between a general unilateral right of exit and the use of the exit right as a remedy where the majority has infringed some norm governing their conduct lies the technique of giving the minority an exit right if the majority take a particular type of decision. In this case, there is no general and unilateral right of exit because the right arises only if the majority take a particular type of decision and the majority can avoid triggering the right by not taking the decision. Further, appraisal is not a remedy (in the legal sense) because the majority do not commit a wrong by taking the decision in question. British company law in fact makes little use of this technique. The principal example is to be found in fact in a set of rules, dating from 1862 and now contained in Chapter V of Part IV of the Insolvency Act 1986. Sections 110–12 of that Act permit the liquidator of

---

[43] See p. 293 for the legal problems to which such provisions in the articles may give rise.
[44] CLR, *Developing the Framework*, March 2000, para. 4.103. On an earlier proposal from the Law Commission see *Shareholder Remedies*, Cm. 3769, 1997, Part 5.

a company being wound up voluntarily[45] to transfer the company's business to another company in exchange for shares in the transferee company, which shares are then distributed among the shareholders of the transferor company. In effect, the businesses of the transferor and transferee companies are merged and the shareholders of the transferor company become shareholders in the combined enterprise. Any shareholder who did not vote in favour of the special resolution needed to implement the scheme may notify his objection to the liquidator within seven days, and the liquidator must then either abandon the scheme or buy out the dissenting shareholder's shares at a price to be fixed by arbitration. The procedure seems to be popular for reconstructing private companies or groups of companies, where there is agreement among the shareholders about what is to be done. However, if shareholder dissent is a potential threat to the scheme, it can normally be implemented through other mechanisms which do not provide an 'appraisal right' for dissenting shareholders, such as a scheme of arrangement[46] or a take-over offer.

As with cumulative voting, the British reluctance to adopt appraisal rights on a widespread basis is in contrast to the laws of the US states, where it is currently common to provide appraisal rights 'in connection with mergers, sales and exchanges of substantially all assets of the corporation, and charter amendments that materially and adversely affect the rights of the dissenting shareholder'.[47] However, just as the City Code on Take-overs and Mergers provides affiliation rights for shareholders as a class, so also the Code provides an exit right for minority shareholders through its mandatory bid rule.[48] This requires a person (normally another company) who has acquired control over 30 per cent or more of the voting shares in a company to offer to buy out the remaining shareholders at the highest price paid for the shares in the controlling block. In this way, the City Code treats a change in *de facto* control of a company as a ground for exit at a fair price for the non-controlling shareholders and so goes behond what the Act requires.

---

[45] Any company can thus make use of this mechanism by the shareholders agreeing to wind the company up.

[46] See p. 125. This will require the scheme to be restructured. If it remains a simple sale of the transferor's assets for shares in the transferee, the court is likely to insist that the IA 1986 procedure, with its appraisal right, be used: *Re Anglo-Continental Supply Co Ltd* [1922] 2 Ch 723.

[47] R. C. Clark, *Corporate Law* (Boston: Little, Brown & Co, 1986), p. 443. See also a somewhat similar set of rules in French law: A. Viandier, *OPA, OPE et autres offres publiques* (Paris: Éditions Francis Lefebvre, 1999) pp. 434 ff.

[48] City Code, rule 9. See above at p. 147 for the role of the Code in relation to shareholders as a class.

CONSTRAINING MAJORITY DECISIONS

Having thus looked at the three legal strategies which empower the minority as against the majority, we now turn to the two strategies which operated directly upon decision-making by the majority. Subjecting that decision-making to constraints contained in rules and standards is, perhaps, an obvious use of the law but at common law there was an initial difficulty in identifying the conceptual basis for the imposition of rules or standards. As we noted in Chapter 6,[49] the fiduciary duties of directors are owed normally to the company, rather than to individual shareholders, so that they do not provide a basis on which minority shareholders can restrain majority power as expressed through the board of directors. Further, as we have noted earlier in this chapter,[50] the common law does not perceive the controlling shareholders to be in a fiduciary position towards non-controlling shareholders, so that basis for the individual shareholder to restrain the power of the majority as it reveals itself in shareholder decision-making is not available.

COMMON LAW CONSTRAINTS ON CONTROLLER/DIRECTORS

Both these propositions remain true of the common law and so statute has had to intervene to provide the main platforms for minority protection. However, even the common law qualified its basic positions to a limited extent, so as to provide some minority protection, and so we need to look at those common law qualifications first. As far as directors' duties are concerned, the basic proposition that directors do not owe duties to individual shareholders, famously associated with the decision in *Percival v Wright*,[51] was intended to preserve the collective nature of the company. It was therefore appropriate to apply it to directors' decisions relating simply to the conduct of the company's business, but less obvious that it should apply where the directors, whether as part of the conduct of the company's affairs or not, were dealing with the shareholders in relation to their shares (i.e., in relation to the property of the shareholders rather than the property of the company). Imposing duties on directors in relation to the property of shareholders individually does not necessarily undermine the collective nature of the company and the corporate nature of its business assets.

This argument removes a reason against recognizing directors' duties

---

[49] At p. 153.   [50] See p. 220.   [51] [1902] Ch 421.

owed to individual shareholders, but does not provide a positive reason for imposing such duties. Why should not directors and shareholders dealing with each other in relation to the latters' shares be treated as operating at arm's length, so that no fiduciary duty is owed by one party to the other? Within the Commonwealth, the principled answer to this question was first provided by the New Zealand Court of Appeal in *Coleman v Myers*,[52] where it was found in the monopoly of the majority shareholder/directors (in a private company) over up-to-date information about the affairs of a private company, coupled with a consequent situation of long-term reliance by the minority on the majority, as both sides recognized. In this situation, the controllers were regarded as under a fiduciary duty and a duty of care to disclose to the minority non-public information which was central to the valuation of the shares of the minority which the controllers were negotiating to buy from them.

This 'special facts' exception to the *Percival v Wright* rule that directors do not owe fiduciary duties to individual shareholders seems now to be fully part of English law as a result of the decision of the Court of Appeal in *Peskin v Anderson*.[53] In fact, the situation facing the English Court of Appeal was more difficult than that which the New Zealand Court of Appeal had dealt with and the former's acceptance of the special facts exception thus more significant. In *Coleman v Myers* the director/controllers were acting in a private capacity in seeking to acquire the minority's shares, whereas in *Peskin v Anderson* the alleged breach of duty to the individual shareholders arose out of the directors' conduct of the company's affairs. This consisted of negotiations to sell the company's business, the non-disclosure of which plans was argued to have caused a loss to shareholders who sold their shares before the project matured, earning a substantial surplus for the company. It is significant, therefore, that, while accepting the 'special facts' doctrine in principle, the English Court of Appeal found no breach of it on the facts of this case.

Probably the most likely situation where the directors' conduct of the company's affairs will also involve a breach of duty to the shareholders under the special facts doctrine occurs in relation to take-overs. As we saw in Chapter 5,[54] a take-over has two facets. It is a transaction between the offeror and the shareholders of the target company, but a successful take-over often has important consequences for the company's business strategy, so that the board of directors is heavily implicated in the transaction. The present policy in the UK is to 'sideline' incumbent

---

[52] [1977] 2 NZLR 225.   [53] [2001] 1 BCLC 372.   [54] See p. 145.

management in the take-over process, as the City Code on Take-overs explicitly provides[55] and as the common law implicitly does through the 'improper purposes' doctrine.[56] Hoffmann J has held that, while directors are not obliged at common law to advise their shareholders whether to accept the offer, if they choose to speak they must give advice in the interests of the shareholders (and not, for example, in their own interests or to promote their view of the company's interests).[57]

More adventurously, Hoffmann J has also suggested that, where directors act for an improper purpose by issuing shares to defeat a take-over bidder, that is a breach of duties owed to individual shareholders, not to the company.[58] This represents a suggestion for a genuine shift in the definition of the beneficiaries of directors' duties from the collective to the individual, but, even if it were accepted, it would be confined to the scope of the improper purposes doctrine which, we have suggested above,[59] is at present limited in scope. However, we also noted there the suggestion of Richard Nolan that the improper purposes doctrine should be developed so as to regulate the 'internal' aspects of directors' decisions and, in particular, to secure fairness between groups of shareholders. Is there, then, a case for tackling this issue head-on and adding to the duties of directors an obligation to act fairly as between shareholders, a duty which might be enforceable by individual shareholders?

There is some slight recognition of such a duty in the case law in the shape of the decision of Goulding J in *Mutual Life Insurance Co of New York v Rank Organisation Ltd,*[60] where a duty to treat the shareholders fairly was said to be an implied term in the articles of association. The Law Commissions included in their draft statement of directors' duties the proposition that: 'A director must act fairly as between different members.'[61]

---

[55] See p. 146.   [56] See p. 164.

[57] *Re A Company* [1986] BCLC 382.

[58] *Re A Company* [1987] BCLC 82. If the duty is owed to individual shareholders, then presumably breaches of the improper purposes rule would no longer be ratifiable by the shareholders as a whole.

[59] See p. 165.

[60] [1985] BCLC 11, where the claimant North American shareholders of the company were excluded from the right to subscribe for new shares in the company, because the company did not wish to incur the heavy costs of compliance with the US securities laws. The judge rejected the argument that the shareholders were entitled to equal treatment; accepted that they were entitled to fair treatment; but thought they had been treated fairly in this case.

[61] Law Commission and Scottish Law Commission, *Company Directors: Regulating Conflicts of Interest and Formulating a Statement of Duties,* Cm. 4436, 1999, p. 186, though it was not clear whether such a duty would be enforceable by individual shareholders.

The CLR was more cautious. As we shall see in the next chapter,[62] the basic duty imposed by the CLR upon directors in its draft statement of principles is to 'promote the success of the company for the benefit of the members as a whole'.[63] Note 2 to this principle makes it clear that one of the matters to which the directors must have regard when discharging this duty is the need 'to achieve outcomes that are fair as between its members'. The comment on this principle[64] states that 'the duty of fairness is thus covered within this "inclusive" list, rather than as an independent duty, so as to make it clear that fairness is a factor in achieving success for the members as a whole, rather than an independent requirement which would override commercial success'. This approach leaves the law on directors' duties playing no significant role in the protection of minority shareholders.

COMMON LAW CONSTRAINTS ON CONTROLLING SHAREHOLDERS

From the point of view of the minority shareholder, the problem with the duties imposed by the common law on controllers as directors is that they are not, normally, owed to the right persons, that is, to the shareholders individually. In the case of controllers as shareholders the problem is the reluctance of the common law to subject shareholder voting to judicial review by reference to a standard at all. This is partly to be explained by the fact that shareholders are not perceived to be fiduciaries,[65] but only partly. The common law could seek to establish limitations on the exercise of the powers of the majority without treating them as fiduciaries, for example by reference to the concept of proper purpose. However, with one important and long-standing exception it has not sought to do so.

The exception is to be found in the decision of the Court of Appeal more than a century ago in *Allen v Gold Reefs of West Africa Ltd*,[66] laying down a standard by which the courts could review the actions of the majority in deciding to alter the company's constitution. Such alterations, it was said, perhaps in a conscious echoing of the rule applicable to directors, should be made 'bona fide for the benefit of the company'. Thus, as far as alterations to the articles are concerned, the law imposes a supermajority requirement,[67] and also gives individual dissenting

---

[62] Chapter 9, p. 276.
[63] *Final Report*, July 2001, vol. 1, p. 345.
[64] Ibid. p. 352.
[65] See p. 220.
[66] [1900] 1 Ch 656.
[67] See p. 222.

shareholders the power to have the majority's decision reviewed against a standard.[68] If the review is successful, the decision taken no longer binds the company.

However, the judges have had tremendous difficulty articulating what this standard requires of majorities. On the one hand, they have been unwilling to allow the rule to lapse into thorough-going subjectivism (that is, that the majority should be prevented from doing only that which they themselves did not believe to be in the best interests of the company), the judges being no doubt aware how this approach has emasculated the similar rule applying to directors[69] and aware that, unlike in relation to directors, the common law seemed to make no other tools available to constrain majorities. On the other hand, they have been uncertain how interventionist a stance they wished to adopt in relation to the internal affairs of companies. Consequently, the interpretation of the requirement has varied over time. At an early stage the judges did seem prepared, by interpreting the test as having an objective element, to use it to impose their view on the majority of what fairness to the minority required.[70] Later the Court of Appeal interpreted the test as a single, subjective test, but nevertheless one which required the majority to have regard to the interests of the 'individual hypothetical shareholder'.[71] In one case in 1976 things went so far awry that the judge interpreted the test as being whether what the majority did was believed to be in the best interests of the minority.[72] This case is also significant in that it involved the application of the bona fides test to a decision other than a change of the articles (namely, a decision to issue shares).

The truth of the matter probably is that there is no sensible half-way house between a subjective test and permitting the court to form its own view of the fairness of the majority's actions (though the latter course then opens up the further question of the basis on which the courts will

---

[68] In the case of alterations to the objects clause in the memorandum, there is a statutory right of appeal to the court, but one exercisable only by the holders of 15 per cent or more of the company's capital (or any class of it), though the company's power of review appears to be open-ended (CA 1985, ss 4–6). The court's review power represents the final gasp of the original view that the objects clause could never be altered. It is rarely invoked.

[69] See p. 159.

[70] *Brown v British Abrasive Wheel Co Ltd* [1919] 1 Ch 290; *Dafen Tinplate Co Ltd v Llanelly Steel Co Ltd* [1920] 2 Ch 124.

[71] *Shuttleworth v Cox Bros & Co Ltd* [1927] 2 KB 9; *Greenhalgh v Arderne Cinemas Ltd* [1951] 1 Ch 286.

[72] *Clemens v Clemens Bros Ltd* [1976] 2 All ER 268.

formulate their views). The former approach, which was recommended by the CLR, means that it will continue to be the case that few decisions will fall foul of the test, probably only those where the majority 'is riding roughshod over the interests of other members for selfish purposes which have nothing to do with the success of the business'[73] or unless a vote of a class of shareholders is involved. In the case of class votes, the duty is to act bona fide in the interests of the class, and this rule does sometimes catch shareholders holding two classes of share, who vote in a class meeting to benefit themselves in their capacity as holders of the other class of share.[74]

The CLR rejected the route taken in Australia, which had inherited the *Gold Reefs* principle, to solve the problem, which was to move explicitly to an objective test. The dangers of so doing were thought to be demonstrated by the decision of the Australian High Court in *Gambotto v WPC Ltd*,[75] where this development occurred and where that Court invalidated a majority decision which would have left the minority economically no worse off and the majority considerably better off. The CLR, with one dissenting voice, also recommended that the subjective test be confined to decisions to alter the articles, that is, the area where it is already well established. The case for so confining the common law test depends in large part on one's assessment of the statutory controls which we discuss next.

STATUTORY CONSTRAINTS ON COMPANY CONTROLLERS: REMEDIES AGAINST 'UNFAIR PREJUDICE'

Some history

Since the common law gives no general protection to minority shareholders through rules and standards, there has been scope for statutory intervention to fill the vacuum, though it is only recently that statute has begun to discharge this task effectively and the statutory intervention is still tightly circumscribed. The legislature might have proceeded by analogy with Part X of the Companies Act,[76] whereby certain transactions between the company and its directors are made subject to shareholder approval. Such transactions with a substantial shareholder might have been made subject to general meeting approval as well, which is the rule

---

[73] Above, n. 63, para. 7.58.
[74] *Re Holders Investment Trust Ltd* [1971] 1 WLR 583.
[75] (1995) 127 ALR 417.   [76] See Chapter 6, p. 176.

applied by the Listing Rules.[77] However, the legislature chose to go down a different track,[78] partly for historical reasons and partly, perhaps, because the problem of majority opportunism was not seen to be confined to self-dealing transactions.

In fact, from the earliest days of modern company law the legislation has contained one tool of intervention, namely, the power compulsorily to wind the company up if the court thinks it is 'just and equitable' to do so. It has long been clear that the phrase just and equitable encompasses oppression of the minority by the majority. This power is now to be found in s 122(1)(g) of the Insolvency Act 1986. This review power, however, had little impact, in part because of its remedial inflexibility. The only remedy the court could give the minority was an exit right arising out of the dissolution of the company and the disposal of its business (though the threat of a just and equitable winding-up might induce the majority to offer the minority something more appropriate).

In 1948 Parliament decided to meet this argument by introducing an alternative remedy to winding-up. By virtue of s 210 of the 1948 Companies Act, if the circumstances were such that a just and equitable winding-up was available but it was inappropriate to grant this remedy, the court could instead grant such other remedy as it thought fit. The impact of this new section was to bring the full force of litigants' and judges' attention to bear on what was meant by 'oppression', the scope of which concept would determine the rigour of the standard by which the majority's conduct was reviewed. In the end, the courts took a cautious line and so that section had less impact than the legislature had probably hoped. In 1980 the legislature had another go: the test for intervention was now stated to be that the affairs of the company were being conducted in a way which was 'unfairly prejudicial' to the interests of any of its members; the express link to the winding-up remedy disappeared; but the wide remedial flexibility of the section was retained. The legislative scheme is now contained in Part XVII of the CA 1985 (ss 459–61). Thus, by 1980 the legislature had laid down a standard by which the courts might review, across the board, the conduct of those controlling

---

[77] Chapter 11: subject to exceptions all transactions with a shareholder holding 10 per cent or more of the company's shares require approval by the shareholders as a whole. The 10 per cent shareholder may not vote. Transactions with a shareholder holding 30 per cent or above must also be 'at arm's length and on normal commercial terms' (para. 3.12).

[78] Part X applies to shareholders only if they have turned themselves into shadow directors (see pp. 176–83).

companies, but the question remained as to the use which the courts would make of their powers.

In fact, the judges this time reacted more positively, perhaps because the current generation of judges is less conservative than their predecessors and perhaps because the legislature's reiteration of the principle of minority protection in 1980 made it clear that it took the matter seriously. In any event, the judges quickly accepted that the section was wide enough to cover acts done by the majority, whether as shareholders or directors, and done to the minority, whether as shareholders or directors.[79] The courts also concluded that the section permitted the court to review actions of the majority which they were, apart from s 459, entitled to take, such as decisions by the majority to exercise their statutory power[80] to remove a minority shareholder from the board. Doubt on both these points had severely reduced the impact of CA 1948, s 210.[81]

Informal agreements

With this ground-clearing task performed, the courts then squarely faced the need to articulate the basis on which their review of controllers' decisions under the heading of 'unfair prejudice' was to proceed. The courts have been able to identify one clear basis for intervention, which is where the courts are acting to support the private agreements or arrangements made by the shareholders and where, thus, the courts are at their least interventionist. The most obvious expression of the agreement among the shareholders is the articles of association, and even under CA 1948, s 210 it was clear that flagrant disregard of the provisions of the articles by a dominant shareholder would provide the basis for a remedy.[82] In small companies, however, it is not uncommon for the shareholders, setting up a company, to have a clear understanding of how the company is to be run, for example on the basis that all the shareholders are to be involved in the management of the company by being directors of the

---

[79] The action must prejudice the interests of the petitioning member, but that prejudice to a member's interests may arise out of acts done to him or her as director, for example where a person has secured a seat on the board in order to protect the investment made as shareholder in the company but is later removed from the board. See *Re A Company* [1986] BCLC 376.

[80] See p. 129.

[81] Ironically, the inspiration for this change of heart in relation to CA 1985, s 459 was a watershed decision of the House of Lords taking the broader view of its 'just and equitable' winding-up powers: *Ebrahimi v Westbourne Galleries Ltd* [1973] AC 360, HL. Since winding-up is not available as a remedy under s 459, the IA 1986 remedy remains important if the petitioner does in fact want a winding-up.

[82] *Re HR Harmer* [1959] 1 WLR 62, CA.

company, but to fail to embody that expectation in the company's articles of association.[83] As we saw with our hypothetical small company, Smith & Jones (Decorators) Ltd,[84] in such cases it is often the opportunity for remunerative work which is more important for those setting up small companies than the opportunity to invest, for the shareholders' contribution to the company's finance may be minimal. The crucial step which the courts have taken in their interpretation of CA 1985, s 459 has been to recognize the existence of informal agreements and arrangements existing outside the articles. The courts have given legal backing to such arrangements by granting the minority a remedy under Part XVII of the Act, if the expectations generated by the informal agreement are later ignored by the majority without good reason. Normally, the remedy is a buy-out by the majority or by the company of the minority's shares at a fair price, for example when a minority shareholder is removed from the board, dismissed from employment with the company, and left merely as a shareholder, but the court is not confined to this remedy.

This use by the courts of the CA 1985, s 459 power is relatively uncontroversial. Section 459 is being used in support of private ordering, not to contradict it. Will the courts be willing to go beyond this basis of intervention? In its first decision on the section, *O'Neill v Phillips*,[85] the House of Lords was particularly concerned not to allow the concept of 'legitimate expectations' to be dissociated from what the parties had (informally) agreed amongst themselves and to be used as a general tool to assess the fairness of the majority's conduct. The basic task for the court was to identify the basis upon which those involved in the small company came together. If the basis of association was 'adequately and exhaustively laid down in the articles',[86] then fair treatment was likely to mean only compliance with the articles. If, as was likely in small companies, there was 'a fundamental understanding between the shareholders which formed the basis of their association but was not put into contractual form',[87] then an argument of unfair treatment could be based on that fundamental, if informal, understanding. Beyond that, however, one reaches the limits of legitimate expectations.

---

[83] This is done partly for cost-saving reasons (the company is bought 'off the shelf' with a standard set of articles) and partly because the shareholders are not psychologically in a position to contemplate their later falling out.

[84] See Chapter 1, p. 25. See also D. Prentice, 'The Theory of the Firm: Minority Shareholder Oppression' (1988) 8 OJLS 55.

[85] [1999] 1 WLR 351, HL.

[86] *Ebrahimi v Westbourne Galleries Ltd* [1972] 2 All ER 492, 500.

[87] *Re Saul D Harrison & Sons plc* [1995] 1 BCLC at p. 19 (*per* Hoffmann LJ).

The main difficulty that arises from the use of CA 1985, s 459 to support informal agreements among the shareholders is the cost of litigation, because establishing what the parties originally agreed and whether the majority have subsequently unjustifiably departed from that agreement may involve an extensive trawl in court through the company's life-history. A number of ways of addressing this problem have been suggested. The courts have sought to encourage minorities to accept pre-litigation offers to buy them out at a fair price, under threat that, if the offer is refused, the majority's conduct will no longer be seen as unfairly prejudicial;[88] the Law Commissions have proposed that the courts should operate a presumption in favour of the minority being entitled to a buy-out if removed from the board in certain types of cases;[89] and the CLR has proposed to foster an arbitration scheme as an alternative to litigation.[90]

Other bases of intervention

However, the more important point about the state of the law after the *O'Neill* case is the very narrow basis for intervention which it appears to afford. The minority will be restricted to their rights under the articles, unless some further informal agreement outside the articles can be found. Outside small companies, such agreements will be rare, because the larger the shareholder body, the more difficult it will be to demonstrate that such informal agreement exists among *all* the shareholders. Section 459 of the CA 1985 has thus become largely a small company remedy.[91] Even in companies with small shareholder bodies such informal agreements will have to be proved and cannot be assumed from the nature of the company.[92] In the absence of such informal agreements, can any other basis of intervention under s 459 be identified? It is suggested that there are two.

First, one may predict that the courts would grant a remedy under s 459 in respect of the sort of self-seeking conduct on the part of the majority which constitutes a breach of the *Gold Reefs* rule, discussed earlier in this chapter in relation to common law constraints on controlling shareholders, whether or not the conduct infringed an informal

---

[88] *O'Neill v Phillips*, see n. 85 above.
[89] *Shareholder Remedies*, Part 3 (see n. 44 above). See also Chapter 10 at p. 292.
[90] Above, n. 63 at para. 2.27.
[91] Small in the sense of having a small number of shareholders. See *Re Posgate & Denby (Agencies) Ltd* [1987] BCLC 8 and *Re Blue Arrow plc* [1987] BCLC 585.
[92] See, for example, *Re JE Cade and Sons Ltd* [1992] BCLC 213.

agreement among the shareholders. In fact, cases falling under the *Gold Reefs* principle are more likely to be brought as s 459 petitions today than as common law claims. Further, the reach of s 459 in such cases would be longer because the section is not confined to majority action consisting of changes to the articles of association.[93]

Second, s 459 may be used to seek redress if the directors of the company act in breach of their duties to the company but are protected by the principle of majority rule from any action against them by the company.[94] In this situation s 459 is being used by the minority to outflank the rule in *Foss v Harbottle*, which normally restricts severely the situations in which the minority may bring a derivative action on behalf of the company.[95] That s 459 should be capable of being used in this way was explicitly advocated by the Jenkins Committee, which proposed the unfair prejudice remedy.[96] In *Re Saul D Harrison & Sons plc*,[97] where the leading judgment was given by Hoffmann LJ, this use of s 459 was also put on the basis of an agreement among the shareholders: '[T]he powers which the shareholders have entrusted to the board are fiduciary powers . . . If the board act for some ulterior purpose, they step outside the terms of the bargain between the shareholders and the company.' However, unlike informal agreements, which have to be specifically proved, the obligation upon the directors to observe their fiduciary duties flows inherently from their appointment as directors.

It is certainly true that s 459 petitions now often contain allegations that the controllers acted both in breach of an informal agreement among the shareholders and in breach of their fiduciary duties, usually by engaging in some form of self-dealing or diversion of corporate opportunities.[98] Some courts have also been prepared to bring at least self-serving negligence within the scope of s 459 petitions.[99] However, there remains an outstanding question of what remedy the petitioner can obtain if the petition is based mainly on allegations of breaches of directors' duties. The legislature seems to have contemplated that, if the petitioner wanted relief for the company, then it would seek, as a remedy in the s 459 petition, authority from the court to bring a derivative action

---

[93] If one accepts this proposition about s 459, then it probably matters little that the CLR proposes to confine the *Gold Reefs* principle to changes of the articles: see p. 236.

[94] See p. 191.

[95] (1843) 2 Hare 461. See p. 225.

[96] Report of the Company Law Committee, Cmnd. 1749, 1962, para. 206.

[97] [1995] 1 BCLC 14, CA, at p. 18.

[98] See Chapter 6, pp. 170 and 183.

[99] *Re Macro (Ipswich) Ltd* [1994] 2 BCLC 354.

on behalf of the company, even though the petitioner did not meet the normal standing rules for a derivative action.[100] However, this course of action has proved unattractive to litigants, perhaps not surprisingly. Bringing and succeeding in one piece of litigation (the s 459 petition) just to obtain permission to bring another piece of litigation (the derivative action) no doubt appears to minority shareholders an expensive and long-winded process.

If, however, a substantive remedy is sought at the conclusion of the s 459 petition, it seems that the court will not grant the petitioner corporate relief but only personal relief. Thus, for example, the successful petitioner may seek to have his or her shares bought out at a fair price but not to have misappropriated assets restored to the company.[101] In effect, s 459 puts the minority under pressure to accept an exit remedy rather than to remain in the company and seek to have it run properly by the majority. This may reflect the fact that, in small companies, any other solution is beyond the powers of the court. The unfair prejudice remedy, like the law of divorce, is much better at bringing relationships to an end on a fair basis than at restoring partnerships which have broken down.

Beyond these three categories of unfairness, it would be rash to predict that the courts will be willing to go. However, it is clear that the limits placed on s 459 are the result of judicial policy, not of any inherent restriction in the wording of s 459. The fear of ending up managing every playhouse and brew-house in the kingdom[102] is clearly one that continues to motivate the courts, and probably rightly so. The CLR was happy with the *O'Neill* decision, on the grounds that 'it is not desirable that, when members of companies fall out, all manner of allegations may be made which might possibly sustain a contention that a particular situation is unfair. This can lead to enormously lengthy and expensive proceedings, which are unsustainable for small companies, producing potentially unfair results at wholly disproportionate expense.'[103] In other words, in relation to private companies, where the CLR saw minority remedies as having the greatest significance, 'clarity, accessibility and cost-effectiveness' were more important than formally perfect justice.[104] Whether the courts continue to take this approach remains to be seen,

---

[100] CA 1985, s 461(2)(c) specifically makes this remedy available to the court.

[101] Cf. *Re Charnley Davies Ltd (No 2)* [1990] BCLC 760. For this reason, the shareholder may bring a s 459 petition even if he does meet the standing rules for a derivative action.

[102] See Chapter 6, p. 160.

[103] *Completing the Structure*, November 2000, para. 5.78.

[104] Ibid., para. 5.60.

though, obviously, the House of Lords has now given a powerful steer in this direction.

ENFORCING THE ARTICLES

When examining the duties of directors, we saw that sticking by the company's constitution was an important element of them.[105] Is there an equivalent rule for shareholder decisions? The rule might be thought to be an obvious one and the Companies Act 1985 at first sight seems to embody it. By CA 1985, s 14, albeit in rather archaic language, the articles of association are treated as a contract between the company and its members, and the courts have interpreted it as also producing a contract among the members.[106] We have seen that everyone agrees that breaches of the articles may constitute a ground for intervention by the court under CA 1985, s 459. It might be thought, therefore, that actions in contract to enforce the articles would be legally unproblematic. It could be said that a very basic form of minority protection is that the controllers should be required to conduct the company's affairs according to its 'rule-book', especially as the majority can always change the articles for the future.[107]

It is the case that the true nature of the articles is only partly captured by a contractual analysis. Externally, by virtue of their public registration, the articles also constitute a statement to investors and those who deal with the company about the rights and duties of the company's shareholders and directors and about the procedures for taking decisions which bind the company. In consequence, some important contractual doctrines are not applied to the s 14 contract because they might defeat the expectations of outsiders,[108] the protection of whose interests, we have seen, has been an increasing concern of company law.[109] But, acceptance of the principle of enforcement of the s 14 contract by the individual shareholder, one might think, should be straightforward.

However, the courts have generated two hurdles for the shareholder who wishes to enforce the CA 1985, s 14 contract, of which the first is probably justifiable and the second is not and, indeed, is incoherent. The

---

[105] See Chapter 6, pp. 160–167.   [106] *Rayfield v Hands* [1960] Ch 1.

[107] As s 9 of the Act permits them to do, albeit subject to a supermajority requirement and the possibility of review by the courts. See above in this chapter at pp. 222 and 234.

[108] See, for example, *Scott v Frank F Scott (London) Ltd* [1940] Ch 794, CA and *Bratton Seymour Service Co Ltd v Oxborough* [1992] BCLC 693, CA, the former refusing the remedy of rectification, the latter refusing to imply terms into the articles from facts unknown to outsiders.

[109] See p. 47.

first hurdle is that s 14 can be used to enforce only 'membership' rights, not 'outsider' rights.[110] A membership right is one which is held in common by all the shareholders of the company or, at least, all the shareholders of a particular class. Thus, a right to vote, attached to a class of voting shares, is a membership right, while a right to be a director of the company, conferred by the articles on a particular individual, is not. The strongest argument in favour of this rule is probably that, if the individual is not a member of the company, there is no question of his or her being able to use s 14 to enforce the entitlement,[111] and that it is not rational to change this position if the outsider happens to become or to be a member of the company.[112] The CLR was content to keep this restriction.[113] In any event, the impact of the rule is easy to circumvent: the individual enters into a separate contract with the company in his or her 'outsider' capacity, as directors do in relation to their executive positions by entering into service contracts with the company outside the articles. That separate contract may even incorporate the terms of the articles, if that is desired, and may incorporate the articles as they stand from time to time, so that changes in the articles automatically produce changes in the separate contract.[114]

The second hurdle is more problematic. Even if the claimant is seeking to enforce a membership right, the claim may fail on the ground that what he or she is seeking to complain of is a 'mere internal irregularity' (which can be put right by a decision of the majority of the shareholders) rather than breach of a personal right. It is wholly unclear why a breach of the articles should be subject to majority control. It is one thing for the majority to forgive a wrong done to the company, quite another for them to purport to forgive a wrong done by the company, which is the essence of a CA 1985, s 14 claim.[115] Perhaps for this reason, the cases have failed to produce a reliable test for predicting which breaches will be regarded as giving rise to complaints of mere irregularities and which breaches of

---

[110] The modern distinction was first clearly drawn by Astbury J in *Hickman v Kent or Romney Marsh Sheep Breeders Association* [1915] 1 Ch 881.

[111] It should be noted that s 6(2) of the Contracts (Rights of Third Parties) Act 1999 provides that that Act does not apply to the CA 1985, s 14 contract.

[112] However, it is not clear that subsequent courts have always observed Astbury J's distinction, and Professor Wedderburn once famously proposed a way wholly to subvert it, by suggesting a membership right to have the affairs of the company conducted in accordance with its articles. See [1957] CLJ 194 at 212.

[113] See n. 103, paras 5.66–5.67.

[114] *Shuttleworth v Cox Bros & Co (Maidenhead) Ltd* [1927] 2 KB 9.

[115] R. Smith, 'Minority Shareholders and Corporate Irregularities' (1978) 41 MLR 147.

rights.[116] Even where the shareholder is complaining of a procedural defect in the taking of a decision by the shareholders, it seems correct in principle that the shareholder should be entitled to have the decision taken properly, unless it is clear that, even if the proper procedure had been followed, the meeting would have arrived at the same conclusion. This last point can be catered for by the court not granting a remedy in any case where this is the situation, rather than by depriving the individual shareholder of the right to sue by some *ex ante* and arbitrary categorization of the articles into those generating rights and those not. The CLR has proposed reform along these lines.[117]

SETTING INCENTIVES

TRUSTEESHIP

The current law

We turn now to the final strategy, altering the majority's incentives, which comes in two forms: trusteeship and reward. The trusteeship strategy involves allocating the decision to some body which is not exposed to the temptations to undertake self-interested conduct to which the majority are subject. Such a trustee may be either internal or external to the company. The obvious candidate for internal trusteeship is the board. The dictates of centralized management, as explained in Chapter 5, often push the company in this direction in any event. Moreover, it is interesting that, in the cases which effected the switch from the agency to the constitutional view of the directors' powers about a century ago,[118] protection of minority shareholders was given as one of the benefits of the change. A simple majority of the shareholders would no longer be able to tell the directors what to do; instead the procedure for changing the articles (requiring a special majority) would have to be followed. It is doubtful, however, whether the argument is any longer a strong one, in the light of the statutory insistence upon removal rights for shareholders

---

[116] The conundrum is exemplified in two similar cases of the 1870s, where the courts went in different directions: *MacDougall v Gardiner* (1875) 1 ChD 13, CA and *Pender v Lushington* (1877) 6 Ch D 70. The modern tendency is perhaps to prefer the rights analysis: *Wise v USDAW* [1996] ICR 691.

[117] See n. 103, paras 5.70–5.74 and *Final Report*, vol. I, paras 7.34–7.40. The company could opt not to give legal enforceability to one or more of its articles, though this would not affect the ability of the shareholder to build a CA 1985, s 459 claim on the majority's failure to follow the articles.

[118] See p. 115.

exercisable by simple majority.[119] In any event, in the type of company under consideration in this chapter, the directors are likely to be the nominees of the controlling shareholder, so that the minority may find that board decision-making simply moves them out of the frying pan and into the fire. Nevertheless, the notion that the board is, or should be, an institutional protection for all the shareholders is reflected in the Listing Rules, which, as a condition for listing, stipulate that 'a company which has a controlling shareholder must be capable at all times of carrying on business independently of such controlling shareholder'.[120]

In the case of the relationship between the board and shareholders as a class the internal trusteeship strategy consists mainly of increasing the importance of independent NEDs.[121] This strategy may also benefit minority shareholders, in that independent NEDs may have some reputational incentives to resist purely self-seeking conduct on the part of the majority shareholder/directors and to take decisions in the interests of the shareholders as a whole. In other words, independent NEDs are capable of operating as a counter-influence not only to a dominant CEO but also to a dominant shareholder. However, as we also noted above, there are reasons for thinking that NEDs are less effective than might be desirable, and in any case they are required only of Listed Companies. To the extent that it is correct to see the problems of minority shareholders as predominantly problems of private companies, the Combined Code does not address the issue.

As far as external trustees are concerned, the Companies Act makes considerable use of the courts in this role. The strategy in these cases is not a pure trusteeship strategy. Normally, there is first a decision of the shareholders in general meeting, which is then subject to confirmation by the court. The court as trustee is thus given a veto right over the decision or transaction but initiation lies with the company, though often the power of confirmation includes the power to approve the decision in terms different from those adopted initially by the company, so that the court's decision is not necessarily a simple 'yes' or 'no'. The veto position of the court is hardly surprising: it would be very odd if the court could take a decision binding on the company without any evidence that the company's decision-making bodies supported the decision, though, as we shall see below, the Law Commissions have recently made a proposal which comes near to this situation.

It may be wondered what the difference is between a court reviewing a

---

[119] See p. 128.   [120] Listing Rules, para. 3.12.   [121] See p. 200.

decision of the company by reference to a standard and a court deciding whether to confirm a company decision. The answer lies in the fact that, with a standard, the grounds for court review are laid down in the standard, whereas, as trustee, the court has an open-ended discretion. However, it has to be conceded at once that the line between these two can be very narrow, as where the standard is imprecise, on the one hand, and the courts acting as trustee have adopted a narrow view of how they will exercise their discretion, on the other.

In some cases confirmation by the court is mandatory. This is so in a proposed scheme of arrangement between a company and its shareholders or a class of them (which normally involves some amendment of the rights of the shareholders), even though the adoption of the scheme requires supermajority approval of the shareholders.[122] A similar set-up is found in relation to proposals to reduce a company's capital.[123] In other cases, confirmation by the court may be something which has to be triggered by shareholders who did not vote in favour of the proposition at the shareholder vote. Sometimes any dissentient shareholder can invoke the right,[124] but normally a percentage requirement is imposed, a somewhat crude way of filtering out unmeritorious cases.[125]

Thus, the court as trustee is a feature of British company legislation, but these provisions have had relatively little impact. In 1948, in a case concerning a reduction of capital, a senior Scottish judge, Lord President Cooper, said: 'Nothing could be clearer than and more reassuring than those formulations of the duties of the court. Nothing could be more disappointing than the reported instances of their subsequent exercise.'[126] He was referring to the dearth of cases in which the courts had refused to confirm a reduction on the grounds that it was substantively unfair (though they are more willing to turn a proposal down on procedural

---

[122] CA 1985, s 425 and see p. 223. A scheme may also be proposed between a company and its creditors, in which case they may be the parties objecting before the court.

[123] CA 1985, s 135. As we saw at p. 90 a reduction of capital may affect the rights of creditors, but objection may also come from the shareholders, often preference shareholders, who are being paid off, while other classes of shareholder remain unaffected by the proposed reduction. The CLR has proposed a substantial down-grading of the role of the court in reductions of capital. See p. 92.

[124] Examples are: objections to resolutions for payments out of capital by a private company to redeem or re-purchase shares (s 176) and to compulsory purchase of shares after a take-over (s 430C).

[125] Examples are: alteration of the objects clause (15 per cent of the shares or any class: s 9); re-registration of public company as private (5 per cent of the shares or any class or 50 members: s 54); resolutions varying class rights (15 per cent of the class: s 127).

[126] *Scottish Insurance Corp v Wilsons & Clyde Coal Company*, 1948 SC at 376.

grounds, such as the failure to make full disclosure of relevant facts at the prior meeting of the shareholders). However, perhaps this should not surprise us. The confirmation provisions present to the court in specific contexts precisely the difficulties which the courts have faced more generally under the open-ended standard embodied in the CA 1985, s 459 remedy, which has also produced limited results.[127]

However, in some cases the specific context in which the court has to apply its discretion has provided some guidance to the courts on how that discretion should be exercised. Thus, a shareholder has the right to appeal to the court where a take-over bidder, who has achieved acceptances from 90 per cent of those to whom the offer has been made, seeks to purchase the remainder of the shares compulsorily, as CA 1985, s 429 in principle entitles the offeror to do. The courts have insisted strongly on the principle that those whose shares are acquired compulsorily should be treated no less well than those who accepted the offer, while being unwilling to be drawn into general arguments about the fairness of the offer which the majority has accepted.[128]

Section 429 of the CA 1985 is interesting, not only because under this section acceptance of the bidder's offer functions as a substitute for a shareholder resolution, but also because it constitutes a recognition on the part of the legislature of the potential 'hold-up' power of the minority.[129] Here the legislature addresses the agency problems of the *majority* by permitting them to appropriate the minority at a fair price. In some other European jurisdictions, there is a buy-out right for an overwhelming majority shareholder (for example, one holding 95 per cent of the shares), whether or not that position has resulted from a take-over offer.[130] The CLR proposes a different approach to this issue. The unfair prejudice provisions[131] should apply to the powers of a minority to block company decisions, for example where supermajority approval of the shareholders is required, as well as to majority decisions.[132] If unfair prejudice were found in such minority action, then a compulsory buy-out of the minority's shares by the majority might be an appropriate remedy.

---

[127] See p. 240.

[128] Contrast *Re Carlton Holdings Ltd* [1971] 1 WLR 918 (an approach now embodied in s 430(4) of the Act) and *Re Grierson, Oldham and Adams Ltd* [1968] Ch 17.

[129] See p. 218.

[130] See Forum Europaeum Corporate Group Law, 'Corporate Group Law for Europe' (2000) 1 *European Business Organization Law Review* at 225 ff.

[131] See p. 236.

[132] CLR, *Completing the Structure*, November 2000, para. 5.102. The restricted approach to 'unfairness', associated with *O'Neill v Phillips* (see n. 85) would still apply.

Proposals for the enforcement of the directors' duties

Despite the low-key role of the court as trustee under current law the Law Commissions have recently proposed a substantial expansion of this function in one particular, but important, area, namely, the enforcement of the company's rights against directors who have acted in breach of the duties owed by them to the company. The unsatisfactory current law, as we have seen, is based essentially on variations of the decision rights strategy. Because the alleged wrongdoers are members of the board, the decision to enforce the company's rights is given also to the shareholders in general meeting. If the wrongdoing directors as shareholders also control the general meeting, this is not likely to represent a significant change. The CLR has proposed, therefore, that interested shareholders should not be entitled to vote on resolutions to enforce the company's rights against the wrongdoers.[133]

However, this proposal does not go far enough entirely to solve all the problems arising with the enforcement of directors' duties. It does not deal with the situation where the wrongdoing directors simply do nothing. If the shareholders are to consider whether to institute proceedings, someone other than the wrongdoing directors needs to summon a meeting of the shareholders. We have seen above that such provisions are contained in the Act,[134] but they require a relatively large proportion of the shareholders (normally 10 per cent) to trigger them. In response to this, company law shifts decision-making on suits against wrongdoing directors into the hands of any individual shareholder, but only in very restricted circumstances. Not all breaches of duty committed by directors against the company can be the subject of derivative actions brought by individual shareholders on behalf of the company. Only non-ratifiable[135] breaches of duty are subject to this procedure, and then only if the wrongdoers control the company and the majority of the non-controlling shareholders are not opposed to the derivative action.[136]

In truth, the decision rights strategy is subject to a contradiction from which it appears impossible to escape. Leaving the decision to sue with the shareholders as a whole, even if interested shareholders are excluded from voting, runs the risk that the shareholders' collective action problems will lead to less than the optimal amount of litigation. Giving an unfettered right to bring a derivative action to any individual shareholder creates the risk that the shareholder, having only a small stake in the company, will bring the action, not because it is thought to be in the best

---

[133] See p. 221.   [134] See p. 136.   [135] See p. 225.   [136] See p. 219.

interests of the company, but to promote some personal objective.[137] This might be thought to be an example of minority oppression of the majority. The latter argument appears to explain why the derivative action is so restricted in current British company law.

In this situation the Law Commission,[138] whose recommendations have been accepted substantially by the CLR,[139] has proposed a conceptually bold move. The power of the individual shareholder to bring a derivative action would be extended to all breaches of directors' duties, whether ratifiable or not, provided the shareholders in general meeting had not actually ratified a ratifiable breach or decided not to sue in respect of it. This deals with the collective action problem of the shareholders at a stroke, but, of course, only at the cost of magnifying the risk that individuals will bring derivative actions which are not in the best interests of the company. In order to counteract this risk, the court is to be brought in as trustee. The action initiated by the individual may proceed only if the court permits it to do so and on the terms set by the court.[140] The court will thus be expected to discharge the task of determining whether the derivative action proposed by the individual shareholder is in fact in the best interests of the shareholders as a whole.

Three brief points may be made about this proposal. First, it holds out the possibility of greater levels of enforcement of breaches of directors' duties, especially breaches of the director's duty of care, which is ratifiable, unless there is a self-serving element in it, and thus excluded currently from the scope of the derivative action.[141] Second, whether this potential will be realized will depend partly on how the courts discharge the discretion entrusted in them. The Law Commission itself evidently approves of the policies which underlie the present restrictive standing rules for individual shareholders,[142] and if the courts simply transfer those policies from the common law to their interpretation of the discre-

---

[137] See *Nurcombe v Nurcombe* [1984] BCLC and *Konamaneni v Rolls Royce Industrial Power (India) Ltd*, [2002] 1 All ER 979 for (very different) cases where this was arguably the situation.

[138] *Shareholders' Remedies*, Cm. 3769, 1997, Part VI.

[139] *Developing the Framework*, March 2000, paras 4.112–4.139.

[140] This builds on the existing Civil Procedure Rules. See p. 219. The terms on which the court permits the action to proceed could include, as at present, a ruling that the company pay for the litigation.

[141] *Pavlides v Jensen* [1956] Ch 565, cf. *Daniels v Daniels* [1978] Ch 406.

[142] See n. 138 at para. 6.4. At para. 6.13 the Commission says: '[W]e do not accept that the above proposals will make significant changes to the availability of the [derivative] action. In some respects, the availability may be slightly wider; in others it may be slightly narrower. But in all cases the new procedure will be subject to tight judicial control.'

tion conferred upon them, then the changes brought about by the reform will be limited. Third, if the courts are effective in weeding out cases where the derivative action is brought to further the personal interests of the individual shareholder, one may wonder what incentive the shareholder will have to seek the court's leave to sue on behalf of the company. The company may be ordered to pay the costs of the litigation, but that does not in itself produce a positive incentive to sue. If the individual has only a small shareholding in the company, that may not act as a big enough positive incentive either. Perhaps the incentive will be on the shareholder's lawyers, not the shareholder him- or herself, but it remains to be seen whether the conditional fee arrangements, being introduced for civil litigation generally, will generate effective incentives for the lawyers involved.

While accepting the Law Commission's proposals in general, the CLR made one additional significant suggestion, this time for a trustee role for the non-involved members of the board. If the board, by a decision of the majority of the non-involved directors, decided not to sue in respect of the breach of duty, the individual shareholder would no longer be free to ask the court for permission to bring a derivative action.[143] At present, the common law rule that the company is entitled to the unbiased advice of all its directors would seem to render a board decision not to sue not binding on the company (unless the articles expressly permitted board decision-making in this situation).[144] The CLR wants to break away from this rule and use the non-involved members of the board in an internal trustee role. We have already noted another example of this technique in its proposal to permit the board to give authorization in advance for the taking of corporate opportunities by a director.[145] The question, which we have already raised, is whether directors, even if non-involved, can always be relied upon to be genuinely independent of the wrongdoers. There might be a case for treating board approval not as a bar to the court giving a shareholder permission to bring a derivative action, but simply as an important factor for the court to bear in mind when deciding whether to give permission.

REWARDS

As applied to the board, the reward strategy involves giving executive directors substantial financial rewards tied to the meeting of performance

---

[143] See n. 139 at Questions 4.6.   [144] See pp. 172 and 193.   [145] See p. 186.

targets which reflect the shareholders' interests.[146] In so far as those targets reflect the interests of the shareholders as a whole, such a reward
strategy may also protect minority shareholders. As for decisions taken by
the shareholders, the risk to the minority is that the majority shareholders
will seek to divert to themselves a disproportionate amount of the economic surplus earned by the company. The most effective way of implementing a reward strategy in this context would seem to be, therefore,
through an equality or sharing rule (though, of course, this is an equality
of shares, not of shareholders). An example of such a rule would be that
distributions by the company to the shareholders should be strictly pro
rata to the number of shares held. If effectively drafted and enforced,
such a rule would prevent the majority preferring themselves when
making distributions, such as dividends.

In fact, neither the common law nor the legislation contains a general
statement of the equality principle in respect of shareholder decisions
and, as we noted above, the courts have rejected the principle in relation
to board decisions having a differential impact upon the shareholders.[147]
The Listing Rules, by contrast, do state that 'a company having listed
shares must ensure equality of treatment for all holders of such shares
who are in the same position'.[148] Further, and more important, equality of
treatment of shareholders of the same class is a central principle of the
City Code on Take-overs and Mergers. Amongst other things, this prevents a majority shareholder from negotiating a higher price from the
bidder than is available to the non-controlling shareholders.[149] Finally, it
would appear that private contracting is often used to secure equality of
treatment in the absence of general legal requirements. Thus, where
preference shares are issued with the certain dividend rights or rights
to return of capital attached, it will not be lawful to make distributions to
the shareholders which contravene those rights.

Occasional instances of acceptance of the equality principle in relation
to shareholder decisions can be found in the Companies Act. As we

---

[146] See p. 207.   [147] See p. 233.

[148] Para. 9.16, though it is doubtful whether the Listing Authority is well placed to
implement this principle except in relation to transactions whose documentation has to be
pre-vetted by the Authority. In all probability, the provision was included simply in order to
meet the requirements of what is now Directive 2001/34/EC, Art 65(1)—the Combined
Admissions and Reporting Directive.

[149] City Code, General Principle 1 and rules 6, 9, and 11. Of course, if the majority cannot
obtain a higher price, they may be disinclined to accept the offer and without the majority's
acceptance the offer will not succeed.

have noted above,[150] the Act in principle requires new s̸
issued for cash) to be offered pro rata to the existing ⸴
though that requirement is concerned more with equality between new
and existing shareholders than with equality between different groups of
existing shareholders. Probably, legal backing for the idea of equal treatment of shareholders of the same class is most often provided within company law proper when the court has to review the majority's conduct by
reference to a standard or acts as a trustee in relation to some decision
of the company. In such cases, proof of unequal treatment is probably
the starting point for persuading the court to take the minority's
side in the dispute, but, even here, unequal treatment is not, in itself,
unlawful.[151]

CONCLUSIONS

It is difficult to resist the conclusion that the law addresses the agency
problems of minority shareholders as against majority shareholders less
effectively than it does the agency problems of the shareholders as a class
as against the board. As we saw in Chapters 5 to 7, in respect of the latter
agency problem the law seems to provide at least two potentially effective
remedies: the removal rights of the shareholders over the directors and
the exit right of the shareholders associated with the take-over offer. For
minority as against majority shareholders neither of these strategies is
highly developed nor do alternative strategies seem to have been
developed to take their place. The most promising recent innovation is
the deployment of the courts to review majority conduct under CA 1985,
s 459, but so far that has become an effective weapon for the minority
only in small, usually 'quasi-partnership', companies. Nevertheless, the
level of litigation which s 459 has triggered suggests that there was a
substantial unmet need for minority protection in these companies before
the introduction of this remedy.[152]

This probably does not matter much in companies whose securities are

---

[150] See p. 213. These are pre-emption rights on issue, as contrasted with pre-emption
rights when shares are transferred. See Chapter 10, p. 293.

[151] For example, *Re Sam Weller & Sons Ltd* [1990] Ch 682—a s 459 case. This case shows
that, given the difficulty of treating shareholders of the same class differently as far as
dividends are concerned, differential distributions in a small company are likely to take the
form of derisory dividends to all shareholders but large payments of fees or salaries to
the directors who are also the majority shareholders.

[152] The Law Commission established that 254 petitions were presented under s 459 in the
three years 1994 to 1996: see n. 138, Appendix J.

publicly traded. Majority control is uncommon in such companies and, where it exists, the pressures of the capital markets, the Listing Rules, and the City Code on Take-overs and Mergers are probably strong enough to keep the worst excesses of majority control in check. As stated, at the opposite end of the spectrum, among the quasi-partnerships, s 459 has made a significant contribution to the protection of the legitimate expectations of minority shareholders. It is much less easy to be confident about the position of minority shareholders in private companies where there is a separation between the majority shareholder/directors, on the one hand, and the minority shareholders on the other. The best protection for minority shareholders in this class of case is careful negotiation of the terms on which the investment is made, plus careful monitoring of the majority's decisions.[153]

[153] For an analysis of what such self-help might require see E. Boros, *Minority Shareholder Remedies* (Oxford: Clarendon Press, 1995), pp. 104–6.

9

Shareholder Control

THE MEANING OF SHAREHOLDER CONTROL AND THE NEED FOR ITS JUSTIFICATION

In chapter 1 we identified shareholder (or member) control as one of the core features of company law. It has now become clearer what are the main features of shareholder control. First, the shareholders have control of the company's constitution, since those who establish the company and who become its first members also adopt its constitution[1] and the members may change the constitution subsequently.[2] By the constitution, the shareholders determine the division of powers between themselves and the board, so that the directors are beholden to the shareholders for the formal grant of their functions. Unlike in many other systems, the directors' powers derive, in the main, from the company's constitution, not from the companies legislation. Second, the shareholders' formal power over the directors is affirmed by their right to remove the directors at any time without cause by ordinary majority vote.[3] Third, and consistently with the previous two points, the directors are required to exercise the discretion which is conferred upon them under the constitution in the best interests of the company, which, in the traditional learning of the common law, is a reference to the interests of the shareholders as a group.[4]

Thus, as far as the allocation of powers within the company is concerned and the accountability of those who exercise management powers, the law places the shareholders in the driving seat. It is sometimes said that the law also entitles the shareholders to the economic surplus earned by the company and, equally, throws its losses first of all on to the shareholders. This is true when the company is wound up. Section 107 of the Insolvency Act 1986 provides that in a winding-up the company's property shall be 'applied in satisfaction of the companies liabilities pari passu and, subject to that application, shall (unless the articles provide otherwise) be distributed among the members according to their rights and interests in the company'. This rule means that, if a company is wound

---

[1] See p. 16.   [2] See p. 116.   [3] See p. 128.   [4] See p. 153.

up with more property than is needed to meet the claims of the non-shareholders, then the whole of the surplus goes to the shareholders. On the other hand, since the non-shareholder claims have to be met before the shareholders become entitled to anything, it is the residual payment to the shareholders which first is diminished if the company has performed poorly. So, on a winding-up, the shareholders go first as far as losses are concerned and go last as far as surplus is concerned.

While the company is a going concern, the law shows less interest in directing the distribution of surplus; indeed, its main concern is to protect creditors' interests by ensuring that only surpluses which exist are distributed.[5] Although it has sometimes been argued that it would be a good discipline on management to do so, the law does not in fact require the whole or any part of the company's profits in a year to be paid out to the shareholders by way of dividend. The articles might impose such an obligation, though in fact the statutory model treats the level of dividend pay-out as a matter for the board, with the shareholders having merely the power to decide to distribute less than the board proposes.[6] Where the company's shares are traded on a public market, this probably does not matter very much to the shareholders. The retained profit should boost the value of the company and thus of its shares, and a shareholder who wishes to realize that profit can do so by selling part of his or her share-holding. Where there is no public market for the company's shares, however, a shareholder may find that, in the absence of dividends, no economic return on the investment is forthcoming. This is a classic method for the majority to seek to 'squeeze out' the minority from a private company (i.e. to induce them to sell their shares to the majority at a low price), but it is now a matter which the courts may be capable of addressing under the provisions of CA 1985, s 459.[7]

The fact that shareholders have formal control of the company does not mean that they are always in a position to exercise it, for example, because of their collective action problems.[8] Indeed, at periods in our history, the boards of large companies have seemed to be firmly in control of them, for example in the 1950s, before the rise to influence of institutional shareholders.[9] Contrariwise, market pressures may lead companies to make steady dividend pay-outs to their shareholders or to return unused capital to shareholders by re-purchasing their shares,[10] in

---

[5] See p. 87.   [6] Table A, art 114
[7] See Chapter 8, p. 253.   [8] See p. 139.   [9] See p. 141.
[10] See p. 213.

order to maintain the market value of the shares, whether or not the law requires them to do this. Although in the 1950s it may have been possible to discount the formal rules on shareholder control on the grounds that they were ineffective in practice,[11] the more recent rise in importance of global capital markets and of institutional investors means that shareholder influence over companies is not purely theoretical, though its exact extent is not easy to determine. Therefore, the substantive question needs to be addressed of whether and how shareholder control can be justified.

It is quite clear that the business which a company carries on requires inputs from a number of groups of people other than its shareholders in order to function successfully. Even within the field of view of company law itself, the role of creditors and senior managers is recognized, in connection with the doctrines of limited liability and centralized management. Further, one does not need to be an expert in business organization to see that the contribution of further groups—employees, suppliers, customers—may also be crucial. So, the question is, can one explain and justify UK company law, in which the shareholders are centre stage, creditors and senior management are given only a supporting role, and no (or very little) mention is made of employees, suppliers, and customers? The old argument that the shareholders have these rights because they are the owners of the company now carries little sway, because its premise is false: shareholders own their shares, not the company. The question is why ownership of shares usually carries control rights over the company: the answer to that question cannot be deduced from the proposition that shareholders own shares in the company.

It is the aim of this chapter to argue that there are good reasons for shareholder control of companies (i.e. that this model of allocation of control rights is not arbitrary); that, however, different allocations of control rights are perfectly conceivable and are to be found in practice, both in the UK and elsewhere; and that the choice among the various possible allocations depends on one's view of how large organizations are best structured for the production of goods and services in the modern economy. In answering this last question, one should bear in mind the possibility that there is no one best solution and therefore no one best set of company laws.

---

[11] This was a central argument in C. A. R. Crosland's influential book, *The Future of Socialism* (London: Jonathan Cape, 1956). See P. Davies, 'Shareholder Value, Company Law and Securities Markets Law' in E. Wymeersch and K. J. Hopt (eds), *Company Law and Financial Markets* (Oxford: OUP, 2002). For institutional investors' shareholdings see Table 1 on p. 141.

DOES THE LAW REQUIRE CONTROL BY THE SUPPLIERS OF RISK CAPITAL?

To ask whether the law requires control by the suppliers of risk capital may seem very odd in view of the explanation in the previous section of how company law facilitates control of the company by its members. However, it is contended that the law does not in fact require those who supply risk capital to the business to be allocated control of the business. Control rights can be, and sometimes are, allocated elsewhere. However, the fact that control rights normally are in fact allocated to the suppliers of risk capital suggests that the explanation for shareholder control is to be found in something more profound than the argument that company law reflects in this respect nothing more than an outdated nineteenth-century view of the allocation of property rights.

CO-OPERATIVES AND MUTUAL SOCIETIES

The argument that the law does not require the suppliers of risk capital to be allocated control rights is two-fold. First, the law does not require business to be carried on through the company form. Other legal entities with limited liability which require or facilitate the assignment of control rights to groups other than the suppliers of risk capital are provided by the law. Thus, the Industrial and Provident Societies Act 1965 permits the incorporation with limited liability of co-operative societies, a crucial feature of which, for present purposes, is that profits, if distributed among the members, are distributed in accordance with the extent to which they traded with or have taken part in the business of the co-operative, not in accordance with the contributions of risk capital. Equally, while a co-operative may issue share capital, governance rights are assigned to members, not to shares, so that the general rule is 'one person, one vote'.[12] Co-operatives may in fact choose as the basis for membership (and thus of ultimate control of the society) one of a number of different tests. For example, the members may be those who are customers of the business (as in the retail co-operative societies which trade in the High Street in competition with supermarkets operated by companies formed under the Companies Act), or who are

---

[12] Registrar of Friendly Societies, *Guide to the Law Relating to Industrial and Provident Societies* (London: HMSO, 1978), p. 3.

suppliers to it (as in the case of agricultural co-operatives), or who are its employees.[13]

Another form of non-company incorporation is provided by the Friendly Societies Act 1992, though friendly societies can exist on an unincorporated basis as well. An incorporated friendly society must include in its purposes the provision on a mutual basis of insurance against loss of income, principally as a result of sickness, unemployment, or retirement. As of 1999 there were some 270 societies, with total funds of some £12 billion. The mutual principle means that the members of the society are those who take out the insurance, so that, in the pure case, a mutual assurance company is one where the members are both the insurers and the insured. An incorporated friendly society is, thus, more restricted in the range of activities it can carry on than is a co-operative, as is the third example of an incorporated body with limited liability, which is not a company. This is the building society, incorporated under the Building Societies Acts 1986–1997. The principal purpose of a building society must be to make loans, secured on residential property. The members of the building society are both those who deposit money with it and those who borrow from it, and votes are allocated, normally, on the 'one person, one vote' basis.

Thus, the law provides a number of non-company vehicles through which a business can be run under the control of its customers, suppliers, or employees, with the benefit of separate legal personality and limited liability, though two of these vehicles are limited to particular types of activity.[14]

CONTROL RIGHTS WITHIN COMPANIES

The second argument in favour of the proposition that the law does not require the suppliers of risk capital to have control of the business concerns the more usual case where the business is carried on through a company incorporated under the CA 1985. Although company law puts the members in control of the company, it does not say that the members

---

[13] The 1965 Act also provides for the incorporation of societies whose activities are for the benefit of the community ('bencoms') but here there must be shown a good reason why the bencom should not incorporate as a company.

[14] The emergence in the nineteenth century of the mutual principle in insurance companies and of depositor control in building societies seems to have been in part because of the absence of effective governmental regulation at that time of such activities and thus of the risk of opportunism on the part of shareholder-controlled companies: H. Hansmann, *The Ownership of Enterprise* (Cambridge, Mass.: Harvard University Press, 1996), chs 13 and 14.

need to be the suppliers of risk capital to it. Indeed, as we saw in Chapter 1,[15] the Companies Act provides one form of the company, the company limited by guarantee, where the company has members but no shareholders. In such companies, where there is no share capital, the criteria for admission to membership, which are chosen by the company itself, can be related therefore to some quality, other than the contribution of risk capital, which is helpful to the running of the business which the company carries on. Equally, decisions are taken on the basis of 'one member, one vote' and not 'one share, one vote.' As we also noted in Chapter 1, such companies are not normally used for carrying on commercial businesses, but they are not excluded by company law from so doing.

A notable recent use of the company limited by guarantee to carry on a commercial business is Glas Cymru, which provides water and sewage services to a substantial segment of the people of Wales. Glas Cymru raised the finance it needed by issuing bonds (i.e. long-term debt), rather than shares, and used the proceeds to buy the water business from its previous owner, a shareholder-controlled company. However, we can expect from what we learned about covenants in loan contracts in Chapter 3[16] that lenders would not be willing to take on such a large financing commitment and without the benefit of an equity cushion, unless they were granted significant control over the company's activities. Indeed, the *Financial Times*[17] reported that the bond covenants in this case would 'set a new precedent in terms of bondholder influence'. So, Glas Cymru can be seen as a company in which there are no shareholders, but where the members have had to cede a substantial influence to the providers of the debt finance who have replaced the shareholders.[18]

Even if the company is formed as one limited by shares, there is no obligation in law to assign control to the providers of risk capital. Like Glas Cymru, such a company could raise its long-term finance through debt or it could issue non-voting ordinary shares[19] to the providers of risk capital. In either case, the voting shares could be allocated elsewhere (say,

---

[15] See p. 31.   [16] See p. 70.   [17] 21 November 2000.

[18] Glas Cymru calls itself the 'Welsh people's company', though it is open to question whether this is a more accurate appellation for a company, whose membership is likely to be no more than 50 people, chosen by the existing board of directors, than for its predecessor, whose securities were traded on a public market and therefore could be bought by anyone.

[19] Non-voting ordinary shares are not prohibited in the UK, either by the Act or by the Listing Rules, though they are fiercely opposed by institutional shareholders, who are reluctant to buy them. For that reason, they are uncommon.

to employees) for a nominal consideration.[20] Other mechanisms to similar effect can be envisaged. In some cases, successful entrepreneurs, reaching retirement without any obvious successors in the family, have handed over the shares to a trust for the benefit of the employees, an arrangement which often comes near to entrenching the management of the company. An example is the retailer, John Lewis.

Although the above disposes of the argument that the law requires companies to be controlled by the providers of risk capital, the fact remains that companies such as John Lewis, Glas Cymru, and even the co-operative societies occupy a minor, and indeed declining, part of the national economy, although mutual companies have traditionally been a powerful presence in the insurance and house-finance sectors. Overall, the dominant form for the conduct of large commercial business in the UK is the company limited by shares, where the voting shares are held by the providers of risk capital. What the above discussion suggests is that, if a business does not need external, long-term finance or if it can obtain that finance through debt, it can either do away with shareholders altogether or allocate the shares to the providers of some other input which the company needs for its success.

In fact, the typical example of this arrangement is to be found, not among the large companies, but at the other end of the size spectrum. Thus, as we argued in Chapter 1,[21] our hypothetical small company, Smith & Jones (Decorators) Ltd, is an example of worker control, because the entrepreneurs who set up the business provided no long-term finance to the company. That came from the bank as lender; the entrepreneurs provided their skilled labour. Many ordinary partnerships can be analysed in the same way: control is with the partners because they have proved to be the most successful workers, not because of their capital commitments.[22] At this bottom end of the spectrum (in terms of size), many small businesses are, in truth, worker controlled. Higher up the scale, however, doing without long-term risk capital is much more difficult. To be successful without long-term risk capital a large company needs either to be able to generate internally all the resources it needs for

---

[20] The Act does not require a minimal nominal value for shares, so shares could be issued with a nominal value of 1p, nor do shares of different classes have to have the same nominal value. However, the total nominal value of the shares issued by a public company must amount to £50,000, a pretty trivial figure. See above, p. 85.

[21] See p. 25.

[22] Partners may have to make capital commitments, but they have to make these commitments because they are partners. They do not become partners because they are prepared to make the capital commitment.

its operation and expansion or to have a predictable income stream against which bond-holders will lend money. This is the basis of the arrangement for financing Glas Cymru, which provides a natural monopoly service to its customers and whose income-stream is thus highly predictable.[23]

WHY ORDINARY SHAREHOLDERS CONTRACT FOR VOTES

So far, the picture which is emerging is that, on the one hand, the law does not require the providers of risk capital to be given control of the company and, on the other, it is difficult for large companies to do without risk capital. We still have to explain why the providers of such finance (the so-called ordinary or equity shareholders) require in practice that they be given such control and, in particular, that the shares with which they are issued should carry voting rights.

At a pragmatic level, the answer to this question of why ordinary shareholders require control rights is that no rational investor would subscribe for or buy ordinary shares in the company if control rights were not attached. The purchase of an ordinary share involves the handing over of a sum of money in exchange for nothing in the way of a legally enforceable promise about the return on the money invested, until the unlikely event of the company being wound up. If the company does badly because of poor management, the ordinary shareholders may receive no or only a very small dividend and the market price of the shares may fall from the level at which they were purchased. Of course, the investor's downside risk is restricted by the doctrine of limited liability,[24] so that the investor cannot normally lose more than he or she invested in the company. However, if that is all the investor can expect from the shares, he or she may as well buy bonds, which also give limited liability but, in addition, carry a promised rate of interest and a promise of the return of the principal at a specific time. Even if the company does well, the ordinary shareholder cannot legally insist on any particular level of pay-out, as we have seen. Instead, the board may reinvest the surplus in some risky project of its own, so that the surplus is not even reflected in the price of the company's shares, because the market realizes that the management is intent on dissipating it.

---

[23] And, of course, regulated by a governmental agency.   [24] See Chapter 3.

To say that no rational investor would buy ordinary shares without the power, ultimately, to remove an under-performing management or to exit the company on fair terms may be a slight exaggeration. An investor may be prepared to buy non-voting shares if there exists a class of voting shares (often held by the founding entrepreneur's family) whose holders, the investor thinks, will keep the management up to the mark and whose tendencies towards unequal appropriation to themselves of the company's surplus will be kept in check by the minority protection provisions of company law. However, this is simply to say that one class of investor may be able to free-ride on the monitoring efforts of another class, and it does not really affect the principle of shareholder control. Alternatively, an investor may be prepared to buy non-voting shares where he or she concludes that the company will have to come back to the market periodically in the future for more capital and so will have to treat the shareholders well if it is to raise risk capital in the future. This is shareholder control through the market rather than through legal rights, but it is still shareholder control.[25]

THE DISTRIBUTION OF VOTING RIGHTS AMONG SHAREHOLDERS AND THE LOSS OF CONTROL

In general, however, the proposition seems robust that the cost to companies of raising risk capital would be substantially greater and the supply of risk capital would be reduced, if purchasers of ordinary shares obtained neither control of the company nor a legally enforceable promise of a return on their investment. Indeed, an argument can be made that the mechanisms of protection for suppliers of long-term finance to companies demonstrate a trade-off between control rights and entitlements to a return on the investment. Two examples can be given, which concern preference shareholders, on the one hand, and bond-holders, on the other.

We have talked above in places, rather loosely, about 'shareholder' control. In fact, where a company has issued preference shares as well as ordinary shares, it is common for the control rights, in the shape of votes, to be either confined to the ordinary shareholders or shared with the preference shareholders only in limited circumstances. There is no fixed set of rights which preference shareholders must have.[26] Their rights are a matter of contract between them and the company. However, it is

---

[25] See p. 213.   [26] *Gower*, pp. 314–15.

common to give them a preference as to dividend, that is, an entitlement to a fixed dividend out of the profits the company makes before a dividend can be declared in favour of the ordinary shareholders.[27] In such a case, it is also common not to give the preference shareholders voting rights, unless their dividends are in arrears. In other words, as long as the promise made to them by the company about the level of return on their investment is being met, they have no rights to control management. Thus, shareholder control, normally, is not control by *all* the shareholders but control by those (the 'ordinary' shareholders) who have no contractual entitlements as to the return on their investment.

By the same token, bond-holders, who normally have a contractual entitlement to regular interest on the loan to the company and to repayment of the principal at a fixed point in the future, do not routinely obtain control rights over the company. However, they normally do obtain such rights when events happen which put in doubt the company's ability to pay the interest due or to repay the loan on time. Thus, the large lender will contract for the freedom to take the management out of the hands of the existing board, where events occur which threaten the lender's entitlements.[28] Where the loan is risky, because there is little equity cushion for the bond-holders if things start to go wrong for the company, the bond-holders' control rights may be particularly extensive, as we saw in the case of Glas Cymru, even while the company is a going concern.

The above explanation of the ordinary shareholder's need for control rights also helps to define the point at which those rights should be lost, that is, when the shareholder no longer has an investment to protect. Even where there is no large lender who has contracted for rights of intervention, insolvency law recognizes this principle, because it operates to transfer control of the company from directors appointed by the shareholders to a liquidator appointed by the creditors when the company becomes insolvent. The precise point at which the incumbent management should lose control of the company is controversial. Nevertheless, the principle is firmly embedded in the insolvency law; indeed, it can be

---

[27] The preference shareholders may become entitled to a further dividend, along with the ordinary shareholders, once the ordinary shareholders have received a dividend equivalent to that of the 'prefs' (in which case the prefs are usually described as 'participating preference shares'). If there are not sufficient profits to pay the preferential dividend in a particular year, the prefs may or may not be entitled to payment in respect of the earlier missed dividend, if profits in a later year are sufficient to pay the preference dividend for both that year and the earlier one. If so, they are called 'cumulative' preference shares.

[28] For a discussion of the position of secured lenders see Chapter 3, p. 73.

said to be the prime function of insolvency law to bring about this shift from shareholder control to creditor control.

The onset of insolvency also affects the definition of the beneficiaries of directors' duties. The shareholders are no longer in pole position. As we noted in Chapter 4,[29] s 214 of the Insolvency Act 1986 lays upon directors a duty of care, owed to creditors, once it becomes clear that the company has no reasonable prospect of avoiding insolvent liquidation, even though at that time no liquidator or administrator has been appointed. Under the CLR's draft statement of principles applying to directors[30] it is clear that this duty, when triggered, replaces that normally owed by the directors to promote the success of the company for the benefit of its members. The CLR also puts forward for consideration a further principle,[31] which would apply at an earlier stage. Where it is 'more likely than not' that a company will be unable to pay its debts as they fall due, the directors would come under a duty to balance the interests of the creditors and those of the shareholders. It is also clear that at some point pre-insolvency, though not precisely when, the power of the shareholders to ratify a wrong done by the directors[32] ceases, because the true parties interested in the property represented by the company's claim are now the creditors.

One can conclude that the basic practice of corporate finance in large companies, though not the requirement of the law, is that the suppliers of long-term finance to the company obtain either a contractual entitlement to a certain return on their investment (by way of interest on a loan or by way of a preferential dividend) or they obtain control rights over the company by way of ordinary shares carrying voting rights. The law facilitates the granting of such control rights but its main mandatory contribution is to *deprive* shareholders of the control rights they have contracted for from the company at the point where their investment has disappeared. At this stage, the law moves the creditors' interests to the centre of the stage, because the main financial question which now faces those who control the company is how the shortfall in the company's assets in relation to its liabilities will be distributed across the various classes of creditor.

---

[29] See p. 95.

[30] Principle 9. See CLR, *Final Report*, July 2001, vol. I, pp. 345–8.

[31] Ibid., Principle 8. Some think the principle is already part of the law: *West Mercia Safety Wear Ltd v Dodds* [1988] BCLC 250, CA.

[32] See p. 192 and *Official Receiver v Stern (No. 2)* [2002] 1 BCLC 119, CA.

ALLOCATING GOVERNANCE RIGHTS TO NON–SHAREHOLDER STAKEHOLDERS

So far, it is hoped, two propositions have been established. The first is that the allocation of control rights to ordinary shareholders is not required by law; and the second is that ordinary shareholders have very good reasons to contract for control rights. But why do not other groups whose contribution is important for the success of the company contract for control rights in place of the ordinary shareholders? The answer in part is that they do, as we noted above, where the business is set up as a co-operative or friendly society or as a partnership. However, such non-shareholder-controlled companies are relatively rare, not only in the UK but in all modern economies, whereas partnerships flourish mainly in the area of professional services. This might be for the reasons suggested above. If a company needs risk capital, it will not be able to acquire it on acceptable terms unless control rights are allocated to the ordinary share-holders. This is a powerful explanation. Ordinary shares are a more flex-ible form of long-term finance for companies than bonds, because if things go badly the dividend can be cut or be suspended entirely and the value of the shares will fall. None of this represents a breach of contract on the part of the company, however, unlike a failure to pay interest on bonds, which is due whether the company has had a good year or not. Certainly, the recent wave of demutualization of insurance companies and, to a lesser extent, of building societies seems to have been driven by the view that access to the capital markets would give these organizations greater resources for expansion than would be available if they remained under the control of their policy-holders (in the case of insurance com-panies) or their depositors and borrowers (in the case of building societies).[33]

However, doubt remains whether this argument fully explains the marginal role of businesses not controlled by shareholders. It is surprising that there are not more companies that seek to raise their long-term finance from loans or internal resources or from their employees, rather than ordinary shares. Bond financing, if less flexible, is cheaper than equity capital, because the bond-holders take on less risk. Not all

---

[33] The legislation, discussed above, dealing with co-operatives and mutuals provides pro-cedures, whereby the members can decide either to transfer the society's business to a shareholder company or to convert the society into a plc. The requirements for shareholder consent vary from statute to statute and have become controversial during the recent wave of demutualizations.

companies operate in such cyclical industries that equity shares are the only possible basis for long-term finance. As suggested above, once the need for equity capital is dispensed with, the question of the allocation of control rights seems to be at large. If John Lewis is a successful retailer, why are there not more employee-controlled department stores and why did John Lewis become run in the interests of its employees because of an act of generosity on the part of the original shareholder/entrepreneur, not because it was built up from scratch by an employee co-operative?

As an alternative to the corporate finance explanation for the paucity of cases where governance rights, at least in industrial companies, are allocated other than to shareholders, Henry Hansmann, in a stimulating book,[34] has suggested that ordinary shareholders are allocated governance rights because they are in a position to discharge the governance function more efficiently than any non-shareholder stakeholder group. This is essentially because the ordinary shareholders are a more homogeneous group, and thus less prone to internal conflicts of interest, than employees, suppliers, or customers. In this explanation, efficiency in discharging the governance function is what marks out ordinary shareholders, not their efficiency in providing long-term finance. It is certainly true that ordinary shareholders will normally have identical securities, whereas those with non-standard rights, for example preference shareholders, are, as we have seen, normally denied votes in the company.[35] Employees, by contrast, in any large company are likely to fall into a variety of categories, with divergent interests. Nevertheless, this argument perhaps falls short of explaining why there are not more equal numbers of large companies controlled by homogeneous groups of (ordinary) shareholders and homogeneous groups of employees (say, the skilled workers) or homogeneous groups of customers or suppliers.

SHARING CONTROL RIGHTS WITH STAKEHOLDERS

In the previous section, we wondered why control rights are not more often allocated to some group other than the shareholders. A variation of this question is also worth posing: why don't ordinary shareholders more often share their control rights with other groups whose input is necessary for the success of the company? Neither the corporate finance nor

---

[34] See n. 14 above.
[35] Note also the modern rejection of cumulative voting (see p. 227) which might operate so as to reveal conflicts of interest *within* a single class of share.

the lack of homogeneity argument completely answers this question. Sharing control with other groups no doubt means diluting shareholder control, but it might be possible to design schemes in which the shareholders have sufficient control to protect their interests, but do not have exclusive control of the company. Indeed, the schemes of co-determination in Germany[36] constitute functioning examples of shareholders sharing control with one other stakeholder group, namely the employees.

The traditional explanation of why shareholders do not share control is that other groups do not need it to protect their interests. If this argument is correct, it also explains, *a fortiori*, why control is rarely allocated wholly to non-shareholder groups. Groups other than ordinary shareholders, the argument goes, can protect themselves fully through contractual provisions. It is certainly true that these groups have substantial contractual entitlements, whereas ordinary shareholders typically have none. The contracts of bond-holders or preference shareholders, as we noted above, give them significant economic rights, whilst employees have important contractual entitlements in their contracts of employment (and, indirectly, in collective agreements, where a union is recognized for the purposes of collective bargaining) and customers and suppliers in their commercial contracts with the company.

However, modern work on long-term or 'relational' contracts, which we discussed in Chapter 5,[37] shows conclusively that it is impossible fully to specify in a contract rules to apply in all the contingencies which may occur over the life-time of a long-term relationship. Suppose a business opportunity arises for a company, which will increase the level of risk to which bond-holders, preference shareholders, employees, suppliers, and customers are subject, but which, if it is exploited successfully, will make the company more profitable, increase the number of workers it employs, produce a better product, and increase its need for supplies. It is inconceivable that the various contracts which the company has with its non-shareholder stakeholders could specify whether the opportunity should be taken up. The question becomes even more difficult if the risks and rewards of the potential business opportunity are differentially distributed across the stakeholder groups, so that the rewards, if the project is successful, will accrue predominantly to some groups, whilst the costs of failure will fall predominantly on other stakeholder groups. What is needed is a mechanism or mechanisms for considering, when the

---

[36] See p. 20.   [37] See p. 118.

opportunity actually arises, whether it is sensible to take the risk or not. In other words, governance mechanisms are needed to supplement specific contractual entitlements if the full range of issues likely to arise in the life of long-term relationships with non-shareholder groups is to be effectively addressed.

On this analysis, the ordinary shareholders appear simply as the most obvious category where governance mechanisms are needed (because they have very little, if any, contractual protection), but it is wrong to conclude from this that other groups are in a position fully to bargain out their relationships with the company. Ordinary shareholders are the 'residual' claimants par excellence, because the return on their invest-ment is almost wholly dependent upon the company's economic success. However, other groups also have residual claims on the company, that is to say, even after their contractual claims have been met, their interests in the business may still be vitally affected by the success or otherwise of decisions taken in the company's name. Does this mean that all those groups which have long-term relationships with the company and which cannot, therefore, fully bargain out the terms of that relationship[38] should therefore be entitled to participate in the governance mechanisms pro-vided by company law? Should all these groups have control rights and be entitled, for example, to place their representatives on the board of direc-tors? It might be said that only in this way will it be possible to protect these groups from the opportunism into which ordinary shareholders, if left in sole control of the company, will be tempted by virtue of the inadequacy of the contracts the non-shareholder groups have negotiated.

One overwhelming argument against giving all stakeholder groups representation on the board is that the board mechanism is very unlikely to be able to operate effectively with such a diverse range of interests represented on it. Setting board policy would become very slow and contentious, perhaps in some cases impossible, and in effect the senior management of the company would either be paralysed or be able to carry on without a significant level of accountability to anyone, through a strat-egy of divide and rule. It is notable that no modern company law system seeks to use the board to provide such a wide representation of interests.

A more plausible alternative is simply to alter the duties of directors. Instead of requiring them to exercise their discretion in what they think is the best interests of the shareholders, that discretion becomes bounded

---

[38] This constitutes, in effect, the definition of 'stakeholding group' adopted in this chapter.

by a requirement to act in the best interests of all the groups having a long-term relationship with the company. This suggestion has been enacted into positive law, in the shape of 'constituency statutes' in a number of US states. Thus, s 717 of the New York Business Corporation Law requires directors, in certain circumstances, to consider, among other things, the impact of their proposed decision on current and past employees, the company's customers and creditors, and 'the ability of the corporation to provide, as a going concern, goods, services, employment opportunities and employment benefits and otherwise to contribute to the communities in which it does business'. It is not clear, however, that shifting the multi-constituency strategy from representation on the board to directors' duties alters the nature of the problem identified in the previous paragraph. So long as the duty on directors to act in the best interests of the company is formulated subjectively, such an expansion in the range of interests to be taken into account is likely to make the duty even more difficult to enforce than it already is.[39] If, to meet this problem, the duty is cast in partially objective terms, then a third party, such as a court, will need to be given the power to review the directors' assessment of the balance to be struck among the competing interests. One might have doubts about whether the outside body would be able accurately to identify where the company's best interests lie, and, in any event, the power of review, if frequently invoked, would slow down substantially decision-making by the board.

It may be significant that this expanded view of directors' duties is applied under the New York law only when the directors are facing a decision which might lead to a change in control of the company, notably, whether to redeem a 'poison pill' so as to allow a take-over offer to be put to the shareholders.[40] The aim and effect of such statutes is not so much to make directors accountable to a wide range of constituency interests as to leave them legally free to oppose a take-over bid which they think is undesirable. In other words, the New York statute embodies the opposite policy to that of sidelining management which is found in the City Code.[41] Of course, non-shareholder interests may benefit in fact from managerial opposition to a particular take-over offer, but only to the extent that the interests of the non-shareholders happen to coincide with those of the managers. This cannot be guaranteed to be the case. If, for example, managerial discretion under a constituency statute simply allows incompetent directors to remain in office while the company

[39] See p. 159.   [40] See p. 146.   [41] See p. 147.

continues to decline, it is far from clear that this is an effective way of promoting the interests of, for example, the employees.[42]

SHARING CONTROL RIGHTS WITH SPECIFIC STAKEHOLDER GROUPS

If it is unlikely that the institution of the board of directors or the law relating to directors' duties could carry the full weight of providing governance mechanisms for all stakeholder groups, then it might be that they could be used to provide governance for one or a limited number of non-shareholder groups. This proposal certainly brings us closer to what is found in practice. In about half the present states of the EU, for example, workers, or their representatives, have the right to appoint some members of the board (usually of a supervisory board under a two-tier system) of a large, private-sector company. Usually only a clear minority of the members are appointed by or on behalf of the employees, but in large German companies half the supervisory board members are appointed in this way.[43] Such provisions have not been adopted in the UK, where employee representation at board level is not mandatory.

However, even the UK makes a nod in this direction through s 309 of the Companies Act, a mysterious provision introduced in 1980. This section requires the directors, in the performance of their functions, to have regard to the 'interests of the company's employees in general, as well as the interests of its members'. The section is mysterious because it is unclear why the Government, in fact a Conservative Government led by Mrs Thatcher (as she then was), introduced it. It is also unclear whether it was intended to put, and whether it has the effect of putting, the interests of the employees on a par with those of the shareholders or whether it simply requires the directors, in pursuing the interests of the shareholders, to have regard to the interests of the employees. In the words of the CLR, does s 309 express a pluralist view of the company or simply enlightened shareholder value? The CLR thought the latter,[44] in part because enforcement of the remodelled duty remains with the

---

[42] On constituency statutes see R. Romano, 'A Guide to Takeovers: Theory Evidence and Regulation' in K. Hopt and E. Wymeersch (eds), *European Take-overs: Law and Practice* (London: Butterworths, 1992) pp. 40–1 and, more generally, R. Gilson, 'The Political Ecology of Takeovers', in the same work, ch. 2.

[43] See p. 20. However, the chair of the board, a shareholder representative, has the casting vote if decisions are deadlocked.

[44] *The Strategic Framework*, February 1999, para. 5.1.21.

shareholders.[45] In fact, the introduction of this section seems to have had little impact on directors' decision-making, perhaps because it did not alter the subjective nature of the duty on directors to act in the best interests of the company.[46]

Thus, it is clearly possible for company law to be used to provide a governance mechanism for a stakeholder group, other than the shareholders, but is company law the most efficient mechanism for providing that governance? It can be argued that the core function of company law is to regulate the input of risk capital (primarily ordinary share capital) and to some extent of loan finance (because shareholders' desire in large companies for limited liability creates extra risks for creditors)[47] and of senior managerial expertise (because of shareholders' reliance in large companies on centralized management).[48] The law needs to provide a framework for the co-ordination of the other inputs upon which business success depends, but the process of contracting for labour or supplies, for example, does not have to be seen as part of company law. Indeed, there are good reasons for not seeing the regulation of all inputs as the task of company law, because that would be to tie regulation to the corporate vehicle. Whatever the legal vehicle used for carrying on business—company, partnership, co-operative—and, indeed, whether the business is carried on through a legal vehicle at all or by an individual acting as a sole trader, it is likely that large parts of the process of contracting for labour, for example, should be regulated in the same way. Thus, in labour law the principal focus is on the 'employer', no matter what its legal form, rather than upon the company; and in commercial law the focus is on the other party to the contract or transaction, no matter what that party's legal status is.

Pursuing the issue of contracting for labour a little bit further, it is worth noting that labour law has two powerful governance mechanisms available to it. Collective bargaining with a trade union can operate as an

---

[45] A decision normally to be taken by majority vote of the shareholders as a whole (see p. 194), so that an employee or trade union which buys a single share will still be in no position to enforce the duty.

[46] See p. 159. In one reported case, the section was used, not so much to require unwilling directors to promote the interests of the employees as to protect the board from a shareholder challenge on the grounds that the decision did not promote shareholder value. See *Re Saul D Harrison & Son Ltd* [1995] 1 BCLC 14, CA.

[47] See Chapters 3 and 4. The extent to which the facilitation of loan capital is a matter for company law depends in part on whether the law on corporate insolvency and on the taking of security over corporate assets is regarded as part of company law or as part of general insolvency law or the general law on secured lending.

[48] See Chapters 5–7.

effective mechanism for adjusting terms and conditions of employment (and perhaps more than that) to the changing environment in which the business finds itself. Collective bargaining traditionally has been widespread in the UK but, depending as it does on levels of membership in the workplace, has retreated to some degree over the past two decades. However, there is now in place a legal procedure requiring the employer to 'recognize' the union for the purposes of collective bargaining where the majority of the workforce in an appropriate 'bargaining unit' desire this. Further, and much under the influence of EC law, there is mandatory consultation with representatives of the workforce (not necessarily trade unions) over strategic issues, on a general basis in respect of businesses operating in two or more Member States and over specific issues for all employers, even if operating wholly within a single Member State.[49]

Both of these mechanisms operate outside company law. What are the issues at stake if it is proposed to supplement collective bargaining and mandatory consultation with employee representation at board level? Probably what is potentially available through board representation is a closer involvement of the employees in the taking of strategic decisions than is achieved by mandatory consultation within a labour law framework. Board-level representation could get the employee representatives further into the heart of corporate strategy setting and provide a much higher quality of information to the representatives of the employees. The board, and thus company law, become the focus of attention here because the board is taken as the ultimate authority for strategic decision-making within the large business. Logically, of course, such schemes should apply to all legal vehicles for carrying on large-scale business, whether they are companies or not.

However, employee representation at board level will dilute the control rights of ordinary shareholders, and they can be expected to oppose it. It is perhaps not surprising that Germany, where board-level representation for employees is the most advanced, has traditionally relied more heavily upon debt finance (or internally generated funds) for large companies and less heavily upon equity shareholdings than has been the case in the UK (though the position may be changing in Germany). Moreover, the providers of debt finance (notably the large banks) have been able also to secure a position where they exercise considerable influence as the voters

---

[49] On both forms of representation see S. Deakin and G. Morris, *Labour Law*, 3rd edn, (London: Butterworths, 2001), ch. 9. The system of national level consultation is about to be generalized by a new EC Directive.

of shares (deposited with them) at general meetings and have used that power in the past to protect their position as creditors rather than to promote shareholder value. Finally, the principle of employee representation at board level was confirmed in Germany immediately after the Second World War when the political position of capital was weak (because of its co-operation with the Nazi regime), whilst the political position of the trade unions, which had opposed Fascism, was strong. By contrast, when in the 1970s a scheme of employee representation on the board was proposed in the UK, with its very different social structure and traditions of corporate finance, shareholder and business interests were able quite easily to mobilize enough political support to prevent legislation.[50]

The previous paragraph may help to explain why things are as they are in Germany and the UK, but it does not answer the point of principle: would the German economy be more productive if employee interests were expelled from company law or, contrariwise, would British productivity be improved if they were included? This is a large issue which can be touched on only briefly here. It is possible to identify three competing positions. The first is that the exclusion of employee representation from the board is the efficient governance solution. The traditional British (and US) division of functions, whereby labour law gives employees governance rights over terms and conditions of employment (broadly) and company law gives shareholders governance rights over corporate strategy, is efficient because each group is thereby given governance rights in areas where 'it has something to contribute'. It is further argued that 'different sorts of governance rights coexist in the firm and relate to one another', so that governance of strategy is not superior to or more important than governance of employment conditions but rather the two proceed on 'parallel tracks'.[51] The only question is which parties can most effectively exercise a particular set of governance rights, the implication being that corporate strategy rights for employees do not constitute an efficient arrangement.[52]

---

[50] See n. 58 below.

[51] E. Rock and M. Wachter, 'Tailored Claims and Governance: The Fit between Employees and Shareholders' in M. Blair and M. Roe (eds), *Employees and Corporate Governance* (Washington, DC: Brookings Institution, 1999).

[52] Though there might be other arguments for employee representation at board level, for example in order to improve the flow of information to such representatives and thus the quality of bargaining over employment conditions. Such an argument would support only minority employee representation, however.

Alternatively, the differences between Germany and the UK in relation to employee representation at board level could be seen as illustrating profounder differences between two ways of providing for the inputs necessary for the functioning of business. In liberal market economies, of which the USA and the UK are the primary examples, that provision is made predominantly through a process of market contracting rather than close co-ordination. Only those without any contractual protection, such as ordinary shareholders, obtain institutional positions of influence instead. In co-ordinated market economies, such as Germany and Japan, a bigger role is played by institutions, sometimes state institutions, oftentimes not, which align the actions of those providing the necessary inputs. In the latter type of economy, representation of non-shareholder interests on the board has a natural affinity with other organizational structures for co-ordinating activities, existing outside company law, whereas in liberal market economies institutional representation seems an unnecessary addition to contractual arrangements. Further, neither type of economic organization can be said to be better in all circumstances in discharging the tasks facing a modern economy. Each has its strengths and weaknesses.[53] Certainly, analyses of the functioning of co-determination in Germany stress the importance of its taking place within a highly co-operative framework of industrial relations, though it is not clear which way the chain of causation runs.[54]

This second analysis seems to have been the one ultimately accepted by the EC in relation to the European Company Regulation and Directive.[55] These EU instruments require employee representation on the board of the European Company only to the extent that this was required by the national laws of the companies forming a European Company.[56] Instead of the various uniform or equivalent systems of board-level representation which had previously been proposed, the adopted version of the Directive is avowedly relativistic: different European Companies will

[53] See P. Hall and D. Soskice, 'Introduction' and S. Vitols, 'Varieties of Corporate Governance: Comparing Germany and the UK' in P. Hall and D. Soskice (eds), *Varieties of Capitalism* (Oxford: Oxford University Press, 2001).

[54] H. Schmidt et al., *Corporate Governance in Germany* (Baden-Baden: Nomos, 1997), Part 2D: 'As employers and employees perceive a mutual dependency, a relation of high trust and low conflict has developed. Thus, German industrial relations take place essentially in a non-conflictual context' (p. 229).

[55] See Chapter 1, p. 4.

[56] Council Directive 2001/86/EC, Annex, Part 3. This is the so-called 'before and after' principle.

have different systems of employee representation at board level according to the national legal cultures out of which they emerge.[57]

The third position is that board representation should be promoted, even within conflictual industrial relations systems, either because the principle of joint regulation should be extended from terms and conditions of employment to corporate strategy or as part of a strategy for transforming a conflictual industrial relations system in a more co-operative direction.[58]

SHAREHOLDER CONTROL AND THE INTERESTS OF OTHER STAKEHOLDERS

At least for the time being, it is clear that UK company law places the shareholders centre stage. This is evident in the CLR's proposed formulation of the core duty which company law imposes on directors. This is that a director should act 'in the way he decides, in good faith, would be most likely to promote the success of the company for the benefit of the members as a whole'.[59] This is a clearer formulation than the common law rule that directors should act 'in the best interests of the company' because it establishes who constitutes the company's interests. Since, however, the CLR's formulation also maintains the subjective approach of the common law, the importance of the duty lies probably more in the realm of values than in the realm of litigation. As we have argued above,[60] the present common law duty is difficult for shareholders to enforce in the courts, and it is doubtful if the new formulation, if adopted, will be more productive of litigation.

Nevertheless, values are important in company law, as in other branches of law. A very considerable part of the work of the CLR was devoted to devising, and putting out to consultation, two different models of company law, designed to elicit from consultees their preferences. One model was that

---

[57] However, UK law transposing the Directive will have to provide for employee representation at board level in order to allow for European Companies with registered offices in the UK, where the companies forming the European Company come from national systems requiring board-level representation.

[58] See the *Report of the Committee of Inquiry on Industrial Democracy*, Cmnd. 6706, 1975 (the 'Bullock' Report), which advocated the introduction of a form of parity representation for employees on the boards of large British companies, but was not implemented by the Government. See P. Davies and M. Freedland, *Labour Legislation and Public Policy* (Oxford: Clarendon Press, 1993), pp. 396–404. For a vigorous recent re-statement of this view see Wedderburn, 'Employees, Partnership and Company Law' (2002) 31 ILJ 99.

[59] CLR, *Final Report*, vol. I, July 2001, p. 345 (Principle 2).

[60] See p. 159.

of the pluralist company, in which the directors, as described above, would owe duties, via the company, to the whole range of stakeholder groups; the other was the 'enlightened shareholder value' model, essentially a re-statement for modern conditions of the traditional approach of the common law.[61] Consultation revealed very strong support for the modernized trad-itional model and only limited support for the pluralist model. As suggested above, such an outcome of a debate focused solely on directors' duties is probably rational. A stakeholder formulation of directors' duties, if accom-panied by nothing else, leaves directors even less accountable, if the duty is subjectively formulated, or transfers inappropriate decisions to the courts, if it is objectively stated. A broadening of directors' duties is a necessary preliminary to institutional reforms, intended to place representatives of stakeholder interests on the board,[62] but by itself it is unlikely to change how directors decide, at least so long as the directors are subject to other mechan-isms of shareholder control, such as the shareholders' removal rights over directors.[63] However, those supporting a pluralist model of directors' duties did not propose the necessary further institutional changes,[64] perhaps because of the difficulty of answering the question of how board-level decision-making could be effective if all stakeholder groups were repre-sented on it or, if only one or two groups were to be represented, of why some stakeholder groups were to be preferred over others.

However, in the CLR's view, enlightened shareholder value does have a content which is not just 'shareholder value' with an approving epithet attached. First, enlightened shareholder value does not require the direc-tors to prefer the short term over the long term, in promoting the suc-cess of the company.[65] This is no more than a restatement of the common law, but stating this explicitly may turn out to be important in the light of a surprisingly wide misunderstanding that the common law does require short-termism.[66] Second, the duty of the directors to promote the success

[61] See n. 44 above, pp. 33–46.

[62] P. Davies, 'Employee Representation on Company Boards and Participation in Corpor-ate Planning' (1975) 38 MLR 254.

[63] See p. 128.

[64] CLR, *Developing the Framework*, March 2000, para 3.29. Paragraphs 3.20 to 3.31 contain a developed statement by the CLR of its reasons for choosing the 'enlightened shareholder value' model.

[65] See n. 30 above, Note 1 to Principle 2.

[66] CLR, n. 64 above, at para. 3.54. The situation may be different, both at common law and under the CLR's proposals, where the main decision is allocated to the shareholders and the directors' decision is ancillary to that of the shareholders. Here, the interests of the company, as far as the directors are concerned, are to be equated with the decision which the current body of shareholders wishes to take: *Heron International Ltd v Lord Grade* [1983] BCLC 244, CA.

of the company for the benefit of the shareholders restricts directors' freedom to give effect to non-shareholder interests when exercising the discretion vested in them by the law and the company's articles, but it does not exempt them from obedience to either that law or the company's constitution.[67] This is an obvious point, and one reflected in the common law, but it is surprising how often it is misunderstood. The importance of the point is that, if the interests of some non-shareholder group are dealt with in some body of law other than company law, for example the interests of employees in health and safety law, the law on directors' duties gives the board no exemption from the mandatory rules of that body of law. If health and safety law requires a certain course of action from employers, the board of a company cannot lawfully ignore that rule, no matter how much it might be in the interests of their shareholders to do so. Third, the draft principle refers to the 'success' of the company and not to the maximization of economic returns. This takes account of the fact that companies may be used for non-profit-making purposes and success for the benefit of the members is to be gauged by what the members have set as its objectives in the constitution.[68]

Fourth, and most important, even in a commercial company the promotion of the success of the company for the benefit of the members of the company is unlikely to be most effectively achieved by riding roughshod over the interests of the other groups whose contribution is necessary for the success of the company. It is difficult to imagine a successful business with disaffected employees, reluctant suppliers, and customers who doubt the quality of the product which the company provides. This, again rather obvious point, has been long recognized by the common law, by means of a permission to directors to take account of the interests of stakeholder groups when promoting the interests of the company. As Bowen LJ said in 1883, when discussing the principles governing gratuities paid to employees, 'the law does not say that there are to be no cakes and ale, but there are to be no cakes and ale except such as are required for the benefit of the company'.[69] The reason why this principle does not turn the company law into a pluralist concept is that it does not give

---

[67] As far as the company's constitution is concerned, this is reflected in the CLR's formulation of Principle 1 and in Note 4 to Principle 2 (see p. 162) and, as far as the law is concerned, in its draft Clause 17(3) (*Final Report*, n. 30 above, at p. 344).

[68] Note 4 to Principle 2 is relevant here as well.

[69] *Hutton v West Cork Railway Co* (1883) 23 ChD 654, CA. (On 'cakes and ale' see *Twelfth Night*, Act II, Scene 3, lines 125–6.) The point was made in the context of the *ultra vires* doctrine (see p. 45) but it seems applicable equally to directors' duties.

non-shareholder interests an independent value: promoting employee welfare is valued not as a thing in itself but as an end to promoting shareholder welfare. If the two diverge, as they might when the company was being wound up, the employees' interests might be allocated a very subordinate place.[70]

The CLR's statement of principles accepts the view of Bowen LJ and arguably extends it by *requiring* directors to take account of stakeholder interests and, indeed, the interests of communities and the environment when considering, in good faith, what will best promote the success of the business for the benefit of the members.[71] The innovative aspect of the CLR's proposals lies, however, more in the mechanism proposed for the enforcement of this requirement. It lies, not in litigation, which is not likely to play an important part, but in expanded disclosure requirements, especially the Operating and Financial Review (OFR). As we have seen above,[72] this is a proposed addition to the mandatory annual reporting requirements for large companies, which will require the board to move beyond financial information and to explain how it has dealt with relevant stakeholders and communities in the formulation and execution of its policies to promote the success of the business.

Two of the six elements of the OFR are relevant to our current concerns: 'an account of the company's key relationships, with employees, customers, suppliers and others' and 'policies and performance on environmental, community, social, ethical and reputational issues, including compliance with relevant laws and regulations'.[73] These will be required to be covered when and to the extent that they are relevant to the business, and it is difficult to envisage many situations in which some account under these headings will not be relevant to large businesses. There are still many issues to be thrashed out in relation to the OFR, two of the most important of which are the extent to which it can and should be audited and whether sensible standards can be developed for presenting the information and thus making it comparable across companies.[74] Nevertheless, the OFR is not a complete step in the dark. The Accounting Standards Board already produces non-mandatory guidance on the

---

[70] Cf. *Parke v Daily News* [1962] Ch 927.

[71] Notes 1 and 2 to Principle 2. Thus, although Principle 2(a) maintains the traditional subjective nature of the duty upon directors to act in the interests of the company, the requirement to take into account the interests of non-shareholder groups, in so far as it is 'practicable in the circumstances' for the director to identify them (Principle 2(b)), constitutes an objective supplement to the duty. Presumably, if this reform is enacted, it will swallow up the present CA 1985, s 309.

[72] See p. 135.   [73] CLR, n. 59 above, at para. 8.40.   [74] *Ibid.*, paras 8.49–8.63.

production of an OFR,[75] and a number of large companies do produce them and/or reports in more limited areas such as environmental or social impact.[76]

Of course, any action within company law in response to the OFR lies with the shareholders, and it may be wondered whether the shareholders will take any action which is not directly in their own interests. However, although probably true as far as it goes, this insight may understate the impact of the OFR. If a company is obliged to explain publicly its policies on stakeholder relations and to do so each year, so that past statements are to some degree tested by subsequent performance, the information thus made available may be capable of effective, direct use by stakeholder groups in other contexts, such as collective bargaining or lobbying of government or even public protest. In other words, although the shareholder-centred philosophy of company law means that the regulation of the relationship of non-shareholder stakeholders with the company is not predominantly a matter for company law, nevertheless, company law, because of its developed mechanisms for the disclosure of information, can be used to meet the information needs of non-company law governance mechanisms.

CONCLUSION

Exclusive shareholder control is a central feature of British company law. It is a feature shared with company law in the United States and many Commonwealth countries. Some substantial degree of control of companies by ordinary shareholders seems to be inherent in the way corporate business is financed. The CLR proposes to retain its central place, while modernizing the expression and operation of the principle. On the other hand, that shareholder control does not have to be exclusive is demonstrated by the company laws of a number of our continental European neighbours, though it is less easy to deduce from them why employees turn out to be the sole beneficiaries of wider representational rights at board level. The debate on the merits of being on one side or another of this great divide in modern company law systems has been, and will no doubt continue to be, long and hard, with predictions that one

---

[75] Reproduced in *Palmer's Company Law* (London: Sweet & Maxwell, looseleaf), vol. 6, para. F.099.

[76] See R. Macve, 'Accounting for Environmental Cost' in D. Richards (ed.), *The Industrial Green Game: Implications for Environmental Design and Management* (Washington, DC: National Academy Press, 1997).

arrangement would triumph over the other changing with the perceived relative success over time of the economies which exhibit one or other of the arrangements. We have not been able to do full justice to this debate, though we have pointed to a third possible analysis, which is that each system is better adapted to the needs of particular industries or production functions and that both may be able to survive in a fast-changing world.

Small Companies and Small Businesses

THE NATURE OF THE SMALL COMPANY ISSUE

When in Chapter 1 we identified the five core features of company law, we saw that only one of them, separate legal personality, was a necessary attribute of companies formed under the Companies Act. The others, while representing distinctive doctrines of company law, could be opted out of in particular cases. We suggested that the full range of core features was typically to be found in practice in 'large' companies, meaning by this companies with a large shareholding body, distinct from the board, where the shareholders had made a significant contribution to the financing of the company by subscribing to or purchasing its shares. Shareholders in such a company are likely to make their funds available at a lower price if they benefit from limited liability and free transferability of their shares and if they have ultimate control of the company. Moreover, a large shareholding body makes centralized management a necessity for the efficient conduct of its business. There are, by contrast, other types of company where these core, but non-mandatory features, are not on display, either not at all or not fully. An example is the company limited by guarantee and used for non-profit purposes.

However, the most significant class of company not displaying the full range of core features is the 'small' company, meaning here the company with a small number of shareholders, all or most of whom expect to be involved in the management of the company. Such companies are sometimes referred to as 'closely held' or 'close' companies. The shareholders in such a company may have contracted out of limited liability at least as regards the main source of their finance (the loan from the bank, which will have taken security over the shareholders' personal assets)[1] and, in any case, they are in a better position to monitor the risks of unlimited liability because of their close involvement in the management of the company. The shareholders in such a company positively reject the idea of centralized management (i.e. that the directors should be a body

---

[1] See p. 69.

entirely distinct from the shareholders), and, further, they are likely to regard the identity of any new shareholder as a matter for concern for all the shareholders and not just the potential transferor (so that the articles will restrict free transfer of shares).

On the other hand, some problems for company law occur disproportionately in small companies, such as opportunistic conduct on the part of majority shareholders towards the minority, as we saw in Chapter 8.[2] With large companies, the capital markets and centralized management reduce the incidence of this problem, at least where shareholdings are dispersed. Further, small companies display one core feature in an even stronger form than large companies, namely, the feature of shareholder control, again because of the members' involvement in management (though we have argued that often in small companies the shareholders acquire their shares in return for their promised contribution as workers rather than as suppliers of risk capital).[3]

While it is wrong to divide the corporate population neatly into two groups, for there are many companies in an intermediate position between 'small' and 'large',[4] it is nevertheless important to ask how, if at all, company law should adapt itself to small companies that display only one or two of the core features which company law provides. The question is pressing for two reasons. First, a large proportion of the companies registered under the Act are in fact small, in the sense in which the term is used above. The CLR reported that 70 per cent of companies have only one or two shareholders and 90 per cent have fewer than five.[5] Thus, in terms of numbers of companies, those not displaying the five core features probably outweigh those that do. Not only is wealth generated by small companies as a group at any one time, but they provide the seedbed out of which the large companies of the future may grow. Providing a legal framework which facilitates the growth of small companies is particularly important in public policy terms.[6]

Second, as we indicated in Chapter 1, the nineteenth-century history of how small companies obtained access to incorporation under the Companies Act is one of subversion of legislative intent, in which the

---

[2] At p. 253.   [3] See p. 261.   [4] See Chapter 1, p. 26.

[5] *Developing the Framework*, March 2000, para. 6.9. Companies which are small in shareholders tend also to be small economically, though the two things are not the same: ibid., para. 6.8 reporting that 65 per cent of 'live' companies had a turnover of less than £350,000.

[6] So-called life-style companies, which provide work for their usually single shareholder and which that shareholder does not wish to expand, are of less concern for the future health of the economy.

legislature acquiesced, rather than a result of an explicit statutory scheme.[7] Consequently, the legislature never addressed in a comprehensive manner the question of how such companies should be regulated by the Act, once its initial policy of excluding them had failed.[8] In fact, as the CLR put it, successive Companies Acts continued to be 'largely structured around the needs of the large public company',[9] with only occasional adjustments to take account of other types of company.

However, the issue of adjustment is not a merely technical one; rather, it has generated some sophisticated policy debates. There are basically four points of view. The first is that the access to incorporation with limited liability for small companies is to be encouraged, to the extent that a separate form of incorporation for small companies should be enacted, either in a separate statute or as a separate part of a general Companies Act.[10] The second, which can be said to be the view of the CLR, is that the free availability of incorporation under a Companies Act applying to all companies is the correct principle, but the statute should be subject to a 'think small first' approach, which would mean more extensive and systematic adjustments of the legislation to meet the needs of small companies and those dealing with them than has historically been the case.[11]

The third and fourth approaches both place greater stress on the fact that carrying on a small business through a legal vehicle other than the company is perfectly possible and that a large number of small businesses are in fact carried on as either partnerships or small traders.[12] The third view is sceptical about the value of making it easier for small businesses to incorporate and would prefer to encourage small businesses to use the partnership, by updating that form,[13] and through education about the

---

[7] See Chapter 1, pp. 28 and 68 on the decision in *Salomon v Salomon* and the subversion of the 'seven member' requirement.

[8] The only area the legislature addressed in any significant way was that of disclosure of information to the public, some private companies being exempted from the full regime. These exemptions were brought to an end by the Companies Act 1967, but, as we shall see below, have been reintroduced in a new form in recent years.

[9] See n. 5 above, at para. 6.10.

[10] The arguments for and against this approach are set out in CLR, *The Strategic Framework*, February 1999, pp. 56–69.

[11] See n. 5 above, at paras 6.15–6.25.

[12] See Chapter 1, p. 29.

[13] See Law Commission and Scottish Law Commission, *Partnership Law: A Joint Consultation Paper*, 2000.

respective advantages and disadvantages of the two forms.[14] Education is said to have an important role here because of research findings which suggest that some business people choose incorporation without a proper appreciation of its costs or, even, of its benefits. The fourth view is an extension of the third, and is more robust about the value of making changes to the companies legislation so as to discourage incorporation thereunder, whilst also being more enthusiastic about creating a new form of incorporation (but without limited liability) in order to provide a tailored vehicle for the small business.[15] Interestingly, proponents of both the third and the fourth view accept that there is no realistic chance of going back to the nineteenth-century starting point of simply excluding small companies from any form of incorporation with limited liability: indeed, it would seem to be inconsistent with EC law to attempt to do so.[16]

We shall look at how these views have played out in recent years, in relation both to reform of the Companies Act and to the promotion of alternative forms for the carrying on of small businesses.

THE SMALL BUSINESS AND THE COMPANIES LEGISLATION

LIMITED LIABILITY

The two core features of company law which are most challenged by the small company are limited liability and centralized management, and their associated public disclosure requirements. Limited liability for small companies is probably the pivotal issue and has been much debated. As we saw in Chapter 3,[17] the arguments in favour of limited liability are least strong in relation to small companies, and also,[18] that the risk of abuse of limited liability is highest where management is combined with shareholding, as it typically is in the small company. However, since the

---

[14] The strongest advocate of this point of view is Judith Freedman. See 'Small Business and the Corporate Form: Burden or Privilege' (1994) 57 MLR 555; 'The Quest for an Ideal Form for Small Businesses—A Misconceived Enterprise' in B. Rider and M. Andenas (eds), *Developments in European Company Law* (London: Institute of Advanced Legal Studies and Kluwer Law International, 1999); and 'Limited Liability: Large Company Theory and Small Firms' (2000) 63 MLR 317.

[15] See A. Hicks, 'Legislating for the Needs of the Small Business' in Rider and Andenas, n. 14 above, and A. Hicks, R. Drury, and J. Smallcombe, *Alternative Company Structures for the Small Business* (London: Certified Accountants Educational Trust, 1995).

[16] See the discussion in Chapter 3 at p. 69 of the Twelfth Company Law Directive.

[17] See p. 66.   [18] See p. 61.

removal of access to limited liability for small companies is not a feasible policy for the reasons just given, the debate has focused instead on the conditions of access to incorporation under the Companies Act and the control of opportunistic conduct.

Some have argued for the introduction of a significant minimum capital requirement for small companies.[19] Others, including originally the DTI,[20] favour a symbolic minimum capital requirement of £1,000, to deter 'frivolous' incorporations, though it is difficult to evaluate this proposal without knowing what, in its supporters' view, makes an incorporation 'frivolous' and how the characteristic of frivolity is related to the need to find £1,000.[21] The CLR did not propose the introduction of a minimum capital requirement for small companies, but was in favour of some strengthening of the law dealing with the abuse of limited liability.[22] Since the policy questions in relation to limited liability have been canvassed above in Chapters 3 and 4, where small company problems were specifically highlighted, it is not proposed to recapitulate the arguments here. The conclusion there was that minimum capital requirements are an unsophisticated instrument for control of the abuse of limited liability and that it has not been demonstrated that *ex post* control over abuse (i.e. the current approach of the law) is less effective than *ex ante* minimum capital requirements.[23]

CENTRALIZED MANAGEMENT

As we saw in Chapters 5 to 7, the existence of a large body of shareholders and a separate board of directors gives rise to problems, to the regulation of which company law has devoted considerable resources. All this, however, is beside the point in small companies where the directors are the shareholders and where the shareholders (or most of them) are the directors. There are no principal and agent problems where the principal and agent are the same persons (or nearly so). In fact, the opposite problem emerges: what is the point of requiring a company to have two

---

[19] Hicks, n. 15 above, at pp. 66–7.

[20] DTI, *Company Law Reform White Paper*, Cmnd. 5391, 1973.

[21] Just as age does not necessarily lead to wisdom, it is doubtful whether the possession of £1,000 in ready cash does so either.

[22] CLR, *Developing the Framework*, March 2000, paras 9.61–9.71 and *Completing the Structure*, November 2000, paras 13.102–13.110 ('Phoenix' companies).

[23] It is insufficient, of course, to point out that the current laws on disqualification of directors, wrongful trading and use of company names (see pp. 93–102) are imperfect, since the same may be said of minimum capital requirements as well. The question is which type of regulation has the greater potential to control abuse at the least cost.

separate decision-making bodies (board and shareholders' meeting) if the same people crop up on both occasions? In fact, it is well established that those involved in small companies often do not distinguish between their actions as shareholders and their actions as directors. They simply come to a decision about the future conduct of the business.

Since it is shareholder meetings which require greater formality (in particular, by way of advanced notice to all those entitled to attend),[24] the tendency is for those running small companies to purport to act all the time as directors. For some years, the law has tried to accommodate this tendency by making it easier for shareholders in private companies to dispense with the meetings the Act requires them to hold and to take informally (i.e. without a meeting) the decisions they need to take as shareholders. One important feature of the design of these rules should be noted. The exemptions can be claimed by the shareholders in any private company, so that the legislature has avoided the task of having to identify situations where there is a sufficient degree of congruence between shareholders and directors for the exemption to apply.[25] On the other hand, the consent requirements built into the rules make it highly likely that the exemptions will in fact be claimed only in companies where there is unity of shareholders and directors (or nearly so), and, by the same token, minority shareholders are protected from overreaching.

Under the current law, the shareholders are entitled, by unanimous vote (the so-called elective resolution),[26] to opt out of some otherwise mandatory meeting requirements of the Act, of which the most important are the requirement to hold an annual general meeting and the need to lay the company's accounts before the members in general meeting.[27] An elective resolution may be rescinded by an ordinary resolution,[28] and, in any event, in any particular year and provided he or she acts quickly enough, any individual member can insist on an AGM being held or the accounts being laid before the members in general meeting, despite the existence of an elective resolution.[29] However, while dispensing with

---

[24] See p. 136.

[25] Obviously, some private companies have significant numbers of shareholders, only a small proportion of whom are involved in the management of the company.

[26] CA 1985, s 379A.

[27] CA 1985, ss 366A and 252. An elective resolution does not dispense the company from the obligation to send the accounts to each member individually, which is separate from the obligation to lay the accounts before the members in a meeting. See ss 238 and 241.

[28] CA 1985, s 379A(3), so that it is easier to repeal than to adopt an elective resolution.

[29] CA 1985, ss 366A(3) and 253(2).

the AGM and the laying of accounts is important for small companies, shareholders, without further reform, would still need to meet to take decisions allocated to them by the Act or under the company's articles.[30] Thus, it is important that the Act goes further and allows the shareholders of a private company, subject to certain minor exceptions, to take binding decisions informally (i.e. without a meeting and without prior notice) by means of a simple written resolution, again provided they act unanimously.[31] As we have seen,[32] this is in part a statutory borrowing from the common law which also allows the unanimous decision of the shareholders to bind the company (whether public or private). The common law is even more informal since it does not require a written resolution, provided the unanimous consent of the shareholders can be shown.

The CLR proposes to develop these rules in three ways, all in the direction of easier decision-making. First, all private companies, upon formation, will be treated as having made the choices currently available to them by means of an elective resolution, unless they choose otherwise, either on formation or later. So, holding an AGM and the laying of accounts become a matter of opting in rather than opting out, but the right of the individual member to have an AGM or to have the accounts laid is retained.[33]

Second, written resolutions would no longer require unanimity but rather the same percentage as would be required if a meeting were held, except that the percentage (half or three-quarters) would be applied to those eligible to vote and not, as at a meeting, to those present and voting.[34] This is a significant change because it means that a single member will no longer be able to compel the holding of a meeting by simply refusing to consent to the written resolution. The justification for this must lie in the view that in small companies the holding of a meeting does not constitute a significant opportunity for the minority shareholder to express his or her view, because other informal opportunities are available to that shareholder. Of course, taking decisions in this way might

---

[30] See p. 115.   [31] CA 1985, s 381A.   [32] See p. 116.

[33] *Developing the Framework*, March 2000, para. 7.93. Subsequent opting in would be by ordinary resolution.

[34] Ibid. paras 7.10–7.15; *Completing the Structure*, November 2000, paras 2.11–2.13; and *Final Report*, July 2001, para. 2.15. All shareholders would be given notice of the resolution and of whether it was adopted. The original proposal was that companies could in their articles adopt a regime for less-than-unanimous informal decision-making, but the final recommendation was for an opt-out: companies could choose to impose higher consent requirements, including the restoration of unanimity, in their articles.

constitute grounds for a successful application under CA 1985, s 459,[35] for example where there was an arrangement among the members that some or all categories of decision should require the consent of all the members, but this would equally be the case if the decision were taken at a meeting without a particular shareholder's agreement.

Third, the unanimous consent rule of the common law should be clarified to remove the uncertainties that surround it and be embodied in the Act. The rule would continue to require unanimity, but that unanimity would not need to be expressed in a written resolution and would apply to any decision which the company was free to take, whether that decision was allocated to the shareholders or not.[36] Thus, unanimity would remain mandatory for highly informal decision-making by shareholders or for decisions not allocated to the shareholders under the company's constitution, but otherwise private companies could take decisions by written resolution by the appropriate majority, unless they chose a more demanding regime.

It is clear from the above that the law has made considerable efforts to adapt the machinery of centralized management for those companies where ownership and control are in the same hands. However, it is arguable that a more radical approach should be taken. The current law, and the CLR's proposals, keep the two-centre decision-making structure in existence (and so require those running small companies still to distinguish between what they do as directors and what they do as shareholders), while making it more convenient for them to operate it. A more radical approach would be to permit the company to opt for rolling the two decision-making bodies into one, as is permitted in some US jurisdictions. Thus, s 351 of the Delaware General Corporation Law permits a close corporation to opt for its affairs to be run solely by the shareholders. This choice may be made on incorporation or subsequently by unanimous vote and may be reversed by an ordinary resolution. In this model the board goes into abeyance while the choice is in effect. An alternative model would be to allow the shareholders to cede the whole of their powers to the board. The CLR thought that one or other of these schemes might be desirable so long as the shareholders and the directors were the same people, and it consulted on possible models for implementing such a scheme in the UK. However, those consulted showed little enthusiasm for the idea. This may have been, not so much because the idea itself was not welcome, but because of the complexity of the

---

[35] See Chaptert 8.   [36] *Final Report*, July 2001, paras 2.14 and 7.17–7.26.

termination arrangements the CLR proposed, because of its desire that the model should not continue in force once unity of shareholders and directors no longer obtained.[37]

MANDATORY DISCLOSURE

As we saw earlier in the book, both limited liability and centralized management naturally generate pressure for compulsory disclosure of information by the board so that both creditors and shareholders (and potential creditors and shareholders) should know the financial state of the company. This impulse expresses itself above all in the requirement for the annual production of financial statements by the company and the verification of those statements through the auditing process. In particular, annual public disclosure of financial information about the company has been argued to be the proper trade-off for limited liability and to explain why the same disclosure rules are not applied to partnerships, where liability is unlimited. Should the rules be modified for small companies?

The one area where there has been a substantial reduction of the requirements on small companies is in relation to the audit. Over a period of less than ten years the law has moved from the position where all companies had to have their accounts audited to one where over 80 per cent of companies filing accounts with the Registrar are exempted from this requirement and, if the CLR's proposals were accepted, the proportion of exemptions would rise to over 90 per cent.[38] In terms of regulatory techniques, it is interesting to note the different criteria used to identify 'small' companies in the audit exemption area. These relate, not to the number of shareholders or the identity of shareholders and managers, but to the economic size of the company. The criteria concern the number of employees, the balance sheet total, and, most important, the size of its turnover, which is a measure of the value of the business done by the company during the accounting year.[39] This is probably a rational set of criteria to use,[40] but they are in any event mandated by the provisions of the Fourth Company Law Directive on accounts.[41]

---

[37] See *Developing the Framework* (n. 22 above), paras 7.95–7.135 and *Completing the Structure* (n. 22 above), paras 2.35–2.36.

[38] DTI, *The Statutory Audit Requirement for Smaller Companies*, URN 99/1115, October 1999, p. 5.

[39] CA 1985, s 249A.

[40] As the CLR put it, 'Economic size . . . is an obvious proxy for economic impact of the company on members, employees and those with whom it interacts': *Developing the Framework*, para. 8.6.

[41] Directive 78/660/EEC, [1978] OJ L222/11, Arts 11 and 51.

Essentially, exemption from audit is based on a cost–benefit analysis. The cost of the audit to small companies is said to be disproportionately high in relative terms. That is, although the audits of small companies cost less than the audit of large companies, that cost represents a larger proportion of the company's turnover than in the case of a larger company. On the benefit side, it is said that the audit is less valuable to shareholders of small companies, because they are more likely to have other access to accurate information about the company, and less important to its creditors, because small creditors do not rely on the published accounts anyway and large creditors can, and do, ask for their own verified information. It is obviously a matter of judgement, and not an easy matter of judgement, to balance costs to the company and benefits to creditors, but in the Government's view the balance has come increasingly to be struck in the company's interests. In 1994, before which date there was no exemption, the turnover figure below which exemption was available was set at not more than £90,000; it was increased to £350,000 in 1997 and again to £1m. in 2000; and the CLR has recommended a further increase to £4.8m., the maximum allowed by the Fourth Directive.[42] Some doubts about the move to making full use of the exemption permitted by the Fourth Directive are perhaps to be found in the CLR's proposal that between turnovers of £1m. and £4.8m., companies should have to produce an Independent Professional Review of their accounts, instead of an audit, if trials show that the IPR produces valuable information at significantly less cost than an audit.[43]

However, audit comes into play only once there is a set of accounts to be audited. Should small company accounts be less demanding than the accounts required of large companies? Here, the CLR thought that there should certainly be a set of statutory accounting requirements tailored to the needs of small companies and the users of their accounts, and so it produced a model of what it proposed.[44] This would replace the provisions of Sch 8 to the Act (Form and Content of Accounts Prepared by Small Companies), which it criticized as simply a cut-down version of something designed for large companies. However, it also criticized the

---

[42] *Final Report*, July 2001, para. 2.32. In fact, the requirement would be that, to qualify as a 'small' company, two of the following three criteria must be satisfied: turnover of not more than £4.8m.; balance sheet total of not more than £2.4m.; and not more than 50 employees, but the turnover figure is normally the most significant.

[43] Of course, exemption from audit is not the same thing as not having an audit. About half of the presently exempted companies do in fact have their accounts audited, often at the behest of creditors: DTI, n. 38 above, at p. 6.

[44] See Annex E to *Developing the Framework* (n. 22 above).

distinction, currently embedded in the legislation, between the accounts produced for members and those filed publicly (which may, if the company wishes, take the form of 'abbreviated accounts').[45] It thought the distinction gave companies little relief from 'regulatory burdens', since they had to produce the full accounts anyway for their members, and, more important, abbreviated accounts short-changed the users of small company accounts because they were 'simply not meaningful to creditors and denied them access to relevant information'.[46] Abbreviated accounts contain no profit and loss account, no directors' report, and only an abbreviated balance sheet. The CLR proposed that the principle to be adopted was that small companies should prepare for shareholders and file publicly the same accounts. If this proposal is accepted, it will increase the amount of information available to those who deal with small companies.

MINORITY SHAREHOLDER PROTECTION

If limited liability and centralized management are features of company law which the small company does not or ought not to need, protection of minorities is something of which small companies make disproportionate use. As we saw in Chapter 8, the law has recognized this and, for example, has developed the provisions dealing with unfair prejudice in such a way as to provide for the special needs of small companies.[47] There is no need to repeat that analysis here, but it is worth noting that it represents an adaptation of the law to the particular situation of small companies, just as much as the changing rules on audit do so.

Two special features of the small company are recognized in CA 1985, s 459 and the cases decided thereunder. The most obvious feature is the strong version of shareholder control which obtains in small companies, namely, that shareholder control is often expected by the shareholders to show itself through participation in the management of the company. The Law Commission recognized this in its proposal that in private companies where all, or substantially all, of the members were directors, there should be a presumption of unfairly prejudicial conduct where a shareholder with at least 10 per cent of the voting shares was excluded from participation in the management of the company.[48] It is important to see that this proposal was made, not in order to bring such

---

[45] CA 1985, Sch 8A.   [46] See n. 42 above, at para. 8.33.

[47] Another strand in the law has been its protective attitude towards private ordering in this area. See, for example, Chapter 5, p. 132.

[48] Law Commission, *Shareholder Remedies*, Cm. 3769, 1997, pp. 30–40.

cases within s 459, but to provide more expeditious handling of cases which already constituted a substantial part of the unfair prejudice workload.[49]

The other feature of small companies under CA 1985, s 459 is rather different. This is that the common law presumption of free transferability of shares is often qualified or excluded in such companies. A shareholder wishing to transfer his or her shares in a 'quasi-partnership' company may find that the shares must be offered first to the existing shareholders at a (perhaps unattractive) price determined under a mechanism contained in the articles or that the board of the company is empowered by the articles simply to refuse to register a transferee of the shares as a member of the company, thus preventing the easy exercise by the transferee of the rights attached to the shares. Section 459 permits both the existing holder of the shares and a transferee of the shares to use the section to challenge the board's decision,[50] and the CLR has proposed that a board refusing to register a transfer should be obliged to give its reasons.[51]

However, whereas exclusion from management in a small company may raise a presumption of unfairness, a refusal to admit a new member to whom the existing members object does not. In fact, involvement in management and exclusion of free transferability are, in many ways, two sides of the same coin. The personal nature of the relationship among the controllers of a small company explains both features. Entitlement to participate in management and some degree of lock-in are functional attributes where the controllers contribute their talents to the company rather than (or as well as) finance. The right to participate in management helps to ensure that those talents can be exercised; the lock-in reduces the risk that one partner to the joint venture will behave opportunistically by moving on (or threatening to do so) when his or her contribution is most in demand. So courts hearing CA 1985, s 459 cases should be suspicious

---

[49] Ibid., p. 25. However, when the CLR consulted on the proposal it was not supported: *Developing the Framework*, March 2000, para. 4.104.

[50] CA 1985, s 459(2) gives *locus standi* to non-members to whom shares have been transferred (or transmitted by operation of law, as upon the death of a member to a personal representative). For unlisted companies, becoming a member is a two-step process: first, the transfer of the share(s) from the current holder to the potential new member, which is normally a transaction between the current shareholder and the prospective member, and then the registration of the latter in the company's register of shareholders in place of the former, a decision of the company which is normally delegated to the board under the company's articles. See CA 1985, ss 22(2), 183, and 352 and Table A, arts 23–8.

[51] *Completing the Structure*, November 2000, para. 5.80.

of exclusion from management, but not use it to give shareholders and their transferees untrammelled affiliation rights (i.e. rights of entry and exit).[52]

SMALL BUSINESSES AND ALTERNATIVE BUSINESS VEHICLES

An alternative focus for debate over small businesses is whether a new form of business vehicle, specially adapted for their needs, should be devised. The four views on the appropriate legislative framework for small businesses, identified above, are relevant here also. However, only the first and the fourth views are strongly in favour of a new business vehicle. The second and third views share the proposition that their aims can be achieved by appropriate amendments to the companies legislation, and differ only in the extent to which they would be prepared to go to alter that legislation to accommodate the needs of small businesses.

Those taking the fourth view wish to discourage incorporation with limited liability for small businesses and so, often, couple the introduction of such disincentives (such as minimum capital requirements for private companies) with the provision of a special form of incorporation (*without* limited liability) which addresses the other needs of small businesses, for example by providing a simple governance system, dispensing with the notion of share capital, and requiring low levels of disclosure of financial information to the public.[53] The CLR did not pursue this idea because, as we have seen, it was not in favour of making incorporation with limited liability more difficult for small businesses.

Those taking the first view also argue strongly for a separate form of incorporation for small businesses, but one available with limited liability. The advantages of a separate form of incorporation with limited liability over incorporation under the companies legislation (and thus with limited liability) are normally seen as lying mainly in the area of a simplified governance arrangement (a single decision-making body).[54] This issue was argued out at an early stage in the CLR and the conclusion was

---

[52] On affiliation rights see Chapter 5 at p. 144. For an expression of this view under CA 1985, s 459 see *Re A Company* [1983] BCLC 126, one of the first reported decisions under what is now s 459, though the judge (Lord Grantchester) chose an unfortunate way of putting the point. For an expression of the same point when the claim is brought at common law consider *Re Smith & Fawcett Ltd* [1942] Ch 304.

[53] Hicks, n. 15 above, at pp. 60–4.

[54] If limited liability is available, then more extensive public disclosure of information than is required of a partnership is necessary.

against a separate form of incorporation with limited liability. The main argument against, in the CLR's view, was that a separate form of incorporation would generate barriers to growth (and indeed legislative traps), as small companies which grew would need to reincorporate in order to maintain an efficient governance structure. As we have noted, the CLR thought that small companies with growth potential were particularly important in public policy terms, so that legislation should be designed to facilitate their growth. Consequently, it opposed a legislative structure which depended upon unity of ownership and control and which, therefore, would become inappropriate as soon as one shareholder ceased to wish to be involved in the management of the business, for example because he or she inherited the shares upon the death of a founding shareholder. It preferred, as we have seen, reforms which, though designed for small companies, did not formally depend upon the company's having any particular structure of relationships between shareholders and directors.[55] It recommended accordingly that small businesses should continue to incorporate under the general companies legislation, but companies legislation better adapted to the needs of small businesses.

However, while the CLR was taking this view, the Government, indeed the same government department which sponsored the CLR, was also promoting legislation which produced the Limited Liability Partnership Act 2000. Despite its name the Limited Liability Partnership (hereafter 'LLP') is much more like a company than like a partnership. Indeed, the Act provides that, unless specifically provided otherwise in legislation, 'the law relating to partnership does not apply' to an LLP.[56] The LLP looks very much like a separate form of incorporation for small companies. It takes from partnership law the simplified internal decision-making structure, so that decisions are prima facie to be taken by the members and there is no board of directors,[57] and each member is prima facie entitled to take part in the management of the LLP.[58] It also takes from partnership law the absence of a share capital, so that, as in an ordinary partnership, the primary qualification for selection for

---

[55] The issue is set out most clearly in CLR, *The Strategic Framework*, February 1999, paras 5.2.23–5.2.36, in which the CLR displays its preference for the 'integrated' over the 'free-standing' approach.

[56] LLP Act 2000, s 1(5).

[57] Though such a structure can be reintroduced by agreement among the members and no doubt will be in large LLPs.

[58] LLP Regulations (SI 2001 No 1090), Part VI.

membership is not the provision of risk capital but, for example, success or promise as a worker in the partnership.[59] For the rest, however, the LLP is governed by company law principles. In particular, limited liability[60] is available and in consequence the disclosure rules for small companies are applied to LLPs as well.[61]

Thus, it might seem that the proponents of the view, that a separate and specially tailored form of incorporation with limited liability should be made available to small businesses, have succeeded in achieving the legislation they want, even though their views did not find favour with the CLR. How did this example of un-joined-up government come about? The answer seems to be by accident rather than design. For a number of years professional partnerships, especially those of accountants, have complained that recent developments in the law of tort relating to negligent misstatement have made the carrying on of business through the ordinary partnership with unlimited liability unattractive. Large judgments, in one case of over £100m., have exceeded the insurance cover easily available in the market, and have thus threatened not only the business carried on by the partnership but also the personal assets of the negligent partner and, through the doctrine of joint and several liability, the personal assets of all the partners, even though they may not have been in a good position to monitor the actions of the negligent partner.

A number of responses to the issue were suggested,[62] but the one that concerns us here is the suggestion that a form of partnership with limited liability be made available for professional firms.[63] After some hesitation, the Government responded with a proposal for the LLP, but a proposal limited to professional firms. Only under pressure from Parliament was the new form made available to all businesses, whether professional firms

---

[59] Partners may be required to put money into the partnership, but this is not effected through the issuance of shares and the amount of the finance contributed does not normally determine the size of the voting rights at partnership meetings.

[60] If, as seems likely, the courts apply the decision in *Williams v Natural Life Health Foods Ltd* (see Chapter 2, p. 51) to LLPs, the personal assets of the negligent partner as well as those of the non-involved partners will be protected in principle, but see the qualification in n. 47 on p. 53.

[61] LLP Regulations (SI 2001 No 1091), reg 3 and Sch 1.

[62] See *Gower*, 6th edn, 1997, pp. 552–61 and J. Freedman and V. Finch, 'Limited Liability Partnerships: Have Accountants Sewn up the "Deep Pockets" Debate?' [1997] JBL 387–423.

[63] For various reasons it was unattractive for the professional firms to secure limited liability by incorporating under the companies legislation.

or not.[64] Only in this rather indirect way was a new form of incorporation made available for small businesses.

CONCLUSION

We identified at the beginning of this chapter four views about the proper approach of the law to the provision of legal vehicles for the carrying on of small businesses. Three out of the four can claim to find something in their favour in recent law reform or proposals for reform. The traditional view that a single Companies Act can accommodate all sizes of business, provided it is properly structured, is represented in the reports of the CLR. The view that business people overestimate the advantages of the company form and should be encouraged to give more consideration to unlimited liability vehicles is represented by the Law Commissions' Consultation Paper on the reform of the law of partnership.[65] Finally, those who want to make it even easier for small firms to incorporate with limited liability can point to the new LLP. The only view not represented among these developments is one which would place significant barriers in the way of small businesses wishing to incorporate with limited liability. However, even with only three views represented, it is difficult to see all this adding up to a coherent policy. Nor is it easy to predict which policy will predominate in practice, for it is too early to know what the relative take-up will be of the LLP, the company incorporated under a reformed Companies Act, and a modernised partnership.

---

[64] The legislative history is given in *Palmer's Limited Liability Partnership Law* (London: Sweet & Maxwell, 2001), ch. 1.

[65] Above, n. 13.

Index

Abuse of power 163–5
Accountability 19–20, 34–5, 255
Account of profits 180–1, 188
Accounts *see also* Operating and
    Financial Review
  auditors 134–5
  directors 14, 134–5, 195
  disclosure 72–3
  format 134
  groups of companies 134
  Independent professional review 291
  interim accounts 135
  limitation of liability 72–3
  small companies and businesses 287–8,
    291–2
  time for filing 135
Affiliation rights
  appraisal rights 229–30
  centralized management 144–9
  exit rights 228–9
  minority shareholders 228–30
  take-overs 148
  transfer of rights 144–5
Agency
  articles of association 46
  attribution 43–8
  authority 43–8
    actual 46
    ostensible 48
    usual 44–5
  centralized management 117–23
  constitution, restrictions in 45–8
  constraining strategy 151–3
  constructive notice, doctrine of 46–7
  contracts 43–9
  decisions 151
  directors 45, 116, 118, 152, 159, 161,
    198, 209–11, 214
  incentive strategy 141
  indoor management rule 46
  memorandum of association 45–6
  minority shareholders 216–17, 226, 253
  remuneration 121
  shareholders 151–3, 159, 209–10, 214,
    216, 248
    minority 216–17, 226, 253

  third parties 44–8
  vicarious liability 49–54
Aggregation 40
Annual general meetings
  directors, removal of 136–8
  piggy-backing on 136–8
  resolutions 137–8
  shareholders' meetings 136–8
  small companies and businesses 287–8
Appointment rights
  board of directors 216
  centralized management 127–44, 151,
    154–5
  directors 127–44, 151, 154–5
    non-executive 204
  shareholders 127–44, 151, 154–5, 216
    minority 226–7
Appraisal rights 229–30
Articles of association
  agency 46
  centralized management 114–16
  conflicts of interest 174
  contracts 243–4
  directors 164–5, 167–8, 197
  enforcement 243–5
  exit rights 229
  fairness 239
  investors, as statement to 243
  secret profits 184–7
  shareholders 16–17, 238–9
    minority 221–2, 240, 243–5
  Table A 16–17
Assets
  creditors 66–7
  groups of companies 67, 102–3
  limitation of liability 62, 81–2
  partitioning 66–8, 102–3
  shareholders 66–7
Assumption of responsibility 52–4
Attribution
  agency 43–8
  aggregation 40
  contracting 41–8
  corporate personality 38–9
  criminal liability 55–9
  knowledge 39–40

primary rules of 41–3
tort 54–5
vicarious liability 39–40, 49–54
Auditors 134–5
Audits for small companies 290–1
Australia 236

Best interests of the company, *bona fide*
    in the 159–60, 168, 198, 276
Board of directors 13–14, 18–19
    business strategy 157
    centralized management 113–16, 151–214
    chair 202–3
    chief executive 202
    Combined Code 157, 202
    committees 202
    composition of 176
    conflicts of interest 174–6
    constraining the 151–3
    corporate governance 15
    delegation 157–8
    incentives, setting 198–214
    Listing Rules 157
    minority shareholders, representation of
        227
    monitoring 203, 212–13
    non-executive directors 202–3
    reward strategy 251–2
    secret profits, approval of 184–7
    self-dealing 171, 174–6
    shareholders 151–3, 255
        appointment to 216
        minority 227
        relationship 217
    small companies 14
    staggered 129
    statutory requirement for 13–14
    structure of 202–3
    trusteeship 245
    two-tier 203
    Turnbull Committee 157
    voting 227
Bonds 8, 264, 266–8
Bribes 190–1
Building societies 259, 266

Cadbury Committee 200–1, 205
Capital
    centralized management 111
    control 258–67, 272
    co-operatives 258–9
    creditor protection 83–92
    definition 83–4
    dividends 87–9

EC law 85
insolvency 83–4, 87
legal 83–4
limitation of liability 83–93, 101–2
maintenance 86–90, 91–2
markets 213–14
minimum 84–6, 286
minority protection 216
mutual societies 258–9
private companies 85
profits, distribution of 258
public companies 85–7
reduction of 90–2, 247
return of 256–7
risk 6, 258, 262
share buy-backs 87–9, 91–2
shareholders 84, 87, 256–62
small companies and businesses 286, 296
wrongful trading 94
Centralized management 13–15, 19, 27,
    111–50
    agent/principal problems 117–23
    affiliation rights 144–9
    appointment rights 127–44, 151
    articles of association 114–16
    board of directors 113–16, 157
        constraining the 151–97
        incentives, setting 198–214
    capital, provision of risk 111
    collective action problems 139–44
    contracts 118–19
    decisions 112–13, 117
        shareholder involvement on 123–7
    development of 112
    directors 123
        agents, as 116, 118
        appointment 127–44
        board of 113–16, 151–97
        defensive steps by 129–33
        removal of 128–9
        remuneration of 126–7
    delegation 118–19
    disclosure of information 122
    Germany 114, 115, 129
    guidance 114
    identification of 111
    incentives, setting 198–214
    information
        disclosure 122
        shareholders, to 133–6
    judiciary 115
    large companies 113, 115
    legal basis of 111–17
    legal strategies, typology of 118–22

Listing Rules 125–6
meetings, convening 136–9
minority shareholders 118, 227
monitoring by 117
private companies 114
public companies 13, 114, 136
shareholders
    appointment and removal rights
        127–44, 151
    consent of 116–17, 125–6
    control by 111–12
    decisions, involvement in 123–7
    empowering 111–50
    information to 133–6
    meetings 116, 118
    minority 118
    monitoring by 117
    small bodies of 112–13
    small companies and businesses 116,
        282–3, 285, 286–90
    United States 129
Champerty 96
Charges *see* **Fixed charges, Floating
        charges**
Charities 31–2
Chief executive officer 111, 199, 202
Chinese walls 40
City Panel on Take-overs and Mergers
        147–8
    code of practice 147–8
    equality principle 252
    function of 147
    non-frustration rule 147
    rules 3
Class rights 222
Close companies 282
Codes of practice *see also* **Combined Code**
    board of directors 157
    City Panel on Take-overs and Mergers
        147–8
    corporate governance 15
    directors 15, 132–3, 161, 208–11
        board of 147
    take-overs 148–9
Codification 2
Collective action
    centralized management 139–44
    directors 194–5
    shareholders 194–5, 256–7
Collective bargaining 272–3
Combined Code 131–2, 157, 208–11
    board of directors 157
        structure of 202
    Cadbury Committee 200–1, 205
    compliance with, level of 203–4

comply or explain 131
    directors 161, 208–11
        board of 157, 202
        non-executive 200–6
        remuneration 204
    impact of 203–6
    institutional investors 204, 205
    listed companies 201, 203–4
    non-compliance 201
    non-executive directors 200–6
    trusteeship 202–3
Common law 2
Company Law Review 1, 152
Conflicts of interest
    articles of association 173–4
    board of directors
        composition of 176
        mandatory disclosure to 174–6
    contracts 172–3
        long-service 177–9
    corporate opportunities 183–90
    decisions 174
    delegation 170
    directors 153, 170–83, 194, 196, 210–11
        board 172–6
        breach of duty 176
        remuneration 178–9
    disclosure 172, 174–7
    judiciary, role of 173
    Listing Rules 176–7
    loans 177
    long-service contracts 177–9
    no conflict rule 172–5
    related party transactions 177
    secret profits 185, 188
    self-dealing 170–83
    shareholders 143–4, 170, 220
        approval 172–9
        disclosure 172
        meetings 172
    substantial property transactions 179–83
    termination payments 177–9
Consolidation 1
Constitution
    agency 45–8
    alteration of 234–5, 255
    constructive notice, doctrine of 46–7
    contracts 41–2
    directors 160–7
    indoor management rule 46
    restrictions in 45–8
    shareholders' control over 15–18, 234–5,
        255
Constructive notice, doctrine of 46–7

Contracts
  agency 43–9
  articles of association 243–4
  attribution 41–8
  breach, inducing 55
  centralized management 118–19
  conflicts of interest 172–3, 177–9
  constitution 41–2
    restrictions in 45–8
  control 262–3, 268–9, 275
  corporate personality 39, 41–8
  decision rights 221–2
  delegation 43
  directors 41, 54–5, 130–1, 162–3, 168–9,
    177–9
  fixed-term 130–1
  good faith 41–2
  limited liability 11, 69–72, 75–6, 109
  long-service 177–9
  minority shareholders 227
  pre-incorporation 43
  relational 268
  self-dealing 170–1
  shareholders 6–7, 41–2
    minority 227
  small companies and businesses 42
  third parties 41–2
  vicarious liability 51–5
  voting 262–3
Control
  bond-holders 264, 266–8
  building societies 258–60, 266
  capital, suppliers of risk 258–67, 272
  centralized management 111–12
  collective bargaining 272–3
  common law constraints on 234–6
  constitution 15–18, 234–5, 255
  consultation 276–7
  contracting out 272–3
  contracts 268–9, 275
  co-operatives 258–60
  corporate governance rights, allocation
    of 266–7, 269, 271–4
  creditors 265, 270
  customers 270
  directors 265
    duties of 269–71, 276–9
  dividends 264
  EC law 275–6
  employees 267, 268, 270, 278–9
    contracting out for 272–3
    interests of 271–2
    representatives 271, 273–5
    terms and conditions 273

  friendly societies 259
  Germany 268, 271, 273–5
  guarantee, company limited by 260
  health and safety 278
  insolvency 264–5
  institutional representation 275
  investment 262–3
  justification for 255–7
  large companies 215
  limited liability 61
  loans 264
  loss of 263–5
  majority shareholders 215, 253–4
  management 18–20, 34, 111–12, 255
  meaning of 255–7
  members 259–60
  minority shareholders 215, 253–4
  mutual societies 258–9, 261, 266
  Operating and Financial Review 279–80
  rights 259–62
  shareholders 15–21, 25–6, 34, 111–12,
    215, 253–81
    capital, suppliers of risk 258–62
    common law constraints on 234–6
    constitution 15–18, 255
    justification for 255–7
    legal and factual control 112
    majority 215, 253–4
    meaning of 255–7
    preference 263, 268
    rights 259–62
    stakeholders 266–80
    value 276–8
    voting 262–5
  shares, ordinary 262–3, 266–7, 269,
    280
  small companies and businesses 261,
    283, 292
  stakeholders
    corporate governance 266–7
    information on 279
    interests of 276–80
    sharing control with 267–76
  take-overs 270
  United States 270, 275, 280
  voting 260–3
    distribution of rights 263–5
Co-operatives 258–9
Core characteristics of company law
  9–34, 282–3, 285
Cork Report 63, 98, 99
Corporate governance
  board of directors 15
  codes of practice 15

control 266–7, 269, 271–2, 274
directors 15, 131–2
  board of 15
  non-executive 200
  limitation of liability 75–6
  resolutions 139
  small companies and businesses 294
  stakeholders 266–7
  trusteeship 199
Corporate killing 58–9
Corporate personality 36–59
  acting 38–59
  attribution 39–59
  contracts 39, 41–8
  corporate veil, piercing the 37
  criminal liability 55–9
  exceptions 37–8
  groups of companies 104, 105, 107
  knowledge 38–59
  limitation of liability 11–12, 36–7
  memorandum of association 10
  separate 9–12, 24–5, 36–59, 104, 105, 107, 282
  shares, transfer of 37
  small companies and businesses 282
  tort 49–54
  vicarious liability 39–40, 49–54
  wrongs, commission of 39, 49–59
Corporate veil, piercing the 37
Creditors 5
  assets, partitioning of 66–7
  capital 83–92
  control 265
  facilitating 72–3
  groups of companies 82, 92
  guarantees 82, 92
  investment 63–4
  involuntary 80, 82
  limitation of liability 12, 68–77, 80
    facilitating 72–3
    opportunistic behaviour, by 76–7
    secured 76–7
    self-help 68–77
  loans 8
  management, monitoring 67–8
  opportunistic behavioiur, by 76–7
  protection of 81–91
  secured 76–7
  self-help 68–77
  small companies and businesses 291
  types of 7–8
Criminal liability
  attribution 55–9
  compliance systems 57–8

corporate killing, offence of 58–9
corporate personality 55–9
directing mind and will 56
health and safety 55–6, 58
identification, doctrine of 56–7, 58
Law Commission 58
management failure 58–9
manslaughter, involuntary 56–7, 58–9
reform 57–9
strict liability 55
United States 58
vicarious liability 56, 57–8

Damages
directors 154
  removal of 129–30, 132
  secret profits 190
Debt instruments 8
Decisions
  agency 151
  allocation to individual 224–6
  centralized management 112–13, 117, 123–7
  confirmation by 246–8
  conflicts of interest 174
  constraints, on 231–2
  directors 156–63, 167–70, 191–4, 197, 211, 272
    constraints, on 231–2
    non-executive 206
  involvement in 123–7, 149
  majority, constraining the 231–45
  non-executive directors 206
  secret profits 187–7
  shareholders 13
    allocation to individual 224–6
    confirmation by 246–8
    involvement in 123–7, 149
    majority, constraining 231–45
    size of majority, altering 222–4
    small companies and businesses 288–9
  size of majority, altering 222–4
  small companies and businesses 287–9
Default rules 7, 68
Derivative actions 219, 225–6, 241–2, 250–1
Directors 5 *see also* **Board of directors,**
    Chief executive officer,
    Non-executive directors,
    Remuneration of directors
  abuse of powers 163–5
  accounts 14, 134–5, 195
  agency 45, 116, 118, 152, 159, 161, 198, 209–11, 214

appointment 127–44, 151, 154–5
articles of association 164–5, 167–8, 197
authority
  abuse of, actions in 163–5
  actions lacking 162–3
best interests of the company, duty to act *bona fide* 159–60, 168, 198, 276
breach of duty 191–6, 249–51
  legitimization of 192
  takeovers 232–4
capital markets 213–14
civil liability 101
centralized management 18–19, 123, 151–97
  agents, as 116, 118
  appointment 127–44, 151
  defensive steps by 129–33
  removal of 128–9
  remuneration of 126–7
collective action 194–5
Combined Code 161, 208–11
competence 153, 154, 158, 210
comply or explain, principle of 131
conflicts of interest 153, 170–83, 194, 196, 210–11
  board 172–6
  breach of duty 176
  end games 177
  prophylactic rules 181
  remuneration 178–9
constitution 160–7
contracts 41, 54–5, 130–1, 162–3, 168–9
  long-service 177
control 265, 269–71, 276–9
Cork Committee 98
corporate governance codes 15, 131–2
damages 129–30, 132, 154
decisions 156–63, 167–70, 191–4, 197, 211, 272
  common law constraints on 231–4
default rules 167–8
defensive steps by 129–33
delegation 157–8, 165, 167–8
derivative actions 225–6, 250–1
disclosure of remuneration 135–6
discretion 159, 161–2, 164–7, 269–70
  fettering 168–70
dismissal 129–30
disqualification 15, 97–8, 101–2, 157–8, 197, 210
duties 151–67, 198, 210, 219–20, 225–6
  control 269–71, 276–9

derivative actions 250–1
enforcement, proposals for 249–51
  shareholders, to 231–2, 249–51
  statutory statement of 152, 233–4, 265
duty of care 15, 154–60, 167
  breach of 191–6, 232–4, 241–2, 249–51
EC law 166
employees 271
enforcement 191–6, 225–6, 249–51
fiduciaries, as 19, 159, 197, 220, 231–2
figurehead 155, 197
fixed-term contracts 130–1
forgiveness 191–6
fraudulent trading 93–102
groups of companies 104, 106
incentives 198–214
insurance 195–6
judiciary 161
  restraint 156–7
Law Commission 152, 156
legal proceedings 191–2, 195–6
liability to the company 163, 192
Listing Rules 131, 169, 208–9, 211
limitation of liability 11–12, 72–3, 97–8
loans 177
long-service contracts 177–8
long-term incentive plans 208–9
loyalty, duty of 153, 160
minority shareholders 219–20, 231–4
misappropriation 225
mutual backscratching 176
negligence 156
nominee 168, 216, 246
opportunities, corporate 183–91
pre-emption rights 214
proper purposes doctrine 164–7, 233
ratification 192, 194–6, 225
relief 195–6
removal of 128–44, 210, 253
  costs of 140
  rolling contracts 131
  weighted voting 132
resolutions 138
reward strategy 207–9
secret profits 183–91
self-dealing 170–83, 195
self-interest 198, 207
shadow 15, 104, 106, 153–4
shareholders 153, 154, 192–3, 196, 207–13
  agents, of 159
  appointment 127–44, 151, 154–5
  approval of 169–70, 173–85, 197, 209
  collective action problems of 194–5, 212

costs to 165
delegation and 167
directors 231–2, 286–7, 289–90, 292
division of powers and 166
institutional 214
markets, protected by 213–14
meetings 132–3, 136–9, 194–5, 249
removal 128–44, 210, 253
remuneration and 161
take-overs 232–4
shares
  buy-backs 89
  sale of 149
skill and care 197
small companies and businesses 286–7,
  289–90, 292
standard of care 154–60, 197
  objective 154–7
  subjective 154–6
substantial property transactions 179–83
take-overs 212, 232–4
termination 129–33
  payments 177–8
trusteeship 198–207
Turnbull Report 158
unfitness 98, 157–8
United States 156, 158, 270
vicarious liability 51, 53, 54–5
voting 226
wrongful trading 93–102, 197
Disclosure
accounts 72–3
centralized management 122
conflicts of interest 172
directors' remuneration 135–6
institutional shareholders 143
limitation of liability 72–3
Listing Rules 136
secret profits 184
self-dealing 174–6
shareholders 172
small companies and businesses 285,
  290–2, 296
voting 143
Disqualification of directors 15, 97–8,
  101–2, 157–8, 197, 210
Dividends
capital 87–9
control 264
limitation of liability 87–9
shareholders 256
Duty of care
breach 176, 191–6, 232–4, 241–2, 249–51
conflicts of interest 176

directors 15, 154–60, 167, 191–6, 232–4,
  241–2, 249–51
enforcement 191–6
take-overs 232–4

EC law
capital 85
control 275–6
directors 166
European Company 4, 275–6
  before and after principle 275
harmonization 3–4
incorporation 4
limitation of liability 69
small companies and businesses 290–1
Employees
collective bargaining 272–3
contracting out for 272–3
control 267, 268, 270, 278–9
  contracting out for 272–3
  interests of 271–2
  representatives 271, 273–5
  terms and conditions 273
directors 271
Germany 20, 271, 273, 275
health and safety 278
insolvency 81
insurance 81
interests of 271–2
limitation of liability 81
representatives 20, 271, 273–5
shareholders 20
small companies and businesses 38
terms and conditions 273
vicarious liability 49–50, 53–4
Enforcement
articles of association 243–5
collective action 194–5
directors 191–6, 225–6
  duties 249–51
duty of care 191–6
shareholders 194–5, 225–6
  minority 219, 225–6, 241
European Union *see* **EC law**
Exit rights 228–9, 237
Extraordinary meetings 138, 142

Fairness
articles of association 239
minority shareholders 236–43, 248,
  292–3
prejudice 236–43, 248, 292–3
self-dealing 171
small companies and businesses 239

Fiduciaries
directors, as 19, 159, 197, 220, 231–2
New Zealand 232
secret profits 183
shareholders, controlling 231–2, 234
substantial property transactions 182
Financial statements 290
Fixed charges 74–6
Fixed-term contracts 130–1
Floating charges 73–5, 76–7
Foss v Harbottle rule 241
Fraud 79 *see also* **Fraudulent trading**
Fraudulent trading
directors 93–102
enforcement 101
liabilities, increase in 93–102
limitation of liability 93–102
Friendly societies 259
Fund managers 142–3

Germany
centralized management 114, 115, 129
control 268, 271, 273, 275
employee representatives 20, 271, 273, 275
groups of companies 108
management 20
public companies 114
two-tier boards 20
Governance *see* **Corporate governance**
Greenbury Committee 200
Groups of companies
accounts 134
assets, partitioning 67, 102–3
creditors 82, 92
directors
shadow 104, 106
Germany 108
insolvency 107
limitation of liability 61–2, 67, 102–10
management 103
New Zealand 107
parent companies 103–7
separate legal personality 104, 105, 107
shadow directors 104, 106
subsidiary companies 103–7
wrongful trading 104
Guarantee, companies limited by
commercial purposes 260
control 260
incorporation 32
'ltd', use of 32
members 31, 260
non-profit-making activities 31–2
small companies and businesses 282
surplus 32

Guarantees 69–70 *see also* **Guarantee, companies limited by**

Hampel Committee 200
Health and safety 55–6, 58, 278

Incentives, setting 198–214
Incorporation
charities 31–2
EC law 4
guarantee, companies limited by 32
small companies and businesses 28–9, 283–6, 294–7
Indemnities 181
Indoor management rule 46
Information *see also* **Disclosure**
centralized management 133–6
non-executive directors 202
public companies 136
reporting 134
shareholders 133–6
small companies and businesses 290
stakeholders 279
Insolvency 2 *see also* **Liquidation**
appraisal rights 229–30
capital 83–4, 87
control 264–5
disqualification of directors 97–8
employees 81
exit rights 237
fraudulent trading 93–102
groups of companies 107
limitation of liability 11–12, 76–7, 80
small companies and businesses 28–9
phoenix companies 99–100
tort 80
wrongful trading 95–7
Institutional representation 275
Institutional shareholders 141–4, 214
activism 142
competition and conflicts of interest 143, 212
concentration of shareholdings 141
takeover bids 144
voice and exit 144
Insurance
compulsory 81
demutualization 266
directors 195–6
employees 81
friendly societies 259
limitation of liability 81, 109
Investment
articles of association 243
control 262–3

creditors 63–4
diversification 64
encouragement of public 63–5
fund managers 142–3
institutional 204, 205, 257
limitation of liability 63–5
majority shareholders 216
protection 216

Judiciary
centralized management 115
directors
discretion 161
standard of care 156–7
minority protection 237–8
restraint 156–7

Knowledge
attribution 39–40
constructive notice, doctrine of 46–7
corporate personality 38–59

Law Commission 58, 152, 249
Legal personality *see* **Corporate personality**
Legal proceedings
derivative actions 219, 225–6, 241–2, 250–1
directors 191–2, 195, 196
informal agreements 240
minority shareholders 219
right to sue 219
shareholders 225–6
minority 219
Legitimate expectations 239
Limitation of liability 10–12, 60–110
accounts 72–3
assets 81–2
partitioning of 66–8
assumption of responsibility 62
businesses having access to, types of 68–9
capital 83–93, 101–2
contracting out of 282
contracts 11, 69–72, 75–6, 109
control 61
co-operative societies 258
Cork Report 63
corporate governance 75–6
corporate personality 36–7
separate 11–12
creditors 12, 68–77
facilitating 72–3
involuntary 80, 82
opportunistic behaviour, by 76–7

secured 76–7
self-help 68–110
default rule, as 68–70
directors 11–12, 72–3, 97–8
disqualification of 97–8
disadvantages of 33
disclosure 72–3
dividends 87–9
EC law 69
employees 81
fixed charges 74–6
floating charges 73–5, 76–7
fraud 79
fraudulent trading 93–7
groups of companies 61–2, 66, 102–10
guarantees 69–70
insolvency 11–12, 76–7, 80–1
insurance 81, 109
investment, encouragement of public 63–5
liabilities, increases in company's 93–102
limited liability partnerships 295–7
liquidation 11–12
loan contracts 70–1
mandatory rules, case for 79–110
members 11–12
opportunism 62–3, 76–7, 78–9
general rules against debtor 80–2
liabilities, increases in 93–102
opting out 69–70
parent companies 61–2, 103–7
partnerships 60, 295–7
phoenix companies 99–100
private companies 72
public companies 72
rationale 60–8
rules, case for mandatory 789
separate legal personality 11–12
shareholders 11–12, 60–2, 75–6
shares
buy-backs 87–9
facilitation of public market in 63–6
small companies and businesses 25, 61, 69, 108, 282, 285–6, 290, 294–7
subsidiary companies 61–2, 103–7
suppliers 71
tort 80–1
unlimited companies 12, 25, 63–4, 224
vicarious liability 53–4
wrongful trading 93–102
Liquidation
limitation of liability 11–12
members, contributions from 11–12
unlimited companies 12, 25

Listing Rules 2–3
  board of directors 157
  centralized management 125–6
  conflicts of interest 176–7
  directors 131, 169, 208–9, 211
    board of 157
  disclosure 136
  equality principle 252
  minority shareholders 246
  reports 135–6
Loans
  control 263–4
  creditors 8
  debt instruments 8
  directors 177
  interests of 8
  limitation of liability 70–1
Long-term incentive plans 208–9

Management *see also* **Centralized management**
  accountability 19–20, 255
  creditors 67–8
  criminal liability 58–9
  directors 155
    board of 18–19
  failure 58–9
  floating charges 75
  fund 142–3
  Germany 20
  groups of companies 103
  monitoring of 67–8
  public companies 34
  senior 199
  shareholders 13, 27–8, 67–8
    control over 18–20, 34
  small companies and businesses 34, 293–4
  take-overs 147–8
  trusteeship 199
Manslaughter, involuntary 56–7, 58–9
Meetings *see also* **Annual general meetings, Shareholders' meetings**
  centralized management 136–9
  convening 136–9
  directors, removal of 132–3, 136–8
  extraordinary 138, 142
Members
  control rights 259–60
  co-operatives 258
  guarantee, companies limited by 31, 260
  limited liability 11–12
  liquidation, contributions from 11–12
  shareholders, as 7

Memorandum of association 10, 16, 45–6
Mergers *see* **City Panel on Take-overs and Mergers**
Minority shareholders 215–54
  agency 216–17, 226, 253
  affiliation rights 228–30
  appointment rights 226–7
  appraisal rights 229–30
  approval 218–19
  articles of association 221–2, 240
    enforcement of 243–5
  Australia 236
  board, representation on 227
  capital 216
  centralized management 118, 227
  class rights 222
  contracts 227
  controllers
    shareholders, common law constraints on 234–6
    statutory constraints on 236–43
  decision rights 218–22, 249–50
    contracting for 221–2
  derivative actions 219, 225–6, 241–2, 250–1
  directors 231–4
    duties 219–20, 241–2, 249–51
    fiduciaries 220, 231–2
    non-executive 246
  enforcement 243–4, 249–51
  equality principle 252–3
  exit rights 228–9, 237
  fiduciaries 220, 231–2
  Foss v Harbottle rule 241
  hold up risks 218
  incentives, setting 245–53
  informal agreements 238–41
  intervention 236–43
  judiciary 237–9
    creativity 218–19
  large companies 215
  legal proceedings, standing to take 219
  Listing Rules 246
  majority shareholders and 215–54
    control, by 215, 253–4
  oppression 237
  personal relief 242
  private companies 215
  rewards 251–3
  small companies and businesses 215, 242, 253, 283, 288–9, 292–4
  supermajority requirement 223–4, 234–5, 248
  take-overs 219
  three-quarters rule 223

trusteeship 245–51
unfair prejudice, remedies against
236–43, 248, 292–3
voting 218
exclusion from 220–1
property right, as 220–1
winding up 237
Mutual societies 258–9, 261, 266
Myners Reports 143

Negligence 95–6, 156
Negligent misstatements 51–4
New Zealand 107, 232
Nominee directors 168, 216, 246
Non-executive directors 45, 167
advice 202
appointment 204
board of directors 202–3
two-tier 203
business strategy 203
Cadbury Committee 200–1, 205
Combined Code 200–6
corporate governance 200
decisions 206
directors
board 202–3
disinterested 206–7
remuneration 204–6
Greenbury Committee 200
Hampel Committee 200
incentives 200
independent 200, 202, 205, 206, 246
information 202
minority shareholders 246
monitoring role of 203
opportunities, corporate 206–7
public policy 200
remuneration 204
trusteeship 199–207, 246
United States 205
Non-profit making activities 31–2

Offers *see* **Public offers**
Operating and financial review 135,
279–80
Opportunism 61

Panel on Take-overs and Mergers *see*
City Panel on Take-overs and
Mergers
Parent companies 61–2, 103–7
Partnerships
limited liability 295–7
limitation of liability 60, 295–7

professional 296
small companies and businesses 28–9,
284–5, 296–7
Phoenix companies 99–100
Prejudice
minority shareholders 236–43, 248, 292–3
unfair 236–43, 248, 292–3
Private companies
accountability 34–5
capital 85
centralized management 114
core features, displaying 26
limitation of liability 72
minority shareholders 215
public companies, as 17–18
share buy-backs 89
size of companies 29–30
Professional partnerships 296
Profit warnings 136
Proper purposes rule 164–7, 233
Public companies
capital 85–7
centralized management 13, 114, 136
core features, displaying 26
Germany 114
information 136
limitation of liability 72
management 34
private companies, as 17–18
profit warnings 136
regulation 18
share buy-backs 88
Public offers 2, 22

Ratification 192, 194–6, 226
Related-party transactions 177
Remedies
codification 182
exit rights 229, 237
minority shareholders 236–43
secret profits 189
substantial property transactions 179–83
unfair prejudice, statutory constraints
on 236–43, 248
winding up 237
Remuneration of directors 130–2, 196,
207–8
centralized management 126–7
Combined Code 126–7
committees 208–9
conflicts of interest 178–9
disclosure 135–6
non-executive directors and 204–6
policies 208–9

rolling contracts 131
shareholders 161, 178–9
trusteeship 206
voting 206
Reports 135–6
Rescission 182–3
Resolutions
  annual general meetings 137–8
  corporate governance 139
  directors 138
  extraordinary 222
  shareholders
    majority 222
  shareholders' meetings 133–4, 137–9
    timing of 137–8
  shares, repurchase of 223
  small companies and businesses 287–9
Results, statement of 135–6

Schemes of arrangement 125, 247
Scope of company law 1–5
Secret profits
  account of profits 188
  articles of association 184–7
  bribes 190–1
  conflicts of interest 185, 188
  corporate opportunities and 183–91
    identification of, criteria for 187–90
  damages 190
  decisions 186–7
  directors 183–91
    board of, approval of 184–7
  disclosure 184
  fiduciaries 183
  no profit rule 184–6
  remedies 189–90
  self-dealing rule 186
  shareholders 184–7
    approval of 185, 187, 191
  United States 189
  voting 186
Securities markets 2–3
Self-dealing
  articles of association 174–5
  conflicts of interest 170–83
  contracts 170–1
  directors 170–83, 195
    board of 171, 174–6
  disclosure 174–5
  fairness 171
  regulation 170
  related-party transactions 177
  secret profits 186
  shareholders 170

  approval 173–7
  meetings 171
  United States 171, 176
  voting 175–6
Senior managers 5
Separate legal personality 9–12, 24–5,
  36–59, 104, 105, 107, 282
Shadow directors 15, 104, 106, 153–4
Shareholders *see also* **Institutional
  shareholders, Minority
  shareholders, Shareholders'
  meetings**
  activism 142–3
  agency 151–53, 159, 209–10, 214,
    216–17, 248
    minority 216–17, 226, 253
  appointment and removal rights 127–44,
    151, 154–5, 216
  approval of 169–70, 173–85, 197, 209
  articles of association 16–17, 238–9
  assets, partitioning 66–7
  audits 291
  board of directors 151–3, 255
    appointment of majority to 216
    relationship 217
  capital 84, 87, 256
    control by suppliers of risk 258–62
  centralized management 257
    appointment and removal rights
     127–44, 151, 154–5
    consent of 116–17, 125–6
    control by 111–12
    decisions, involvement in 123–7
    empowering 111–50
    information to 133–6
    minority 118
    monitoring by 117
    small bodies of 112–13
  class rights 222
  collective action problems of 194–5, 256–7
  common law constraints on controlling
    234–6
  conflicts of interest 143–4, 170, 176–8, 220
    consent 173–4
    disclosure 172
  consent of 116–17, 125–6
  constitution
    alteration of 234–5
    control over 15–18, 255
  contracts 6–7, 41–2
  control 15–21, 25–6, 34, 111–12, 215,
    253–81
    capital, suppliers of risk 258–62
    common law constraints on 234–6

constitution 15–18, 255
  justification for 255–7
  legal and factual control 112
  majority 215, 253–4
  management 18–20, 34
  meaning of 255–7
  preference 263, 268
  rights 259–62
  small companies and businesses 292
  value 276–8
  voting 262–5
co-operatives 258–9
corporate personality 37
creditors 257
decisions 13
  allocation to individuals 224–6
  confirmation by 246–8
  involvement in 123–7, 149
  majority, constraining 231–45
  size of majority, altering 222–4
  small companies and businesses 288–9
delegation and 167
directors 153–4, 192–3, 196, 207–14
  agents, of 159
  appointment and removal rights
    127–44, 151, 154–5
  approval of 169–70, 173–85, 197, 209
  collective action problems of 194–5
  costs to 165
  delegation and 167
  division of powers and 166
  duties 231–2
  removal of 127–44, 210, 253
  remuneration and 161, 178–9
  shareholders, as 231–2, 286–7,
    289–90, 292
  take-overs 232–4
disclosure 143, 172
dividends 256
division of powers and 166
empowering 111–50
enforcement 194–5, 225–6
fiduciaries 231–2, 234
information to 133–6
institutional 141–4, 214
  investors 257
investor protection 216
legal proceedings 225–6
legitimate expectations 239
limitation of liability 11–12, 60–2, 75–6
listed companies, control of 215
majority 215–54
  control, by 215
  decisions, constraining 231–45

size of, altering the 222–4
  standard required of 235–6
management 13, 27–8
  control over 18–20, 34
  monitoring 67–8
  senior 257
memorandum of association 16
members, as 7
monitoring 117
mutual societies 258–9
nominee 28
number of 26
opportunistic conduct 223
pre-emption rights 213–14, 253
preference 263–4, 268
public offers 22
remuneration 161
resolutions 133–4
  extraordinary 222
reward strategy 251–3
rights 6–7
secret profits 184–5, 187
self-dealing 170, 173–7
small bodies of 112–13
small companies and businesses 25–6,
    282–3
  audits 291
  control 292
  decisions 288–9
  directors, as 286–7, 289–90, 292
substantial property transactions 179–83
supermajority 223–4, 234–5, 248
surplus, entitlement to the 20–1, 255–6
take-overs 19, 146–8, 232–4
trusteeship 199
voting 222–4, 255
  contracting, for 262–3
  control 262–5
Shareholders' meetings
AGMs, piggy-backing on 136–8
centralized management 116, 118
conflicts of interest 172
convening 136
directors 132–3, 138–9, 194–5
  duties, enforcement of 249
  removal of 136–8
resolutions 133–4, 137–9
  timing of 137–8
self-dealing 171
small companies and businesses 287–9
Shares *see also* **Public offers,
    Shareholders**
buy-backs 87–9, 91–2
  directors and 89

directors 89, 149
limitation of liability 63–6, 87–9
ordinary 262–3, 266–7, 269, 280
private companies 89
public companies 88
public market in, facilitation of 65–6
purchase of 144–6
    compulsory 248
repurchase 223
resolutions 223
sale of 149
small companies and businesses 293
take-over 248
trading 22–3
transfer of 21–4, 144–5, 293
Size of companies 24–30
Small companies and businesses 282–97
accounts 287–8, 291–2
annual general meetings 287–8
audits 290–1
board of directors 14
capital
    minimum 286
    risk 296
centralized management 116, 282–3,
    285, 286–90
close companies 282
contracts 42
control 261, 283, 292
core features of company law 282–3,
    285
corporate governance 294
corporate personality 282
creditors 291
decisions 287–9
directors
    board of 14
    shareholders, as 286–7, 289–90, 292
disclosure 285, 290–2, 296
EC law 290–1
employment 38
exit rights 229, 237
fairness 239
financial statements 290
guarantee, company limited by 282
incorporation 28–9, 283–6, 294–7
Independent Professional Review 291
information 290
legislation and 285–94
limited liability partnerships 295–7
limitation of liability 25, 61, 69, 108,
    285–6, 290, 294–7
    contracting out of 282
lock in 293

management 34, 293–4
    centralized 116, 282–3, 285,
        286–90
minority shareholders 215, 242, 253,
    283, 288–9, 292–4
nature of issue 282–5
opportunistic conduct 283, 286
partnerships 28–9, 284–5, 297
    limited liability 295–7
    professional 296
phoenix companies 100
professional partnerships 296
quasi-partnerships 253, 293
resolutions 287–9
shareholders 25–6, 282–3
    audits 291
    control 292
    decisions 288–9
    directors, as 286–7, 289–90, 292
    meetings 287–9
    minority 215, 242, 253, 283, 288–9,
        292–4
shares, transfer of 293
squeeze outs 256
United States 289
vehicles, use of 30–1, 284
    alternative 294–7
vicarious liability 54
Sources of company law 1–4
Specialized management *see*
    Centralized management
Stakeholders
control
    corporate governance 266–7
    information on 279
    interests of 276–80
    sharing control with 267–76
corporate governance 266–7
information on 279
interests of 276–80
operating and financial review 279–80
Standard of care
directors' duties 154–60, 197
objective 154–7
subjective 154–6
Strict liability 55
Subsidiaries 61–2, 103–7
Substantial property transactions
account of profits 180–1
conflicts of interest 179–83
directors 179–83
fiduciaries 182
indemnities 181
remedies 179–83

rescission 182–3
shareholder approval 179–83
third parties 180
voidable 179–80
Suppliers 71
Surplus, entitlement to 20–1, 32, 255–6

Table A 16–17
Take-overs *see also* **City Panel on
Take-overs and Mergers**
affiliation 148–9
codes of practice 148–9
control 270
directors 212, 232–4
improper purposes doctrine 233
management 147–8
minority shareholders 219
shareholders 19, 146–8, 232–4
minority 219
shares, compulsory purchase of 248
United States 270
Third parties
agency 44–8
contracts 41–2
good faith 41–2
substantial property transactions 180
Tort
attribution 54–5
corporate personality 49–54
insolvency 80
limitation of liability 80–1
negligence 95–6, 156
vicarious liability 49–54
Transfer of shares 21–4, 37, 144–5, 293
Trusteeship
chief executives 199
Combined Code 202–3
corporate governance 199
courts and 246–8, 249
directors 198
board of 199–200, 245
nominees 246
non-executive 199–207, 246
remuneration 205–6
external 246
incentives 245–51
senior management 199
shareholders 199
minority 245–51
Turnbull Committee 157–8

United States
appraisal rights 230
business judgment rule 156

control 270, 275, 280
criminal liability 58
directors 156, 270
non-executive 205
secret profits 189
self-dealing 171, 176
small companies and businesses 289
take-overs 270
voting 227
Unlimited companies 12, 25, 63–4, 224

Vehicles, companies as 30–2, 284, 294–7
Vicarious liability
agents 49–54
assumption of responsibility 52–4
attribution 39–40, 49–54
contracts 51–5
corporate personality 39–40, 49–54
criminal liability 56, 57–8
default rule 52
directors 51, 53, 54–5
employment 49–50, 53–4
individual liability 51–4
limited liability 53–4
negligent misstatement 51–4
small companies and businesses 54
tort 49–54
Voting
contracting, for 262–3
control 260–5
cumulative 227
directors 226
board of 227
remuneration 206
disclosure 143
minority shareholders 220–1
property rights, as 220–1
secret profits 186
self-dealing 175
shareholders 255
control 262–5
size of, alteration of 222–4
supermajorities 222
United States 227

Winding up 237, 255–6
Wrongful trading
capital 94
directors 93–102, 197
enforcement 96, 101
groups of companies 104
liabilities, increase in 93–102
limitation of liability 93–102
negligence 95–6